KU-588-134

World Population Growth and Response

1965-1975 • a decade of global action

A publication of the Population Reference Bureau, Inc.
1754 N Street, N.W.
Washington, D.C. 20036
April 1976

UNIVERSITY LIBRARY NOTTINGHAM

i

cc

This publication was produced under contract (AID/pha-C-1096) with the U.S. Agency for International Development.
Contents of this publication may be reprinted without permission; appropriate credit to source will be appreciated.

For sale by the Population Reference Bureau at $4.00 per copy.

Foreword

Since its founding in 1929, the Population Reference Bureau has pioneered in analysis and reporting of changes in population in the United States and the world, assessment of the effects of these changes on the quality of human life and the environment, and in reporting of key developments relating to population dynamics, including population growth and other changes.

The present publication is a major example of the Bureau's work, illustrating the broadening services of the Bureau to other population agencies and institutions. Although the publication was prepared under a contract funded by the U.S. Agency for International Development, the Population Reference Bureau is solely responsible for the information and analysis presented here. The views expressed do not necessarily represent those of the Agency for International Development, and should not be considered as representing official policy of the U.S. Government.

This report was prepared by the PRB editorial staff including the following principals: W. Bert Johnson, Project Director; Harry W. Henderson, Deputy Project Director; Kenneth K. Krogh, Senior Writer-Editor; Kenneth W. Olson, Senior Writer-Editor; Elinor Sylvester, Senior Writer; James Meem, Statistical Researcher; Paul Myers, Chief Demographer; Alice Fray Nelson and Faith Payne, Senior Editors; and Milton S. Fairfax, Coordinator.

The Bureau acknowledges with deep appreciation the valued contributions of each of these individuals in a necessarily difficult task. Appreciation is also extended to members of the Bureau's Board of Trustees, its specialist-advisory committee, its library staff, and other staff members who have also assisted in this undertaking.

The Bureau specially acknowledges the cooperation and information provided by numerous agencies and institutions including the United States Agency for International Development, the United Nations, U.N. specialized agencies, the embassies of numerous countries in the United States; the International Planned Parenthood Federation, the Population Council, the Ford Foundation, the Rockefeller Foundation, The Pathfinder Fund, the Population Crisis Committee, and many other international, national, and church-related and other private groups concerned with population matters.

Robert M. Avedon, President
Population Reference Bureau

Preface

Presented in this book is an overview of major population developments in 1965-75—worldwide, regional, and in individual countries. In the decade, world concern and action have been on the rise and these years have seen greatly increased emphasis on responsible parenthood, the rights of women, improvement of maternal/child health and family well-being, and the need for accelerating economic and social advances in less-developed countries.

This report is designed as a benchmark document covering population changes, policy actions, and program developments up to mid-1975. As such, it is expected to be a continuing reference source in the population field. Although it will be of current interest to all who are concerned with world population dynamics—legislators, administrators, journalists, teachers, and leadership groups as well as population workers—it will also have long-time usefulness here and in other countries.

Family planning programs are the means by which global-scale action is conducted for direct support of voluntary action by individuals to control their fertility. The report focuses on the development of these programs and their services. Although the importance of supportive policies and measures beyond the program sphere is recognized—that is, legal or institutional and other developmental factors which influence fertility behavior—selected references to these are made only in the summaries where such measures are used for this purpose.

Population Reference Bureau

The Bureau gathers, interprets, and publishes information about population trends and their economic, environmental, and social effects. Founded in 1929, it is a private non-profit educational organization that is supported by foundation grants, individual and corporate contributions, memberships, and subscriptions. It consults with other groups in the United States and abroad and provides library and information services.

Officers

*Robert M. Avedon, President
Leon F. Bouvier, Vice President

Trustees

*Conrad Taeuber, Chairman of the Board
*Caroline S. Cochran, Chairman of the Executive Committee
*Mildred Marcy, Secretary of the Board
*Bert T. Edwards, Treasurer of the Board

*Paul F. Bente, Jr., Michael P. Bentzen, Barbara L. Carter, Jacob Clayman, *James R. Echols, Louis M. Hellman, Kathleen McNamara, Francis X. Murphy, David O. Poindexter, Patricia Rambach, John Reid, Caroline S. Saltonstall, James H. Scheuer, William O. Sweeney.

Advisory Committee

Samuel Baum, Calvin L. Beale, Donald J. Bogue, Georg A. Borgstrom, Lester R. Brown, Philander P. Claxton, Jr., Mercedes B. Concepcion, Douglas Ensminger, J. George Harrar, Philip M. Hauser, Snowden T. Herrick, Thomas B. Keehn, David Kline, Malcolm H. Merrill, Russell W. Peterson, Stephen Viederman, Benjamin Viel, Robert P. Worrall.

---

*Members of the Executive Committee of the Board of Trustees.

Contents

The World Population Situation

The explosive growth of population in this century, long given only sporadic notice, has in the past decade become a focus of world concern and action. Since the mid-1960's, new and stronger population policies and programs leading to reduction in high birth rates have been initiated by scores of national governments and by the United Nations, other international agencies, and many non-government organizations and institutions. As a result, by mid-1975 over two-thirds of the world's people were living in countries with positive programs for family planning and control of excess fertility.

The rapid spread of population action, especially since 1965, is itself a historic development. It marks the 1965-75 decade as the period of world awakening to the problems of rapid population increase and their effects for individuals and societies.

World population is now the largest in history and is rising at a pace that if not reduced could double human numbers in the next four decades. From mid-1965 to mid-1975 alone, the increase was 658 million—equal to the world total of two centuries ago. Just since 1900, population has increased from about 1.5 billion to the present level of about 4 billion.

It is the effects of these increases, present and future, that have compelled the attention—albeit belated—of so many governments, institutions, and agencies.

In the developing countries of Asia, Latin America, and Africa, there have been gains—some of them impressive—in *total* gross national product, industrialization, agricultural output, educational facilities, and health services. These are the gains through which the poorer countries had hoped to relieve widespread poverty and accumulate the savings necessary for self-sustaining national development. For many developing countries, however, the unpreceden-

Plenary meeting of World Population Conference, Bucharest, Romania, August 1974. This largest international population conference brought together representatives from 136 countries.

ted increases in population have frustrated this hope by holding *per capita* gains to distressingly low levels. The majority of the people in the developing countries, their discontent intensified by unrealized expectations, are continuing to face the traditional problems of unemployment, poverty, and hunger.

The more advanced nations, including the United States, have population growth rates substantially lower than those of the developing countries. Yet many of the industrialized countries also have problems tracing in part at least to population factors. These problems come into sharpest focus in the cities, where all too often there is overcrowding, a lack of jobs for all wanting to work, inadequate health and education services, rising crime rates, and pollution.

Thus it is that most major countries, developing and advanced, have initiated population/family planning programs as one means of attacking economic and social problems stemming in some degree from excessive or poorly distributed populations. These activities are having a measurable effect on birth rates and percentage rates of population increase throughout the world.

Decline in World Birth Rates

Between 1965 and 1974, world birth rates dropped significantly—and for the first time in many years declined faster than death rates.

The world figures reflect widely diverse situations. An increasing convergence of birth and death rates in the industrialized countries is bringing natural increase to low levels. In the developing countries there was some slowing of growth over the 1965-75 decade in Asia and the Caribbean Islands, but the rate of natural increase in Latin America and the Near East was stationary and rose slightly in Africa.

The contrast in the approach to population growth is sharp as between the industrialized and the developing countries. Some of the industrialized countries of Europe, for example, tend to be pronatalist out of concern for their low rates of natural increase, although few have placed restrictions on the contraceptive practices of their people. Among the developing countries, the aim (with a few exceptions) is to dampen population growth—and some, especially in Asia and the Caribbean area, have met with considerable success. Population programs are having a marked effect on birth rates and percentage rates of population increase in many countries, including the People's Republic of China, India, Indonesia, Korea, China (Taiwan), Hong Kong, Cuba, Costa Rica, and Jamaica. The differences in results among countries reflect largely the degree of official support for population and family planning programs—support

being shaped, in turn, by economic, cultural, and religious considerations.

Worldwide, continuing reductions in annual percentage growth seem expectable for some time ahead as existing population programs become stronger and additional ones are undertaken. Some specialists in this field now believe, based on program experience to date, that reduction of the world birth rate to about 20 per 1,000 population, from 30 in 1974, is feasible within another 10 years, given adequate program resources and initiative.

Shrinking rates of natural increase are essential to moderation of population growth. Therefore, the slowing of the percentage rise since 1965, including lower birth rates in countries conducting population programs, is a major advance.

Although awareness of the world's high annual rate of population growth—it was still 1.8 percent annually in 1974—has increased greatly, views on that growth show wide variation. Some see rapid growth as leading to certain future disaster for mankind—a fear that has given the language such expressions as "population crisis" and "population explosion." Others feel that if economic and social development can be brought to poorer countries, population growth will slow of itself. The more general view, based on program experience, is that programs to dampen population expansion must go hand in hand with social and economic development.

Family planning and health programs have demonstrated that they can reduce high birth rates, improve maternal and child health, and strengthen family well-being. Also, economic development programs have demonstrated that they can expand the total of resources available for human use, including per capita gains when population increases are held to moderate levels. Both approaches are clearly essential to a balanced development drive.

Population Momentum

But any consideration of current population problems must take into account the rise in total numbers of people. This rise, in contrast with the percentage rate, is continuing at a record level. By itself, the present decline in percentage rate of increase is only a beginning toward the greater decline in numbers of people that will be needed. There must be slower growth in total numbers if humanity is to achieve in the remainder of the Twentieth Century an improved balance between population, the environment, and the resources necessary for decent living.

Unfortunately, current signs of slowing growth, though highly encouraging to those who fear a catastrophic over-peopling of the globe, do not point to any early stabilization of world numbers. High fertility, reflecting long-established religious, cultural, and economic factors, is resistant to change. Of more importance is "population momentum," which might be likened to the momentum of a speeding passenger train that cannot be brought to an immediate stop even with full application of the brakes. Population momentum is great in many countries—largely developing countries—that have in their age structures a high proportion of young people who will be forming families and producing babies at a faster rate than older persons will be dying. This process will continue until the age structure can be shifted to one that contains about as many old people as young ones.

Bernard Berelson, former President of the Population Council, has noted: "Such is the momentum of population growth that even if the replacement level were reached in the developed world by 1980 and in the developing by 2000, the world's population would go to 8 billion. Where will such growth end: 8 billion? 10 billion? 15 billion? More? Whatever the figure, our children and certainly our grandchildren will look back at today's world of 3.5 billion (in 1972) as the good old days."

Since population increases of major proportions will continue for decades to come, despite efforts to moderate fertility, society must accommodate to the continuing growth. The struggle in the coming decades will be mainly one of trying to stay abreast of new requirements. More of everything will be needed in the remainder of this century and in the next—more food, housing, medical services, education, employment. Migration to cities—urbanization—has already intensified population problems and will continue to do so to an increasing extent. International migration, which served well as a population pressure safety valve in the late 1800's and early 1900's, appears to offer fewer opportunities in the years ahead. Economic and social development is a "must" in the accommodation process. A gross failure to accommodate the expected population growth could lead to such calamities as famine, epidemics, and anarchy. A partial failure to meet demand for essentials of rising populations would, at the very least, mean a further erosion of the quality of life in many developing countries.

The declines in birth rates and natural increase levels taking place between 1965 and 1974 indicate that the world is at least headed toward, rather than away from, a more slowly increasing population.

Demographic Highlights of the Decade

The world's population increased by an annual average of about 66 million people in the 1965-75 decade although the rise may have been slower since about 1973. The increase was from 3,289 million on July 1, 1965 to 3,947 million on July 1, 1975.

A feature of the world demographic situation over the decade was a drop of 6 percent in the annual rate of natural population increase, which measures the excess of births over deaths. During the last 5 years, world birth rates have declined faster than world death rates.

The world birth rate declined from an average of 34 per 1,000 people in 1965 to 30 in 1974.* The decreases were widespread. Birth rates dropped in 127 countries, including many of the most populous.

Birth rates of the industrialized countries, already low, dropped still further between 1965 and 1974. The U.S. birth rate dropped from 19 to 15 per 1,000 people and Canada's from 21 to 15. All countries of Western Europe showed declines except Ireland and Norway. But increases were reported for some Communist countries, including Bulgaria, Czechoslavakia, Hungary, Poland, and Romania. The Soviet Union's birth rate held steady at 18.

Asia and the Near East made substantial progress in controlling fertility. Declines in birth rates took place in all the densely populated countries, including the People's Republic of China, India, Indonesia, Japan, Korea, Pakistan, the Philippines, Taiwan, and Thailand.

For the Caribbean area as a whole, birth rates declined from 36 to 31, every country (including Cuba) showing decreases.

Central and South America made only moderate headway in damping fertility, birth rates for the area as a whole declining from 39 per 1,000 people to 38. The sharpest decreases were reported for Chile, Costa Rica, Panama, and Venezuela. Birth rates increased slightly in populous Mexico.

The decrease for Africa as a whole also was small—from 48 to 47. Tunisia's birth rate declined rather sharply, and Liberia's increased. But changes in most countries were small.

World death rates have been declining for many years, a trend that has contributed significantly to population expansion. The trend line leveled off somewhat between 1965 and 1974, but death rates declined nevertheless, offsetting in part the de-

---

*Based on an estimated 1974 birth rate of 27 per 1,000 population in the People's Republic of China. Some experts believe a 1974 rate as low as 17 per 1,000 is more accurate for the P.R.C. At this lower birth rate for the P.R.C.'s millions, the world birth rate for 1974 would be 28 per 1,000.

cline in birth rates. The overall death rate fell from 15 per 1,000 people in 1965 to 12 in 1974 for the world as a whole. In some developing areas—Latin America, the Caribbean islands, and East Asia—death rates reached levels comparable with those of Europe and Northern America, but remained especially high in Africa at 21 per 1,000 persons. Africa's infant and child mortality rates are the highest in the world.

For the world as a whole, the 1974 rate of natural increase indicated that the number of people would double in 38 years, but there were substantial differences among geographic regions. For Northern America and Europe the doubling process would take 116 years, but for Africa 27 years, and for Latin America as a whole only 25 years.

Life expectancy at birth in 1974 also showed wide variations from the world average of 59 years. In Northern America and Europe it was 71 years, and in Oceania 68, Caribbean islands 64, Latin America 62, Asia 56, Near East 54, and Africa 45.

World gross national product per capita rose from $920 in 1965 to $1,250 in 1973, the latest year for which information is available in most countries. Northern America led in 1973 with an average per capita GNP of $6,130. The U.S. average of $6,210, however, was no longer the world's highest; it was exceeded by Kuwait's $7,050, the United Arab Emirates' $6,740, and Switzerland's $6,350. Northern America was followed by Oceania with $3,330, Europe $3,010, Caribbean islands $780, Latin America $770, the Near East $710, Asia $410, and Africa $310.

Beginning of Official Activity

Official concern about population growth eventually was manifested especially about rapid population growth in the developing countries and its diluting effect on efforts that were going into development programs to improve living conditions and national stability in developing countries.

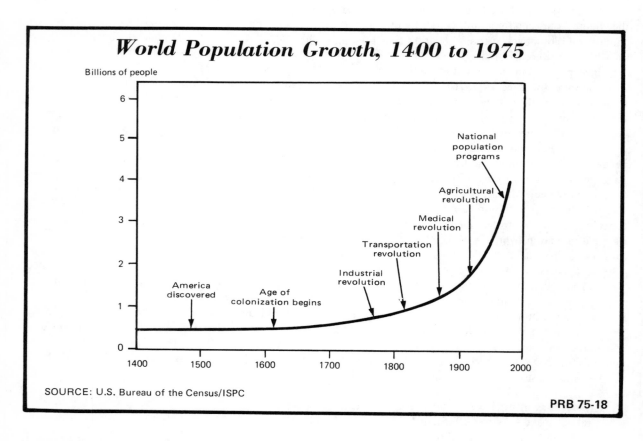

World Population Growth, 1400 to 1975

Billions of people

National population programs

Agricultural revolution

Medical revolution

Transportation revolution

Industrial revolution

America discovered

Age of colonization begins

SOURCE: U.S. Bureau of the Census/ISPC

PRB 75-18

Beginning about 1750, world death rates began to decline and world population rose.
Over the next 200 years major "revolutions" accelerated population growth. Some, by improving job opportunities, transportation facilities, and food production created conditions leading to lower mortality rates.
Generally death rates continued to decline more rapidly than did birth rates, especially in the advanced countries. By the 1960's decade, however, birth rates began to decline faster than death rates throughout the world—declines tracing in major part to the initiation of national population programs.

Concern about population subsided somewhat in the late 1800's and early 1900's, probably because very heavy international migration during that period reduced population pressures, notably in Europe. In the years between World Wars I and II some activists in the United States, Europe, and elsewhere, among them Margaret Sanger, pressed for responsible and planned parenthood, emphasizing the inherent right of women to control their fertility, family welfare, and the need for prevention of too-frequent pregnancies because of their effects on the health of mothers and children. This work has led to establishment of many national family planning associations and the International Planned Parenthood Federation.

The population question received prominent attention through activities of President Eisenhower's Committee to Study the U.S. Military Assistance Program, established in 1958 under the chairmanship of the late General William H. Draper, Jr. The Draper Committee eventually came to believe that excessive population growth in developing countries was hampering world recovery. In 1959 the Committee recommended that the United States help countries receiving U.S. aid work out plans to deal with population growth; to step up U.S. aid relating to maternal and child welfare programs; and to support population research in the United States and elsewhere and make the findings available to countries having rapidly expanding populations. Draper later became chairman of the Population Crisis Committee.

The sensitivity of this subject at that time prevented endorsement of these recommendations. However, in the period between 1960 and 1965 there was increasing awareness by governments, international organizations, and others that population problems retard economic and social development.

In 1962, Sweden sought U.N. approval of a resolution calling for studies of population and development and for technical assistance to national population programs when requested. The resolution was not adopted, but the U.S. statement supporting it was a landmark expression of U.S. policy.

Sweden announced in 1962 that birth control would be a major part of its expanding foreign aid program. In 1963 U.S. legislation said that funds "may be used to conduct research into the problems of population growth." In 1962 and 1963 the Population Council sponsored three overseas advisory missions—to Korea, Tunisia, and Turkey; and in 1964 it established a new Division for Technical Assistance, reflecting the growing interest of other governments in family planning. The First Asian Population Conference, held in New Delhi in late 1963, concluded with an appeal to all United Nations agencies to provide technical assistance on request for research and action "in all aspects of population problems." In January 1964 a Population Office was established within the U.S. Agency for International Development, and AID missions in Latin America were instructed to "consider the population program as a priority area."

Coming of Age of World Population Programs

It was in the 1965-75 period that population awareness and resultant activity came of age.

One index has been the strong support given by the industrialized nations to population programs of the developing countries. Through fiscal 1975, the United States, through its Agency for International Development, provided $732 million in such assistance. Through fiscal 1974, grant aid of other countries, notably Canada, Norway, Sweden, and the United Kingdom, amounted to $224.2 million, and of private agencies $207.2 million. The grand total for the 1965-74 period was $1,054.0 million (which does not include the even more substantial outlays of countries, including the United States, carrying on population programs to control growth within their own borders). Bilateral aid has been provided to developing countries by some nations but the substantial portion of external assistance has been provided through multilateral organizations, such as the United Nations Fund for Population Activities (UNFPA) and other U.N. agencies, and through private organizations.

The year 1965 was important in the history of population programs. In January 1965 President Johnson said in his State of the Union Message, "I will seek new ways to use our knowledge to help deal with the explosion in world population and the growing scarcity in world resources." In June 1965 the Supreme Court overturned the Connecticut law prohibiting sale of contraceptives. By the end of 1965 more than a dozen U.S. projects, developed largely by Planned Parenthood affiliates, were receiving Government financing for medical personnel, clinics, and contraceptive supplies for indigent women.

World interest in population growth intensified in the mid-1960's when a serious food shortage developed in South Asia. Weather played a prominent role. Monsoon rains failed in 1965; agriculture in India and in other South Asian countries had been somewhat neglected in the drive for industrialization; and the situation was aggravated, certainly, by continued population increase. It was a period described by some writers as "a genuine Malthusian crisis." Heavy shipments of grain from the United

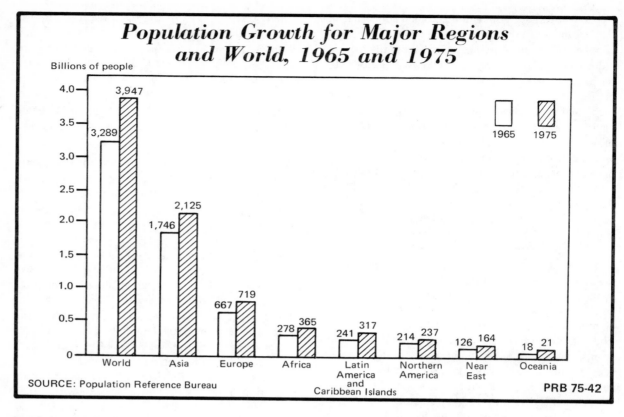

Population Growth for Major Regions and World, 1965 and 1975

Billions of people

	World	Asia	Europe	Africa	Latin America and Caribbean Islands	Northern America	Near East	Oceania
1965	3,289	1,746	667	278	241	214	126	18
1975	3,947	2,125	719	365	317	237	164	21

SOURCE: Population Reference Bureau

PRB 75-42

Populations expanded in all parts of the world between 1965 and 1975. But declining birth rates and some decrease in the overall world rate of natural population increase indicate that the percentage rate of population expansion was slowed in the 1965-75 period.

States, plus some from other countries, averted famine.

The crisis focused attention on the population-food equation. Legislation providing authority for U.S. food donations to needy countries (Public Law 480) was amended in 1966 to provide resources to promote voluntary activities in other countries dealing with the problem of population growth. Further attention was directed to population through a continuing series of Senate hearings by the Senate Government Operations Committee's Subcommittee on Foreign Aid Expenditures, under the chairmanship of Senator Ernest Gruening of Alaska.

In 1966 a Population Branch was created in the Health Service of AID's Office of Technical Cooperation and Research. The U.S. Congress in that year expressed its support of assistance to voluntary family planning efforts overseas in two laws—the Foreign Assistance Act of 1961, as amended, and the Food for Peace Act of 1966. The Secretary of State, the AID Administrator, the Acting Director of the

Peace Corps, and the Director of the U.S. Information Agency also announced jointly in 1966 that their agencies would give high priority to helping limit excessive rates of population growth and to increasing food production. U.S. Ambassadors and AID Mission Directors were instructed to consider population problems and requirements among their principal concerns and responsibilities.

Early in 1967 the Office of the War on Hunger was established in AID, focusing attention on the problems of population, food production, health, and nutrition. A Population Service was created within that Office to provide technical guidance and leadership for AID's population work. Along with expansion of the Population Service staff, population staffing was begun by the Regional Bureaus of AID in Washington and in AID Missions and U.S. posts abroad.

In fiscal year 1968, with passage of the amended Foreign Assistance Act of 1961, including Title X—Programs Relating to Population Growth—broadening

A lowering of the world's fertility rate from present levels to the replacement rate of two children per family by 1990 would mean a difference of 7 billion people in the world's total by the year 2020.

6

World Population Growth, 1970–2020

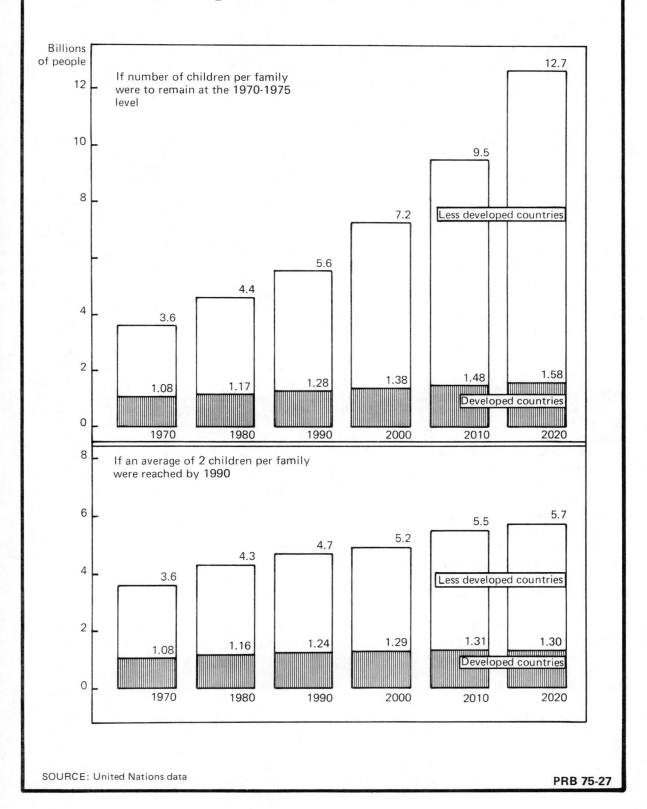

SOURCE: United Nations data

PRB 75-27

action was begun to help developing countries and institutions to carry out population programs. The present Office of Population, now part of the Bureau of Population and Humanitarian Assistance, was established in 1969.

World population activities continued to expand in the early 1970's. Existing private agencies stepped up their operations; new agencies entered the field. Multilateral involvement in population programs expanded through the work of the United Nations Fund for Population Activities (UNFPA) and other U.N. agencies and through entry of the World Bank into the population arena. Other countries joined the United States in providing bilateral population assistance to the developing countries or by channeling funds through multilateral and private organizations. For example, the 1974 report of UNFPA lists pledges from 52 different nations.

World Population Conference

The United Nations in 1973 designated 1974 World Population Year. The World Population Conference, held in Bucharest, Romania, in August 1974, was calculated to focus world attention on population problems. It succeeded in doing that. At Bucharest 136 governments were represented, the largest international population meeting ever held, and reports of the debates went out to all parts of the globe.

The Conference met shortly following the Sixth Special Session of the U.N. General Assembly, at which many developing countries had outlined proposals for a new world economic order. These faced severe problems—scarce food supplies, inflation stimulated by rising prices for imported oil, unfavorable terms of trade—and in most countries increasing populations were cancelling out or diluting, in per capita terms, hard-won economic and social gains.

But it became apparent early in the Conference that, while most nations recognized the existence of population problems within their own borders and in the world community, there was much disagreement about causes of the problems and workable solutions. A World Population Plan of Action was agreed to only after intense debate.

A number of participating countries held that lack of economic and social development is itself responsible for high birth rates in disadvantaged areas and that emphasis therefore should be on development rather than on population/family planning programs. They pointed to Europe's demographic transition as showing that fertility declines are a natural concomitant of social and economic transformation, even in the absence of any govern-ment support or policy. The fact that Europe experienced substantial population growth during its development was often noted as evidence that demographic growth does not affect development negatively.

Heard frequently at Bucharest was the slogan, "Take care of the people, and population will take care of itself." Significantly Paragraph 1 of the final World Plan closely links development with population:

The explicit aim of the World Population Plan of Action is to help co-ordinate population trends and the trends of economic and social development. The basis for an effective solution of population problems is, above all, socio-economic transformation. A population policy may have a certain success if it constitutes an integral part of socio-economic development; its contribution to the solution of world development problems is hence only partial, as is the case with other sectoral strategies. Consequently, the Plan of Action must be considered as an important component of the system of international strategies and as an instrument of the international community for the promotion of economic development, quality of life, human rights, and fundamental freedom.

Development was at the heart of the position expressed by Algeria, supported by a few African countries; by Argentina, backed by several other Latin American countries; by an Eastern European group of eight socialist states; and by the People's Republic of China.

A different position was taken by a number of countries, including most Western European nations (except France and Italy), Canada, the United States, some Latin American countries, Australia, New Zealand, Japan, and Iran. All of these countries were strong supporters of economic and social development for the Third World and most of them had contributed substantial sums to promote development; but it was their position that reductions in population growth could make a substantial contribution to development in countries where population growth is very rapid.

This interrelationship was spelled out in Paragraph 14 (c) of the final World Population Plan of Action:

Population and development are interrelated: population variables influence development variables and are also influenced by them; thus the formulation of a World Population Plan of Action reflects the international community's awareness of the importance of population trends for socio-economic development, and the socio-economic nature of the recommendations contained in this Plan of Action reflects its awareness of the crucial role that development plays in affecting population trends.

A more lucid explanation of this relationship has been expressed by Dorothy Nortman, Population Council, in that agency's October 1975 "Report on Population/Family Planning." She notes, "Whatever the stance on the political stage, the most ardent family planning advocates recognize that contraception 'alone' will not produce housing, schools, or steel mills; and among the staunchest supporters of the 'new economic order,' many appreciate the demographic value of legitimate and government-subsidized family planning services."

The final World Plan did endorse the concept of family planning by recommending in Paragraph 29, that all countries:

(a) Respect and ensure, regardless of their overall demographic goals, the right of persons to determine in a free, informed, and responsible manner the number and spacing of their children.

(b) Encourage appropriate education concerning responsible parenthood and make available to persons who so desire advice and means of achieving it.

At the Conference there was almost universal recognition of family planning practice as a human right, regardless of its demographic merits or demerits.

The Roman Catholic Church, through the representative of the Holy See, did not fully support the World Population Plan of Action. The Church objected to the World Plan's emphasis on the human rights of *individuals* in the matter of family planning, an emphasis which seemed to be a departure from previous U.N. stress on the human rights of *families*. More importantly, the Holy See felt that its position on artificial contraception was incompatible with family planning recommendations of the World Plan.

The position of this body on contraception had been set forth in detail by the Encyclical Letter, "On the Regulation of Birth"—Humanae Vitae—of Pope Paul VI in July 1968.

The Letter states, in part: ". . . we must once again declare that the direct interruption of the generative process already begun, and, above all, directly willed and procured abortion, even if for therapeutic reasons, are to be absolutely excluded as licit means of regulating birth."

"Equally to be excluded . . . is direct sterilization, whether perpetual or temporary, whether of the man or of the woman. Similarly excluded is every action which, either in anticipation of the conjugal act, or in its accomplishment, or in the development of its natural consequences, proposes, whether as an end or as a means, to render procreation impossible."

The Letter recognizes natural means as distinct from artificial contraception: "If, then, there are serious motives to space out birth, which derive from the physical or psychological conditions of husband and wife, or from external conditions, the Church teaches that it is then licit to take into account the natural rhythms imminent in the generative function for the use of marriage in the infecund periods only, and in this way to regulate birth without offending the moral principles which have been recalled earlier."

The Letter recognized the serious difficulties of public authorities, especially in the developing countries, but added, "The only possible solution to this question (population growth) is one which envisages the social and economic progress both of individuals and of the whole of human society and which respects and promotes true human values."

The World Plan comes out strongly for women's rights. It declares sweepingly in Paragraph 14-h:

Women have the right to complete integration in the development process particularly by means of an equal participation in educational, social, economic, cultural, and political life. In addition the necessary measures should be taken to facilitate this integration with family responsibilities which should be fully shared by both partners.

But the Conference's commitment to principles far outdistances any related commitment to their implementation. For example, the Conference did not address itself to the question of how quickly to increase education for women when overall educational improvements are painfully slow and costly. Nor did it have answers for questions of how to increase job opportunities, when one of the major problems in many of the developing countries is the growing unemployment and underemployment of their labor force, or how to influence local leaders in the more conservative areas to encourage additional general development opportunities for women.

(Some of these deficiencies were corrected at the World Conference of the International Women's Year held in Mexico City June 19-July 2, 1975. The delegates agreed on a program that mandates increased access to education, training, income-generating activities, better health care, and fertility control service for women, so that they can achieve their full potential and participate in all aspects of national life. Fuller access to family planning services is one of the goals targeted for achievement by 1980.)

The Bucharest World Plan contains a series of recommendations to stabilize migration within countries, particularly policies to reduce the undesirable consequences of excessively rapid urbanization and to develop opportunities in rural areas and small towns, recognizing the rights of individuals to move freely within their national boundaries.

The World Plan advocates agreements to regulate the international migration of workers and to assure nondiscriminatory treatment and social services for these workers and their families, plus other measures to decrease the "brain drain" from developing countries.

The Plan recommends that population censuses be taken at regular intervals and that information concerning births and deaths be made available at least annually.

The Population Council, in its "Report on Bucharest," notes that the World Plan of Action recognizes many problems. The Report says, "It is clear that the inevitable population growth of the next decades requires rapid socio-economic development if tragic loss of life is to be avoided. It is clear that death rates remain high, particularly among children in many parts of the world, and that their reduction must be high on the agenda of international action. It is clear that, while respecting the right of persons to determine the number and spacing of their children, all countries should encourage appropriate education concerning responsible parenthood and make available to persons who so desire advice and means of achieving it. It is clear that no marrriage should occur without the consent of the contracting parties, that child labor should be opposed, that education should be fostered for both boys and girls, and that economic opportunity outside the home should be made available to women as rapidly as possible. It is clear that there is much to be done in the fields of internal and international migration that will serve to rationalize the movements and foster the lot of the movers. It is clear that governments should take steps to study their demographic situations, should educate their publics about its meaning, and constantly reappraise the form and functioning of their population policies."

Philander P. Claxton, Jr., former Special Assistant for Population Matters to the Secretary of State and a U.S. delegate to the Conference, stated after the Conference ended that "By any reasonable standard, (the Conference) was a remarkable success." He also observed that "the World Population Plan

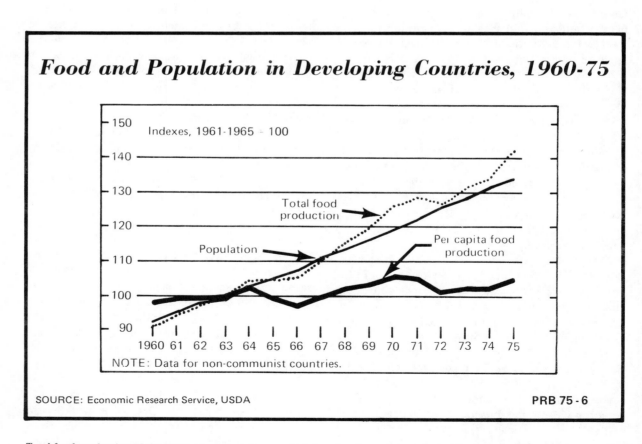

Total food production of the developing countries as a whole has risen in most recent years. But population increase has tended to keep pace. As a result, per capita food production as a whole has increased but little.

of Action, despite its wordiness and often hesitant tone, contains all the necessary provisions for effective family planning programs and population growth control programs at national and international levels. It lacks only plain statements of quantitative goals with time frames for their accomplishment. These can be added by individual national action and by development in future U.N. documents."

The Bucharest Conference was a trail blazer. It represented the first time that virtually all the countries of the world faced up to population problems and their relationship to other important economic and social issues. But population problems are of a continuing nature. Other conferences undoubtedly will be needed in the decades ahead if the potential of the agenda for action set forth at Bucharest is to become a reality.

Health Care Systems and Family Planning

Especially in the less-developed countries, provision of public services has not been able to keep pace with population growth and the consequent greater needs for services in such fields as health, education, transportation, and communication. Particularly hard hit is the field of health where increases in trained personnel and facilities have been far outstripped by population growth.

Most of the family planning programs are conducted through, or are importantly dependent upon, the existing infrastructures of health and health-related facilities. To overcome the scarcity of family planning/health resources, extensive training programs have been necessary at virtually all program levels. Also, the programs have moved increasingly toward wider dissemination of contraceptive supplies and information through field workers, village midwives, and other community-based personnel, as well as through commercial channels.

Officials of the U.N. World Health Organization in Geneva have noted that, owing to shortages of trained health personnel, many developing countries will not be able within the foreseeable future to extend conventional health services with family planning to cover the majority of the population in rural areas.

Less sophisticated integrated health delivery systems are needed that are suited to local conditions and that use less trained personnel for simpler health care matters, with referral of complicated cases to service points that have better equipment and more qualified personnel. Health systems of this kind would probably utilize indigenous health workers, including local midwives, after some limited training in relevant subjects and procedures. Recent reports indicate that rural health care in China makes major use of "barefoot" doctors with limited training and technical responsibility. This general approach has been adopted with modifications by several programs and is under consideration by others faced with scarcity of medical personnel and facilities.

Family Planning

Contraception has been a major factor in the reduced rate of population growth. A key element in "family planning," "planned parenthood," or "responsible parenthood," fertility control is being practiced to a greater extent than ever before. Family planning, although including fertility control, also importantly involves family welfare as a whole, including maternal and child health.

When, at the Bucharest Conference, 135 nations approved the recommendation that all countries "encourage appropriate education concerning responsible parenthood and make available to persons who so desire advice and means of achieving it," the Conference in large part was recommending something that was already in effect. Most of the industrialized countries in recent years have relaxed or removed legal restrictions on contraception. Among the developing countries, 65 now have population and family planning programs, many of them far advanced.

In the industrialized countries, which already had relatively low birth rates, widely practiced birth control has brought further reductions in fertility over the 1965-75 period. The birth rate in Europe dropped from 18 per 1,000 people in 1965 to 16 in 1974, while the decline in Northern America was from 20 to 15. Birth rates have dropped so low in some countries as to engender pronatalist thinking. Yet, it appears that less than a dozen countries have interposed total prohibition to distribution of contraceptives and that about half of the countries have provisions for legal induced abortion.

But fertility control is receiving special emphasis in the developing countries, which in the aggregate account for over four-fifths of the increase in the world's population. The People's Republic of China has a comprehensive birth control program that includes official encouragement of late marriage and small families, plus a broad spectrum of readily available contraceptive services. Among other countries carrying on vigorous and effective programs are Colombia, Costa Rica, Egypt, El Salvador, Hong Kong, Indonesia, Pakistan, Panama, the Philippines, Singapore, South Korea, Thailand, and Tunisia. In almost all of these, birth rates have dropped significantly. India, with a population of over 608 million, also has experienced a significant drop in birth rates. Family planning, generally speaking, has not yet been implemented in the countries of central Africa. The combined drop in birth rates for Africa, Asia, the Caribbean islands, Latin America, and the Near East was from 41 per 1,000 people in 1965 to 37 in 1974.

Rapid improvement in contraceptives and fertility control technology has played a key role in the widespread adoption of family planning. Biomedical and operational research programs by governments, private foundations, international organizations, pharmaceutical firms, universities, and other groups have contributed to the safety and effectiveness of contraceptive methods and their delivery.

Great improvements have been made in oral contraceptives. Around 1960, when the "pill" was first introduced, the formulations were relatively strong. All women using them were advised to remain under close medical supervision. Today the hormonal content of these preparations has been decreased, their relative safety has been widely studied and measured, and iron pills have been added to the monthly cycles. Objections to distribution of oral contraceptives without medical prescription have largely subsided in a number of countries—for example, in Pakistan, the Philippines, etc.

Now sought is a nontoxic and completely effective substance which, when self-administered on a single occasion, will ensure the nonpregnant state at completion of a monthly cycle. A 1975 research report indicates that success may be near.

The condom, an ancient contraceptive device, has been made more reliable through manufacturers' modern quality control. Diaphragms and vaginal chemicals have been improved. Research on different types of intrauterine devices—IUD's—has indicated that the Lippes Loop, one of the earliest types, is the most widely accepted.

Considerable research has been done on the "rhythm method" of contraception—sexual abstinence except during the "safe" phase of the menstrual cycle. But no reliable means has yet been found for accurately predicting the safe period for each individual.

Little improvement has been made in male sterilization; but the technology of female sterilization has been greatly simplified, and the operation is now being performed by one of several methods as a low-cost, outpatient procedure. Successful research has been conducted on devices for menstrual regulation. New and safer techniques have been developed for pregnancy termination through abortion.

Delivery of Family Planning Services

Between 1965 and 1975 there was a marked improvement in methods of delivering family planning services.

Experience of governments and intermediary organizations working in the population field has shown that effective family planning programs involve a number of related elements: development of effective and safe contraceptives along with adequate delivery systems; determining the suitability of contraceptives and procedures in each country; furnishing information and education designed to motivate acceptance of family planning and to inform potential acceptors of the services available and where and when they can be obtained; measuring results through the collection and analysis of demographic data (some countries have never taken a census of their populations); evaluating and shaping population policy; and training professionals and other personnel.

Dr. R. T. Ravenholt, Director of AID's Office of Population during the past decade, gives particular emphasis to the importance of country program delivery systems' assuring that effective means for fertility control are fully available to all people who want them. Establishment and maintenance of these systems are viewed as a primary program necessity.

Being tried in at least a dozen countries is extensive use of village or household distribution points for condoms, foams, and oral contraceptives. These can be supplied without clinical procedures and with new, more flexible patterns of supervision. Variously referred to as community distribution, village and household availability, continuous motivation, contraceptive inundation, subsidized sales, and social marketing, the new distributive methods are aimed at extending family planning services and supplies beyond the clinics and making them easily available to everyone.

The aptly named Contraceptive Inundation Scheme in Pakistan is illustrative of the new approaches. Basically a subsidized sales activity, it uses both shops in 40,000 villages and door-to-door distributors to sell contraceptives—at 2½ cents (U.S.) for a monthly cycle of pills or the same price for 12 condoms. Some 700 clinics employ female high school graduates to insert IUD's, provide pills and condoms, and dispense simple medicines. Program employees also do educational work, handle some demographic registration, and distribute contraceptives at about 400 Government hospitals and at the 40 hospitals which have postpartum family planning programs. Some 2,000 physicians are providing pills and condoms for free distribution to patients. Government-sponsored, the program has had major assistance from the U.S. Agency for International Development, and other direct aid has come from the United Nations, West Germany, the United Kingdom, Australia, and Norway.

Population and Food

An inexorable equation functions with respect to population and food: *total food availability divided by population equals per capita food availability.*

If a nation can increase its food supply by stepping up production or imports or both—and if the population stays the same—the average quantity of food available for each person is increased. But, as has happened frequently in the heavily populated developing countries, gains in food availability have been canceled by equal or increased gains in population, thereby leaving per capita supplies no larger, and sometimes smaller, than they were before.

This relationship was recognized at the World Food Conference at Rome in November 1974 when delegates of 24 nations sponsored a resolution calling for governments and people not only to produce more food but also to support population policies "which would assure the right of all couples to decide freely and responsibly the spacing and size of their own families . . . ." The Conference also called for a larger role for women in the war against hunger.

Concern about population growth in the 1960's and 1970's was heightened by two major food crises.

In 1965 and 1966, failure of the monsoons, the seasonal rains, brought disastrous drought to heavily populated South Asia—India, Pakistan, Nepal, and what is now Bangladesh. Only heavy imports of grain—the United States alone supplied about 11.5 million metric tons on concessional terms—averted major famine.

But in the years from 1967 through 1971, the food situation in the developing countries improved dramatically, especially in South and Southeast Asia. The so-called Green Revolution—use of new high-yielding varieties of wheat and rice with fertilizer, other chemicals, and irrigation—plus a period of good weather raised new hopes that the world food problem was on the way to solution. In terms of the 1961-65 average, total food production in all developing countries rose 15 percent from 1967 to 1971. Even per capita production rose about 4 percent.

Then, in 1972, food production dropped off almost everywhere. Sharp declines took place in many developing countries, especially in South Asia, which again suffered from drought. In parts of Africa, where production already was low because of prolonged dry weather, crops, livestock, and people suffered further setbacks. Output also declined in Canada and Australia—major grain exporters—and in the U.S.S.R. The U.S.S.R. became the world's largest grain importer, purchasing a total of 30 million metric tons (net) in 1972 and 1973, as compared with net exports of 8.6 million tons in the previous 2 years.

Reflecting operation of the population-food equation, per capita food production in the developing countries dropped off to the level of 1961-65. World food production rose substantially in 1973, but not enough to rebuild stocks. Production in 1974 was below expectations, especially in the United States, and stocks remained low. In 1975 food production was up sharply in the United States, but world stocks remained low. In 1975 food production was up sharply in the United States, Canada, India, and the People's Republic of China, but the U.S.S.R. again experienced widespread drought and was forced to obtain very large supplies of grain in the world market, and production also declined in Western Europe and some areas of Latin America.

Reversal of the world food situation from one of surpluses and low prices to one of relative scarcity and high prices has aroused considerable population-food pessimism Others, however, see cause for optimism if countries follow the population and food policies that will make for effective use of available resources. A wide spectrum of opinion exists.

But most would probably agree with the program suggested below, a program that comes to grips directly with the population-food equation:

". . . we urge governments . . . to consider realistic and purposeful measures such as the following:

1. Give high priority to programs in each country which will increase the production of grains, legumes, and other staple food crops; ensure the availability of protein-rich foods, particularly to the more vulnerable population groups; expand the production of fertilizer; and improve the opportunities for small farmers to make a reasonable living . . ."

2. Support sound population policies relevant to national needs which respect national sovereignty and the diversity of social, economic, and cultural conditions; accept and assure the human right of each couple to decide for themselves the spacing and size of their families; and recognize the corresponding responsibility of governments to provide their peoples the information and the means to exercise this right effectively . . ." (Declaration on Food and Population, Apr. 25, 1974, Population Crisis Committtee, Washington, D.C.)

Some developments in the 1970's support the gloom of the pessimists. Thousands of people have died of famine in the African Sahel and in Ethiopia.

Severe malnutrition, according to estimates of the Food and Agriculture Organization, is the lot of 460 million of the world's people. Food demand has increased, not only as a result of population growth, but also because of rising affluence, particularly in the developed countries; this has stimulated increased consumption of livestock products and, in turn, an increased use of grain for livestock feed. Prices of food have risen sharply everywhere, a circumstance which has tended to reduce the volume of concessional food aid to developing countries—and to diminish the ability of poor people in every country to buy as much food as they did a few years ago. The rise in fertilizer prices has hampered efforts of the developing countries to produce more of their own food. There has been some concern about the possibility of major changes in climatic patterns.

"Although the world has potentially cultivable land not in crops," states Lester R. Brown, internationally known economist, "this fact is illusory because 'cultivable' leaves out of account the cost of making land productive and also the food-price levels that would be needed to make production economically feasible. There is little potential for new cropland in Asia and Europe, and relatively little in the Soviet Union. Sub-Saharan Africa and the Amazon Basin of Brazil are the only regions with much new cropland potential, and tropical farming is often not economically feasible."

But the optimists also have much to encourage them.

The U.S. Department of Agriculture points out in its "World Food Situation and Prospects to 1985" that total food production has tended to increase over the past two decades. Growth in the developing countries has roughly paralleled that in the industrialized nations. Although populations have grown fastest in the developing countries, there was nevertheless an annual rate of increase in per capita food production in these countries of 0.4 percent.

In fact, the food situation in some developing countries is fairly good. Some have traditionally produced food surpluses; others, though not producing enough food to meet domestic demand, are able to pay for imports with manufactured goods or raw products like petroleum, copper, bauxite, and tin.

Yield-increasing techniques show promise as a means of expanding food production. Between 1973 and 1980, unless the energy shortage tightens, world fertilizer output and consumption are expected to increase at a compound annual rate of 5½ percent. High-yielding varieties of wheat and rice, although they have not solved the food-deficit problems of developing countries, have contributed greatly to a solution

of those problems. For example, India in 1965 produced about 12 million tons of wheat; but in 1975 it produced something over 24 million tons, thanks to high-yielding varieties, fertilizer, and irrigation, and that difference helped to feed India's population increase over the decade.

The oceans are providing large quantities of fish and can provide more if the countries of the world can agree on a cooperative approach to sound management of this great resource. Cooperation is imperative. Fishing fleets, equipped with modern electronic equipment for detecting fish, make it possible for some countries, notably the Soviet Union and Japan, to dominate fishing in many areas. This has forced a number of countries to extend their territorial control as much as 200 miles to sea, resulting in "tuna wars," "cod wars," and other frictions as nations try to stake out and police expanded fishing grounds.

"Hard core" population-food problems, in brief, are less widespread than such frequently used expressions as "worldwide famine" or "global starvation" would indicate. Hunger is endemic in most developing countries; famine is not. The population-food balance is most critical in densely populated India, Bangladesh, and Sri Lanka, where material shortfalls in food production can rapidly pose threats of famine. The balance also is precarious in some smaller countries, including the Sahelian area of Africa and, in the Western Hemisphere, Guyana, Haiti, Honduras, Jamaica, Paraguay, and Trinidad and Tobago. But these large and small countries are relatively few in number; their people in the aggregate account for less than 20 percent of the world's total. Viewed in this light, the "hard core" problems would seem to be manageable, eventually, with more energetic efforts by the vulnerable countries themselves, supplemented by expanded assistance from the international community.

The country with the largest population—the People's Republic of China—is taking energetic action not only to increase food production but also to slow its rate of population increase. The Chinese have developed their own high-yielding dwarf rice varieties. They have devoted much attention to fertilizer production. They import grain, sometimes in rather substantial quantities, but have been able to finance imports from their own resources. While strengthening their agriculture, they have taken vigorous steps to reduce their birth rate—from an estimated 50 per 1,000 population in 1950 to an estimated 27 in 1974.* Family planning has been a

*PRB estimate. Another source estimates the 1974 PRC birth rate at 17 per 1,000.

part of the national policy for more than 10 years; birth control methods include condoms, intrauterine devices, oral contraceptive pills, sterilization, and abortion. China also emphasizes postponement of marriage and "ideal" two-children families.

India, with a population about three-fourths as large as that of China, has been in a precarious food situation for many years.

Although India has adopted some elements of the Green Revolution technology, it has not been able to achieve a major agricultural breakthrough. There was promise of that when India's food production per capita rose from a near-disastrous 89 percent of the 1961-65 average in 1966 to 109 percent in 1970, one of the country's few good agricultural years. But since 1970, per capita food production has tended to decline despite gains in total output.

Population, the other factor in the picture has continued to rise at a rapid rate. Prime Minister Indira Gandhi has voiced concern about this trend, has spoken about it over nationwide networks, and has sent letters to village leaders, asking for their help in lowering birth rates. Condoms have come into

wider use, and abortion has been legalized, but services are far from fully available and the program has not yet realized the progress that is sought and much needed. In 1973 for a time India de-emphasized its sterilization campaign, and use of IUD's decreased. Oral contraceptives have not been made generally available under the Government's program, and condoms are of poor quality.

The contrast between the population-food programs of China and India seems to reflect differences in policies followed by Governments of the two countries rather than differences in resources or capabilities of the people. Policies are important everywhere. The U.S. Department of Agriculture has noted that:

. . . much of what has happened in the development of the world food situation can be traced to government policies and basic human conditions (such as income distribution and poverty), and suggests that governmental and individual choices will continue to be critical in the future. The world food situation can be changed to the extent that governments and individuals see needs for change and are willing to modify those policies and conditions

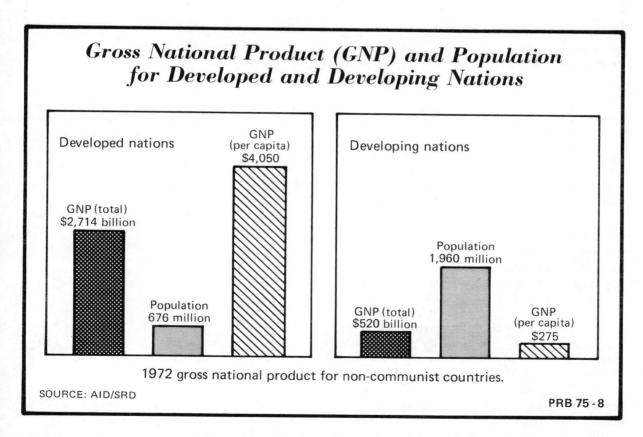

Gross National Product (GNP) and Population for Developed and Developing Nations

Developed nations

GNP (total) $2,714 billion

Population 676 million

GNP (per capita) $4,050

Developing nations

Population 1,960 million

GNP (total) $520 billion

GNP (per capita) $275

1972 gross national product for non-communist countries.

SOURCE: AID/SRD

PRB 75-8

When national resources are inadequate and must be shared by many, the proportion per person is often extremely small. A relatively small total gross national product in most developing countries is restricting individual savings and country revenues, and retarding capital accumulations needed for self-generating development in these countries.

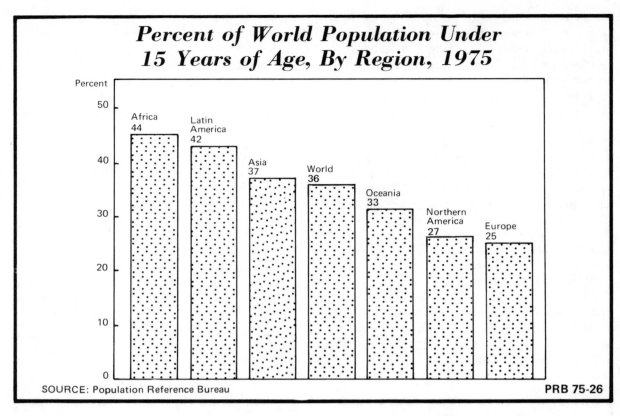

Percent of World Population Under 15 Years of Age, By Region, 1975

Percent

Africa 44
Latin America 42
Asia 37
World 36
Oceania 33
Northern America 27
Europe 25

SOURCE: Population Reference Bureau

PRB 75-26

The developing countries, with a high proportion of young people in their population and high annual rates of natural increase, will provide the bulk of the world's population gain in the next 60 years and possibly beyond.

that influence food production and consumption.

How the individual developing countries modify their policies could well shape the volume and nature of assistance granted by the industrialized nations, which seem increasingly disposed to grant substantial aid to the developing countries.

U.S. Secretary of State Kissinger, in an address to the U.N. General Assembly in September 1975, urged establishment of a world reserve system for grain. He also announced that President Ford would seek Congressional authorization for a $200-million direct U.S. contribution to an International Fund for Agricultural Development provided other countries support a combined goal of at least $1 billion. The Secretary noted that massive new concessional resources need to be mobilized to expand agricultural production in the poorest countries because of the growing gap between their needs and their own production—a gap that food aid cannot possibly fill completely. He also stated that traditional bilateral aid programs for agriculture remain indispensable and announced that the President would ask Congress to double U.S. agricultural assistance in fiscal 1976 to $582 million.

But food aid probably will not be provided on the same scale in the future as it was in the 1950's and 1960's, when grain stocks in the major grain-producing countries were large. Global grain stocks are down, largely because of a generally increased world demand and the need to fill drought-shorted granaries in the Soviet Union and elsewhere. Also, prices of grain have risen, which increases the tendency of grain-producing countries to sell commercially to offset increased prices for imported petroleum and other raw materials. It would appear that, out of necessity, countries that once relied rather heavily on concessional supplies must sooner or later take action to step up food output and, at the same time, adopt meaningful measures to slow down the increase in the number of people eating at national dinner tables.

Time has a major role to play in this population-food race. It is urgent that population actions be initiated as early as possible because of the long lead time required to make an impact, especially in the countries with very large populations. Action to produce more food must be undertaken early also, because of the need to "buy time" for the population actions to take effect. For many countries of this world with serious problems relating to food and population, the hour already is late.

Urbanization

The movement of people within the borders of their own countries—internal migration—has generally been from rural to urban areas. This urbanization phenomenon reflects in considerable degree the gregariousness of humanity as well as many social and economic factors.

Urbanization dates far back into history; Athens, Babylon, Rome, Peking, and other cities of the ancient world attracted migrants long before the Christian era. Cityward movements were accelerated by the Industrial Revolution; the rise of the factory system attracted large-scale migration to cities, especially in Europe and Northern America. Urbanization today is taking place not only in the industrialized nations but also in the developing countries.

Ronald Freedman, University of Michigan sociologist, and Bernard Berelson note that urbanization "presents causes for concern: urban congestion, unemployment, environmental deterioration, problems of housing and sanitation and transportation, lack of social services, political unrest, and difficulties of acculturation."

Robert S. McNamara, World Bank president, has commented on problems of urban poverty with specific reference to the developing countries. He says:

To understand urban poverty in the developing world one must first understand what is happening to the cities themselves. They are growing at a rate unprecedented in history. Twenty-five years ago there were 16 cities in the developing countries with populations of one million or more. Today there are over 60. Twenty-five years from now there will be more than 200.

How has this happened? Fundamentally, of course, it is a function of population growth. But it is more than just that. For though the total population in the developing world is increasing by about 2.5 percent a year, the urban population is growing at nearly twice that rate. Half the urban growth is due to natural increase, and half is due to migration from the countryside.

What this means is that many millions of additional people have been absorbed into cities, through birth and migration, in a single generation—something wholly without parallel. In contrast, the developed world urbanized at a leisurely and less pressured pace at a time when its national populations were growing very slowly, at only about half a percent a year.

Latin America is already 60 percent urbanized, and Asia and Africa about 25 percent. But by the end of the century, three out of every four Latin Americans will live in a city and one out of every three Africans and Asians. Thus, at current trends, over the next 25 years the urban areas will have to

absorb another 1.1 billion people, almost all of them poor, in addition to their present population of 700 million.

Life for the urban poor today is unspeakably grim. Though they spend up to 80 percent of their income on food, they typically suffer from serious malnutrition. It is estimated that half the urban population of India is undernourished. Up to 15 percent of the children who die in Latin American cities, and up to 25 percent of those who die in African cities, are victims of malnutrition.

Now what do these figures imply?

They make it certain that the cities of the developing world are going to find it incredibly difficult to provide employment, and minimally decent living conditions for the hundreds of millions of new entrants into urban economies which are already severely strained.

An even more ominous implication is what the penalties for failure may be. Historically, violence and civil upheaval are more common in cities than in the countryside. Frustrations that fester among the urban poor are readily exploited by political extremists. If cities do not begin to deal more constructively with poverty, poverty may well begin to deal more destructively with cities.

It is not a problem that favors political delay. Freedman and Berelson describe attempts to limit the growth of large urban centers including:

. . . regional development (Greece and Finland), decentralization of government activities (the Netherlands), relocation of the capital (Brazil and Tanzania), support of new towns (Japan and Britain), damping of wage differentials between urban and rural areas (Zambia), reorientation of education toward agricultural interests (Indonesia and Tanzania), subsidies for industrial location (France, Sweden, and Togo), rural land reclamation (Kenya) and even a "citizenship tax" on living in the city (Seoul in South Korea).

The effect of such efforts, although difficult to measure, has not been striking, and the further modernization of agriculture will intensify the pressures. The cities can only be expected to grow even more, with all the problems that implies. Again there is the (reported) counter example of China, where as a matter of national policy migration to the cities is stringently controlled and many people are actually exported for various periods from the cities back to the land.

(The settlement of agricultural areas in Australia, Argentina, South Africa, the United States, and other countries in the 1800's possibly slowed the world trend toward urbanization—but only temporarily.)

The worldwide pace of urbanization has been rapid. Kingsley Davis, University of California sociologist, cites figures:

In 1970 the earth had approximately 1,725 cities of 100,000 or more inhabitants. By 1975 there will probably be about 1,950—a rise of 13 percent in 5 years—and, if development continues to follow a smooth course, by the year 2,000 there will be approximately 3,600 such cities. As recently as 1950 the number of these cities was only 962.

Davis observes:

Whether viewed in terms of population size, density, or mass, the city represents a habitat extremely different from the migratory camp or small village that characterized 99 percent of human history. The transition to a city mode of living is therefore a major turning point in human evolution. The fact that this transition is occurring now and is quickly running its course permits us to be first-hand observers of a fundamental alteration in the human condition. Our ancestors could only dream about this change; our descendants can only read about it.

International Migration

Migration, births, and deaths are factors in population dynamics. In some periods, in some countries, migration has been a major element of population growth or decrease. In recent years, however, it has been less important in the world population equation than formerly, largely because a declining proportion of the world's people are moving from one country to another.

Migration encompasses voluntary and forced movements. Its overall effect on population growth depends on such factors as permanence of the move, age and sex of the migrants, and their fertility and mortality. "Pull" and "push" forces—the relative advantages and disadvantages of migrating or staying at home—play a part in determining with respect to voluntary movements the size and direction of migratory streams.

Migration policies of nations, influenced by economic and political considerations, are increasingly shaping the size and the direction of migrant movements. Prosperity in a country may create a demand for labor and bring about an easing of immigration restrictions, whereas a business recession often results in tightened restrictions on immigration. The sharp rise in the number of independent countries following the post-World War II decline of colonialism in Asia, Africa, and the Caribbean area has tended* to increase restrictions on emigration, immigration, or both. A United Nations questionnaire circulated at the 1974 World Population Conference revealed that 116 countries restrict permanent immigration while only 32 permit it. Two of the heavily populated countries, the People's Republic of China and the Soviet Union, discourage both emigration and immigration.

Migration flows over the years have often shifted direction.

A major flow took place in the 1840-1915 period when an estimated 52 million people left Europe—

about 31 million for the United States and the others for such distant destinations as Argentina, Australia, Brazil, Canada, and South Africa. This movement reached a peak in the years between 1900 and 1914.

In the 1965-75 period, there was still considerable migration from Europe but, at the same time, other European movements had appeared. For example, establishment of the European Economic Community in 1968 led millions of workers from Southern and Eastern Europe, Turkey, and North Africa to migrate to Western Europe in the 1960's; Western Europe had a net in-migration of 4.9 million workers who were drawn there by job opportunities and attractive rates of pay.

In the meantime, the flow of Western Europeans to such traditional destinations as Canada, the United States, and Latin America declined partly because of improved opportunities in their own countries. Increasing unemployment in the mid-1970's however, brought about reassessments in Western Europe; "anti-immigration" attitudes made their appearance in some countries, notably Switzerland, but also to some extent in Belgium, Denmark, France, Luxembourg, West Germany, and the United Kingdom.

The United States in the 1965-75 period remained the leading country of immigration in terms of total intake, with 395,000 immigrants admitted legally in 1974. There have been great increases in immigration from Latin America and the Caribbean islands, especially from Mexico, and from Asia, particularly from India, Korea, the Philippines, and Taiwan.

Migration to South Africa and Australia, mainly from Europe, increased in the 1951-75 period. South Africa has encouraged the entry of white immigrants; 37,000 entered the country in 1975, about half from the United Kingdom. Australia, which also has encouraged immigration, has had some second thoughts following an increase in unemployment. As compared with the previous "target" for immigration of 110,000 per year, Australia set a ceiling of 80,000 immigrants in 1974, and lowered that to 55,000 in 1975.

There has been a drastic drop-off in the traditional migrant flow from Southern Europe to Latin America. Totals dropped from 800,000 in 1951-55 to 131,000 in 1966-70, and a further decline took place in 1971-75. Workers from Italy, Spain, and Portugal have found the job market in Western Europe more attractive than that of Latin America. Also a factor, several Latin American countries have taken action to reduce the inflow of workers without special skills. In the mid-1970's, much of the intracontinental migration in Latin America consisted of

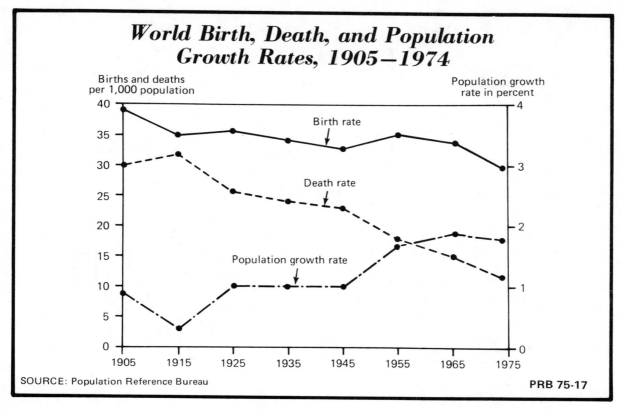

World Birth, Death, and Population Growth Rates, 1905–1974

Births and deaths per 1,000 population

Population growth rate in percent

Birth rate

Death rate

Population growth rate

1905 1915 1925 1935 1945 1955 1965 1975

SOURCE: Population Reference Bureau

PRB 75-17

Birth rates since 1965 have declined to a greater degree than death rates, possibly denoting the beginning of a down-trend in the population growth rate.

movements between rural areas.

From 1950 into the 1970's, there were heavy out-movements of people from a number of the newly independent countries of Africa, involving some repatriation to Europe and elsewhere. Also, these years included population movements in India, Pakistan, and Bangladesh involving a total of many millions of people.

In summary, the major migration streams since 1960 have been from Southern and Eastern Europe, Turkey, and North Africa to Western Europe; from Europe to Australia, Canada, South Africa, and the United States; from Latin America, the Caribbean countries, and Asia to the United States; and from Asia and Latin America to Canada.

Countries registering the largest net migration gains in 1950-70 were the United States with a net intake of about 6.9 million, West Germany with 4.8 million, France with 3.3 million, Australia with 1.9 million, Canada with 1.8 million, and Switzerland with 630,000. The countries with the heaviest net outflows were East Germany with 2.5 million, Italy and Portugal with 2.0 million each, Spain and Yugoslavia with 1.2 million to 1.5 million each, Greece with 651,000, and Ireland with 558,000.

Between 1960 and 1970 about 5 million people moved from one country to another. Major world regions losing migrants included Latin America, 1.9 million; Africa, 1.6 million; Asia, 1.2 million; and Europe, 300,000. Regions gaining migrants were Northern America, 4.1 million and Oceania, 900,000.

Illegal immigration has become an increasingly vexatious problem for many nations. It has been estimated that more than half a million foreigners were illegally working or living in various European countries in 1973. The United Nations reported in 1974 that there was illegal migration from North Africa into Italy and Greece and from Portugal to France. Large numbers of black workers have moved illegally into South Africa. Thousands of illegal immigrants, mainly from the People's Republic of China, have crossed the border into Hong Kong. Several hundred thousand illegal workers from Colombia and the Caribbean islands are reported in Venezuela. Estimates of the "illegals" in the United States, many of them from Mexico, range to 7 million or more.

Complaints about illegals are varied: they take jobs that could otherwise be filled by the native-born or by migrants who entered the country legally;

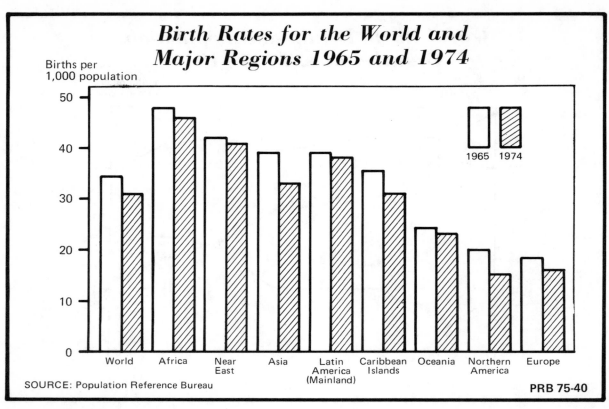

Birth Rates for the World and Major Regions 1965 and 1974

Births per 1,000 population

Legend: 1965, 1974

Regions (left to right): World, Africa, Near East, Asia, Latin America (Mainland), Caribbean Islands, Oceania, Northern America, Europe

SOURCE: Population Reference Bureau

PRB 75-40

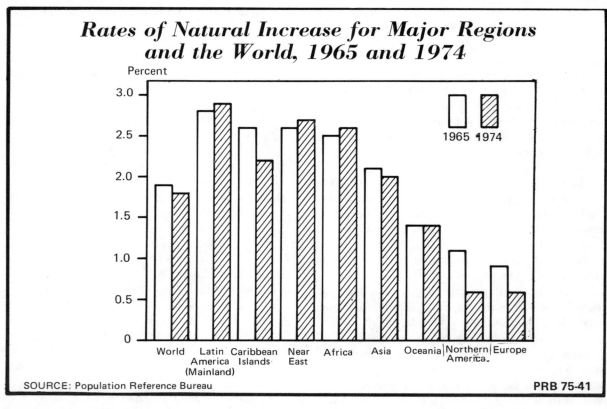

Rates of Natural Increase for Major Regions and the World, 1965 and 1974

Percent

Legend: 1965, 1974

Regions (left to right): World, Latin America (Mainland), Caribbean Islands, Near East, Africa, Asia, Oceania, Northern America, Europe

SOURCE: Population Reference Bureau

PRB 75-41

The world rate of natural population increase declined between 1965 and 1974. Declines in the developed countries, the Caribbean area, and Asia were offset in considerable degree by increases in Latin America, Africa, and the Near East.

Birth rates appear to be associated with per capita gross national product. In 1974, Europe, Northern America, and Oceania had an average birth rate of 16 per 1,000 people and a per capita GNP of $3,456, whereas all other regions, mainly developing countries, had a birth rate of 32 and a composite per capita GNP below $450.

they overburden social services; they pay few taxes; they send money out of the country in the form of remittances. Currently the arguments against wider action on illegals in the United States emphasizes humanitarian considerations including avoidance of family breakups and other hardships for individuals.

Forced migrations have been an unfortunate factor of life for mankind since the dawn of history. One of the oldest examples of forced movement is the enslavement and transport of human beings; it is estimated that 9.6 million slaves—those that survived the voyages—were imported into the numerous slave-using areas between 1450 and 1970; most of them were from Africa. There have been other forms of forced migration: Compulsory resettlement, expulsion and flight from political persecution, or war.

Forced migrations are still part of the world population picture. About 10 million refugees were involved in the conflict between India and Pakistan in the early 1970's. In 1972, Uganda, as part of its campaign to "Africanize" trade, the professions, and government, expelled some 40,000 Asians. Many thousands of Portuguese-speaking people, fleeing from civil war in Angola, have taken up residence in Portugal and elsewhere. Over 200,000 Cuban refugees have been admitted to the United States, and the U.S. refugee total was increased still further in 1975 by the addition of some 120,000 Vietnamese men, women, and children.

Whether migration is "good" or "bad" has been debated often but inconclusively. Few of the victims of forced migration would see any good in it. And developing nations that have lost scientists, skilled technicians, and other high-caliber people through voluntary migration argue that this "brain drain" works to their detriment. Some demographers have doubts about the benefit of immigration to receiving countries. But immigration, in filling the empty spaces of the world, unquestionably has improved the balance between population and resources. Certainly for millions of migrants who have found good jobs and improved living conditions in receiving countries, migration has been advantageous.

Migration does affect population trends in individual countries. It has been estimated, for example, that Ireland's population of 3.1 million in 1974 would have been about 12 million without emi-

gration over the past 100 years and with the birth and death rates that prevailed. On the other hand, the population of the United States today would be substantially smaller in the absence of the 46.7 million immigrants admitted between 1820 and 1974, plus their offspring.

Because international migration can be significant in increasing or decreasing the rate of population growth in individual countries, it has been suggested from time to time that migration be made a keystone of international population policy. At the World Population Conference, representatives from Argentina and some other nations suggested that heavily populated countries would be helped if their citizens were encouraged to move into countries having smaller populations. But this proposal would seem to have little chance of universal adoption—not with 116 countries opting for restrictions on immigration.

But even if there were no political restrictions against the movement of people from one country to another, the logistics involved would make migration an utterly impracticable way of solving the problem of excessive population pressures. For example, if the developed nations should try to accept as immigrants the excess population growth of the developing countries, they would have to receive scores of millions per year. Relocating such an enormous number of immigrants—year after year—would, of course, put an impossible burden on the world's transport, housing, health, education, and other services. The answer to the problem of excessive population growth obviously continues to involve fertility and mortality primarily. In the economic, social, and political climate existing today, international migration can contribute relatively little to easing the global problems of population growth—and that in only a few limited parts of the world.

Women's Rights and Fertility

The United Nations in its Charter and in the Universal Declaration of Human Rights, stressed that all men and women are born free and equal in dignity and in rights.

The U.N.'s first specific reference to family planning came in 1966 when the United Nations stated that the size of the family should be the free choice of each individual family.

The International Conference on Human Rights, in 1968, expanded on this tenet by declaring that couples have a basic human right to decide freely and responsibly on the number and spacing of their children and a right to education and information in this domain.

In 1969 a U.N. General Assembly resolution

Changes in Birth Rates Since 1960 in 63 Countries

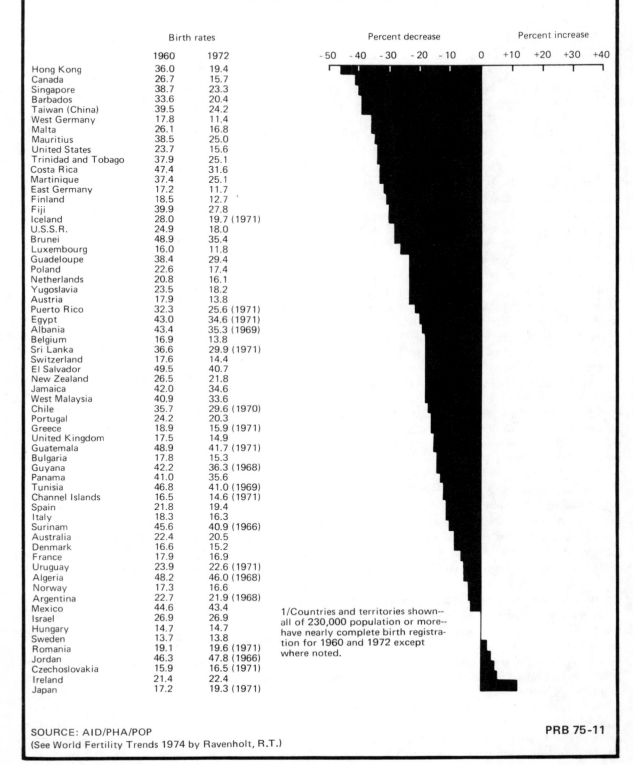

	Birth rates	
	1960	1972
Hong Kong	36.0	19.4
Canada	26.7	15.7
Singapore	38.7	23.3
Barbados	33.6	20.4
Taiwan (China)	39.5	24.2
West Germany	17.8	11.4
Malta	26.1	16.8
Mauritius	38.5	25.0
United States	23.7	15.6
Trinidad and Tobago	37.9	25.1
Costa Rica	47.4	31.6
Martinique	37.4	25.1
East Germany	17.2	11.7
Finland	18.5	12.7
Fiji	39.9	27.8
Iceland	28.0	19.7 (1971)
U.S.S.R.	24.9	18.0
Brunei	48.9	35.4
Luxembourg	16.0	11.8
Guadeloupe	38.4	29.4
Poland	22.6	17.4
Netherlands	20.8	16.1
Yugoslavia	23.5	18.2
Austria	17.9	13.8
Puerto Rico	32.3	25.6 (1971)
Egypt	43.0	34.6 (1971)
Albania	43.4	35.3 (1969)
Belgium	16.9	13.8
Sri Lanka	36.6	29.9 (1971)
Switzerland	17.6	14.4
El Salvador	49.5	40.7
New Zealand	26.5	21.8
Jamaica	42.0	34.6
West Malaysia	40.9	33.6
Chile	35.7	29.6 (1970)
Portugal	24.2	20.3
Greece	18.9	15.9 (1971)
United Kingdom	17.5	14.9
Guatemala	48.9	41.7 (1971)
Bulgaria	17.8	15.3
Guyana	42.2	36.3 (1968)
Panama	41.0	35.6
Tunisia	46.8	41.0 (1969)
Channel Islands	16.5	14.6 (1971)
Spain	21.8	19.4
Italy	18.3	16.3
Surinam	45.6	40.9 (1966)
Australia	22.4	20.5
Denmark	16.6	15.2
France	17.9	16.9
Uruguay	23.9	22.6 (1971)
Algeria	48.2	46.0 (1968)
Norway	17.3	16.6
Argentina	22.7	21.9 (1968)
Mexico	44.6	43.4
Israel	26.9	26.9
Hungary	14.7	14.7
Sweden	13.7	13.8
Romania	19.1	19.6 (1971)
Jordan	46.3	47.8 (1966)
Czechoslovakia	15.9	16.5 (1971)
Ireland	21.4	22.4
Japan	17.2	19.3 (1971)

1/Countries and territories shown-- all of 230,000 population or more-- have nearly complete birth registration for 1960 and 1972 except where noted.

SOURCE: AID/PHA/POP
(See World Fertility Trends 1974 by Ravenholt, R.T.)

PRB 75-11

22

Birth rates in most countries are lower than a decade ago. For the world as a whole birth rates declined from 34 per 1,000 people in 1965 to 30 in 1974. Natural increase, the excess of births over deaths, also is beginning to drop despite the continuing decrease in the mortality rate.
The world rate of natural increase declined from 1.9 percent in 1965 to 1.8 percent in 1974.

broadened this concept to include the right to the means to space and limit births.

At the World Population Conference in 1974, and at the International Women's Year Conference in 1975, the close interrelationship between fertility and women's rights was clearly delineated. The importance of family planning to women's status was emphasized in the International Women's Year Plan of Action as follows:

Individuals and couples have the right freely and responsibly to determine the number and spacing of their children and to have the information and means to do so. The exercise of this right is basic to the attainment of any real equality between the sexes and without its achievement women are disadvantaged in their attempt to benefit from other reforms.

However, a number of legal, economic, social, and cultural factors keep women from fully exercising their right to plan births and some encourage large families. Often, there are legal and other restrictions which prevent the relevant education, information, and services. Inadequate family planning programs deprive many women, particularly the rural poor, of the knowledge and means of safe, reliable fertility regulation. Cultural definitions of woman's role as sexual partner, homemaker, and mother restrict her rights rather than affording her equal participation in the social and economic life of her community. Lack of alternative roles for women, and male dominance in decision-making, including decisions concerning childbearing and all other facets of home life, are the current reality in most of the world's nations.

An official of the Office of Population, U.S. Agency for International Development, has described the actual plight of women in the poorer areas of the world:

The daily pattern of women in the developing countries has changed very little for centuries. For instance, the average woman in South Asia or Africa rises at 5 a.m. every morning. Shortly thereafter, with a small baby on her back, she leaves her rural hut for the fields. There she bends her back to planting, ploughing, and farming for most of the day, pausing occasionally to quiet and nurse her child. Returning home, she gathers firewood along her way and once home, pounds grain, walks a mile to fetch water, and cooks the family meal. After a fifteen-hour, nonstop working day, she finally sleeps.

She does not know this is women's year and has been unaffected by it. She has never learned to read and write, was married off by her father at 14 years of age, will have eleven pregnancies, six surviving children, and may live to be fifty. She has had no access to family planning services and does not understand the reproductive process. Her property and money, if she has any, are controlled by her husband. She has few, if any, rights. This woman bears the heavy home and work responsibilities of her family and has far less chance for education and advancement than her husband or brother. In Bangladesh, for example, the literacy rate for men is 20 percent, while for women it is only 2 percent. The women are kept closely in the home, and are not allowed even to worship in the mosques where only men are deemed worthy to pray.

The International Women's Year Conference (IWY), with its central theme of equality, development, and peace, was attended in Mexico in June 1975 by representatives of 133 countries. Central to the demands expressed for equal rights, opportunities, and responsibilities was the insistence on a woman's right to determine the number and spacing of her children.

With the ability to delay the first birth, to space births several years apart, to stop childbearing when desired family size is reached and to limit the total number of births (or choose to have no children), it was stated a woman gains considerable control over her health, the health of her children, her opportunities for employment and education, and the exercise of her economic, social, and political rights in the society and in the family; that by exercising her right to control her fertility, a woman also contributes to the economic well-being of her family, her village, her country, and the world. Freedom from care of the family, be it small or large, was discussed in terms of freedom to gain education and add to the economic output of the family and larger economic entities. The view was widely held that fewer children per family can enable a better quality of life for family members and savings and capital formation for the family, village, and nation. It was stated also that by mobilizing women fully into economic production, increased output and more rapid economic growth results, as well as smaller families.

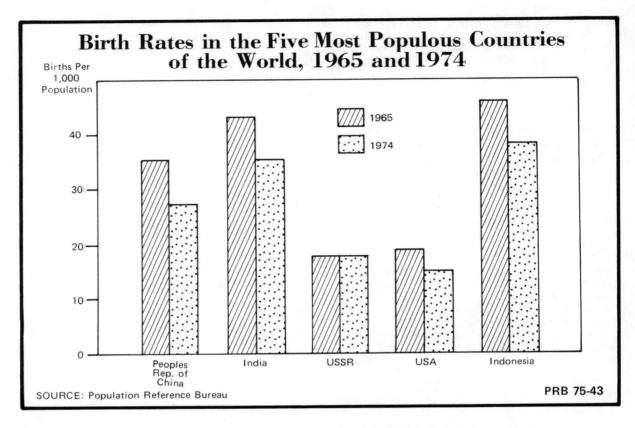

Birth Rates in the Five Most Populous Countries of the World, 1965 and 1974

Births Per 1,000 Population

- 1965
- 1974

40

30

20

10

0

Peoples Rep. of China   India   USSR   USA   Indonesia

SOURCE: Population Reference Bureau

PRB 75-43

Of the five most populous countries in the world, four showed significant decreases in birth rates over a 10-year period. These four countries, with a combined population of 1,778 million in 1975, account for 45 percent of the world's total population. (Estimates of China's current birth rate vary considerably.)

Abortion Situation*

Induced abortions have long affected significantly the world rate of population increase as well as the rate in individual countries. For this reason the following information is presented regarding the estimated worldwide incidence of abortion and its current legal status in most countries.

The world total of abortions—legal and illegal—is not known for any year, since statistics even on legal abortions are not fully reported in many countries and illegal abortions are mostly unrecorded. However, health records, data on legal abortions, and related information indicate that abortion continues to be widely used.

Probably indicative of the annual world total is the estimate for 1971 reported by John Robbins of

the Planned Parenthood Federation of America. With calculations based on data from 87 countries included in the International Planned Parenthood Federation (IPPF) survey of 208 countries in 1971, Robbins estimated that "... more than 55 million women terminated their pregnancies by abortion —legal and illegal—during the year (1971), for a worldwide total of 4 abortions for every 10 babies delivered."

Because estimating the extent to which abortions reduce the number of births which would otherwise have occurred in a population depends upon knowing the level of contraceptive practice, it is impossible to calculate for the world as a whole the current demographic impact of abortion, particularly as based on admittedly controversial estimates of annual incidence. However, analysts of abortion statistics relating to population growth have noted that none of the world's industrialized countries has ever brought its birth rate down substantially without significant recourse to abortion. These analysts conclude that developing countries will be unable to

*Most information given here is drawn from *Population Reports:* Law and Policy, Series E, No. 3, January 1976, by Margot Zimmerman, published by George Washington University Medical Center, Washington, D.C.

reach desirable demographic goals for the future without such recourse.

Although abortions are prohibited absolutely in some countries and are subject to varying restrictions in most others, considerable liberalization of abortion laws has occurred in this century, a trend which has accelerated in the 1970's. As a result, legal abortion services are now theoretically available in many populous countries, although availability in actual practice varies considerably.

In January 1976, Margot Zimmerman, of the Population Information Program of George Washington University Medical Center, concluded that "Today 60 percent of the people of the world live in countries where abortion in the first trimester of pregnancy is legal either for social and economic reasons, or on request without specific indication."

The following countries permit abortion "on request" during a specified period, usually the first trimester of pregnancy, without the applicant's specifying any reason: Austria, The People's Republic of China, Denmark, France, the German Democratic Republic, Singapore, the Soviet Union, Sweden, Tunisia, the United States, and the Democratic Republic of Vietnam. In these countries, the decision usually rests with the woman and her doctor. (Generally, abortions beyond the period prescribed by law for elective abortion are permitted when medically indicated.)

In addition, 19 other countries or states allow abortions for social and socio-medical reasons. As reported by Zimmerman, these include South Australia and the Northern Territories of Australia, Bulgaria, Cyprus, Czechoslovakia, Finland, Germany, Great Britain, Hong Kong, Hungary, Iceland, India, Japan, Norway, Poland, Romania, Uruguay, Yugoslavia, and Zambia. In these, in evaluating the threat to a woman's health, doctors are permitted to consider social factors, such as marital status, economic condition of the family, and family health and housing conditions. In some countries, adverse social conditions unrelated to the woman's health may also be taken into account.

Also 36 other countries are identified by Zimmer-

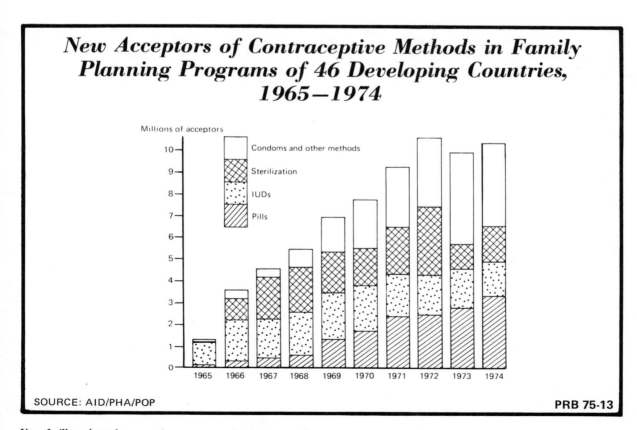

New Acceptors of Contraceptive Methods in Family Planning Programs of 46 Developing Countries, 1965—1974

Millions of acceptors

Condoms and other methods
Sterilization
IUDs
Pills

1965 1966 1967 1968 1969 1970 1971 1972 1973 1974

SOURCE: AID/PHA/POP

PRB 75-13

Use of pills and condoms continues to expand, while use of IUD's has just about held its own. The sharp decline in sterilization in 1973 and 1974 reflects India's decision to de-emphasize its mass camps for vasectomies, while sterilizations were increasing elsewhere. The upswing in sterilization in 1974 is apparently continuing.

man as permitting abortion under "moderately restrictive" conditions. These include: In North America—Canada; in Europe—Albania, Greece, Italy, and Switzerland; in Africa—Cameroon, Ethiopia, Ghana, Kenya, Mauritius, Morocco, Nigeria, Sierra Leone, South Africa, Sudan, Swaziland, and Uganda; in Oceania—Australia; in the Near East—Israel, Jordan, Lebanon, Syria, and Turkey; in Asia—the Republic of Korea and Thailand; and in Latin America—Argentina, Brazil, Costa Rica, Cuba, Ecuador, El Salvador, Guatemala, Honduras, Mexico, Peru, and Chile. In these, abortions are permitted on one of several grounds: (1) To preserve the health of the woman (in some countries mental as well as physical health); (2) on humanitarian or juridical grounds if pregnancy resulted from rape or incest; or (3) on eugenic grounds if it is believed the fetus has been impaired and/or the child would be born with serious physical or mental defects. In this group of countries, the written consent of two physicians and/or an abortion board is usually a prerequisite.

In another 45 countries, abortion is permitted only to save the life of the pregnant woman. These are: In Europe—Luxembourg, the Netherlands, Northern Ireland, and Spain; in Latin America—the Canal Zone, Jamaica, Nicaragua, Paraguay, Trinidad and Tobago, and Venezuela; in Asia—Bangladesh, Malaysia, Pakistan, the Khmer Republic, Sri Lanka, the Republic of Vietnam, and Nepal; in the Near East—Iran, Iraq, and Kuwait; in Oceania—New Zealand; and in Africa—Algeria, People's Republic of Benin, Botswana, the Central Africa Republic, Chad, the People's Republic of Congo, Egypt, Gabon, Gambia, Guinea, Ivory Coast, Lesotho, Liberia, the Malagasy Republic, Malawi, Mali, Niger, Rwanda, Senegal, Somali, Tanzania, Togo, Upper Volta, and Zaire.

On the other hand, 15 countries and areas have laws prohibiting abortion under all circumstances: In Europe—Belgium, the Republic of Ireland, Malta, and Portugal; in Latin America—Barbados, Bolivia, Colombia, the Dominican Republic, Haiti, Guyana, and Panama; and in Asia—Burma, Indonesia, the Philippine Republic, and the Republic of China (Taiwan).

In addition, Zimmerman identifies other countries whose laws do not mention abortion but where abortion is presumed to be illegal or very restricted. Among these are: In Latin America—French Guiana and Surinam; in Asia—Afghanistan, Laos, and North Korea; in the Near East—Bahrain, Muscat, Oman, Qatar, Saudi Arabia, the United Arab Emirates, and the People's Republic of Yemen; in Africa—Burundi, Equatorial Africa, Libya, Mauritania, and Rhodesia; and in the Pacific area—the Gilbert and Ellice Islands, the New Hebrides, Western Samoa, and the Cape Verde Islands.

The increase in permissiveness for abortion in recent decades, in the face of opposition from religious sources and related groups, is attributed to a varying "mix" of reasons in different countries—improvement in maternal and child health; growing recognition of the rights of women; need for more women to work outside the home; desire to reduce high birth rates for improvement of social, economic, and family welfare conditions; need to reduce deaths and illness associated with illegal abortions; and desire for correction in cases of contraceptive failure.

Africa

The population of Africa in 1975 (including Egypt) was estimated at about 402 million, or about 10 percent of the world's total. By 1974 it was increasing at an estimated 2.6 percent per year, up slightly from 2.5 in 1965; this growth if continued would double Africa's population in just 27 years.

Birth rates are extraordinarily high in nearly all African countries. For the region as a whole, the birth rate in 1974 was about 47 per 1,000 population, accompanied by a high death rate of 21 per 1,000. Unless the birth rate declines sharply, the expected reductions in mortality owing to improved health measures over the years ahead will accelerate the present pace of growth.

Fully half of the region's increase from 1965 to 1975 has occurred in the 20 countries with the lowest incomes per person—per capita Gross National Product (GNP) ranging from $60 to $120 per year—and over two-thirds the total rise was in countries and areas with per capita GNP below $300 per year. In these, the problems of poverty, hunger, ill health, and inadequate public services are especially acute. In most of them, the public revenue base is necessarily thin and the accumulation of savings, public and private, is too small to allow enough indigenous investment for improvement of their economies.

At the same time, population is shifting to the cities from rural areas where living conditions are poor—often primitive. Although over 70 percent of its labor force is still in agriculture, the African Continent is seeing urban population increase by over 5 percent a year and by 10 percent in some areas. In some countries, people have been crowding into cities faster than urban jobs, housing, and social services can be provided.

Official concern with population increase has thus far been slow to develop in most countries in Africa. Many of them, having emerged from colonial status only a few years ago, are largely preoccupied with other problems. Some leaders feel that population increases are needed in their countries; and many hold the view that only rapid economic and social development, with expanded foreign assistance, can create the conditions needed for reduction in fertility. A group of African countries were among those presenting this view at the World Population Conference in 1974.

Even so, the burgeoning populations of recent years have drawn widening attention to family planning, especially for the improvement of maternal and child health and for family welfare. As a result, by 1975 nine of the region's 54 governments had

Population in Africa may double in 27 years if present growth rates continue.

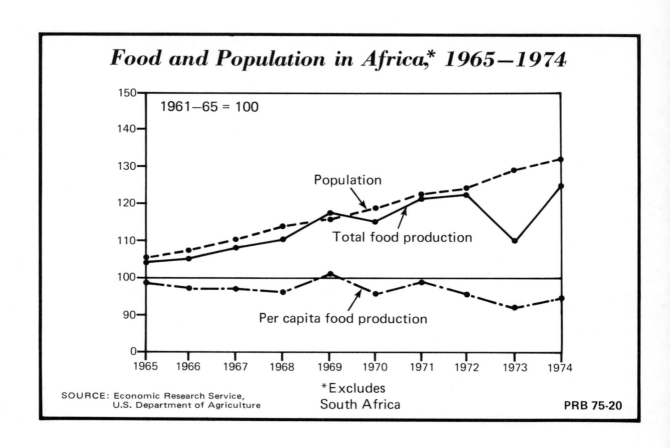

Food and Population in Africa,* 1965—1974

1961—65 = 100

Population

Total food production

Per capita food production

*Excludes South Africa

SOURCE: Economic Research Service, U.S. Department of Agriculture

PRB 75-20

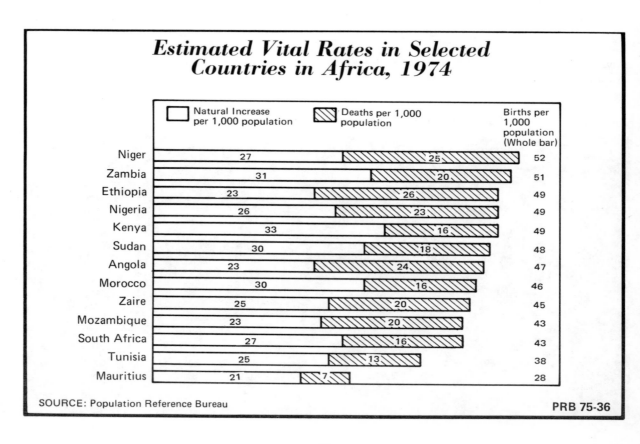

Estimated Vital Rates in Selected Countries in Africa, 1974

	Natural Increase per 1,000 population	Deaths per 1,000 population	Births per 1,000 population (Whole bar)
Niger	27	25	52
Zambia	31	20	51
Ethiopia	23	26	49
Nigeria	26	23	49
Kenya	33	16	49
Sudan	30	18	48
Angola	23	24	47
Morocco	30	16	46
Zaire	25	20	45
Mozambique	23	20	43
South Africa	27	16	43
Tunisia	25	13	38
Mauritius	21	7	28

SOURCE: Population Reference Bureau

PRB 75-36

Africa's population has tended to expand faster than its food production, resulting in a downward trend in per capita food output. In 1972 and 1973, drought brought food shortages and famine to a number of countries, particularly those in the Sahel as well as in Ethiopia. Thousands starved despite large relief shipments of food from the United States and other developed countries. Rains were near normal in 1974 and 1975.

initiated policies and programs for family planning—seven since 1966. Also, family planning activities sponsored by indigenous private organizations and church-related groups have come into being or have been expanded in about 25 other countries.

Family planning services differ widely among African nations. Governments assist programs in Egypt, Morocco, and Tunisia in northern Africa, Kenya and Mauritius in eastern Africa, Ghana and Liberia in western Africa, Zaire in central Africa, and Botswana in southern Africa. Several other countries without official population policies have, nevertheless, incorporated family planning into their maternal and child health programs. Each country's policies and programs are explained under the country headings later in the chapter.

External Assistance

The growing interest in family planning has been accompanied by increased international support for both individual countries and regional programs. The assistance each country receives, if any, is listed under the country heading.

The **U.S. Agency for International Development** (AID) has had a most important role in such assistance. AID has channeled support chiefly to maternal and child/health family planning projects of national governments but has also indirectly assisted governments and private groups through such organizations as the International Planned Parenthood Federation, The Pathfinder Fund, the Population Council, and the Planned Parenthood Federation of America. Further, it has funded demographic and research projects, usually through American universities, and assistance to African regional programs.

In Africa, AID also has a Special Population Activities fund, which was set up in 1971 mainly to assist countries not receiving bilateral assistance through U.S. AID programs. In fiscal 1975, some $173,000 was granted under this program to Chad,

The Gambia, Lesotho, Malawi, Mali, Mauritania, Niger, Rwanda, Senegal, and Swaziland.

AID funding for population/family planning activities through regular bilateral assistance to African countries totaled $3,162,000 in fiscal 1975. This went to Botswana, Ethiopia, Ghana, Kenya, Liberia, Nigeria, Tanzania, and Zaire. The funds provided for the operation of clinics, contraceptives and other supplies, information-education programs, training and research, and maternal and child health extension work.

Regional activities funded by AID have included:

• Participant training and research at Meharry Medical College in Nashville, Tenn., for African medical, paramedical, and other personnel. Through fiscal 1975, the College conducted four 19-week maternal and child health/family planning sessions for 77 participants. In addition, short courses were offered to 20 Africans, and consultants were provided for maternal and child health/family planning programs.

• A maternal and child health extension program involving pilot programs developed jointly with the Governments of the Gambia, Benin (Dahomey), and Lesotho. This assistance has gone for participant training in both the United States and the African country in question, contraceptives, clinic supplies, vehicles, and other costs.

• Assistance to selected African universities in introducing population instruction and research into their curriculums. So far, assistance has centered on the University of Ghana, which is to develop a population center. The University of North Carolina has been a contracting partner in this program.

• A project with the Association of Medical Schools in Africa to help African health-training facilities to develop and implement family planning and health curriculums. The project, to extend through 1978, is to assist 20 medical and 35 nursing/midwifery schools and other allied institutions. Workshops for nurse/

Africa's rate of natural increase was 2.6 percent in 1974, substantially above the world level of 1.8 percent. Africa's birth rate of 47 per 1,000 people was the highest of any major region—but so was its death rate of 21 per 1,000.

midwives already have been held in Ghana, Kenya, and Nigeria. A working conference in Kenya was held for six east African medical schools. As of June 1974, 91 instructional units had been developed and were being tested or approved, and 113 faculty people from 71 institutes in 16 countries were involved in the program.

• Administration of a Special Population Activities fund for projects, primarily in countries not receiving bilateral assistance, with support usually ranging from $5,000 to $25,000 per project.

Plans for fiscal 1976 include training courses for 10 African participants, aid in developing training programs in Africa, consultant services, and short-term classroom training plus clinical training for up to 30 African nurses and/or nurse midwives.

The **United Nations Fund for Population Activities (UNFPA)** assists programs in individual countries and also gives support to a number of regional projects. It especially furthers the work carried on by the **U.N. Regional Economic Commission for Africa (ECA)** and by other specialized U.N. organizations.

The ECA—a key force today in African population/family planning efforts—has among its member-ship practically all the independent nations of Africa. One leading ECA undertaking is the African Census Program, financed mainly by UNFPA, which also has supported demographic censuses and surveys in over 20 African countries. Recent projects have included studies on migration in selected countries.

Other regional African organizations involved population-related analysis and associated activities include the **Population Association of Africa**, and the **Union Douaniere et Economique de l'Afrique Centrale**.

In addition, **Family Planning International Assistance** has provided funds for church-related programs in African countries; the **World Assembly of Youth** has sponsored African regional seminars on "Youth and Family Planning" in Nigeria, Kenya, Mauritius, and other African countries; and **World Education** has assisted in incorporating family planning concepts into functional literacy and adult education programs.

The **International Confederation of Midwives** has sponsored a number of regional workshops, such as one in Accra for Anglophone west African countries in 1972 and the 16th International Congress of

Most African countries show gains in total gross national product. But growth of per capita GNP is being slowed by high rates of natural population increase, which averaged 2.6 percent for the continent as a whole in 1974, as compared with 0.6 percent for Northern America and Europe.

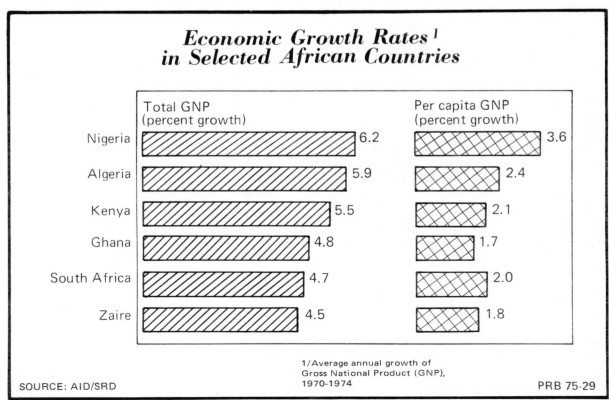

Economic Growth Rates [1]
in Selected African Countries

	Total GNP (percent growth)	Per capita GNP (percent growth)
Nigeria	6.2	3.6
Algeria	5.9	2.4
Kenya	5.5	2.1
Ghana	4.8	1.7
South Africa	4.7	2.0
Zaire	4.5	1.8

1/Average annual growth of Gross National Product (GNP), 1970-1974

SOURCE: AID/SRD

PRB 75-29

The Gabonese Government has established new maternal and child health services as part of the national health development scheme. Near Libreville, a WHO nurse gives advice on child care to mothers. Gabon has the lowest rate of natural increase in Africa because of poor health conditions.

Midwives, October 28-November 3, 1972, in Washington, D.C. Over 40 nurse-midwives from a number of African countries attended the latter conference.

Regional medical seminars have also been held by the **African-American Labor Center** through an AID grant. One was in Bathurst, The Gambia, in September 1972 with labor leaders, family planning officials, and representatives of Government ministries and international organizations attending. Countries represented included Nigeria, Ghana, Sierra Leone, Liberia, and The Gambia. Another seminar was conducted in Paris, France, in January 1973, discussed health projects, including family planning services, in Francophone countries.

A number of voluntary agencies, foundations, and foreign countries have also given extensive assistance. These include: the International Planned Parenthood Federation, the Ford Foundation, Oxfam and Oxfam-Canada, The Pathfinder Fund, the Population Council, and the Governments of Canada, Denmark, the Netherlands, Norway, Sweden, and the United Kingdom.

Algeria

The population of Algeria in mid-1975 was estimated at 16.8 million, up 4.4 million from a decade ago (1965). Based on a birth rate of 49 per 1,000 population and a death rate of 15 per 1,000, the rate of natural increase is 3.4 percent.

With large oil income available to finance its further development, Algeria's leaders see little need to slow population growth. This is reflected in official statements that high birth rates are the result of underdevelopment, not the cause. Yet despite the sensitivity surrounding population issues in Algeria, Government health programs encourage wider spacing of births and make contraceptives available to people seeking them. And the Government allows voluntary and multilateral assistance to private family planning.

Family planning projects, called pilot programs, are operated at university hospitals in the cities of Algiers, Constantine, and Oran. The clinics offer contraceptive service (mainly orals and IUD's) and training for medical and paramedical workers.

External Assistance

The United Nations Fund for Population Activities (UNFPA) is helping to finance a national census and related activities. UNFPA also is helping to fund construction of maternal child health/family planning centers, and is paying for the services of two consultants to the Government.

The World Health Organization (WHO), with UNFPA financing, has provided consultants to conduct training in child spacing.

The International Planned Parenthood Federation (IPPF) has provided training for doctors and paramedical personnel and has supplied contraceptives and literature to clinics. To date, however, there has been no formation of a Family Planning Association of the type organized in many other countries throughout the world.

A number of other voluntary organizations have been active in Algeria. Church World Service has provided limited assistance for planned parenthood activities. The Pathfinder Fund has supplied contraceptives and literature. The Population Council, with Ford Foundation financing, has provided a resident advisor to the Ministry of Finance. The advisor has assisted in such studies as the relationship between population growth and economic planning and between population growth and vital rates. The Council also has provided demographic consultants and fellowships funded by the Ford Foundation to qualified Algerians.

The Swedish International Development Association has provided contraceptives and equipment for the three pilot family planning clinics.

Angola

The population of strife-ridden Angola, until recently a colony of Portugal, is estimated at 6.3 million, and birth and death rates are high—47 and 24 per 1,000, respectively—resulting in a natural increase of population of 2.3 percent annually. Continuation of this rate of increase would double the population within 30 years. Life expectancy at birth is a low 38 years. The infant death rate is 203 per 1,000 live births—one of the highest in Africa.

The dependency ratio is also high; 42 percent of Angolans are below age 15. Although the high proportion of young people would indicate, under normal conditions, that further rapid growth of the population is in prospect, the effects of the continuing conflict in Angola cannot now be assessed. Even before the present internal conflict, health conditions were poor and now are more so.

There are no organized family planning activities.

People's Republic of Benin

The People's Republic of Benin, formerly Dahomey, whose mid-1975 population was estimated at 3.1 million, has a rate of natural increase of 2.7 percent per year. If this rate continues, Benin's population would double in 26 years. As of 1974, births per 1,000 of population stood at 50 and deaths at 23 per 1,000. Contributing to this death rate is Benin's high rate of infant mortality—185 per 1,000 live births. High infant mortality, in turn, lowers overall life expectancy to 41 years. These statistics also indicate that Benin could experience accelerating population growth in the future if it follows the typical developing-country pattern of reducing death rates more rapidly than birth rates. This likelihood is increased by the country's high dependency ratio; 45 percent of the population is under 15 years of age.

Although the Government apparently feels that the country's population is growing at an acceptable rate, population and family planning activities have increased in intensity during the last decade. In 1965, such efforts included a single private clinic and some individual doctors offering family planning advice. Today, the Government is including the concept of child spacing in its maternal and child health program, and a private family planning association is active. It was established in 1971 and is a member of the International Planned Parenthood Federation (IPPF).

In the demographic field, the Government undertook a nationwide population census in 1975; a sample survey will follow in 1976.

External Assistance

Since 1972, the U.S. Agency for International Development (AID) has assisted a project to expand Government maternal/child health services, including child spacing and training of personnel. This help is provided through a contract with the University of California (Santa Cruz) and includes funds for personnel, participant training, commodities, and other services.

The United Nations Fund for Population Activities (UNFPA) provided funds for population censuses being conducted in 1973-75.

The IPPF supports the local family planning group with most assistance going for administration, information-education, and training—and The Pathfinder Fund has provided equipment for the presentation of films on family planning and sex education.

The World Assembly of Youth has sponsored conferences and seminars on population, development, family planning, and responsible parenthood for various youth groups. It also has sponsored team visits to rural areas to provide information on population problems and family planning, help establish youth family planning clubs, and conduct panel discussions.

The Smithsonian Institution, through its Interdisciplinary Communications Program, is assisting the study of the influence of Vodun practices on the fertility of people in southern Benin.

Botswana

Botswana's population totaled 677,000 in mid-1975, or about 111,000 more than 10 years earlier. Its current birth rate is 46 per 1,000 of population and the mortality rate is 23 per 1,000, resulting in a natural increase of 2.3 percent a year.

A nation with no family planning activities 10 years ago, Botswana today gives priority to family planning in its development plans and extends these services through some 64 health clinics. The change in position came in 1970 when the Government included family planning in its National Development Plan for 1970-75. A later scheme, for 1973-78, calls for a rapid expansion of the rural health service, including family planning, noting that "at Botswana's stage of development, economic growth is in no way assisted by the rapidly rising population." Goals of the 1973-78 plan include offering family planning services at 11 hospitals, 8 health centers, 90 clinics, and 178 health posts by 1978.

Earlier, Botswana—like many other African nations—had not related the world population problem to its own situation because its overall population density is relatively light. However, much of Botswana's 220,000 square miles is arid and inhospitable to human habitation, and most of the people are concentrated in a narrow belt in the eastern part of the country. Moreover, the rapidly growing population has a large proportion of dependents (46 percent of Botswana's population is under 15 years of age) and mounting urban population pressures as people move to cities from the countryside in an effort to join the cash economy.

To meet its 1973-78 goals, Botswana is currently training personnel to deliver family planning services to small towns and rural areas. Efforts so far have included an annual conference for family welfare educators as well as training and refresher courses. These educators were to number 130 by the end of 1974, 183 by 1975, and are to reach 240 by 1976. Education campaigns are also an important part of the program, which is designed to improve the quality of life while lowering the population growth rate.

Total inputs into the program in 1975 are estimated at $583,000, including $102,800 from the International Planned Parenthood Federation (IPPF). Botswana's Government is an affiliate member of IPPF and is represented on the regional Council.

External Assistance

Much of the assistance for family planning in Botswana comes from the U.S. Agency for International Development (AID), which began its help in 1971 soon after the Government launched its family planning program. First, a training program for Botswana family planning personnel was set up in 1972 at Meharry Medical College in Nashville, Tenn. AID followed up with advisory assistance in 1973 and 1974. At present, the major areas of AID assistance are manpower and institutional development, including training in maternal and child health, family planning education for medical and paramedical personnel, and establishing a health education unit.

The International Planned Parenthood Federation (IPPF) provides direct assistance to the Government of Botswana with technical services, training, information and education, and contraceptives.

The United Nations Fund for Population Activities (UNFPA), working through the World Health Organization (WHO) and the United Nations Children's Fund (UNICEF), is helping to strengthen the programs of clinics offering health and family planning services. It also provides technical personnel.

Norway has paid the construction and operating costs of 40 health clinics and 120 health posts.

Burundi

The total population of Burundi was estimated at over 3.7 million as of mid-1975, an increase of over one-fifth from 10 years earlier. Although the death rate is high (25 per 1,000) owing to inadequate diets, low incomes, lack of social services, and overcrowding, the birth rate (48 per 1,000) is twice as great and causes a population increase of 2.3 percent per year—a rate that would double the present total in 30 years. Reflecting the poor health conditions and inadequate services, the average life expectancy at birth is 39 years. Annual per capita GNP is $70, and the literacy rate is 10 percent.

The decade has seen little change in Burundi's family planning activities. The country in 1965 had no organized family planning activities, and today only limited services are offered by missionary groups and some maternal and child health centers. There is no official population policy.

External Assistance

The United Nations Fund for Population Activities (UNFPA) financed the services of a population advisor to help with the 1972 census, but no direct external assistance has been provided. At Government request, the International Planned Parenthood Federation has supported a doctor in Bujumbura doing family planning work as a part of his duties since 1970. The Pathfinder Fund has given limited aid.

Cameroon

The country's mid-1975 population was approximately 6.4 million—a count that could double by 2013 at the present rate of growth of 1.8 percent.

Birth and death rates are estimated at 40 per 1,000 and 22 per 1,000, respectively. As of 1974, 40 percent of the country's population was under 15 years of age, and the average life expectancy at birth was 41 years. GNP per person is estimated at $230 per year.

At the start of the decade, Cameroon had no organized family planning activities, no population policy, and maintained a basically pronatalist position based on a belief that the country was under-populated. These conditions still exist at the end of the decade although some private physicians prescribe contraceptives, including orals and IUD's.

The Government is, however, attempting to improve its demographic statistics and statistical services, and its Bureau of Statistics is undertaking several demographic studies.

External Assistance

The U.S. Agency for International Development (AID) is assisting the University Center for Health Sciences with a multi-donor effort to train doctors, nurses, and paramedical staff in preventive and community medicine relevant to rural health needs in Cameroon and neighboring countries. AID funding includes assistance in construction of University facilities for out-patient care, as well as pediatrics and maternity hospitalization; provision of four U.S. faculty members to the University for 4 years each; advanced training of Cameroon health personnel in the U.S. and elsewhere; and scholarships for other Central Africans. AID also has assisted with an urban fertility study and training for a Cameroonian at the U.S. Bureau of the Census.

The United Nations Fund for Population Activities financed a population census, census communication, improved maternal-child care services, and a council of women seminar.

In 1961, the U.N. Economic Commission for Africa established in Yaounde the International Statistics Center, which includes training in demographic analysis.

The Canadian and French Governments are assisting Cameroon in the development of a regional training center for health services.

Church World Service has a limited family planning program in Cameroon. The Ford Foundation, Population Council, and The Pathfinder Fund have also supplied assistance.

Central African Republic

The Central African Republic in the heart of the continent has an estimated population of 1.8 million.

Births per 1,000 population are estimated at 43, deaths at 22. Infant mortality is a high 175 per 1,000 live births, and 42 percent of the population is under age 15. The present rate of natural increase is 2.1 percent per year.

While some official interest has been shown in family planning, there are no organized official activities. Some doctors provide family planning advice. However family planning by individuals is limited by lack of information and the cost of contraceptives.

External Assistance

The United Nations Fund for Population Activities provided $712,000 in the 1973-75 period for a population census.

Chad

The population of Chad is estimated at 4 million, over four-fifths of which is rural. At the 1974 growth rate, the present total would double in 35 years. Birth and death rates are estimated at 44 and 24 per 1,000, respectively, giving a growth rate of 2 percent per year, and 41 percent of the population is under age 15. Annual GNP per capita is only $88.

No organized family planning activities exist. While sale of contraceptives is prohibited, private physicians provide family planning information and services on request.

The Office de la Recherche Scientifique et Technique Outre-Mer (Paris) and the National Museum at Fort Lamy have conducted some economic and social research on Chad's population and related problems.

External Assistance

The United Nations Fund for Population Activities financed a population census in the 1973-75 period. The Population Council supported a knowledge, attitudes and practices survey. The French Government has funded demographic research.

Comoros

The Comoro islands, with a population of 298,000 and birth and death rates of 44 and 20 per 1,000 respectively, have a growth rate of 2.4 percent a year. If the same rate continues, the population could double in 29 years. The present dependency rate is high, with 43 percent of the people under 15 years of age. Per capita income (GNP) is $170 per year.

This newly independent country has no official population policy. A small family planning association was organized in 1969 but is not now active.

External Assistance
In 1970 The Pathfinder Fund made a small study of IUD insertions as part of its international program.

Congo

At its current rate of natural increase, 2.4 percent annually, Congo would double its present population of 1.3 million in 29 years. Birth and death rates are estimated at 45 and 21 per 1,000, respectively.

No family planning activities have been organized.

The United Nations Fund for Population Activities has financed a census and an educational planning seminar.

Egypt

Population pressure in the Arab Republic of Egypt shows up not so much in the total number of people (37.2 million) as in the fact that 99 percent of them are compressed into the 3.5 percent of the country's area that comprises the Nile Valley and its delta. In this crowded area, population density is more than 2,500 people per square mile. By the most recent estimates, the population is increasing by 2.3 percent per year, the birth rate is 38 per 1,000 people, and the death rate is 15 per 1,000.

In an effort to slow its rapid population expansion, Egypt launched a nationwide population family planning program 10 years ago. All elements of Government were to be involved including health services, education, social welfare, information and local bodies. The program had the support of the late President Nasser, who had said in 1962 that "the problem of population increase is the most serious obstacle to the efforts of the Egyptian people in their drive to increase levels of production . . ." And it has continued to receive the support of President Sadat, who in 1971 spoke of the family planning program as a "national cause in the full meaning of the phrase" because rapid population growth "if it continues will not only condemn all our hopes for evolution and progress, but threaten the simple maintenance of our present level."

The family planning effort is credited with a small reduction in population growth rates in recent years. The current growth rate of 2.3 percent compares with 2.8 percent in 1970. Nevertheless, the present rate of increase would double the country's population in 30 years.

Some—not all—Egyptian leaders view the country's population growth with alarm. Many who are concerned with economic development see population

This woman of Chad and her four children, with one to come, are refugees from drought, a disaster that left the husbandless family destitute.

growth as their leading obstacle. A major Egyptian newspaper, *al-Ahram*, which usually speaks with Government acceptance, said in 1975 that current population growth statistics "are disturbing, not to say ominous." It spoke of the nation's doubtful future if the present rapid increase continues. And, it declared "the time has come to call things by their right name; we need birth control, not family planning."

Other leaders, however, believe the population will double in the next few decades no matter how strong the family planning efforts. They speak of the need for developing industry and technology as quickly as possible to meet the requirements of an increasing population. Some add, as one Government official put it, that "industrialization is said to be the best contraceptive."

The problem presented by this passive attitude that nothing much can be done about population growth is that, if widely shared, it could lead to less determined effort by those responsible for working toward Egypt's official family planning goal. The goal is to reduce the current annual rate of 38 births per 1,000 population per year to 24 births per 1,000 by the year 1984.

Population Programs

The Egyptian Government's involvement in family planning began in 1965 with the creation of the then Supreme Council for Family Planning (changed to the Supreme Council for Population and Family Planning in January 1974). The Supreme Council, with members at the ministerial level, is concerned mainly with the policy formulation and symbolic support of the program. The Population and Family Planning Board acts as the Secretariat of the Board. Program activities are carried out through the Health Ministry's existing network of clinics and hospitals as well as centers established by the Social Affairs Ministry.

Family planning services are nominally available to all areas of the country through the national health network. In addition to health clinics in the cities, somewhat more than 2,000 rural health clinics serve Egypt's thousands of rural villages. Although many villages are some distance from the nearest clinic, apparently three-fourths of the people are within walking distance of a hospital clinic, or family planning center.

The country's development plan for the 1970's calls for the establishment of 4,058 new rural health units by 1980 and an extensive program to train the necessary staff. Including already existing clinics, this indicates an ambitious total of some 6,000 rural health centers with each unit reaching about 4,000 people.

In 1973 the number of acceptors of family planning was estimated at 843,000, or almost triple the participation of 5 years earlier. Oral pills and IUD's are the main forms of contraception in use.

A reasonable level of Government support for the national program seems to have been provided. As of 1970, total Government contributions to population/family planning came to nearly $10 million. This included some $4.2 million for the family planning program itself, funds contributed by the various ministries to population/family planning projects, and Government fundings of private family planning activities.

These sizable inputs notwithstanding, the program has been plagued by a number of drawbacks, including inadequate training, little information-education support in the program's early years, and only part time service by the staff attached to rural clinics in spite of an incentive pay system.

In addition to the national program, Egypt has a private Family Planning Association, which was founded in 1958 and became a member of the International Planned Parenthood Federation (IPPF) in 1963. The Association provides family planning services in about 500 clinics. The Association is an independent body, but it works within the framework of national policy laid down by the Supreme Council for Family Planning. The Association uses the Alexandria Family Planning Training Institute for its central training programs. As well as training courses for physicians, nurses, paramedicals and social workers, seminars are held for youth and family guidance leaders, parents, youth leaders in universities, teachers, directors of social welfare agencies and of cultural centers, agricultural societies and for trade union leaders.

External Assistance

The United Nations Fund for Population Activities (UNFPA) provides the main outside support for population and family planning in Egypt. Under a 4-year assistance program ended in 1975, UNFPA grants have totaled approximately $7.1 million. Projects have included: fellowships and observation tours; direct assistance to the national program; funding through the U.N. Educational, Scientific, and Cultural Organization (UNESCO) of an information, education and communication program; and research assistance. Negotiations have been underway for a new long-term program to begin in 1976.

The World Bank/International Development Association has provided a $5-million loan for building, equipping, and furnishing health and training centers and clinics in the period of 1973-77.

IPPF has provided financial assistance to the Egyptian Family Planning Association for its overall program, including information-education, training, operation of clinics, and other activities.

Church World Service has given financial support for a rural mobile team of family planning trainers in Middle Egypt under sponsorship of the Coptic Evangelical Organization for Social Service.

Some funding by the U.S. Agency for International Development (AID) has been provided through intermediaries in support of family planning pilot programs. A substantial amount of AID assistance was channeled through the International Planned Parenthood Federation (IPPF) to Egypt's Family Planning Association and to several individual research projects, one of the most important of which was in cooperation with the American University, Cairo. Pathfinder Fund has given some assistance.

The Ford Foundation has made grants to the Government of Egypt for family planning and reproductive biology research and training at Cairo and Alexandria Universities and Ain Shams University and to the American University, Cairo, for population research.

The Population Council has made a $236,000 grant to the Cairo University for research on the effect of hormonal contraceptives on the pituitary-ovarian axis in patients with bilharzial disease.

The Danish Secretariat for Technical Cooperation has assisted the program in materials for contraceptive pill production and in facilities for family planning training.

Ethiopia

The mid-1975 population of Ethiopia totaled over 27.9 million, an increase of almost 7 million, or 33 percent, since 1965. This growth, arising wholly from the excess of births over deaths, has continued at the rate of 2.3 percent annually for the last 10 years despite high mortality from famine, disease, and population dislocations due to political troubles. The birth rate has continued at 49 per 1,000 population, accompanied by mortality of about 26 per 1,000.

Although curbing population growth is still not a national priority, Ethiopia has seen some progress during the last decade in family planning activities.

As of 1974, some 120 clinics offered family planning services as part of Ethiopia's maternal and child health program—24 in Addis Ababa and 96 in the provinces. The number of acceptors during 1973 doubled to 4,200 with two-thirds of them using orals and most of the rest IUD's. The number reportedly rose another one-third in the first half of 1974.

The private Family Guidance Association of Ethiopia (FGAE), affiliated with the International Planned Parenthood Federation (IPPF), was founded in 1966 and has seen its activities expand rapidly after 1969 despite the recent political upheaval. The FGAE facilitates family planning services in municipal clinics in Addis Ababa and Asmara and works closely with the Government program. It has Health Officer/Coordinators operating in two provinces as liaisons with Government and other institutions offering family planning services. A main responsibility of the FGAE is information-education work, including seminars and meetings, publication of family planning literature, exhibitions, and assistance with family-life education programs. In-service training has been given medical and paramedical personnel in Government and church-related clinics.

The country had planned to undertake its first general census in 1974, with funding from the United Nations Fund for Population Activities (UNFPA). The census, however, was postponed owing to political changes and other conditions. Heretofore, sample surveys carried out by Ethiopia's Central Statistics Office have been the main vehicle for obtaining population data.

At this point, the new Government's future policies regarding population growth are not defined, although there appears to be increased interest in population matters, including family planning. The Government is especially interested in action to overcome some of the many problems facing Ethiopia. Among these are a literacy rate of barely 5 percent, health services that reach only about 15 percent of the people, widespread malnutrition—reaching the point of starvation in areas hit by the devastating drought of the past few years—and an annual per capita GNP of less than $100.

External Assistance

The IPPF, with a 10-year input estimated at $783,000, supports the Family Guidance Association. UNFPA has approved outlays of $3,500,000 for Ethiopian projects, including a census and sample survey. Family Planning International Assistance has been active in family planning efforts during the last 2 years with a cumulative contribution of $60,000, and the Swedish International Development Association has provided a total of $46,000 in support of child health/family planning clinics in Addis Ababa. Other organizations lending assistance over the past decade include the Population Council, The Pathfinder Fund, World Education, Inc., and the U.S. Bureau of the Census.

U.S. Agency for International Development assistance—totaling $81,000 in the last decade but concentrated in 1971 and 1972—has financed contraceptives and other clinic supplies, a statistical and demographic advisor in fiscal 1972, and advisory help in developing proposals for integrated maternal health/family planning projects.

French Territory of Afars and Issas

The French Territory of Afars and Issas (French Somaliland prior to 1967) has a population of about 106,000. Natural increase is estimated at 2.1 percent per year, which could double population in 33 years.

Most of the people are Muslims, and slightly more than half live in Djibouti, the capital. The remainder are mostly nomadic herdsmen. About 89 percent of the country's 9,000 square miles is desert wasteland.

The Government places emphasis on social services—primarily elementary education and health. No family planning activities have been reported.

Gabon

Gabon's population as of July 1975 was estimated at 528,000. The country has an area of 102,000 square miles and straddles the Equator. Birth and death rates are 32 and 22 per 1,000, respectively. Owing mainly to poor health conditions and services, the natural growth rate is only 1 percent per year, the lowest in Africa.

In a period of marked economic development, the Government is endeavoring to improve medical care and social services. Per capita GNP is reported at $1,250 annually, one of the highest in Africa.

Gabon has no organized family planning activities. The Government considers the country to be underpopulated and opposes family limitation.

External Assistance

The World Health Organization (WHO) has a basic health program including maternal and child health. The United Nations Fund for Population Activities has financed a sample census survey.

The Gambia

This small but densely populated country had a 1975 population of 516,000. As of 1974, the population was expanding at the rate of 1.9 percent a year as a result of a birth rate of 43 per 1,000 and a death rate of 24 per 1,000. It is estimated that 41 percent of the nation's population in 1975 was under 15 years of age. Despite the still-high death rate—including an infant mortality rate of 165 per 1,000—the country can expect to see accelerated population growth in the next few years.

The Gambia has no official population policy but has shown a growing interest during the past decade in family planning activities. Ten years ago, for instance, no family planning programs existed. In 1969, the Family Planning Association was founded, and today it works closely with the Government's Ministry of Health. In fact, the Government allows the Association to use its health clinics, provides personnel and publicity for the Association's work, and permits the duty-free import of contraceptives and supplies.

Representatives from The Gambia attended the World Assembly of Youth's African Regional Seminar on Youth and Family Planning in Lagos, Nigeria, during March 1972.

External Assistance

The U.S. Agency for International Development (AID) in 1972 launched a project (under contract with the University of California, Santa Cruz) to help The Gambia expand maternal and child health/child spacing services and develop publicity-education campaigns aimed at motivation in family planning. AID provides personnel, commodities, participant training, and related assistance to the project.

Assistance for the 1973 census in The Gambia came from the United Nations Fund for Population Activities (UNFPA) and the British Ministry of Overseas Development. The latter provided funds for the purchase of eight vehicles for use in census activities. And the Population Council made a grant to the Central Statistics Division, Bathurst, to evaluate The Gambia's 1973 population census.

Among private organizations, the International Planned Parenthood Federation (IPPF) gives assistance to the Family Planning Association for clinic operating expenses, education and publicity, training, and other activities. Pathfinder has also provided assistance to the Family Planning Association and has contributed some medical supplies and literature.

Ghana

By mid-1975, Ghana's population had risen to a little over 9.8 million compared to about 7.5 million a decade earlier. Annual population growth, mainly from natural increase, is estimated at 2.7 percent based on an estimated birth rate of around 49 per 1,000 population and a death rate of about 22 per 1,000. Official reports indicate that the formerly important in-flow of people from nearby countries has ceased to be a serious factor in population increase; the issuance of the 1969 Alien Compliance Order compels the departure of non-Ghanaians who lack residence permits.

The potential for continuing rapid population increase is inherent in the age structure of Ghana's residents. Approximately 47 percent are under 15 years of age, and the proportion will probably increase with declines in infant mortality. The average life expectancy at birth has been rising with improvements in health measures and is expected to rise further. It is believed to be expanding at the rate of 0.6 percent per year, which is above the world average. Average life expectancy at birth is now about 44 years in Ghana.

The difficulties of improving the living conditions of the people—in employment, housing, health, nutrition, education, and social services—are evident in light of presently and potentially expanding numbers. And the difficulties are intensified by the high proportion of dependents.

Meanwhile, if the present growth rate continues, the country's population could double in 26 years, and serious problems could arise of food production, employment, energy use, education, and urban-rural disparities.

The Government of Ghana is aware of the situation, and, in the last decade, has moved from little involvement in family planning efforts to sponsorship of a program that is one of the most comprehensive in Africa. The pioneering work of the Planned Parenthood Association of Ghana (PPAG) contributed importantly to this development. It was formed in 1966 and became a member of the International Planned Parenthood Federation (IPPF) in 1968. It has branches in Accra, Kumasi, Takoradi, Koforidua, and Tamale.

In 1969 the Government became the first in West Africa to formulate a national population policy, and a year later it launched the present Ghana National Family Planning Program (GNFPP) with the aim of slowing population growth to 1.7 percent annually by the year 2000. The program seeks to alter the traditional reproductive habits of Ghanaians by emphasizing the benefits of responsible parenthood and by providing contraceptives to enable couples to regulate the size of their families.

GNFPP began its first full year in 1971 with family planning programs in seven regions and a massive information campaign. By the end of that year, 80 clinics were in operation. Family planning information and services are now offered through some 187 clinics serving urban and rural people. These clinics are operated by the Ministry of Health, the Planned Parenthood Association of Ghana (PPAG), and the Christian Council of Ghana (CCG) under the coordination of the Secretariat of the GNFPP in the Ministry of Finance and Economic Planning. The Secretariat also administers and coordinates public information programs, training of family planning workers, commercial distribution of contraceptives, and postpartum family planning in three Ghanaian hospitals.

Under the program, the number of new acceptors at Government clinics has risen from 8,300 in 1969 to an estimated 34,100 in 1974 and a cumulative total of about 138,000 as of April 1975. It is estimated that programs by private voluntary groups account for over 50 percent of all acceptors recruited;

it is also probable that 100,000 acceptors have not been reported because recordkeeping has been incomplete.

Oral contraceptives are the most popular ones offered through the clinics, and an estimated 19,200 women chose this means in 1974. Condoms and foam also have found wide acceptance commercially as a result of a program in which such contraceptives are provided by AID and sold at subsidized prices at retail outlets of the Ghana National Trading Corporation.

Much effort also has been spent in carrying the family planning message to the populace by means of special seminars, lectures, and annual "Family Planning Weeks." The latter activity—initiated in 1971 to function at national, regional, and local levels—includes exhibits on services available, lectures on population problems and family planning methods, and plays. The country has also served as a host to international meetings on population and family planning, such as the 1973 meeting of the International Labor Organization (ILO) at Accra. This was the first seminar of its kind in Africa, and 10 countries participated.

External Assistance

Ghana's strong concern with population growth problems has brought extensive outside interest and assistance.

The first assistance from the United States was AID's in 1968-69, when that agency worked with the Ghana Ministry of Health and the Ghana Medical School to prepare proposals for a research project on methods of providing family planning/health services and supported a sample survey of family planning knowledge, attitudes, and practices.

Through fiscal 1975, AID has provided some $5.6 million in assistance for GNFPP, or almost half of the $11.4 million total input. AID funding of GNFPP went for contraceptives, participant training, and other activities.

AID has also contributed funds for the Danfa Project, a rural health and family planning demonstration, teaching, and research program. Developed in 1965 by the Department of Preventive Medicine of the Ghana Medical School, this 8-year program was initiated in 1970 under a contractual agreement with the School of Public Health, University of California (Los Angeles) and with U.S. AID. Its aims are to improve the health and welfare of the rural population while providing training for Ghanaian medical students, physicians, and other health personnel. Cumulative AID obligations for the project stood at over $3.7 million as of fiscal 1975.

In addition, a number of regional AID activities benefit Ghana. One of these is the Population Dynamics Program designed to develop an interdisciplinary approach to population activities.

The IPPF, with a cumulative budget for 1965-75 of $1.9 million, has given major assistance to the Planned Parenthood Association of Ghana (PPAG) and to the Christian Council of Ghana (CCG) toward operation of their 23 clinics.

Family Planning International Assistance has budgeted a total of $161,000 in the last 2 years for Government clinical services in the Volta region and for other activities. One grant of $23,000 went toward establishing three new clinics in the Volta region for use as bases for mobile teams working in the surrounding area.

The Population Council has provided a total of $589,000 over the last 10 years, with a grant of $240,000 aiding the establishment of a demographic research and teaching unit at the University of Cape Coast. Other grants have been for postpartum family planning programs.

The World Assembly of Youth has helped sponsor conferences and seminars on population, development, and responsible parenthood for students, young workers, rural leadership, and youth groups to make this large segment of the population aware of the relationship between rapid population growth and economic and social progress. The Assembly has also sent teams into rural areas and sponsored youth family planning clubs, essay contests, and films.

Other voluntary associations providing assistance over the past decade include the Association for Voluntary Sterilization, the Ford Foundation, The Pathfinder Fund, the Rockefeller Foundation, and World Education.

Bilateral assistance in the last decade has included $204,000 from the United Kingdom for equipment for 100 family planning clinics, for the communication programs of the GNFPP, and for operating mobile cinema vans. Canada contributed $130,000 for a film on family planning and other communication-public information activities. Limited assistance also has come from the Swedish International Development Authority.

The United Nations Fund for Population Activities (UNFPA) has provided a total of $454,000 for a number of population-related studies plus a project with the University of Ghana aimed at integrating national educational efforts to improve all aspects of family life. A major project funded by UNFPA and carried out by the International Labour Organisation (ILO) provides assistance to Ghana's Executive Department of Manpower for formulating plans and policies for development, education, and effective utilization of human resources in all sectors of the national economy.

Equatorial Guinea

Guinea's population in mid-1975 was 4.4 million and is currently increasing at the rate of 2.4 percent annually. Continuance of this pace of growth would double its population in 29 years. Birth and death rates are 47 and 23 per 1,000, respectively.

All but 10 percent of the people are dependent directly or indirectly on subsistence agriculture, and the per capita GNP is estimated at $140 annually.

Guinea has no family planning or population programs. The Government considers the country underpopulated and believes rapid increase would encourage political and economic development.

The United Nations Fund for Population Activities is funding health services.

Guinea-Bissau

Guinea-Bissau has one of the lowest rates of natural population increase in Africa—1.5 percent a year. The population totals 522,000 with birth and death rates of 40 and 25 per 1,000, respectively. The proportion of the population under age 15 (37 percent) is one of the lowest in Africa, and so is the life expectancy at birth—only 38 years. Both reflect the poor health conditions and services in Guinea-Bissau. Per capita GNP is estimated at $280 annually.

There are no organized family planning activities.

Ivory Coast

The country's mid-1975 population was reported by the Government of the Ivory Coast at 6.7 million. Its population growth rate is about 2.5 percent, with births per 1,000 population at 46 and deaths at 21—a rate that would lead to a doubling of population in 28 years. Although the birth rate has declined since 1963-68, when it was 55 per 1,000 population, the death rate has fallen even more sharply from its earlier level of 33 per 1,000. As a result, the rate of population increase is greater than in 1963-68. The proportion of the population under 15 years of age is estimated at 43 percent.

The Ivory Coast has no organized family planning activities and throughout the decade has held the view that population is growing at an acceptable rate. Indeed, some see population growth as a means of bringing economic progress to the Ivory Coast. The existence of unusued natural resources plus recurring labor shortages foster this attitude.

Some doctors have shown interest in encouraging child spacing, and limited quantities of contraceptives are available through some pharmacies, hospitals, and clinics.

External Assistance

In June 1973, the U.S. Agency for International Development granted $33,000, through the Ivoirian Ministry of Finance, to the National Institute of Public Health for a study of factors affecting the Ivoirian child.

The United Nations Fund for Population Activities (UNFPA) is assisting with the population census scheduled for 1975.

The Pathfinder Fund and the Ford Foundation have provided travel grants to Ivoirians participating in international health/family planning conferences. The World Assembly of Youth has sponsored seminars for young people on population, development and family planning, and responsible parenthood. It also has sponsored teams to rural areas to provide information about population problems and family planning.

Kenya

With an area of 22,000 square miles, Kenya had a mid-1975 population estimated at 12 million increasing over 3 percent per year (official Government data). If the current fertility (49 births per 1,000 population) and mortality (16 deaths per 1,000) were to continue, population would double in 21 years. Almost half (46 percent) of the present population is under 15 years of age. Nine-tenths of the people are rural and are concentrated on the 17 percent of the Nation's land that is suitable for cultivation. However, rural migration to cities has been increasing, creating and intensifying social and economic problems.

Kenya began limited official action in the population field almost a decade ago to follow up and supplement the work of private family planning groups. In 1967, it announced a national population policy and started the first government-sponsored family planning program in sub-Saharan Africa.

The voluntary Family Planning Association of Kenya (FPAK), established in 1961, provides information and education support for the Government program and operates eight clinics to supplement the services of the Ministry of Health. The FPAK staff also provides family planning information to rural areas, trains its own and some Government personnel, and conducts information and publicity campaigns.

In addition, the city councils of Nairobi and Mombasa provide family planning services, with the Nairobi effort accounting for 15 to 20 percent of the country's total acceptors each year. Private family planning associations have operated in these two cities since 1955.

In 1974, Kenya launched a new and more comprehensive family planning program with the stated goal of reducing population growth to 3 percent by 1979 and to 2.8 percent by 1999. The 1979 target is based on plans to recruit 640,000 family planning acceptors, prevent 150,000 births, lower the birth rate by 5.5 per 1,000, and reduce the death rate by 2.5. Toward this end, the Government hopes to have some 400 service points providing family planning help on a full-time basis and 190 providing it part-time. Funding is estimated at $39.7 million with the Government providing $14.3 million and outside donors $25.4 million.

The new program will build on the family planning program introduced in 1966 but endeavor to solve some of the difficulties it encountered, such as lack of high- and mid-level manpower, need for better coordination of family planning efforts, and a traditional bias toward large families.

Results between fiscal 1968 and 1975 included a cumulative total of 235,400 new acceptors; but the first decline in new acceptors since the program's inception occurred during 1974 when they dropped to 37,899 from 46,499 in 1973. This was the lowest number of acceptors since 1970. Nearly 80 percent of the new acceptors in 1974 chose oral contraceptives.

External Assistance

The International Planned Parenthood Federation (IPPF) has provided $2.36 million in assistance since 1969. This funding has gone toward activities of the Family Planning Association of Kenya (FPAK), including the operation of eight mobile units serving 90 clinics throughout the country. IPPF also operates the Family Welfare Training Center in Nairobi and maintains a regional office in the same city.

The Population Council conducted the study on which Kenya's family planning program is based and has provided a total of $225,000 in assistance since 1969. Family Planning International Assistance has provided $454,000 since 1973. Financial support also has come from the Ford Foundation, The Pathfinder Fund and the Association for Voluntary Sterilization.

The International Bank for Reconstruction and Development (World Bank Group) provided $360,000 for family planning activities in 1974 and 1975 and has pledged loans totaling $12 million in support of the Kenyan program for 1975-79.

The United Nations Fund for Population Activities (UNFPA) made $3.5 million available in 1974 for general support of Kenyan family planning efforts through 1979. Previous UNFPA funding included $794,000 through fiscal 1975. In addition, the Children's Fund (UNICEF) is providing assistance through its maternal and child health programs.

Assistance from the U.S. Agency for International Development between fiscal 1969 and 1975 totaled $1.93 million; about $329,000 is budgeted for fiscal 1976. Funding has gone toward training of family planning personnel, technical and commodity assistance for the Government program, and technical assistance in demographic studies.

Specific activities have included: tests of three different delivery systems in the Special Rural Development Project in Vihiga; advisory assistance in preparing information, education, and training materials for the Ministry of Health; production of a prototype family planning calendar; establishment of a major demographic project through a contract with the University of North Carolina; and a regional project to test the potential for commercial marketing of contraceptives. The latter project included sales of condoms through established markets in the Meru District, which has a population of some 500,000.

Among individual countries providing bilateral assistance, the Swedish International Development Authority has provided $2.4 million in the last 19 years for advisory assistance, contraceptives, and support for the education and information activities of the Government program. The Netherlands has supplied $819,000 in the last decade—mainly for a 1968-72 project in Nairobi to provide training for medical officers and a paramedical staff. Since then, the Netherlands has paid the salary of an obstetrician-gynecologist assisting the national family planning program. Denmark has pledged $426,230 to the school for district nurses in Eldoret. The Norwegian Agency for International Development provided $240,000 in 1974 and 1975—mainly for clinic equipment. In addition, it has committed $3.1 million for 1974-77 for the establishment and operation of six rural health training centers and has programmed $1.9 million for the building of three demonstration health centers and to cover current expense of family planning clinics. West Germany provided $498,000 in assistance from 1969 through 1972.

Lesotho

Lesotho—a small republic bounded on all sides by South Africa—had a population of just over 1 million in mid-1975. With the birth rate at about 39 per 1,000 population and a death rate of 20 per 1,000, Lesotho's citizens increase in number 1.9 percent each year. Some 38 percent of the population is under 15 years of age.

Lesotho has no official population policy, and the traditional Government position has been that the country has no population problem despite high unemployment and low per capita GNP ($100 per year). But the Government has shown increased interest in the past decade in population/family planning efforts.

The private Lesotho Family Planning Association (LFPA) was organized in 1966-67 and offers family planning services through its clinic in Maseru. It is an affiliate of the International Planned Parenthood Federation (IPPF). Some private physicians provide contraceptives, and IUD's are inserted at Scott Memorial Hospital.

External Assistance

The U.S. Agency for International Development (AID) is providing assistance to Lesotho through a regional maternal and child health/family planning project initiated in 1972 under a contract with the University of California, Santa Cruz. The program is designed to introduce the concept of child spacing into the health service and to seek ways of motivating families in child spacing. AID support—to extend through 1976—pays for advisory personnel, commodities, participant training, and local program costs. Funds also have gone toward the construction of lecture rooms at the maternal/child health center at Tsakholo in the Mafeteng District.

The United Nations Fund for Population Activities (UNFPA) has provided assistance for a demographic survey and family planning projects. The World Health Organization has assigned a family planning doctor to the Ministry of Health and Social Welfare.

The International Planned Parenthood Federation (IPPF) supplies financial support to the Lesotho Family Planning Association (LFPA) for fieldworkers, education and publicity, training, and the operation of two clinics. The Pathfinder Fund supplied office equipment for the LFPA, and World Neighbors has also helped the Association.

Liberia

This country of 1.6 million people is experiencing accelerated population growth. While population increased an average of 1.4 percent a year for the decade 1956-65, the growth rate is currently estimated at 2.9 percent annually. This change reflects both a rise in the birth rate (50 per 1,000 population in 1975 compared to 43 per 1,000 in 1965) and a drop in mortality (21 deaths per 1,000 people in 1975 compared to 24 per 1,000 in 1965). Further, the trend will probably continue as nutrition and health services improve. Even with the present rate, Liberia's population will double by century's end.

Liberia's people are chiefly rural (72 percent), and about 42 percent are under age 15. As population increases, many young people will leave rural areas, and the proportion of the population that is young will also increase. Both trends could create social and economic problems. However, the Government recognizes the seriousness of the situation and publicly supports family planning.

A decade ago, Liberians were just beginning to have access to such services through the Family Planning Association of Liberia (FPAL), newly affiliated with the International Planned Parenthood Federation (IPPF). Today, these services have been expanded, and the Government is following through on President Tolbert's May 1973 endorsement of family planning. In it, he said that integrated development plans, including maternal and child health and family planning, were necessary to achieve improved standards of living and that "We owe it to ourselves and to posterity to take advantage of modern technology wherever it is available."

Current Government plans are to provide these services through the AID-sponsored Lofa County Rural Health Project and eventually to incorporate them into all maternal/child health and general health programs. FPAL, which was founded in 1956, works with the Government family planning program and extends services to previously unreached areas. It also

Nurse describes various contraceptives to mothers at a Kenyan health clinic.

Cooking demonstration in a village of Lesotho. Some 38 percent of the population is under 15 years of age, and malnutrition here is widespread. Many African governments believe social development will create conditions needed for a reduction in fertility.

43

assists industries interested in offering family planning services to their employees. Among these have been the Lamco Iron Mine and the Bong Mines.

In 1974, seven clinics were offering family planning services. Plans are currently underway to integrate family planning into public health clinics throughout the country, and a new FPAL clinic was to open in Bong County during 1975. New acceptors in 1973 totaled 2,614, with 6,075 revisits. Orals were the main type of contraceptive used.

The information-education work of FPAL has included production of audiovisual materials, sponsorship of seminars and conferences, participation in radio and television programs along with officials of the Ministry of Health and Welfare, and production of the FPAL's own radio program. Also, a Family Planning Health Program in 1973 reportedly reached 20 percent of the 10-to-14 age group in urban areas and 15 percent of the 15-to-44 group in rural areas. FPAL also conducts in-service training.

External Assistance

The United States, through the U.S. Agency for International Development committed a total of $1.4 million between fiscal 1968 and 1975 for family planning in Liberia and has budgeted another $99,000 for fiscal 1976. Past assistance has included training of Ministry health workers in maternal/child health and assistance in developing demographic data via household surveys. Current assistance is going toward the Lofa County Rural Health Project—an experimental program including family planning services, which, if successful, may be extended to other countries.

The International Planned Parenthood Federation (IPPF) has provided $629,000 since 1969 toward the operations of the private Family Planning Association of Liberia (FPAL). Limited assistance also has come from Family Planning International Assistance, The Pathfinder Fund, and the World Assembly of Youth.

The United Nations Fund for Population Activities (UNFPA) has budgeted a total of $770,000 since 1971 for population assistance in Liberia. Part has helped support several demographic projects; the remainder has provided a family health advisor (through the World Health Organization) for the Ministry of Health and Welfare.

Libya

One of the wealthiest of the African nations, Libya had a population of 2.4 million (mid-1975) and the high rate of natural increase of 3 percent annually. The birth rate is 45 per 1,000 and the death rate 15 per 1,000. Owing largely to its oil resources, per capita GNP is approximately $2,980 per year.

The Republic has no organized family planning. The official view is that the country is under-populated and the Government has no commitment to population programs. Pharmacies are not permitted to sell contraceptives without medical prescriptions, and doctors are instructed to prescribe them only for medical reasons. Further, traditional attitudes favor large families. However, some awareness of potential problems is developing in the wake of increased migration from rural to urban areas. At present, 90 percent of the people live in 10 percent of the total land area—primarily along the Mediterranean coast.

External Assistance

The International Planned Parenthood Federation (IPPF) has provided some training for medical and paramedical workers.

Madagascar

The Madagascan Government has recently moved from its traditional pronatalist position to positive encouragement of family planning activities. This island country's population of 7.5 million at mid-1975 was expanding by 2.9 percent annually with a birth rate of 50 per 1,000 and a mortality rate of 21 per 1,000. About 45 percent of the people are under 15 years.

The Government has created a National Council on Population and includes family planning in the maternal and child health program. A Director of Population, in the Ministry of Social Affairs, maintains close ties with the local Family Planning Association of Malagasy (FPAM). Partly because of improved relations with the Government, FPAM—founded in 1967 and a member of the International Planned Parenthood Federation (IPPF) since 1971—has seen a sharp pickup in its activities during the 1965-75 decade. For instance, the number of new acceptors reached by FPAM rose 50 percent in the first half of 1974 from those in the same 1973 period. As of 1974, FPAM was operating clinics in two parts of Tananarive, in nearby rural areas, and in three other cities. Clinics are being established in four additional cities this year.

Information-education activities have included meetings in 1974 to celebrate World Population Year and in 1975 to celebrate International Women's Year. Other efforts have been the preparation of filmstrips, several booklets, a newsletter, and a calendar.

External Assistance

The United Nations Fund for Population Activities (UNFPA) has provided a fellowship for training in census techniques and for demographic research at the U.S. Bureau of the Census.

The International Planned Parenthood Federation (IPPF) supports the programs of the Family Planning Association of Madagascar (FPAM) with $190,400 budgeted for activities in 1975. Oxfam has provided funds through IPPF for salaries for medical staff and other costs of FPAM and for training two doctors.

Oxfam-Canada has provided more than $5,000 for conferences, educational and motivational work, and medical and clinical activities. Also, the World Assembly of Youth has given assistance for seminars on population, education, and community development.

The U.S. Agency for International Development provides no direct family planning assistance to the Malagasy Republic.

Malawi

The country's population in mid-1975 was slightly above 5 million with a rate of natural increase estimated at 2.4 percent per year. The birth rate is 48 per 1,000 population, and the death rate is 24 per 1,000. Some 45 percent of the population is under 15 years of age. Per capita GNP is about $110 annually.

Little has changed during the past decade in Malawi's view of population growth. The Government is basically pro-natalist, prohibiting wide dissemination of family planning services or publicity. Nonetheless, some family planning assistance is offered by private doctors and hospitals.

External Assistance

The U.S. Agency for International Development has provided support for the Government's maternal and child health extension projects, with cumulative funding through fiscal 1974 of $113,500.

The United Nations Fund for Population Activities (UNFPA) is funding assistance for a national census and improved labor statistics.

The International Planned Parenthood Federation (IPPF) has supported a baby clinic at a mission hospital near the national capital, Zomba. Services of the clinic include advice on child spacing. World Neighbors has also provided limited assistance for family planning.

Mali

Mali's mid-1975 population was estimated at 5.6 million increasing about 2.4 percent a year. Of the total, 44 percent is under age 15. Per capita income (GNP) is estimated at $70 per year—among the lowest in Africa.

The birth rate is 50 per 1,000 and the death rate is 26 per 1,000. Both these rates are among the highest in the world with the latter caused not only by health and nutrition problems but also by the devastating Sahelian drought. Mali was one of the countries most severely affected, and thousands of its people were forced to migrate, enduring great hardship, to other countries while others remained to suffer the effects of malnutrition and—in some instances—starvation.

In the last decade, Mali has shown some movement away from its traditionally pro-natalist position. In 1972, the Government removed some of the restrictions of a long-standing French law that prohibited abortion and the sale and distribution of contraceptives—the first such move by a Francophone country in Africa. The Government is now permitting family planning services at several pilot clinics.

External Assistance

The Canadian International Development Agency (CIDA) gives primary support to the pilot clinics offering family planning services. One is full-time and five are part-time, and the program apparently has been quite successful. Although the Government is not officially involved, it has control of the program through a board of directors, whose president is the Malian Minister of Production.

CIDA also supports a 2-year pilot family planning project in Bamako, the national capital. Funds have provided for operations of the clinics, training, and a national statistical survey.

The Pathfinder Fund has provided contraceptives.

The U.S. Agency for International Development gives no family planning assistance to Mali, but the United Nations Fund for Population Activities (UNFPA) has given assistance for a demographic census and for a family health program.

Mauritania

Mauritania's mid-1975 population, over two-thirds nomadic, is estimated at 1.3 million. Some 42 percent is under age 15. The Mauritanian Government reports a rate of natural increase of 1.4 percent per year and a birth rate of 39 per 1,000 population. The death rate is a high 25 per 1,000, to which the prolonged Sahelian drought has contributed. Income (GNP) per person is about $200 annually.

Little change has taken place during the past decade in the Mauritanian Government's view that the country has an acceptable rate of population growth. Still, a maternal and child health clinic at Nouakchott gives family planning advice—and contraceptives on request for medical reasons. Family planning information is offered by private physicians, and oral contraceptives are sold in drug stores.

External Assistance

The United Nations Fund for Population Activities (UNFPA) supported a population census in 1975 and a followup sample survey of the nomad population.

Mauritius

The tiny (720 square miles) island country of Mauritius, with a population of 885,000 in mid-1975, has had an official population policy and a Government family planning program since 1966. The birth rate of 28 per 1,000 people and the death rate of 7 per 1,000 are unusually low for an African country. Life expectancy at birth in Mauritius is 66 years—the highest in the region. Mauritius also has achieved considerable success in slowing the rate of population increase, which is now about 2.1 percent per year. However, this rate is still unacceptable to the Government, which hopes to cut it to 1.2 percent annually between 1980 and 1985.

While the current growth rate would double the nation's present population in 33 years, it is down sharply from the 1950's. In that period, the rate of increase rose to over 3 percent as post war eradication of malaria brought a precipitous drop in mortality. By the 1960's attention was being focused on the economic and social consequences of such rapid growth and paved the way for the Government's entry into population/family planning.

As of 1975, the Government was operating clinics throughout the country. A total of 269,000 clinic visits were recorded in 1972—80 percent to receive oral contraceptives.

The country also has the private Mauritius Family Planning Association (MFPA), formed in 1957, that is a member of the International Planned Parenthood Federation (IPPF). Although its activities were largely taken over by the Government program in late 1972, the MFPA still runs two model clinics and is responsible for most of the national program's information-education work. Recently, MFPA has begun assisting industrial family planning projects. One industry, for instance, has lent its clinics facilities 4 days a week to the MFPA for the extension of family planning services to the company's 1,000 women of child-bearing age. In addition, the MFPA has launched a pilot project to distribute contraceptives through small shops.

Information-education work has included sega shows (dance and song acts) in rural areas containing family planning messages and extensive use of radio and television for publicity.

Also at work in the country is Action Familiale (AF), a Catholic organization that gives advice primarily on the rhythm method.

External Assistance

The International Planned Parenthood Federation (IPPF) supports the work of the MFPA and contributed $145,900 to its 1975 budget for information-education work, operation of two pilot clinics, training, and other activities.

The United Nations Fund for Population Activities provided $1,204,000 for a population and housing census and for health and family planning projects.

The U.S. Agency for International Development has helped provide training in the United States for several Mauritians and the purchase of equipment.

Other aid has come from the Population Council, which has provided IUD's and inserters. The World Assembly of Youth (WAY) conducts seminars for young people on populations problems and family planning and other relevant issues, and representatives from Mauritius attended WAY's 1972 International Youth Seminar on Environment in Vienna, where family planning was one of two major topics discussed.

The United Kingdom has provided medical personnel for the Mauritian Government family planning program. The Population Investigation Committee of the London School of Economics has evaluated the Government program. The Swedish International Development Authority has supplied orals and condoms to the MFPA.

The World Bank has provided consultant help in planning the national program. The Pathfinder Fund has assisted the program.

Morocco

Morocco's population of 17.4 million, as of mid-1975, was increasing by 3.0 percent per year. This high rate is down only slightly from the annual average of 3.1 percent for 1965. The combination of a high birth rate of 46 per 1,000 people and a death rate that has declined to 16 per 1,000 chiefly accounts for this pace. Other factors also involved, however, include the high proportion of young people in the population (44 percent are below age 15) and the rising number of women of reproductive age. Their number is estimated at 3.99 million, as of mid-1974, compared with 3.53 million in 1970. Further, tradition encourages large families in this conservative Moslem country. This feeling is especially strong in the rural areas, which contain 63 percent of the country's people.

This rapid population growth has brought a strong commitment in Morocco to population and family planning activities. A growing number of Government, religious, and industry leaders have recognized the negative consequences of rampant population growth. This commitment began about a decade ago and has developed to the point where family planning is a vital part of the Government's health network.

However, in the intervening 10 years, many people have left the countryside for the cities and created new difficulties in the form of urban crowding, high unemployment, strained social services, and health and sanitary problems. In addition, with population outrunning food production, the country must pay out increasing amounts of foreign exchange for food and agricultural imports.

The family planning program itself has had a number of problems, the foremost of which is a lack of medical personnel trained in family planning. Although family planning is now included in the curriculums of the Medical School and all para-medical schools, attempts to provide training for practicing personnel have been sporadic.

Nevertheless, the national family planning program has developed from a small pilot project in 1966 into one that is beginning to be integrated into the health service. The program became nationwide in 1968 after the Government's inclusion of family planning in its 1968-72 development plan. The goal was to reduce the birth rate from 50 per 1,000 to 45 per 1,000 by obtaining 500,000 new acceptors of the IUD and 100,000 acceptors of other contraceptives. Results have fallen somewhat short of these goals although the annual number of new acceptors has risen from 21,304 in 1969 to 41,700 in 1974. As of October 1974, current users were estimated at 83,900; orals were used by an estimated 55,600 of these and IUD's by 28,300.

Under the current population policy set forth in the 1973-77 development plan, the program aims to educate, motivate, and inform the people about family planning. Today, family planning services are offered by 180 or more health centers as well as by new Family Planning Reference Centers in urban areas. By 1977, the end of the current 5-year plan, a majority of the 25 provinces is to have one of these Centers, staffed with obstetrics/gynecology personnel. The Government plans to augment these services with 570 dispensaries staffed with paramedics and to offer family planning services once a week. It

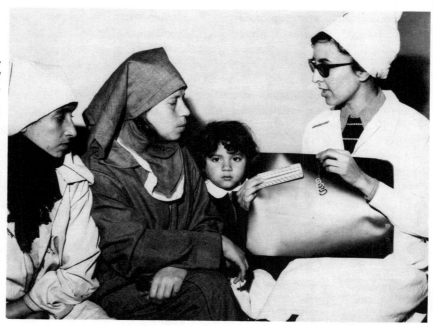

In Morocco, the goal is to find 500,000 new acceptors of the IUD, here being shown to two mothers. The Government wants to reduce the country's birth rate, emphasizing education, motivation, and information.

also plans to increase the number of health centers to 230 by 1977.

Specific goals for 1977 include reducing the crude birth rate to 45 per 1,000 and the annual population growth rate to 2.9 percent. An estimated 400,000 new acceptors will be required to meet these targets.

In addition to the growing Government program, interest by voluntary, religious, and industry groups is mounting.

In 1970, the private Moroccan National Family Planning Association (MNFPA) was formed. It is a member of the International Planned Parenthood Federation (IPPF) and carries out information, communication, and education programs in addition to providing services through four clinics. In May 1973, for instance, the MNFPA sponsored a booth and distributed information at the International Casablanca Fair. This led to a surge in requests for family planning information at MNFPA-sponsored clinics in Casablanca, Tangier, and Rabat-Sale.

Religious leaders also have come to accept family planning activities despite the conservative stance of the dominant Moslem religion. For example, Rabat, in 1971, was the scene of an IPPF-sponsored conference on Islam and family planning. The conference—attended by some 80 Islamic scholars, scientists, and politicians from 24 Islamic countries—issued a communique endorsing the Moslem family's right to space its children through legitimate and reversible contraceptive methods.

In the industrial sector, the Phosphate Office conducted a survey a few years ago of 3,000 women workers or dependents in the mining town of Khouribga. Ninety-nine percent of the interviewees expressed some knowledge of family planning, and 58 percent favored it; some 19 percent even wanted to be sterilized. The Office has since opened a family planning clinic in Khouribga—one of the first industry-backed family planning clinics in Africa.

Demographic research in Morocco has been carried out at a center established in May 1971 with technical assistance from the University of North Carolina under an AID contract.

External Assistance

The U.S. Agency for International Development (AID) has provided a total of $2.35 million in assistance to Morocco's national family planning program between fiscal 1969 and 1975 and has budgeted funds for fiscal 1976. Expenditures have gone toward technical assistance with the 1971 census, support for the national family planning program through provision of advisory help, contraceptives, and a $300,000 local currency grant toward construction of the new National Family Planning Center. AID also has supported a program of training some 600 "monitrices" in family planning motivation and education. The "monitrices" are now working in the 200 women's centers and in a smaller number of others.

The United Nations Fund for Population Activities (UNFPA) provided $128,000 between fiscal 1971 and 1974 for a law and population study and toward activities of the Moroccan National Family Planning Association (MNFPA). And the United Nations Children's Fund (UNICEF) has provided assistance to help develop the national maternal and child health/family planning program.

The International Planned Parenthood Federation (IPPF) provided $900,000 between 1971 and 1975 to assist the MNFPA.

The Population Council has provided $620,000 in funds since 1971. This included a grant to the Institut National de Statistique et d'Economie Appliqué for various research projects and some in demography. Assistance has been given by The Ford Foundation and The Pathfinder Fund.

Mozambique

Mozambique has an estimated population of 9.1 million, about 90 percent of which is rural. The annual rate of natural increase is 2.3 percent. With its present birth rate of 43 per 1,000 and death rate of 20 per 1,000, the population would double in 30 years. The population is young—43 percent under 15 years. GNP per person is estimated currently at $330 per year.

Mozambique has no organized family planning activities.

Niger

Niger's mostly rural population in mid-1975 was increasing at the rate of 2.7 percent annually—a rate that would double the present 4.6 million population in 26 years. This derives from a birth rate of 52 per 1,000—the highest in the world—and a high death rate of 25 per 1,000. About 46 percent of the population is under 15 years of age. Poverty is widespread, and the per capita GNP is only $120 per year. Health facilities and services are scarce for all.

The rapid rate of population increase is posing severe problems, present and future, for a country already suffering from inadequate capital and social services and limited natural resources. Further, Niger was not only one of the West African countries struck by the severe Sahelian drought, but, in addition, received thousands of Tuareg drought refugees from Mali.

Nevertheless, the Government has maintained a

Making ends meet in rural Africa, where most of the Continent's people live, is often difficult. Clockwise from right: Large family to feed, Cape Verde Islands where birth rates are very high; in Mauritania a farmer hoes a thin stand of millet and a herdsman draws water from a small well for his cattle.

strong pronatalist position throughout the past decade, holding that the population growth rate, fertility rate, and expected population size are acceptable. This is reflected in a general lack of family planning activities.

Some family planning information is distributed informally. Contraceptives are sold in urban pharmacies and dispensaries at comparatively high prices.

As one of the African Francophone countries, Niger has a 1920 French law on its books prohibiting the publicizing or selling of contraceptives.

External Assistance

The U.S. Agency for International Development (AID), through the American Organization for Rehabilitation and Training Federation (ORT), assisted the Government of Niger in establishing a pilot maternal/child health project to: develop methods for expanding and improving present services, motivate people to space their children, and train health personnel. AID funding provided personnel, commodities, participant training, and other necessities. AID also has provided $25,000 to the Niger Center for Social and Scientific Research for production of a family planning film.

The United Nations Fund for Population Activities (UNFPA) is supplying assistance for a population census scheduled for 1976.

Nigeria

Although ambitious official plans have been outlined and private family planning activities have been conducted for more than a decade, Nigeria—the most populous nation of Africa and potentially one of the wealthiest—as yet has made no firm commitment to curb population growth.

The former head of state, General Yakubu Gowon, maintained that Nigeria needed a lower rate of population increase in order to facilitate social and economic development and that population growth was outpacing food production. This growth now stands at around 2.7 percent a year, and the country's population of 63 million would reach over 126 million just after the turn of the century. The 1974 birth rate is 49 per 1,000 people, and the death rate is 23 per 1,000.

The growing pressure of population on resources is already evidenced by extensive soil erosion in some heavily populated rural areas, a general inability of public services to keep up with population growth, and high rates of unemployment and dependency.

Yet because of Nigeria's abundance of natural resources, there is a common national feeling that the country can easily absorb the expected population increase. Recently high prices for petroleum—of which Nigeria is a large producer—have strengthened this view.

Nigeria's 1970-74 development plan called for integration of family planning activities into maternal and child health programs, but little progress was actually made. The goals may yet be accomplished, however, since the Government presently hopes to develop a national family planning program out of a maternal and child health/family planning training project. In addition, 10 of the country's 12 States are reported making family planning services available. Among these are Lagos, Western, Kwara, Mid-West, and several of the northern States.

Private family planning services have been offered since 1964 through the Family Planning Council of Nigeria (FPCN), a member of the International Planned Parenthood Federation (IPPF). In addition to services available through clinics, the FPCN conducts widespread information, education, and communication activities stressing the relationship between small families and family well-being.

Efforts of the FPCN are supported by the Universities of Lagos and Ibadan, which have demonstration clinics for student nurses and doctors as part of their curriculums. For example, the Lagos University Teaching Hospital operates a family planning training clinic in Lagos. Here, student nurses, physicians, and paramedics from Nigeria and other countries are trained in family planning and the treatment of infertility.

In addition, a number of Christian mission hospitals offer family planning services, while universities are carrying on research in maternal and child health/family planning.

At a local market in Ibadan, Nigeria, a country where petroleum wealth is bringing the urban congestion familiar in the Western world. Nigeria's Government hopes to develop a national family planning program out of a maternal and child health/family planning training project.

External Assistance

The International Planned Parenthood Federation (IPPF) has provided $3.5 million since 1969—mainly in support of the activities of the Family Planning Council of Nigeria (FPCN).

U.S. AID budgeted a total of $1.62 million for family planning in Nigeria during 1973-75, mainly for an experimental project to integrate family planning into maternal/child health programs and for improvements in preventive and curative medicine for children under 5 years of age. The family planning effort, which will end in 1976, is being carried out by Nigeria's National Institute of Child Health with assistance from Johns Hopkins University under AID contract.

Other AID assistance in the past decade has included: an $84,000 grant to the University of Lagos for an expanded demographic training and research program, $10,000 for training five nurses in family planning, $84,000 under a regional grant to help the Federal Ministry of Health improve its data gathering system, and $114,000 to the University of Michigan to help the University of Ibadan conduct a study of rural-urban migration in Nigeria.

The United Nations Fund for Population Activities (UNFPA) in 1975 approved the outlay of $1,345,000 to assist the Government's rural maternal and child health and family planning program. The estimated equivalent value of the Government's contribution is $3,337,000, for a 5½ year period beginning in July 1975. Earlier, UNFPA had provided funds for the 1973 population census, financing for a law and population study, and other population/family planning projects.

WHO has supplied funds for training and research.

The Population Council has given a total of $1.3 million in assistance, chiefly to improve and maintain demographic and research facilities at the Universities of Ife and Lagos and the Ahmadu Bello University. It also has assisted the rural family planning project at Zuma Memorial Hospital in Urrua, post partum family planning programs, and a demonstration clinic at Ahmadu Bello University.

The Ford Foundation has provided a total of $1.1 million in population assistance since 1966. It maintains a resident West African advisor in its Lagos office, operates an informal population information service, and has made a number of grants for family planning training and demographic projects.

Family Planning International Assistance, with $116,000 in assistance since 1972, has provided support for regional conferences of the Christian Council of Nigeria and other activities.

The Pathfinder Fund's $194,099 in cumulative assistance has gone toward a female sterilization clinic, a family planning information center and clinic at Enugu, a medical student's conference, and a study of maternal and child health services offered by rural health workers in East-Central State. It also has provided contraceptives for family planning activities in the North-Eastern State of Nigeria and at Zuma Memorial Hospital.

Other voluntary assistance has come from the Mennonite Central Committee, the Smithsonian Institution, the World Assembly of Youth, and World Neighbors and the Rockefeller Foundation.

In addition, Finland—through the United Nations Children's Fund—has provided $144,000 during 1972-76 for a pediatric training unit at Ahmadu Bello University Medical School.

Reunion

The birth rate has been falling on the island of Reunion since 1967, but the population of 493,000 is continuing to increase by 2.1 percent annually. At that rate, total population could double in 33 years. Reunion has a low death rate of 7 per 1,000 population and a birth rate of 28 per 1,000. Per capita GNP is a relatively high $1,210 a year, and the literacy rate is 63 percent—the highest in Africa. Its urban population is 43 percent of the total, and 43 percent is also under age 15.

An overseas dependency of France, Reunion comes under the provisions of a French law that encourages local governments to support family planning. Reunion's attitude has been favorable, and support has been provided all during this decade.

Orientation Familiale, a family planning organization funded by the French Government, was organized in 1966 and operates 11 clinics on a daily basis. Attendance has increased steadily. For example, an intensive education/publicity campaign in 1969 brought a 57 percent increase.

The Association Reunionaise pour l'Education Populaire, a primarily Catholic organization, gives marriage guidance and teaches the rhythm method.

More than 30 private physicians prescribe oral contraceptives. Abortions are common although illegal.

External Assistance

The International Planned Parenthood Federation has sent personnel, at the Government's request, to give guidance and advice to Orientation Familiale concerning its educational and family planning information program.

Rwanda

As Africa's most densely populated nation—with 560 people per square mile of agricultural land—Rwanda is feeling the shocks of rapid population growth. In this desperately poor country, the population (estimated 4.2 million in mid-1975) is expanding by 2.6 percent annually. Both birth and death rates are unusually high at 50 and 24 per 1,000, respectively, and about 44 percent of the population is under 15 years of age. Although it is encouraging to note that the overall growth rate has declined from the 3.1 percent annual average reported for 1963-68, the "young" age structure of the population is conducive to future rapid population growth.

With food production lagging behind population expansion, food shortages are an ever-nagging threat forcing the Government to rely on the international community for increasing food aid. At the same time, the country finds itself unable to bring about needed development as money goes toward merely maintaining present services. These conditions are reflected in a per capita income (GNP) of only $70 a year and a literacy rate of 10 percent.

Some leaders have shown concern about the country's rapid population increase. Although the Government has traditionally been opposed to family planning by methods not approved by the Catholic Church, at a 1968 seminar sponsored by the Ministry of Health, agreement was reached that the concept of child spacing should be incorporated into national health education. Also, some doctors provide family planning information on request.

External Assistance

The U.S. Agency for International Development (AID) has provided assistance for construction of dispensary/maternity projects in Rwanda.

The International Planned Parenthood Federation (IPPF) has provided for the training of two nurse-midwives at IPPF's Family Welfare Training Center in Nairobi, Kenya, and it helped finance a Government-organized international symposium on the African family.

The Pathfinder Fund supports a project at the University of Rwanda Medical School in Butare aimed at incorporating family planning services into the public health structure. The United Nations Fund for Population Activities supported a population census in 1975.

World Neighbors includes family planning education in its rural development program.

Senegal

Senegal's population (4.4 million in mid-1975) is growing by some 2.4 percent a year—up from an annual average of 2.1 percent in 1963-68. Both the birth rate (48 per 1,000 people) and the mortality rate (24 per 1,000) are unusually high.

Population growth is continuing to outstrip the country's social services and resources. Per capita income (GNP) is $250 annually. The proportion of dependents in the population is high, with 43 percent of all people under age 15. In addition, growth in critically important agricultural production has been curtailed for most of the decade by the prolonged Sahelian drought.

The Government sees the country's population growth rate as acceptable. However, some leaders are now showing an interest in family planning. A private family planning clinic in Dakar—the first for French-speaking Africa—has been given informal encouragement by the Government and has received assistance from The Pathfinder Fund. It has established two satellite clinics—one in a Dakar suburb and one in the interior of Senegal, and its staff extends services to other parts of the country. Another private family planning clinic existed in Dakar during 1970-71 but was closed because of organizational difficulties.

A few local doctors provide family planning information and insert IUD's.

External Assistance

The U.S. Agency for International Development (AID), through the Special Population Activities Fund, provided support for a maternal and child health/family planning program.

The United Nations Fund for Population Activities (UNFPA) is supporting two demographic projects—the 1975 population census and an investigation of fertility trends.

The International Planned Parenthood Federation (IPPF) has provided limited assistance. The Pathfinder Fund helped establish and continues to support the private family planning association in Dakar as well as a training center for paramedical personnel. The center offers 1-month courses for nurses and midwives of Francophone Africa. Pathfinder also has supported training in the United States of paramedical staff and supported a trip to Moslem countries of North Africa and the Middle East for six Senegalese opinion leaders to enable them to visit family planning programs there.

Seychelles

Seychelles, a small island group and British colony, has a population of about 60,000. Birth and death rates—30 and 9 per 1,000 population (in 1974), respectively, are among the lowest in Africa. At the present 2.1 percent rate of natural increase, the population would double in 33 years. While the birth rate has been declining the last several years, the age structure of the population—with 43 percent of the people under age 15—could allow a sharp reversal of this trend. The current per capita GNP is $370 per year.

While Seychelles has no official population policy, reportedly the Government is showing some interest in family planning.

An English woman doctor, with a grant from the United Kingdom Ministry of Overseas Development, has been working since 1965 to promote family planning. Four clinics, offering all methods of contraception, serve more than 500 patients per month. The doctor also distributes literature and provides education and guidance for maternal and child health.

Two trained nurse-midwives, a nurse, and a fieldworker are also engaged in family planning services.

External Assistance

The International Planned Parenthood Federation (IPPF) has helped a local association set up a nonofficial family planning program and since 1970 has supported the four private clinics. It also provides literature. The Pathfinder Fund has assisted by providing contraceptives.

Sierra Leone

Sierra Leone's population of 3 million, as of mid-1975, is increasing at a rate of 2.4 percent a year. The birth rate for the country is 45 per 1,000, and the death rate is 21 per 1,000. Some 43 percent of the population is under 15 years of age. Based mainly on agriculture and mining, per capita GNP is estimated at $160 a year.

A decade ago, it was widely felt that Sierra Leone would benefit from rapid population growth; but that view has changed considerably. The Government—in most recent years—has encouraged the activities of the private Planned Parenthood Association of Sierra Leone (PPASL).

PPASL was founded in 1960 and became a member of the International Planned Parenthood Federation (IPPF) in 1968. As of the end of 1974, it was operating 11 clinics; as of 1973 new acceptors

totaled 2,182 and continuing acceptors 3,592. Orals have proved to be the most popular contraceptive—with a new acceptor rate in 1973 double that of 1972.

Among its other activities, PPASL sponsored an international seminar on the health of the family unit in 1973; has planned parenthood weeks, exhibits at fairs, and showings of family planning films; has printed and distributed leaflets and pamphlets, posters, calendars, and Christmas cards carrying family planning messages; and has used the mass media for extensive planned parenthood publicity.

The Government allows PPASL free use of radio and television as well as some maternal and child health facilities. The Government also has sponsored participants for maternal and child health/family planning training programs, and has removed the duty on imported contraceptives.

External Assistance

The U.S. Agency for International Development (AID) has provided funds for training Sierra Leoneans at the U.S. Bureau of the Census and at the Meharry Medical College Maternal and Child Health Family Planning Center.

The United Nations Fund for Population Activities (UNFPA) has helped Fourah Bay College establish a demographic unit and, through UNESCO, has provided fellowships for training in the communication aspects of population education. It has also provided assistance for the 1972 population census and a seminar at Fourah Bay College on the health of the family unit.

CARE has given food and medical packages to the Planned Parenthood Association of Sierra Leone (PPASL) for distribution to women visiting parenthood clinics. The International Planned Parenthood Federation (IPPF) assists the PPASL's program and budgeted $212,200 in 1975 for fieldwork, information-eduction, clinic operations, and other activities. The Pathfinder Fund in 1972 sponsored participation of six PPASL officials in a 7-week Government Affairs Institute seminar in Washington, D.C., on planning and management of population/family planning programs.

Family Planning International Assistance has provided contraceptives and medical equipment to church-related family planning programs.

The Population Council has sponsored the training of a Central Statistics Office official in demographic data processing and provided grants for Master's degree students in population and geography at Fourah Bay College. It also has funded a national survey of population knowledge, attitudes, and practices.

Sierra Leone was represented at the World Assembly of Youth African regional seminar on Youth and Family Planning in Lagos, Nigeria, in 1972. The Pathfinder Fund has given some assistance.

Somalia

Somalia's present population of 3.2 million would double in 28 years at the present rate of natural increase (2.5 percent annually). The birth rate is 47 per 1,000 people and the death rate 22 per 1,000. With 45 percent of the people under age 15, the per capita GNP a low $80, and the literacy rate (5 percent) one of the lowest in Africa, Somalia faces severe economic, educational, and social problems. Public services—including health—are already far short of the needs of the people. Life expectancy at birth is 41 years.

No organized family planning or population programs are underway; but with the population 26 percent urban, some urban interest exists in child spacing and limiting family size.

The United Nations Fund for Population Activities has contributed $1,398,000 for a population census and related demographic support.

South Africa

The mid-1975 population of South Africa was estimated at 25.0 million with a birth rate of 43 per 1,000 as of 1974 and a death rate 16 per 1,000 resulting in a natural increase of 2.7 percent a year. South Africa's population could double in 26 years. The average per capita GNP is $1,080 a year. However, that figure conceals large differences between areas and between the white minority and the black majority in the population.

The South African Government has supported family planning throughout the decade by helping to finance family planning services as part of its health program.

The National Council for Maternal and Child Welfare (NCMCW), founded in 1932 and a member of the International Planned Parenthood Federation (IPPF) since 1953, is the coordinating body for regional family planning associations and is supported by the Government and by local authorities. Regional associations are responsible for opening clinics which, when well established, are turned over to local management. At the last report, about 100 clinics had been transferred, and some 130 were being run by regional associations.

The Council is seeking to expand its educational programs and to reach more women in child-bearing years. Special clinics have been established in rural areas and in factories as part of this effort.

External Assistance

The International Planned Parenthood Federation (IPPF) has made a grant to the Transkei branch of the National Council for Maternal and Child Welfare (NCMCW).

World Neighbors has supported a project in Transkei and Zululand involving general economic and social development along with food production—a total approach to meet family needs. It has been strongly emphasized that family welfare includes maternal/child health, nutrition, and sanitation. Where possible, family planning education is incorporated into the program.

None of the above assistance includes funds from the U.S. Agency for International Development.

Namibia

Namibia in south-western Africa has a population of 852,000, and its rate of population increase is 2.2 percent a year. Birth and death rates are 46 and 23 per 1,000 population, respectively. At the present rate of growth, the population would double in 32 years.

Urban centers contain 23 percent of the people, and modern education and medical care have been extended in various degrees to most tribal areas in the last few years. However, social development is limited under the present political situation. Per capita GNP is estimated jointly with South Africa at $1,080 year.

There is no organized family planning activity.

Rhodesia

If the present rate of natural increase of 3.4 percent a year does not slacken, Rhodesia would double its present population of 6.3 million in 20 years. The overall birth rate is a high 48 per 1,000 while the death rate is 14 per 1,000, and 46 percent of the whole population is under age 15. All three indicators, however, are higher for the black majority than for the white population.

The Government takes a positive attitude toward family planning and has supported such programs and activities throughout the last decade. Family planning has been incorporated into the Government's maternal/child health services since 1966 and is part of routine health service in hospitals and clinics.

A family group in rural West Africa awaits the meal being prepared at far left. Among the countries in this region, Ghana and Liberia are giving Government support to family planning programs and others have begun to show interest.

The Family Planning Association of Rhodesia (FPAR) has been active since 1957 and receives substantial grants from the Government. At first, FPAR concentrated mainly on education through films, pamphlets, and talks. As public interest developed, clinics were established by the FPAR's seven branch organizations. Much of this clinical work has now been transferred to the Government. At present, family planning services are available in more than 400 locations offered by clinics of the Government, FPAR, industries, missions, etc.

FPAR now is responsible for family planning education throughout the country. It has seven urban and three mobile clinics. It provides literature in several languages and maintains units for traveling talk and film shows. Field workers visit thousands of families in their homes and talk to thousands more in groups. In other efforts to reach the public, weekly radio programs are broadcast in two vernacular languages and exhibits are set up at agricultural and industrial fairs. FPAR also has a sex education program.

Training courses for family planning workers have been conducted by FPAR and at the University College. Government nurses receive family planning training, and the Spilhaus Family Planning Center—situated at the entrance to Harari Maternity Hospital—began courses for field workers, paramedicals, and medical assistants in 1970. It also gives family planning education to patients in the hospital.

External Assistance

The International Planned Parenthood Federation (IPPF) gives financial assistance to the Family Planning Association of Rhodesia (FPAR). From 1968 through 1972, Oxfam provided funds for FPAR's educational film unit, for furnishing and equipping a clinic in Salisbury, for a nurse's salary, and to provide contraceptives to women who could not pay for them. Oxfam-Canada helped FPAR in 1968-69 with a grant for equipment and medical supplies.

Family Planning International Assistance (FPIA) has provided medical equipment to church-related family planning programs.

The Pathfinder Fund has completed a series of long-range IUD evaluation projects that were started in the late 1950's.

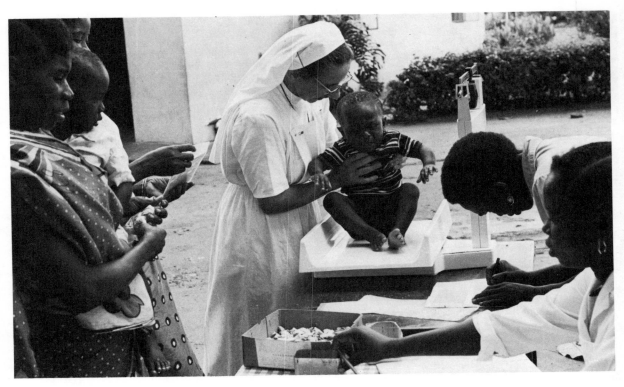

Tanzanian baby is given weight check at the Nutrition Clinic at Pugo, near Dar-es-Salaam. The clinic was established to fight malnutrition and raise health standards. Maternal and child health and family planning services are part of the country's health program.

World Neighbors has assisted the Hlekweni Rural Training Center in a program carried out in cooperation with the Young Women's Christian Association. Specially trained personnel work with women in educational programs that include family planning information.

None of the above assistance includes funds from U.S. AID.

Sudan

The mid-1975 population of Sudan was estimated at 17.8 million with a very high rate of natural increase of 3 percent. Births were 48 per 1,000 people, and deaths 18 per 1,000, and 45 percent of the people were under 15 years of age. If the present rate of increase were to continue, the population would double in 23 years. Present per capita GNP is $140 per year.

The Sudanese Government seems at some times to favor population control and at others to oppose it. In a report prepared for the 1970 Conference of the U.N. Economic Commission for Africa, the Government stated that "... the country cannot afford the rise in fertility which might follow economic develop-

ment. It is necessary to emphasize that unless measures are initiated at this stage to control. . .the rate of population growth, a continuously increasing amount of effort. . .will have to be used to maintain existing standards of consumption. . .In these circumstances it is necessary to stress the need for population policy as part of economic development planning." And Sudan's 1970-75 Development Plan stated that family planning should be incorporated into the maternal and child health services of the country.

The Sudan Family Planning Association (SFPA), founded in 1965, opened its first clinic in 1966 and became a member of the International Planned Parenthood Federation (IPPF) in 1971. It runs clinics in three cities and in some clinics uses Government facilities and personnel. The Sudan Medical Association, the Khartoum Nursing College, Khartoum physicians, and the University of Khartoum cooperate with the Association.

External Assistance

The United Nations Fund for Population Activities (UNFPA) gave assistance for a population census in 1972. The World Health Organization (WHO) has given advisory help in vital and health statistics to the Ministry of Health.

The International Association of Schools of Social Work has included Sudan in its pilot project to develop qualified social work manpower for population/family planning activities.

The International Planned Parenthood Federation (IPPF) has given financial assistance to the Sudan Family Planning Association (SFPA) for information-education, training, clinic operations, and fieldwork.

The International Fertility Research Program has supported introduction of new technologies in the Sudan and relevant training.

The Pathfinder Fund has assisted parts of the program.

Swaziland

Rapid population growth continues in Swaziland although the rate of increase has fallen slightly to 2.7 percent compared with 2.9 percent in 1972. The birth rate is estimated at 49 per 1,000 and the death rate at 22 per 1,000 people. This means that the population of 493,000 could double in 26 years. Further, because of the high birth rate, some 46 percent of the Swazi are under 15 years of age, creating added demands on the Government for schools and other services and providing the potential for continued strong population growth in the future.

The Government, which a decade ago opposed family planning, has shown increased interest recently in slowing population growth. The country's 1969 Development Plan gives authority for a family planning program in the Ministry of Health. Toward this end, the Government has been working to launch a low-key family planning program based around a rural clinic.

Some individual doctors also give family planning advice.

External Assistance

The U.S. Agency for International Development (AID) has provided money from a Special Population Activities Fund for two Government projects: construction in the Hlatikulu area of a public health center that will provide maternal and child health/family planning services; and expansion and renovation of the existing rural health clinic in the Shiselweni District to provide maternity/family planning services.

The United Nations Fund for Population Activities is providing assistance for maternal health/family planning and a census. The United Nations Children's Emergency Fund (UNICEF) has provided contra-

ceptives and transport, and the World Health Organization (WHO) has provided assistance for a family planning program in the public health service. The Pathfinder Fund has been a source of assistance for the program.

Tanzania

The Tanzania population, estimated at 15.2 million in mid-1975, is increasing at the annual rate of 2.8 percent. The birth rate is 50 per 1,000 population, and the death rate is 22 per 1,000. If the above rate of increase were to persist, the population would double to 30.4 million by the year 2000. With 47 percent of Tanzanians under age 15, or just approaching the years of parenthood, further rapid increase in numbers is clearly in the making despite the already heavy pressures on employment opportunities and public services. Per capita GNP is already low at $130 per year.

Although the Government still has no official population policy, activity in the population/family planning field has expanded slowly in the past decade. Maternal and child health and family planning services are integral parts of the basic health program, and the Government in the last few years has given more financial support in this area than most African governments.

Among the direct results of population growth are the country's rising imports of food for immediate comsumption needs. These imports totaled $150 million in 1974 compared with an annual average of $20 million in the late 1960's and $50 million in 1972. Meanwhile, it is estimated that if population growth continues at the present rate, Tanzania's cultivated area would have to expand 64 percent by 1992 to supply the same amount of food per capita in that year as is grown today.

President Nyerere has spoken several times on the problems of rapid population growth. In a September 1973 address he stated, "Whatever we produce has to be divided between an increasing number of people every year. . .It is no use saying that these extra 380,000 people have hands as well as mouths. For the first 10 years of their lives, at the very least, children eat without producing."

The national health program includes midwife services and nutrition and family planning information. Private efforts have been carried on since 1959, when the Family Planning Association of Dar es Salaam was formed. In 1966, the Dar es Salaam Association became the Family Planning Association of Tanzania (FPAT) and joined the International Planned Parenthood Federation (IPPF).

The FPAT provides family planning advisors, conducts training courses, and provides supplies and equipment for the more than 100 maternal and child health/family planning clinics in Tanzania. Over 50 of these are in Government hospitals; the largest and most active clinics are in the capital city, Dar es Salaam. FPAT also produces family planning literature and radio programs.

Other agencies involved in family planning are the Dar es Salaam School of Medicine, which conducts population studies, and the East African Statistical Training Center, which offers Government employees a course in statistics, including census taking and vital statistics.

In line with the Government focus on rural development, there is expanding emphasis on maternal and child health/family planning programs in rural areas.

External Assistance

The U.S. Agency for International Development (AID) has provided $4.74 million for population activities in Tanzania since fiscal 1973 and has budgeted another $958,000 in assistance for fiscal 1976. Much of this money is going toward the construction of 18 regional training centers and 64 outstations, which will provide training for an estimated 2,600 paramedical personnel.

The United Nations Fund for Population Activities has financed census publications and other projects in the family planning field.

The International Planned Parenthood Federation (IPPF) has provided a total of $1.93 million since 1969 in support of the Family Planning Association of Tanzania (FPAT). It also supports work at three mission hospitals in the Masasi area. Oxfam, through IPPF, provided funds to FPAT in 1972 for three vehicles, their operating costs, and 2 years of staff salaries. Additional funds were approved for vehicle operating costs, maternal and child health work, and program expansion.

The Population Council, with a cumulative input of $324,000 since 1969, has provided demographic assistance, support for a project to analyze census data on migration, and assistance for private agencies in Tanzania.

Other private organizations lending assistance during the past decade include Family Planning International Assistance, The Pathfinder Fund, and World Neighbors.

Countries other than the United States also have provided considerable assistance since 1973: Canada contributed $600,000 between fiscal 1973 and 1975; Denmark, $1.33 million; Finland, $1.54 million; Norway, $1.24 million; Sweden, $4.63 million; and Switzerland, $240,000. These countries all have budgeted additional assistance for fiscal 1976, including $3.1 million and $1.03 million, respectively, by Sweden and Finland.

The World Bank has conducted preinvestment studies as a prelude to a possible project.

Togo

Togo's population of 2.2 million is expanding at an annual rate of 2.7 percent as of 1975. Birth and death rates are both unusually high—51 and 23 per 1,000, respectively. If Togo follows the usual pattern of developing countries of reducing deaths faster than births, its rate of population growth would accelerate. Another factor is that 46 percent of the population is under 15 years of age and will move into the reproductive age group over the next decade and a half.

The Government has held the view that the country's population is growing at an acceptable rate. Like most other countries of French-speaking West Africa, Togo has an anticontraceptive law. Still, family planning appears to be on the rise. A family planning clinic is operating in Lome, and some health officials make family planning information and contraceptives available to interested women on an irregular basis. Recently, a private family planning association was established, and it has been approved by the Government. In addition, some private physicians provide contraceptives.

External Assistance

The U.S. Agency for International Development (AID) has provided funds for printing a maternal and child health/family planning manual. In addition, the Ministry of Health and AID have discussed plans for constructing a new health center at Lomé.

The United Nations Fund for Population Activities has financed improvement of demographic statistics, a seminar on education, and a law and population project.

Among private organizations, The Pathfinder Fund has sent medical supplies and contraceptives to the Lomé family planning clinic, and the Population Council and the Ford Foundation have provided fellowships in family planning. At the request of the Togolese Government, the Unitarian Universalist Service Committee has helped develop maternal and child health services and education with family planning to be introduced when it is considered an appropriate time.

Peace Corps volunteers teach family planning, along with other health subjects, in schools and adult education classes.

Tunisia

Tunisia during the last decade has mounted one of Africa's most comprehensive population/family planning programs, moving from a limited pilot project to a nationwide Government program. Its mid-1975 population was almost 5.8 million, and an annual birth rate of 38 per 1,000 people and a death rate of 13 per 1,000 result in a yearly population growth of 2.5 percent.

Although this is a high rate of increase, it is below the 2.7 percent reported for 1965 so that Tunisia is making some progress in slowing population growth despite the general impetus given to fertility by a declining death rate and the large number of women in the reproductive age group. The country's current death rate of 13 per 1,000 is the lowest on the African mainland, while the average life expectancy of 54 years is the highest. In addition, 44 percent of the population is under 15 years of age and will further swell numbers in the reproductive age group as they reach maturity.

Tunisia's national family planning program has grown from a pilot project launched in Bizerte during 1964 to a nationwide program offering free family planning services through some 300 Government health clinics and additional mobile units. Since 1964, the program has undergone a number of changes and reorganizations, including extension to a nationwide program in 1968-69 and the creation of the National Office for Family Planning and Population (ONPFP) in 1974. ONPFP is a semiautonomous Government agency under the Ministry of Health. A further change was the decision in November 1974 to rely more heavily on midwives in carrying out fieldwork.

The primary responsibilities of the ONPFP are to promote population policies and standards of service; to develop adequate training programs; and to provide central support for health and family planning education, communications, research and evaluation, and certain administrative services.

Since the program's extension nationwide, the number of new acceptors has risen from an estimated 15,700 in 1968 to 52,700 in 1974. The cumulative total was estimated at 215,000. The total of continuing users was estimated at 80,200 in 1974, over six times the 1965 level of 13,100. Some 47,800 of these were using IUD's, followed by an unusually high 20,800 receiving sterilizations, and 8,400 were on the pill.

Current program goals are to reach 62,000 new and continuing acceptors in 1975 and 69,000 in 1976. The long-term objective is to slow population growth from the current level of 2.5 percent a year to 1 percent annually by the year 2001.

Toward this end, the Government has passed some milestone legislation aimed at encouraging smaller families. Tunisia was, for instance, the first Moslem nation to legalize abortions, with current legislation permitting abortion on request during the first 12 weeks of gestation. All family planning services—including abortion and tubal ligation—are free. The Government also has outlawed polygamy, raised the legal marriage age to 17 for women and 20 for men, limited child support payments to a family's first four children, and legalized the import, sale, and advertising of contraceptives. In mid-1975 the legal requirement for prescriptions for low-dosage oral contraceptives was lifted.

Also active in the country is the Tunisian Association for Family Planning (ATPF), an affiliate of the International Planned Parenthood Federation (IPPF). The organization was formed in 1969 and currently works closely with the national program. It operates the Ministry of Health's Montfleuri clinic, offering family planning consultations and services and tubal ligations, vasectomies, and abortions. The clinic also conducts family planning training programs for medical and paramedical staff.

In addition, the ATPF carries on much of the education work for the national program, conducting education and family planning campaigns through local chapters organized throughout the country.

External Assistance

U.S. AID has provided a total of $8.25 million in financial assistance for family planning in Tunisia between fiscal 1968 and 1975 and is providing another $878,000 for fiscal 1976 with the overall aim of helping the Government to obtain its demographic goals. Expenditures have covered the whole spectrum of family planning activities: provision of contraceptives, medicines, and audiovisual and surgical equipment; advisory help; local and third-country training; budgetary support for special projects; and financial assistance toward the local currency costs of an International Bank for Reconstruction and Development (World Bank) loan for building clinics and teaching facilities. Support also included help in rehabilitating some 100 health facilities to improve maternal and child/health family planning services.

The United Nations Fund for Population Activities (UNFPA) has provided $4 million in grant funds for the period 1974-78 for a number of demographic and family planning projects. The World Health Organization (WHO) has provided nursing/midwifery consultant services, commodities, and

Tunisian mothers, right, learn about family planning. The program hopes to attract 69,000 new acceptors in 1976. A city mother, below right, would like to keep her family a small one.

funds for training medical and paramedical personnel.

The World Bank made a loan of $4.8 million in fiscal 1971 for the construction of clinics and training facilities.

The Ford Foundation has provided $1.18 million in assistance, including payments to the Population Council for support of two resident advisors in Tunisia from 1968 through 1972 and a demographic advisor since 1972.

The Population Council has furnished technical assistance in demography, public health medicine, and health education.

The Pathfinder Fund furnished the first IUD's in Tunisia and in 1972 supplied Dalkon Shields for research purposes.

The Canadian International Development Authority during the past 8 years has furnished medical teams of 12 to 50 persons for work in medical schools, children's hospitals, maternal/child health clinics, and other health facilities to train Tunisians and improve the delivery of services.

The Netherlands has provided $647,000 between fiscal 1970 and 1974 in family planning assistance, including the support of a team offering maternal/child health and family planning services in the Le Kef region.

Belgium provided $175,000 in assistance during fiscal 1975, including support for a similar team in the Gafsa area.

The Swedish International Development Authority budgeted $2.22 million in assistance between fiscal 1966 and 1972. This went toward advisory help from an expert in the production of

communications/audiovisual materials, communications supplies and equipment, a large offset printing press, and the costs of a nurse-midwife advisor to the national program.

West Germany has provided subsidies to cover the operating costs of the Montfleuri clinic.

Uganda

Although the Government of Uganda has no national population policy or program, it is increasingly concerned at its population growth rate. This has accelerated from an average of 2.5 percent per year in 1956-65 to a yearly 2.9 percent by 1975.

Clockwise from below:
Social worker talks
to Tunisian mother
with large family;
camel, symbol of
birth control, carries
family planning poster;
farm workers get
instruction on family
planning; Minister
of Health cuts ribbon
for new clinic;
talking over family
planning with rural
family.

Declining death rates—now 16 per 1,000—in conjunction with a birth rate of 45 per 1,000 account in part for the pace of population increase.

If the current growth rate were to continue, Uganda's present 11.5 million people would double to 23 million in just 24 years. And since 44 percent of the population is under age 15 and approaching the years of fertility, this doubling is sure to occur in the absence of developments that would reduce birth rates or increase death rates or both. In light of the difficulties in the way of quick economic development in Uganda, such a rapid rise in population would be most likely to depress even further the present GNP of $160 per person.

In its third 5-year development plan, the Government examined the problems caused by the high population growth rate and budgeted an initial sum of $145,000 in 1972 for the activities of the Family Planning Association of Uganda (FPAU).

FPAU was founded in 1956 and is a member of the International Planned Parenthood Federation (IPPF). It is the main source of family planning work in Uganda. As of 1974, it ran a total of 28 clinics, using—in addition to its own facilities—some Government and mission hospitals and municipal health centers. The majority of these are in the Kampala area. The number of clinics, however, is down from 38 in 1972 as a result of the departure of Asian doctors. In addition, it gives support to a cytologist at the Medical School of Makerere University in Kampala.

The FPAU also carries out an information, communication, and education program by producing films, leaflets, and other materials in English, Luganda, and four vernacular languages.

Family planning services and training also are offered at the Makerere Medical School.

External Assistance

U.S. AID budgeted a total of $821,000 in assistance for Ugandan family planning activities between fiscal 1969 and 1973 when aid was discontinued. Funds have gone for various projects: to the Uganda Computer Center for processing the 1969 census, for participant training and advisory services, and for some support of the Family Planning Association of Uganda (FPAU). In addition, AID has given extensive assistance to Makerere University for prostaglandin studies and—through a contract with the University of California (Berkeley)—for maternal and child health/family planning training and services.

The United Nations Fund for Population Activities (UNFPA) has provided a total of $97,000 in assistance since 1972 for a demonstration project in improving family health.

The International Planned Parenthood Federation (IPPF) in 1970-75 provided $948,000 in assistance for the FPAU. It also supports training programs at Makerere University.

Among other voluntary organizations, the Population Council provided $105,000 between 1969 and 1972 for fellowships, a demographic advisor at Makerere University, and research into vital registration and differential growth in Uganda. The Pathfinder Fund has paid for the services of a doctor, supplied contraceptives and films, and provided travel grants. It has also analyzed IUD insertions as part of its international IUD program. The Rockefeller Foundation has provided fellowships to the Medical School of Makerere University for research on blood-clotting mechanisms in relation to ovarian steroid hormones and for an exchange training program between the University of California (Berkeley) and Makerere University. Oxfam, through IPPF, has given financial assistance to FPAU, and World Neighbors has worked with FPAU as well as with the Martyrs Community Center in Kampala and the Christian Rural Service Provincial Program. Family Planning International Assistance has provided limited support since fiscal 1972.

The Government of Denmark has given $219,000 in assistance during the last decade, most of it a lump sum payment in 1969 for building costs and equipment of a family health training center at Makerere University.

Upper Volta

Upper Volta's population, somewhat over 6 million, is increasing by 2.3 percent per year. The high birth rate—49 per 1,000 population—is accompanied by a high death rate—26 per 1,000. The economic situation of the people is indicated in part by the very low GNP per person per year—$80. Over 40 percent of the population is under age 15.

Upper Volta has no official policy on population growth or family planning, and no mention of either was made in the 1972-76 National Plan. However, the Government is aware that a relationship exists between population and economic development.

Some doctors give family planning advice, but contraceptives are not for sale.

External Assistance

The United Nations Fund for Population Activities in 1974 budgeted $1,033,000 for a population census in Upper Volta over a 4-year period.

The American Friends Service Committee funded a family planning seminar in 1972.

U.S. AID provided $16,000 from its Special Population Activities fund for construction of two maternity dispensaries where maternal/child health programs are operating.

The Population Council assisted with a survey of population and family planning knowledge, attitudes, and practices and has provided fellowship support.

Zaire

As of 1975, Zaire had a birth rate of 45 per 1,000 population and a death rate of 20 per 1,000, making for an annual population increase of 2.5 percent. If continued, this would double the country's 24.9 million population in 28 years. Some 44 percent of the country's population is under age 15, setting the stage for further increases.

Zaire, the most populous country in central Africa, is already suffering some of the repercussions of uncontrolled population growth. The needs of the people are outrunning food production; vital social services are lacking; disease and malnutrition are widespread; and mortality rates, especially among children, are high. And each new citizen adds to the demand for jobs, public services, schooling, and food.

The overall problem is attracting increasing attention. In the last decade, Zaire has moved from having no organized family planning activities to offering expanding services through Government facilities. National leaders have indicated a growing commitment to curtailing population growth. For instance, President Mobutu, in a national statement on population in 1972, expressed interest in limiting births to "desirable births."

Later, in March 1974, at a Kinshasa seminar, the Minister of Health stated "We believe...that a moderate demographic growth limited to desired births is a part of the basic equilibrium of a modern country in full development."

The Government currently has a pilot maternal and child health/family planning program under the auspices of Fonds Medical de Coordination (FOMECO). The program operates three clinics (another two have been approved) in Kinshasa. As part of the FOMECO program, the Mama Yemo General Hospital also offers training in family planning.

Additionally, maternal and child health/family planning radio tapes and films are being produced for national distribution by RENAPEC, the national radio education-television production agency.

A recently formed National Council of Health will determine future health and family planning priorities for Zaire and formulate needed programs.

External Assistance

The U.S. Agency for International Development (AID) obligated $1.63 million in fiscal years 1972 through 1975—and budgeted $593,000 for fiscal 1976—for family planning programs in Zaire. Much of this has gone toward the Government's pilot project of maternal and child health/family planning services, including training, information-education work, contraceptive distribution, and development of model clinics.

The United Nations Fund for Population Activities (UNFPA) provided $209,000 between fiscal 1973 and 1975 for a demographic and rural fertility survey and for a civil registration project. Funds also have gone toward strengthening the Demographic Division of Zaire's Department of Statistics and toward the salary of a professor of demography at the Territorial School of Likas.

The Population Council in 1973 provided $40,000 in grant assistance to the University of Zaire for partial support of a Department of Demography.

Canada's International Development Research Center granted $99,500 to the Government's National Institute of Statistics for a demographic survey in three major cities and for development of techniques applicable to other African nations.

Limited assistance also has come from The Pathfinder Fund, Family Planning International Assistance, and the Mennonite Central Committee.

Zambia

Zambia's mid-1975 population of 4.9 million is increasing at the very high rate of 3.1 percent a year—the same as reported for 1963-68. This reflects continued high rates for both births and deaths—51 and 20 per 1,000, respectively. The present pressures on employment opportunities, housing, educational facilities, health facilities, and social services are intense. Further, with 46 percent of its population below age 15, the dependency load on productive workers is extremely heavy. The 1975 per capita GNP is about $500 per year, or above that of most African countries. But a continuing surge in population would tend to diminish this average and intensify many related problems.

Zambia has witnessed a quickening acceptance of family planning activities in the last decade on the part of both the Government and the general public.

A decade ago, the only formal activity was a local family planning association operating in Lusaka, the capital city. Today, the Family Planning and Welfare Association of Zambia (FPWAZ) provides services throughout the country; the Government has moved to offer family planning services through national maternal and child health facilities; and abortions are permitted under certain conditions as a result of a 1972 abortion law.

There is, nonetheless, still some hesitation on the part of the Government, which qualified its announced intent to make family planning services available with the note that they should not be considered as birth control but rather as help in child spacing. Apparently, most people continue to favor large families although a 40 percent increase in use of contraceptives during the past 2 years has been reported.

The FPWAZ was organized in September 1971 and became an associate member of the International Planned Parenthood Federation (IPPF) in 1973. It provides free contraceptives to family planning acceptors and assists with dissemination of family planning services through the Government health program.

The FPWAZ also carries out extensive informa-tion-education work, which has been strengthened by the appointment of an information-education officer in 1974. Among the efforts planned for 1975 are the local production of slides on family planning, the publication of a newsletter, and a greater use of posters and exhibits at agricultural shows. Other activities have included national seminars on the role of family planning in social and economic develop-ment and training courses for paramedical staff.

Results include an estimated 1,684 new acceptors in the first half of 1974—well above the 1,264 reported for all of 1972. Orals are the main type of contraceptive used.

External Assistance

The U.S. Agency for International Development (AID) has provided $35,372 direct assistance through fiscal year 1975. It has funded special population activities projects for training seminars and vehicle purchase.

The United Nations Fund for Population Activi-ties (UNFPA) is helping the Government to improve demographic data collection, analysis, and evaluation.

Private groups have also offered assistance. The International Association of Schools of Social Work has a pilot project to develop qualified manpower for population and family planning activities. The Inter-national Planned Parenthood Federation (IPPF) gives financial assistance to the Family Planning and Welfare Association of Zambia (FPWAZ), including funds for information work, training, and fieldwork. It also has provided contraceptives for dissemination by the FPWAZ. Budgeted expenditures for 1975 were $376,000 compared with $160,000 in 1974. The Pathfinder Fund has sponsored a family planning clinic project and a training program in the Copper Belt. The Population Council has made two grants to the University of Zambia for research on rural-urban migration and for a survey on population growth in selected areas. It also provides fellowship support.

Asia

Asia contains over half of the world's people, with their number increasing rapidly. The estimated rate of increase among South and South East Asia's 1.1 billion people is about 2.3 percent annually and 1.7 percent among East Asia's 1 billion. Just since 1965 Asia's increase has totaled 379.3 million.

If these rates were to continue, in another 35 years Asia's population would be greater than the present world's total.

The population is expanding not only because of high birth rates but also because better conditions have lowered mortality. More babies are surviving and growing to adulthood, and adults are living longer than before.

Although national development programs have made notable progress in most Asian countries since 1950, rapidly rising numbers have prevented the intended improvement in average levels of living and have retarded economic and social development.

Asian leaders have become increasingly concerned. Within the past decade (longer in some cases) most Asian countries have initiated programs to slow population growth and improve maternal and child health. Nineteen today have national family planning programs. Most are administered by governments, and all receive at least some government support. Several countries, notably Singapore, are also working to bring development policies and programs in the "beyond family planning" sphere to bear on fertility (housing allocations, restrictions on maternity leave after birth of a specified number of children, etc).

The early work in Asia was done by voluntary agencies. The later pattern in many countries is for the government to provide the actual services with the private agencies concentrating on public information and personnel training.

In some East and South East Asian countries— the People's Republic of China, Hong Kong, Malaysia,

Variations in Asia's vital rates are wide. Some heavily populated countries—the People's Republic of China, South Korea, Taiwan, Japan, Hong Kong, Singapore—have made progress in reducing birth rates, death rates, and the rate of natural increase. But other countries, as the chart shows, still have far to go in dampening their rates of natural increase.

Estimated Vital Rates in Selected Countries in Asia, 1974

Legend: Natural increase per 1,000 population | Deaths per 1,000 population | Births per 1,000 population (Whole bar)

Country	Natural increase per 1,000	Deaths per 1,000	Births per 1,000 (Whole bar)
Bangladesh	27	20	47
Pakistan	29	15	44
Afghanistan	22	21	43
Philippines	30	11	41
Burma	24	16	40
Indonesia	21	17	38
Thailand	25	11	36
India	20	15	35
South Korea	20	9	29
China (P.R.)	17	10	27
China (Taiwan)	19	5	24
Singapore	15	5	20
Hong Kong	14	5	19
Japan	12	6	18

SOURCE: Population Reference Bureau

PRB 75-38

65

These heavily populated countries account for almost a fifth of the world's people.
Although there were gains in annual growth of total gross national product over 1970-74,
the pressure of rapid population increase brought either very small gains or declines in per capita GNP.

Singapore, the Republic of China (Taiwan), and South Korea—birth rates have dropped significantly. In India the birth rate in 1974 was estimated at 35 per 1,000 people compared with 43 in 1965. In Bangladesh and Pakistan the programs have suffered from political dislocations associated with severance of the two countries.

Important, however, is the fact that in most of Asia inaction about population problems has been replaced by action and that a major and growing movement is underway to curb the wave of additional human beings that will be appearing in the years ahead. Also significant is the fact that out of the Asian experiences are emerging many innovations and conclusions that are useful not only to Asian countries but to all others around the world that are trying to slow excessive population growth.

A large number of external organizations and countries are assisting the development of family planning in Asia. The United States has been a major donor over a 10-year period. More recently, the United Nations Fund for Population Activities (UNFPA) has become highly active on both an individual country and a multilateral basis. Multilateral allocations in 1973 to Asian and Pacific projects now being carried out totaled $3 million.

East and South East Asia

Several countries of East Asia have made notable progress in recent years in initiating and expanding family planning programs designed to reduce population growth.

For example, Singapore has lowered its birth rates from a 1965 level of 31 births per 1,000 population to a current level of about 20 or less per 1,000.

The People's Republic of China, though it does not issue population data, is carrying out a vigorous and far-reaching program thought by some Western observers to have dropped its rate of population increase to near that of Western Europe.

The Republic of China (Taiwan) has a strong family planning program that has dropped birth rates

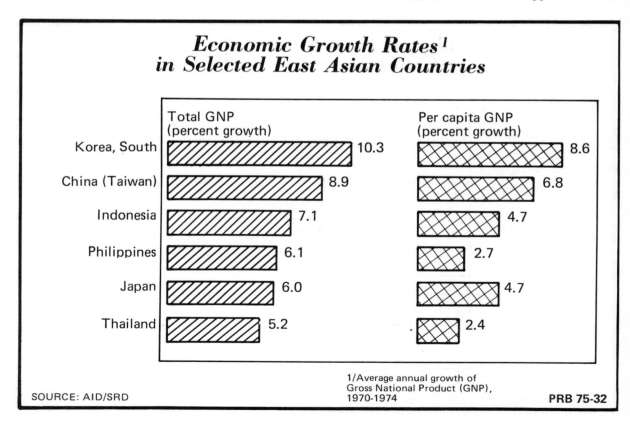

Economic Growth Rates[1]
in Selected East Asian Countries

	Total GNP (percent growth)	Per capita GNP (percent growth)
Korea, South	10.3	8.6
China (Taiwan)	8.9	6.8
Indonesia	7.1	4.7
Philippines	6.1	2.7
Japan	6.0	4.7
Thailand	5.2	2.4

1/Average annual growth of Gross National Product (GNP), 1970-1974

SOURCE: AID/SRD

PRB 75-32

Economic Growth Rates [1]
in Selected South Asian Countries

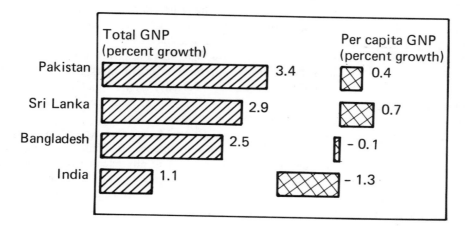

	Total GNP (percent growth)	Per capita GNP (percent growth)
Pakistan	3.4	0.4
Sri Lanka	2.9	0.7
Bangladesh	2.5	- 0.1
India	1.1	- 1.3

1/Average annual growth of
Gross National Product (GNP),
1970-1974

SOURCE: AID/SRD

PRB 75-31

from 45 per 1,000 population in 1956 to 23 per 1,000 in 1974.

Hong Kong has achieved even more spectacular results. Its 1960 birth rate of 36 per 1,000 population per year has been reduced to 19 per 1,000.

Japan, a pioneer in population program efforts, has made similar progress—cutting its birth rate from 34 per 1,000 population after the end of World War II to a 1974 level of 19 per 1,000.

In general, family planning in East and South East Asia has encountered remarkably little opposition. Most people recognize that smaller families are desirable both for family and national well-being. Even the best of family planning efforts, however, faces difficult challenges. One is that of reaching people with supplies, information, and motivation to begin practicing birth control. This is particularly difficult in countries that have large rural populations. Another challenge that several countries face is the exceptionally large number of young people now

reaching marriageable age. Unless most decide to have exceptionally small families, they will add to the population burden. For this reason, some of the countries in this area are placing maximum attention on reaching young people in their family planning programs.

Two small South East Asian countries do not believe that their populations are too big or growing too rapidly, and they do not have national family planning programs. These are Burma and Cambodia. In Burma, family planning services are available only through limited private sources. In Cambodia, even such private sources may no longer be available.

External assistance has played an important part in the establishment of family planning programs in most East and South East Asian countries—with the exception of the People's Republic of China. The United States, through the U.S. Agency for International Development (AID) has been a major donor. Several European countries and Japan also have

These six countries have made excellent progress in reducing fertility of their populations. For example, between 1965 and 1974, birth rates declined in South Korea from 35 to 29 per 1,000 people; in China (Taiwan) from 33 to 23; and in Indonesia from 46 to 38. As a result, a substantial part of the growth in total GNP in 1970-74 was retained in terms of per capita GNP.

contributed. Numerous private organizations have given start-up help and continuing assistance. And the United Nations Fund for Population Activities (UNFPA) is playing an increasing role.

South Asia

Despite strong interest in and a growing commitment to family planning, the countries of South Asia have not yet achieved the breakthroughs evident in many parts of East and South East Asia. Birth rates continue to be above 40 per 1,000 except in India (35 per 1,000) and Sri Lanka (28 per 1,000). Population growth in all South Asian countries continues at 2 percent or more per year.

The "green revolution," with its increases in food production, has helped India and other countries that face extreme population pressure—but the bad weather of 1972 and again in 1974 showed the narrowness of the margin between barely enough food and dire shortage.

Basic to South Asia's problems of reducing population growth rates is the fact that many parts already were overcrowded when—a few years ago—large-scale family planning efforts began. In these, as in most countries of the subregion, widespread poverty, illiteracy, and numerous other conditions make it difficult to provide family planning services,

supplies, and information to many millions of people—especially in rural areas.

Despite difficulties, however, most governments of South Asia today have population policies and are directly involved in carrying out national family planning programs. Most have sought assistance from external sources, in both the start-up and continuation of family planning programs. The United States, through AID and private foundations, has been in the forefront in providing this assistance. More recently, the United Nations Fund for Population Activities (UNFPA) has been giving increasing aid to the programs.

South Asian countries—recognizing that conventional approaches to family planning, such as the use of clinics and physicians, have not brought hoped-for results—are trying new approaches. In such innovations, the U.S. AID program has given considerable guidance and help.

Bangladesh and Pakistan, for example, have concluded that large numbers of trained family planning "contact teams" may be a key to gaining participation. The Pakistani teams, each composed of a man and a woman, seek to motivate couples to practice family planning. Both governments provide their teams with contraceptive supplies (largely from foreign donors) to be given away or sold at minimal

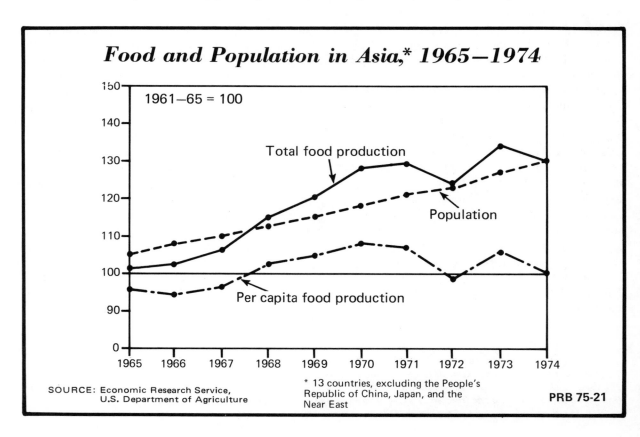

Food and Population in Asia,* 1965—1974

1961—65 = 100

Total food production

Population

Per capita food production

SOURCE: Economic Research Service, U.S. Department of Agriculture

* 13 countries, excluding the People's Republic of China, Japan, and the Near East

PRB 75-21

prices. Both Governments organize the teams to work closely with general health programs directed to mothers of young children. Both governments are seeking to make contraceptives easily and cheaply available by licensing thousands of small shops in cities and villages to sell supplies at low, subsidized prices. Both plan to follow up with evaluation studies to see whether the approach of expanded family planning services plus inexpensive and easily available contraceptive supplies are giving them new progress toward their family planning objectives.

Afghanistan

Afghanistan's population was estimated, based on a 1974 demographic survey, at 19.1 million. The birth rate was estimated at 43 per 1,000 population and the mortality rate at 21 per 1,000. These would result in an annual increase of population of 2.2 percent.

Afghanistan's economy is based primarily on small-scale agriculture and considerable arable land is not yet under cultivation. Its limited stage of development is reflected in the low average per capita Gross National Product (GNP) estimated at $80 per year.

The Government, aided by considerable foreign economic assistance, has been carrying out a series of 5-year economic development programs since 1956. The current program (1973-79) aims at achieving an annual economic growth of 5 percent. Major handicaps are the low literacy rate (estimated at 8 percent), insufficient technical training, and inadequate financial resources. Nevertheless, highway and air facilities are being expanded, natural gas production has been developed, and agriculture has been upgraded to some degree.

Although Afghanistan does not have an official policy on population growth, the Government is aware of the economic hazards of overrapid population expansion. The Ministry of Public Health has long recognized the importance of family planning and has promoted its integration into the basic health services. A decade ago almost no contraceptive services were available; now the Afghan Family Guidance Association (AFGA) delivers services through a national system of clinics serving both rural and urban areas. While growth in participation is slow, it appears that a fairly solid base for further action is being laid. The number of visitors to AFGA clinics increased from 7,670 in 1969 to an estimated 53,700 in 1974. Oral contraceptives and IUD's are the main types of contraception currently being utilized.

AFGA is a semiprivate agency that came into being in 1968 through the efforts of a few physicians and women concerned about social and health problems. It is an affiliate of the International Planned Parenthood Federation (IPPF) and draws support from that organization as well as from the U.S. Agency for International Development.

AFGA has reached an agreement with the Afghan Government to expand the number of AFGA clinics from 19 to 35 over a 3-year period and thereby make family planning available in all 26 provincial centers. (AFGA already maintains 9 clinics in Kabul and 10 in the provinces.) The expansion will include increasing the number of male and female "Family Guide" teams who represent the clinics as family planning teachers and as suppliers of contraceptives. Targets of the expansion include gaining 17,000 new contraceptive acceptors in 1975, 28,000 in 1976, and 31,000 in 1977.

Accompanying the expansion of services at health centers and clinics is an active training program for personnel. During the 1973-77 period, some 36 instructors of auxiliary nurse-midwives and about 500 students are scheduled to be trained. In addition to the home guidance and contraceptive services provided by the "Family Guides," family planning lectures and discussions are scheduled for the regular employees of hotels and a variety of other institutions on a programmed basis.

Meanwhile, the Government's current 5-year plan has a target of making maternal and child health, health education, and family guidance services available at the urban and rural clinics and the outpatient clinics of Government hospitals. Also targeted is the financing of 180 basic health centers planned to include such services.

The Government has also sponsored visits by local religious leaders with their counterparts in Cairo, Teheran, and Ankara to discuss formulation of an international Muslim policy in support of family planning. Afghanistan is a Muslim country.

Dense populations of India, Indonesia, Bangladesh, Pakistan, and other Asian countries keep a constant pressure on food supplies. Crop shortfalls in the mid-1960's, 1972, and 1974 sharply reduced per capita food production, making large-scale grain imports necessary. Even during years when food production rose faster than population, the increase fell far short of closing the nutrition gap for the majority of the people.

Acceptance of the program by religious leaders and leading Afghan citizens has helped to bring progress in family planning.

External Assistance

Afghanistan's population program has received major support from external sources throughout its development period. At the end of fiscal 1975, assistance from leading sources totaled $6.7 million. A principal contributor has been the U.S. Agency for International Development (AID), whose help has totaled nearly $5.4 million through fiscal 1975.

Funds from the United Nations Fund for Population Activities (UNFPA) have totaled $230,000. Other United Nations contributors include the Children's Fund (UNICEF)—which has supplied equipment, vehicles, and drugs to the health clinics—and the World Health Organization (WHO)—which has assisted in maternal and child health development and public health and nursing education. The Asia Foundation has helped fund a provincial pilot education project.

AID has given considerable support to helping build up a demographic knowledge and a knowledge of family planning information, attitudes, and practices. Better information on the nation's population status and growth will help Government agencies to define their problems and plan for the future and can lead to the setting of a national population policy. For example, AID support has included a contract with the State University of New York (SUNY) to conduct a national sample survey, develop a basic demographic description of the population, and conduct a knowledge, attitude, and practices (KAP) survey. This work has been carried out within the Ministry of Planning by a specially trained Afghan staff. Also, SUNY has developed a client record system and made studies to determine why some Afghan people become acceptors of family planning and others do not.

AID also has contracted with a second group, Management Sciences for Health, to work within the Health Ministry and help to improve the administrative capacity of the Ministry to operate the basic health clinics which will be public contact points for family health services.

Development of training schools for auxiliary nurse-midwives is another feature of AID's support. AID also provides contraceptives for use in programs.

As part of the overall U.S. assistance to Afghanistan, AID also is giving support to the country's improvement of health and education, both of which can be important foundation stones for an improved family guidance program. Discussions are underway

between AID and the Afghanistan Government on how AID can support Afghanistan's efforts to bring health services to rural areas.

Also, AID with non-Title X Funds has helped the government in its reform of the primary school system. This has involved writing new primary textbooks about health, agriculture, and crafts; building new schools which include teacher hostels so as to attract teachers to the rural areas; improving attendance; and awakening children to new ideas, including health needs and family future.

The Pathfinder Fund has assisted the country's program.

Bangladesh

As Bangladesh, formerly East Pakistan, struggles to become a viable new nation, it faces the handicap of a rapidly expanding population that is already very large for available resources. The Government esti-

Far left, mothers and children in a Dacca slum pose for their photograph. In a small Bangladesh village a midwife explains the pill to a young mother. In this small country, population is growing at the rate of 2.7 percent a year; per capita income is $100 a year.

mates the population, as of mid-1975, at 77 million persons. Living in an area about the size of the State of Wisconsin, this population is increasing at a rate of 3 percent a year. Unless abated, this rate would mean a doubling of the country's crowded population by the year 2000. Bangladesh estimates its birth rate at 47 per 1,000 population and death rate at 17 per 1,000. Life expectancy is about 47 years.

Over 90 percent of the population is rural. But although the land is fertile and the farmers industrious, food production is insufficient and large imports are necessary. Most of the land is low-lying, subject to heavy rains, and often prey to devastating floods. Some areas, now heavily populated because of population pressure, were considered uninhabitable prior to this century.

With a GNP per capita of about $100 a year, Bangladesh is considered among the world's poorest countries, and much of its population experiences poverty and misery.

Population Programs

The national leadership of Bangladesh is well aware of the nation's growing population problems. Evidence of increasing concern on the part of the national leadership is to be found in the provisions set forth in the country's First Five-Year Plan (1973-78), which aims at reinstating large-scale facilities to bring family planning to the masses. Although the population program leaders of Bangladesh have reservations about the philosophy and approaches of the earlier

population program efforts of former East Pakistan, it is true that these efforts—which began as early as 1952—are providing some helpful background which, with modifications, can be applied today.

Bangladesh's overall aim for the 1973-78 planning period is to sharply cut the current rate of population growth, now 3 percent. A longer range goal is to reach replacement fertility level in 25 to 30 years. In a traditional society such as that of Bangladesh, this is obviously an ambitious target. The scope of the problem is indicated by the estimate that about 15 million couples are of reproductive age with 65 percent of the women in the 15 to 30 age group and contributing 87 percent of all births. Further, although approximately 85 percent of the target population is reported "aware" of family planning, only an estimated 15 percent has effective knowledge and only 7 to 8 percent has ever practiced family planning.

The 1973-78 campaign for achieving population growth control is spearheaded by the Ministry of Health, Population Control and Family Planning. Integrated with national health services prior to June 1975, but now following an independent family planning program, it aims at bringing information, education, and family planning services into every home. Important educational and motivational roles are given to all developmental ministries in contact with the public. The Five-Year Plan envisions legalization of abortion, establishment of abortion clinics, raising the age of marriage, and training a core of professional family planning workers. The Plan anticipates a possible future need to consider stringent legislative measures if the voluntary approach to fertility control is not effective soon enough.

Immediate action aims of the program are: delivery of information and conventional contraceptives to homes in rural areas by approximately 12,000 family welfare workers (trained in both health and family planning) plus some 16,000 family planning workers yet to be trained; clinical services in rural areas and in urban clinics and hospitals; introduction of oral contraceptives on a large scale; and use of paramedical personnel to screen candidates, issue orals, and insert IUD's. The Government has approved commercial marketing of orals and condoms.

Reinforcing the Government family planning program is the work of the private Bangladesh Family Welfare Association (BFWA). Its primary activities include family planning education, motivation, and operation of model clinics in urban areas.

The Government of Bangladesh, within its limited resources, has made yearly increases in its financial support of family planning. Beginning in 1973, it made available $640,000; and in 1975 this had grown to $1.6 million.

Acceptance and practice of contraception, which were making hopeful growth during pre-independence days, appear to be making a slow (though insufficient) comeback as indicated by the fact that only 16,000 new acceptors were listed in 1972 and 41,000 new users in 1974. As of 1974, Bangladesh had a total of about 550,000 users of contraceptives. (This included a substantial number of males who had undergone sterilization.)

External Assistance

Bangladesh is highly dependent on external assistance for financing family planning programs. The United States—both through the Government and private agencies—has been in the forefront in helping to reinstate family planning after the upheavals of achieving independence. A number of other countries and organizations also are assisting.

U.S. Government help has been channeled through the U.S. Agency for International Development (AID). During fiscal years 1973-75, such assistance under Title X totaled $6.25 million. For fiscal 1976, AID has proposed population program grants to Bangladesh totaling $4.6 million to be spent chiefly for contraceptive supplies and for training field, hospital, and clinical population program personnel.

AID is the major contributor of contraceptive supplies to Bangladesh's population growth control program. It provided 3 million monthly cycles of oral pills and 30.7 million condoms in fiscal 1973; 7.4 million monthly cycles of orals and 6.9 million condoms in fiscal 1974; 870,000 monthly cycles of orals and 1.1 million condoms in fiscal 1975; and 5.2 million monthly cycles of orals and 27 million condoms in fiscal 1976.

Other projects receiving AID support are an innovative test program for marketing nonclinical contraceptives through established retail outlets, the establishment of a model fertility control clinic, the work of the private Bangladesh Family Planning Association (BFPA), and an experimental program to secure the support of village leaders in the promotion of family planning. In addition, AID is providing advisory services, equipment, and training.

The United Nations is also providing major assistance. Its Fund for Population Activities (UNFPA) has given considerable advisory assistance as Bangladesh sets up its new population program, and UNFPA has signed a country agreement with the Government of Bangladesh which, over a 3-year period is expected to total $10 million. The U.N. assistance to be given under UNFPA includes several different efforts. The World Health Organization (WHO) will provide guidance in strengthening the family planning clinical program, with special emphasis on maternal/child health aspects and instruction in medical colleges. The United Nations Children's Emergency Fund (UNICEF) will help in developing national maternal/child health services in support of family planning, including training personnel and developing teaching aids. Also, the United Nations will offer consultant services for population census planning, including sampling design and tabulation. The International Labour Organisation is assisting population activities in the organized sectors of industry.

Bilateral assistance is being given by four countries other than the United States. Great Britain is offering advisory assistance on a demographic survey; Denmark is donating contraceptives and equipment for midwives; Norway is financing training institutions for paramedical personnel; and Sweden is supplying condoms and financing family planning seminars.

Many nongovernmental organizations are assisting, in varying degree, the Bangladesh population program. Most active has been the International Planned Parenthood Federation (IPPF), which helped finance and establish the earlier family planning activities of the area when Bangladesh was part of Pakistan. IPPF now gives financial assistance to the BFPA for its overall program. This includes support of mass communication, in-service training for project officers and field motivators, operation of model and mobile clinics and motivation centers at industrial units and factories, and operation of family planning projects with cooperatives and women's centers. IPPF contributions have been $127,000 for 1972, $221,000 for 1973, and $182,000 for 1974.

The Asia Foundation has given small travel and training grants preparatory to the expansion of family planning information, education, and communication activities.

The Association for Voluntary Sterilization has given a grant to the Bangladesh Association for Voluntary Sterilization Polyclinic to help establish nationwide information, education, and communication activities and a pilot clinic for male and female voluntary sterilizations.

Family Planning International Assistance, the international division of the Planned Parenthood Federation of America, has given a grant for a community development pilot project providing family planning through village leadership and another grant for a workshop on family planning project design for voluntary agencies.

The Population Council is providing assistance.

The Ford Foundation maintains a population advisory staff and office in Bangladesh.

The International Association of Schools of Social Work has a pilot project to develop qualified population and family planning social workers carried out with the country's schools of social work.

The Pathfinder Fund has sponsored work to reopen the postpartum program that was closed down by hostilities and to develop a major clinic for the city of Dacca. The clinic would provide complete fertility regulation services and serve as a training facility for the delivery of services.

The World Assembly of Youth has sponsored, in cooperation with the Bangladesh Youth Council, various seminars on population, family planning, and responsible parenthood to help make young people aware of rapid population growth and the problems it brings to family life, community development, and national progress.

World Education has assisted the Bangladesh Rural Advancement Committee in a pilot project on adult functional education. The project includes not only literacy training but also promotes changes in attitude toward family planning.

The International Bank for Reconstruction and Development (World Bank Group) has initiated a program of assistance in 1975 with the following objectives: to construct health facilities; to provide population education, training, and salary support for village health workers; to supply vehicles and equipment; to develop population programs in five different ministries; to supply technical advisor assistance and fellowships.

Burma

The Socialist Republic of the Union of Burma is unusual among Asian nations in that its Government considers the country to be relatively underpopulated and welcomes the nation's annual population growth rate of 2.4 percent. With continuation of this rate, the country's 30.5 million population, as of mid-1975, would double in less than 30 years. The birth rate for 1973-74 is estimated at 40 per 1,000 population and the death rate at 16.

Burma's population density is relatively low— about 110 people per square mile. It has suitable additional land that could be brought under cultivation and has important mineral resources together furnishing a strong potential for economic development. The Government welcomes the present high rate of population increase and views its problem as one of equipping and mobilizing people for economic growth rather than one of reducing the birth rate. The economic development that is sought, however, continues to be elusive. Little expansion is being made and, as one key indicator, per capita GNP of about $80 per year is one of the lowest in the world.

Although health officials consider family planning desirable for maternal and child health reasons, Government controls on importation of contraceptives and restrictions on sterilization inhibit the broadening of services. The oral contraceptives and condoms that are available are expensive. A number of individual physicians give family planning advice, but there is no organized family planning activity.

External Assistance
The United Nations Fund for Population Activities (UNFPA) is helping Burma in a population census. An allocation of $1,493,000 has been made to help collect and analyze data relating to composition, distribution, and growth of the population.

Family Planning International Assistance has provided contraceptives to church-related family planning groups.

The Pathfinder Fund helped set up the Family Planning Association of Burma some years ago, but in the face of Government resistance, Pathfinder has discontinued its aid.

People's Republic of China

Over one-fifth of mankind lives in the People's Republic of China—the most populous of all countries. However, the actual population total is unknown. The Republic's latest census was taken in 1953, over 20 years ago, and the absence of later comprehensive data has led to widely divergent estimates of population size and rate of increase.

The Population Division of the United Nations has estimated the mid-1975 total at about 823 million—an increase of 41 percent, or 240.4 million, from the 582.6 million enumerated in 1953. This estimate is reasonably consistent with the "nearly 800 million" reported in 1974 at the World Population Conference in Bucharest by the leader of the Republic's delegation and with a statement by Premier Chou En Lai in 1972 that the population was then above 700 million but not yet close to 800 million. At the same time, it should be noted that two respected U.S. analysts, working from nonofficial information, have developed separate and widely differing estimates that place the total at many millions more than the above figures would indicate.*

Family Planning

The Republic's apparent lack of demographic information does not stem from lack of interest in the problems of population increase as they affect individuals, families, and national development. It is widely reported, on the contrary, that the Government is strongly encouraging and assisting family planning activities on a wide scale with the aim of voluntary reduction of fertility. Moreover, observers from other countries in recent years have reported a sharp reduction in birth rates—particularly in urban areas. On the basis of these reports, it appears that the People's Republic is making strong and effective efforts to discourage couples from having large families.

The Government first endorsed birth control in the 1950's. It de-emphasized this during the so-called Great Leap Forward beginning in 1957, and then

---

*Leo A. Orleans "China's Population: Can the Contradiction be Resolved?" in *China: A Reassessment of the Economy,* Joint Economic Committee, Congress of the United States, July 10, 1975, pp. 69-80; John S. Aird "Population Policy and Demographic Prospects" in *The People's Republic of China: An Economic Assessment*, Joint Economic Committee, Congress of the United States, May 18, 1972, pp. 220-231.

began to promote it actively again in 1962. In 1966-1969 the Red Guard movement frowned on family planning, but fertility control has remained a national policy—though with fluctuating emphasis.

Today, the concept of the two-child family as the desirable norm is widespread and perhaps pervasive. Western visitors have commented that wherever they went in recent times, they saw younger parents who had only one or two children, never more.

China's continuing effort to build a modern state and improve the living conditions of its people has given fertility control high status. Official support for limiting the size of families is based on the Government's desire to improve the health of mothers and children, give mothers more time to work outside the home, make education available to all, and build a stronger nation. These goals are continuously kept before the people through their communes and local brigades and production teams. The local units in particular appear to exert considerable pressure for conformity to goal-oriented behavior. As a result, a majority of couples, at least in the cities, are believed to be practicing birth control.

Of special attraction to the women of the People's Republic is the fact that family planning releases them from their traditional role of continual childbearing and enables them to enjoy the new opportunities opened to them in recent years. Under the present regime, education of women has been greatly expanded, and all branches of industry and the professions are open to women. They receive equal pay for the same work as men.

The population program of the People's Republic of China has a number of interesting aspects. Some of them are listed in the following paragraphs.

Late marriage. A law setting the minimum age of marriage at 18 years for women and 20 for men was adopted as early as 1950. This law tends to delay childbearing and reduce births overall. More recently, Chairman Mao has asked Chinese women to postpone marriage until at least age 23 and men until after age 26. Although not part of the law, this request is widely known and respected. Also, since premarital intercourse is strongly frowned upon in the Chinese culture, pregnancies among unmarried women are reported to be relatively few. In such instances, there is often strong encouragement for the women to have abortions.

Readily available contraception. At marriage, couples are given detailed advice about contraception. This advice is further reinforced through meetings and health services wherever people work and by the so-called barefoot doctors (paramedics) who work in the numerous health stations and also make home visits—particularly in the rural areas.

All the conventional means of contraception are readily available, including oral pills, IUD's, diaphragms, condoms, and foams (the latter two are available at very low costs in local shops). Oral contraceptives are the most frequently used. Considerable research is being done on low-dosage pills, postcoital pills, monthly pills, and pills for men. Recently, the "paper pill" has been developed and is reported to be successful.

Contraception is backed up by readily available abortion. If a woman suspects contraceptive failure, she is expected to visit her health clinic for a diagnosis of pregnancy. If the tests are positive and she does not want to have a baby, an abortion is performed—usually by vacuum aspiration.

Sterilization is also widely used. There appears to be some reluctance among men to have vasectomies, but tubal ligation is well accepted by women and particularly by those between 35 and 40 who already have had two or more children.

Motivation. China's family planning program has been in operation long enough for a new generation to reach reproductive age. This group has widely accepted the teaching of Mao that limiting family size is a patriotic duty. This is evidenced especially by low birth rates in the cities. The older generation is reported as gradually accepting the change in norms governing family size.

In villages and communes, loudspeakers provide family planning messages along with music and educational features. In urban areas, the family planning messages are frequent, too, though they may vary seasonally and appear most often before the vacation time of year. Everywhere, these messages are further repeated through posters that stress the "ideal" family size—father, mother, and two children.

As one Western observer has stated China's population program is "unequivocal and direct"; people know that they are not supposed to have big families, and most of them are influenced by this knowledge.

National family planning services. Fertility control is made relatively easy for married couples to practice. It is an integral part of a national health system. In the countryside, each basic production team of 200 to 700 persons has a health station that offers contraceptive services along with general health services. Several of these teams comprise a production brigade and this larger work unit has a larger health center. About 20 of these brigades comprise a commune, which has a hospital. It is reported that there are over 70,000 commune hospitals.

In the cities, family planning services are available both at factories and in neighborhood and district hospitals and stations. The smaller stations are manned by the "barefoot doctors," male and female, who are trained in the basics of health care and family planning. The larger centers and hospitals are staffed by health professionals, including doctors, nurses, midwives, and medical assistants.

The health service system is reported to be decentralized, with local units having considerable voice in how they perform. Through these many institutions, family planning reaches almost all city people and an increasing number in rural areas.

China has made great progress in setting up a nationwide family planning structure and in changing the public attitude in favor of small families. Birth rates below 10 per 1,000 population are now reported in many of the largest cities, such as Canton and Shanghai. Considering the large number of young adults in the population, the attainment of such low fertility rates is most remarkable. However, while family size limitation is widespread in the cities, this is less true in many rural areas. As the country is predominantly rural, the overall birth rate for the PRC as a whole is probably higher than in the above cities.

Rates of Population Growth

Fertility control has obviously contributed to a slowing of population growth in China. However, with so little information on total population, it is difficult to estimate birth and death rates. Even if the recording of births were complete and available, uncertainty as to the population total precludes determination of vital rates.

However, it is relatively certain that birth and death rates have declined considerably since 1953. United Nations demographers, U.S. Bureau of the Census experts, as well as Leo Orleans—all are in agreement that in 1965 the birth rate was in the vicinity of 33 to 35 per 1,000 population while the death rate was approximately 15 to 17 per 1,000. The continuation of such growth would mean a doubling of the population in some 35 years to about 1½ billion by the turn of the century.

According to United Nations estimates, the birth rate for the 1970-75 period averaged 26.9 per 1,000 population while the death rate was 10.3. Orleans' estimates are very similar—27 and 12. Aird's high estimates differ significantly. He apparently assumes that little progress in fertility control has occurred over the past decade and fixes the recent birth and death rates at 37.1 and 13.2 per 1,000, respectively. Except for this estimate, there is a general consensus among demographic experts that the birth and death rates have declined considerably over the past 10 years. Leon Bouvier, of the Population Reference Bureau, estimates that by 1975 the birth rate was probably in the vicinity of 25 per 1,000 population for the whole country but substantially lower in the major cities and that the death rate was in the vicinity of 10 per 1,000 population.

The drop in fertility in the past few years is impressive. However, the rate of growth probably remains close to 1.7 percent annually. This would mean a doubling time of only 41 years if the present rate were to continue.

The age structure of the Chinese population is such that continuing increases can be expected. China, despite its advances in fertility control, is still growing relatively rapidly, and it will be necessary for the birth rate to drop much more if population equilibrium is to be reached within the next two centuries. Indeed, Frejka* has calculated that even if replacement level fertility was achieved immediately (in other words, the two-child family), China's population would continue growing and would reach 1.2 billion in the year 2125 before, in fact, attaining an end to growth.

Conclusions

When compared to other large countries facing great population pressure, the People's Republic of China is conducting an outstandingly effective effort in fertility reduction. This is the result of combining the availability of contraceptives, supplies, and services with the development of social pressures and motivations for young couples to limit family size.

The 1974 World Population Conference in Bucharest highlighted the controversy that has emerged between the so-called family planners and the so-called developmentalists. China's program appears to encompass both family planning and development.

---

*Thomas Frejka, *Reference Tables to the Future of Population Growth*, New York, The Population Council, 1973, p. 50.

China, Republic of (Taiwan)

Taiwan, or the Republic of China, had 16 million inhabitants as of mid-1975, who live on an area of about 14,000 square miles. The present total is 3.4 million above the 12.6 million reported in 1965—an increase of more than one-fourth. The 1974 birth rate was estimated at 23 per 1,000 population—down sharply from the 1965 rate of 33 per 1,000. Mortality in 1974 had also decreased to 5 per 1,000 people per year from 6 per 1,000 in 1965. The present rate of population increase is estimated at 1.9 percent annually.

At best, Taiwan faces a crowded future. Along with insufficient land, Taiwan is short of water, which is needed for all irrigated crops but particularly for rice. Taiwan tries to be self-sufficient in rice, its main staple of diet, and it has industrious and efficient farmers to grow the crop. But growing 1 ton of rice on Taiwan is said to require an average of 3,500 tons of irrigation water and the water limit is nearing. If Taiwan must supplement its home-grown rice by imports because of increased population, the cost of this basic food (and thus labor costs) will rise and the island's manufactured products will become less competitive in world markets.

On the other hand, Taiwan's national family planning effort, often viewed as one of the world's most successful, did achieve a goal of reducing the population growth rate from 2.7 percent as of 1965 to 1.9 percent by 1974. In this effort, Taiwan had some advantages not possessed by most Asian countries. About 89 percent of the population over the age of 6 is literate and thus reachable with family planning messages; 63 percent of the population is urban and thus reachable with family planning services; and the per capita GNP of $840 (estimated by the Taiwan Government), while not high by Western standards, indicates an improved standard of living that is thought to be an inducement for smaller families. But future reductions will be more difficult. Whereas in some Asian countries, the two-child family is becoming accepted as the "ideal," in Taiwan a large part of the population continues to think of the ideal family as comprising an average of nearly four children.

Taiwan's first population program began as a voluntary family planning effort of fairly small scope more than a decade ago. In 1968 the Government assumed responsibility for a national program and declared family planning as a national policy. A Family Planning Institute was set up under the Provincial Health Department and made responsible for administering and evaluating the program. All Government agencies were asked to assist. Two voluntary groups—the Planned Parenthood Association of China and the older but smaller Family Planning Association—were included on an assisting basis.

Family planning services are provided throughout the island by public and private institutions. About 450 family planning field workers refer potential acceptors to some 700 private doctors (contracted by the Government), 380 health stations, and about 30 public hospitals. Mass communication is used extensively to promote interest and participation in family planning.

Generally, the program has succeeded in bringing contraceptive services to all wives aged 30 and over who have achieved their desired family size. It is estimated that more than half the island's married women between 15 and 45 years of age are using contraceptives.

The IUD is the main form of contraceptive used, but other methods also are available. Some studies indicate that emphasis on the use of the IUD has automatically brought enlistment of larger numbers of older women, rather than younger women, as acceptors of contraception—and therefore birth rates may not have gone down as much as they could have had the program also emphasized other means, including the pill.

In addition to its own domestic program, Taiwan also serves as a training center for population workers from other countries. The Chinese Center for International Training in Family Planning, established in 1968, provides orientation and practical training to those from other countries who are working in or have an interest in family planning. A number of Asians use the facility.

External Assistance

The Government of the Republic has given strong financial support to the national family planning program. It also accepts external assistance.

U.S. bilateral assistance to Taiwan, through the U.S. Agency for International Development (AID), was terminated in 1965, but AID continues to help fund several organizations that provide some assistance to Taiwan's program. These include the Population Council (technical and evaluation program activities, vital data processing, and international training) and The Pathfinder Fund (oral contraceptives). Various U.S. universities, some with AID support, also assist in the behavioral research being undertaken increasingly by Taiwanese universities.

Other external contributors to the program include Church World Service, the Family Planning Federation of Japan (an affiliate of the International Planned Parenthood Federation), Family Planning International Assistance, Lutheran World Relief, Oxfam, and the United Nations Children's Emergency Fund (UNICEF).

Hong Kong

Hong Kong, a British Crown Colony consisting of two islands and a small strip of mainland, in mid-1975 had a population of 4.3 million—nearly all urban. The 1975 total is almost one-fifth larger than the 3.6 million of 1965.

Although the 1974 birth rate of 19 per 1,000 population was reduced sharply from the 1965 rate of 29 per 1,000 (mortality held steady at 5 per 1,000), natural increase alone has been adding to the population by 1.4 percent annually. The reduction in natural increase since 1965, when it was 2.4 percent, is attributable mainly to the Colony's vigorous family planning program.

Heavy immigration continues to add to population growth, with refugees making up about one-fourth of the total population. In addition, Hong Kong has a large number of young women of reproductive age—the product of earlier years when birth rates were higher and families were larger than they are now.

At around 100,000 people per square mile, there is hardly enough room for the present inhabitants to live in even minimum comfort in the limited area which comprises Hong Kong. The future is further complicated by chronic water shortage.

The Government of Hong Kong, which until recently gave its support to family planning by subsidizing voluntary efforts, has formalized its interest by taking over responsibility for the national program and providing family planning services through clinics located in Government maternal/child health centers.

Previously, family planning services were made available through the work of the Hong Kong Family Planning Association, established in 1936 and an affiliate of the International Planned Parenthood Federation (IPPF).

Hong Kong's program has been and continues to be highly active. Clinics not only offer services but also hold special sessions to present family planning information to married couples and young people. Welfare workers promote family planning at maternal/child health centers. All media are used to attract public attention, including radio and television. Family planning education has been introduced into schools. Posters stress the "ideal" two-child family.

Oral contraceptives for women have become the most popular means of contraception in Hong Kong. They are available at low cost and do not require a medical prescription for purchase at commercial outlets.

External Assistance

Hong Kong finances much of its own family planning work but also accepts external assistance. The Family Planning Association, as an affiliate of IPPF, has long received financial aid from this international organization. In 1974, IPPF gave an estimated $1 million to support the Association's overall program, including a mass communication effort to reach the public with family planning information, the operation of clinics, offering vasectomy services, and the distribution of contraceptives.

The Asia Foundation made available about $46,000 in 1973 and 1974 to support the preparation of educational materials on family planning. Work included the compilation of a glossary in Chinese of English terms on population and family planning and the production of a family planning motivational film.

Others, through the years, also have assisted in various degrees. They include the Church World Service, the American Friends Service Committee, The Pathfinder Fund, the Population Council, Oxfam, and CARE.

India

India is the world's second most populous country, next to the People's Republic of China. It had 608.5 million people at mid-1975. A decade ago (1965) the total was 487.7 million, indicating a growth since then of over 120 million, or more than the total population of Japan and about twice that of Mexico.

National policy in India has consistently favored slower population growth, beginning in 1952 under the first Five-Year Plan of the Republic. Benefitting from the nationwide family planning program initiated by the Government, the birth rate in 1974 declined to 35 per 1,000 people compared with 42 per 1,000 in 1951-61—an achievement offset in part by lower mortality.

As a result of these vital rates, India's already enormous population is expanding by 2 percent annually. If this rate continues, India's present population would be doubled in 35 years.

The tide of population increase in recent decades is recognized as a major deterrent to economic and social development. Despite its population problem, however, India during the past quarter century has made considerable gains in industry, agriculture, education, and public health. Life expectancy has risen to about 50 years, reflecting the continuing investment in medical care and sanitation and the improvement in diets. The literacy rate has risen to

about 35 percent. It is estimated that 80 percent of the children in ages 5 to 11 are in school—a vast increase in number since 1952.

While the Gross National Product (GNP) has risen significantly in most years since the mid-1950's, the GNP per capita has been held to a poverty level owing to the increasing numbers of people. The average per person in 1973 was about $120.

Population Programs

India's population/family planning program has grown to a nationwide effort of high national priority.

In 1965 the Indian Government established a new Department of Family Planning under the Ministry of Health and Family Planning. Under the current Five-Year Plan (1974-79) the total budget allocation for the period is $688 million (rupee equivalent), up sharply from $374 million for 1969-74. The present goal is to reduce the birth rate to 30 by 1979 and to attain an annual growth rate of 1.4 percent in 1986.

The Central Government provides the funds for family planning, but the work is largely carried out by the individual States. The delivery system currently encompasses 1,919 urban centers, 16 central family planning field units, 5,132 rural centers, 33,048 subcenters, and 505 mobile teams—staffed by some 5,200 physicians, 20,000 auxiliary nurse/midwives, about 3,500 public health nurses and lady home visitors, 13,500 family planning health assistants, and more than 12,000 statistical workers, information/education officers, demographers, and social scientists.

Participation in the family planning program is voluntary. Sterilization has been the mainstay of the program, but it offers IUD's, condoms, and other conventional contraceptives to those who desire them. Oral pills have hitherto been available only through limited pilot projects; but plans are to distribute them soon through an increasing number of rural and urban family planning centers. A liberal abortion law was passed by the Parliament in 1971, but so far abortion as a birth control measure has not been widely available to Indian women.

Official Indian estimates indicate that 14 percent of the population of reproductive age is "protected" by various available means of contraception. According to 1974 official reports, a total of 16.5 million Indian couples were practicing family planning. Birth rates reportedly have been reduced from their earlier 43 to 45 per 1,000 to 39 per 1,000 per year in rural areas and 30 per 1,000 per year in cities. The current goal of the national program, more realistic than earlier goals, is to reduce the national

Top to bottom: In a small Indian village, Mrs. Sudha Kaldate surveys attitudes of the villagers to family planning . . . From these surveys, participants are chosen to take part in population and family welfare education; a young Indian stands beside India's well-known sign promoting the small family; doctors and nurses volunteer to work in Bombay slums.

average crude birth rate to 30 per 1,000 by 1978-79.

In 1974 the Indian program began converting its then-80,000 specialized family planning personnel at various service levels into a corps of multi-purpose health workers, who are to provide a total "health package" (including family planning information and services) to people in cities and villages in all parts of India. The stated intention is to increase the number of these workers over time to a level of about 130,000, providing a nationwide network of locally based information and services.

One aspect of India's current family planning efforts is the search for a contraceptive device, or devices, more suitable for use in rural areas.

A second aspect of current efforts is to improve the quality of existing family planning services and link them more closely with community affairs.

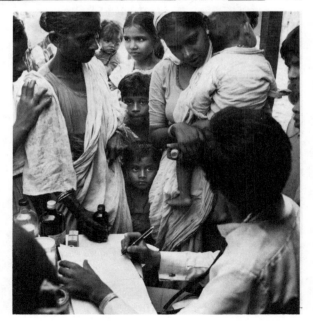

A third aspect is remodeling "communications and motivation," or succeeding better in changing people's minds about the desirable size of a family. Most Indian people continue to associate happy families with large families. The typical marrying age for an Indian girl is 16 years. To help bring about change in such attitudes, India is pressing into service its various channels of communication and urging a wide variety of private organizations to help spread the family planning message. Sex education is being added to curriculums of schools and adult education centers. An emerging trend toward higher marriage age of young people may be reinforced by law.

External Assistance

India has sought and received considerable advisory and tangible assistance for population program development from numerous outside organizations and other nations.

From 1965 through 1975, while India was putting the rupee equivalent of about $655 million into family planning, it also accepted about $57 million from outside sources.

Multilateral assistance. India has been moving increasingly toward favoring multilateral external support for its population programs rather than country-to-country support.

In July 1974 the Government of India signed an agreement with the United Nations Fund for Population Activities (UNFPA) whereby the UNFPA will provide $40 million in support of the Indian program during the next 5 years.

As forerunner to this agreement, UNFPA funded somewhat over $2 million in projects in 1973 through the World Health Organization (WHO) and the United Nations Children's Fund (UNICEF). Projects included: the strengthening of medical college instruction in family planning and population dynamics; assistance to training of auxiliary nurses and midwives; health education in schools, including family life education; strengthening family planning aspects of nursing administration; and the holding of a demographic seminar.

Another multilateral agreement is the loan to the Indian family planning program of $21.2 million, covering the years 1972-78, made by the International Development Association of the World Bank Group. Accompanying the loan has been a grant of $10.6 million by the Swedish International Development Authority. The joint funding is being used to carry out a comprehensive applied research project in two States to test and evaluate approaches to extending family planning services.

Bilateral assistance. The U.S. Agency for International Development (AID) through fiscal 1972,

assisted the Indian family planning program in the amount of $30 million. Emphasis was on broadening and accelerating the family planning effort. AID provided an advisory staff in India, a training program in the United States and other countries, and local currency for research and demonstration activities as well as supplying contraceptives, vehicles, and other needed materials.

With termination of direct U.S. assistance in 1973, India's program has benefitted through AID support of such nongovernmental organizations as the International Planned Parenthood Federation, Family Planning International Assistance, and various American universities. The last includes a contract with Johns Hopkins University School of Hygiene and Public Health for a long-term study to determine which health service elements bring the best participation in family planning.

The Swedish International Development Authority has supported the program with a total of somewhat more than $7 million. In addition to the cooperative program with the World Bank Group, it has provided condoms and other supplies.

The Norwegian Agency for International Development, through 1975, has advanced supporting funds totaling $5.3 million. This aid has included the establishment and operation of postpartum units at Indian hospitals and the initiation of centers and health stations in rural areas.

The Danish International Development Agency, through 1975, has supported India's family planning program in the amount of $850,000. Assistance has included funding the construction of an administration building for the Family Planning Association in New Delhi and the establishment of family planning clinics in Calcutta.

Nongovernmental assistance. The Church World Service promotes family planning in India by working with Christian hospitals and clinics. It provides mobile teams of family planning trainers, supplies contraceptives, and encourages greater involvement of church members in family planning education in rural areas.

The Ford Foundation has supported India's program since 1959. Its grant funding has been principally for technical assistance and support of research training in population, social science, and reproductive biology.

The International Planned Parenthood Federation (IPPF) has been supporting India's family planning movement for 23 years, its financial assistance having totaled about $3.7 million. IPPF support is extended to the Family Planning Association of India for its overall program run through its headquarters and 30 branches. The Association operates model clinics, produces publications and other educational materials on family planning, and provides advanced courses on surgical techniques.

The Mennonite Central Committee helps to support the Shyamnagar Christian Hospital on the outskirts of Calcutta, which provides family planning information and materials as part of its medical program.

Oxfam has supported India's family planning program since 1966. Much of its aid has been channeled through the Protestant mission hospitals of the Christian Medical Association. Projects supported are usually part of an integrated mother and child health, public health, and family planning program.

The Pathfinder Fund, one of the early supporters of India's program, has helped to sponsor a population education project, the introduction of family planning into an industrial slum area in Bombay, a demonstration of the feasibility of outpatient female sterilization using culdoscopy, and a research project to compare desirability of various female sterilization methods.

The Population Council, also an early supporter of India's program, has helped to finance basic research on fertility control in several universities and hospitals.

The World Assembly of Youth has helped to sponsor national, regional, and local conferences and seminars on population problems.

The Rockefeller Foundation funded a study of population and family planning services.

World Education helps produce family life education materials and workshops.

World Neighbors gives financial assistance to several local private organizations, including the Young Men's Christian Association, to support their interest and work in family planning.

Indonesia

Indonesia's 131.9 million people make it the most populous country in South East Asia and the fifth most populous country in the world as of mid-1975. The current rate of increase is 2.1 percent per year—down from 2.5 percent in 1965. The birth rate is 38 per 1,000 population compared with 46 per 1,000 in 1965. Over the same period, the mortality rate has declined from 21 per 1,000 in 1965 to 17 per 1,000.

Although Indonesia is fortunate in having increasing foreign exchange earnings, largely from its oil exports, it is nevertheless beset with serious economic and social problems. Indonesia's annual Gross National Product (GNP), even with increasing oil income, is estimated to be about $120 per capita;

45 percent of the populace is illiterate; 44 percent is less than 15 years old, which means that some 58 million young people are the dependents of earners; unemployment is high; and health and nutrition conditions are primitive. Agricultural production is inadequate, and dependence on food imports is substantial. In other words, Indonesia has a serious problem of rapid population growth.

Population Programs

Family planning efforts were initiated in Indonesia in 1957 by the Indonesian Planned Parenthood Association (IPPA), now an affiliate of the International Planned Parenthood Federation (IPPF). Its work was restricted, however, by the policies that then existed, and IPPA largely devoted itself to information work and very limited family planning services.

Changes in Government brought changes in attitude. In 1965 the family planning policy of the Indonesian Government was reversed. The IPPA was able to expand its activities, and before the end of the decade had 85 branches with 225 clinics on the islands of Java, Madura, and Bali alone.

In 1968, to strengthen and speed the growing national family planning efforts, the Government created a National Family Planning Institute within the Ministry of People's Welfare. Its purpose was to coordinate family planning programs, make recommendations affecting the national program, work with other countries in the area of family planning, and develop a national family planning system on a voluntary basis.

In 1970 the Institute was superseded by the National Family Planning Coordinating Board (BKKBN), which came under the direct responsibility of the President. It was made responsible for coordinating the work of the several ministries, institutions, and agencies that were conducting family planning work. Since its creation, the BKKBN has moved with increasing vigor in generating policies, drawing up guidelines, and coordinating foreign aid.

The family planning program offers services through the 2,400 Ministry of Health clinics. Other Government ministries, including Information, Religion, and Social Affairs, give supporting help. Efforts are being made to bring clinic services more closely to the villages.

The Indonesian Government's family planning annual budgetary obligations have risen from $75,000 in fiscal 1969 to $12.5 million in 1975 for a total during the period of $36 million.

The Government program has as its present target a total of 6 million acceptors and 2,450 family planning clinics by 1976. Its longer range goal is to reduce the country's crude birth rate by 50 percent by the year 2000. This would demand reducing the present rate of about 38 births per year per 1,000 population to 19 births per 1,000 and would require substantial increases in annual numbers of new acceptors.

The national program has been giving special attention to the crowded islands of Java and Bali. An estimated 2.8 million women, representing 20 percent of all eligible couples in these two islands, are now believed to be practicing contraception.

In fiscal 1974 the national program gave 1.5 million as the total number of new acceptors that year. Nearly 70 percent of acceptors have favored use of oral contraceptives, with condoms and IUD's next in use.

Indonesia's family planning effort, as in many other countires, faces the serious obstacle of traditional behavior. Girls tend to marry young (22.5 percent marry under the age of 15, and the median age for girls to marry is 16.8 years). Fairly large families (four to five children) are considered desirable by almost everyone.

Under a "transmigration" program, people from crowded Java have been resettled on more sparsely populated outer islands. The program has been only minimally successful. Population increase on Java and considerable in-migration from the outer islands has tended to offset out-migration.

External Assistance

From 1969 through 1975, foreign aid to Indonesia's family planning programs has totaled $48 million. Inputs have come from bilateral, multilateral, and nongovernmental assistance.

Bilateral assistance. The U.S. Agency for International Development (AID) has assisted the Indonesian Government's family planning program since fiscal 1968, supplying a total of $23 million in direct assistance through fiscal 1975. AID's assistance was $4.2 million in fiscal 1975 alone. It has supplied large amounts of contraceptives, has helped to develop a logistics system and a service statistics program, has helped to initiate pilot projects for commercial sales of contraceptives, and has supported numerous training projects.

AID's support is scheduled to continue with the objectives that include: furnishing the bulk of the contraceptives distributed in the Indonesian family planning program; providing technical assistance to strengthen program management; and promoting experiments to develop new methods of delivering family planning services suitable to local conditions.

The Japan International Cooperation Agency has given support to the Indonesian program in the form of vehicles, contraceptives, and help in producing informational and educational materials. Such assistance through 1975 totaled at least $291,000.

The Netherlands Government has helped the Indonesian program in two specific areas. One contribution of $333,000 supports sociological and medical research, clinical work, and staff training as they relate to family planning. A second contribution of $359,000 (through the Netherlands Organization for International Assistance) has helped to build and equip a center in Djakarta for training nonmedical family planning staff.

The Norwegian Agency for International Development has funded the production of films on family planning.

Multilateral assistance. A multilateral family planning assistance program of substantial size has been signed with Indonesia as a joint undertaking of the United Nations Fund for Population Activities (UNFPA) and the International Development Association (IDA) of the World Bank Group. The 1972-77 program provides for a $13.2 million loan from IDA and a $13.2 million grant from UNFPA. Its goal is to help Indonesia achieve a major expansion in its family planning program. The wide-ranging loan/grant program calls for: constructing and equipping 277 maternal/child health family planning centers, 16 family planning training centers, and 7 family planning administration centers; supplying vehicles; supporting training, motivation, evaluation, research, and population education; and providing family planning technical assistance. UNFPA, the United Nations Children's Fund (UNICEF), the World Health Organization (WHO), and the United Nations Educational, Scientific, and Cultural Organization (UNESCO) are administering various aspects of the program.

Nongovernmental assistance. The largest private contributor to Indonesia's family planning programs has been the International Planned Parenthood Federation (IPPF). This support is given through the affiliated Indonesian Planned Parenthood Association. IPPF helps to finance the Association's overall work including training, development of services to the outer islands, and the operation of clinics. Obligations through 1975 totaled $5.6 million.

The Asia Foundation has made grants to help finance seminars, training of social workers, publications, and mass media utilization.

Church World Service has supported a traveling exhibition which uses puppetry to convey the family planning message. In addition, Family Planning International Assistance has assisted the Council of Churches in Indonesia in the latter's efforts to educate and motivate the public in family planning by utilizing puppet displays, posters, demonstrations, and publications.

The Ford Foundation has made grants to the Government program and to the University of Indonesia in support of census data analysis, family planning research and training, and demographic training. Such grants through 1975 totaled at least $497,000. The Rockefeller Foundation has made grants to universities to enable teaching of population and family planning.

Oxfam has made grants in support of IPPA's work, as well as that of specific family planning clinics. Grants total $92,775.

The Pathfinder Fund has sponsored numerous projects throughout Indonesia with the objective of introducing fertility regulation services into health clinics where they had not been available before. Also the Fund has supported motivational projects, field testing of IUD's, and publication of demographic data for leaders. Support through 1975 totaled $878,000.

The Population Council has made grants to support Indonesia's expanded postpartum family planning program, the manufacture and use of IUD's, and the training of provincial personnel. Grants through 1975 totaled at least $726,000.

The World Assembly of Youth has helped to sponsor seminars and meetings intended to help make young people more aware of population growth and the need for family planning.

Japan

Japan's population in mid-1975 was 111 million, or 12.1 million more than in 1965. The crowding is severe since Japan's area is smaller than that of California. While some decentralization appears to be taking place with people leaving the largest cities for smaller cities and towns, the urban areas are among the most densely populated in the world.

Japan's current rate of natural increase is 1.2 percent annually and the lowest of any country in Asia. Its birth rate, sharply reduced from the 1950's, is 19 per 1,000 people a year, and the death rate 6 per 1,000.

The Japanese people are noted for their industriousness—but in creating a good living for themselves (the average per capita GNP of $3,810 is the highest in Asia), pollution of air and water in the industrial cities is an increasing difficulty. The deteriorating quality of life in the large cities has become a matter of nationwide concern. Japan, at its existing growth rate, would double its population by about the year 2033. Should this happen, the nation would be hard pressed to provide a livelihood for its addi-

In Indonesia, a trained health worker instructs village midwives in family planning, so they can help women in their villages. These midwives play an important role in helping change traditional behavior. Some 22 percent of the girls marry under the age of 15; the median age for marriage is 16.8 years.

tional citizens and at the same time maintain an acceptable environment.

Population Programs

The Government of Japan has been concerned about the nation's evergrowing numbers for many years. After the end of World War II, birth rates had risen to 34 per 1,000 population per year. With the legalization of abortion in 1948, births decreased and had fallen to 20 per 1,000 by 1955. The rate was reduced—to 17 per 1,000 by 1957—and since then has risen slightly to about 19 per 1,000. The rate of natural increase (about 1.2 percent) is by comparison only half of that of most parts of South and South East Asia.

Family planning has become an accepted part of Japanese life. It is practiced by well over half the fertile population. While the National Government does not have a specific family planning program, it supports voluntary and local government efforts, promotes responsible parenthood, and has urged women to use contraception rather than abortion to control the size of their families.

Some controversy exists over the most desirable rate of population growth. Some booming industries have experienced shortages of labor, and some business firms have indicated fear that limited population growth would mean a shrinking labor force. Also, official reservations exist with regard to the use of contraceptive pills and IUD's were approved for contraceptive use only in 1974.

Condoms are by far the most popular method of contraception—used by 77 percent of contracepting couples, according to a nationwide survey of 1975. Commercial outlets are the main source of supply. However, family planning services are also available through more than 800 health centers maintained by prefectural and municipal governments. Condoms are also sold by member organizations of the Family Planning Federation of Japan (FPFJ). A member of the IPPF since 1954, FPFJ puts major emphasis on education, training, research, and fund raising for overseas family planning programs. Although abortions have been declining, it is estimated that there may still be close to a million annually. Abortion is readily available and inexpensive.

The Japanese Government gives financial support to IPPF. It has also given some bilateral assistance in family planning to other Asian countries that have requested it.

Cambodia

The population of Cambodia was estimated at 8.1 million at mid-1975. The estimate, however, does not take special account of the changes in government during the 1970's. In this setting, the rate of natural increase is estimated at 2.8 percent annually with the birth rate at 47 per 1,000 and the death rate at 19.

Prior to the recent change of government, the Cambodian leadership had indicated that the country's anticipated population would be too small in relation to the nation's resources and that officials would welcome a larger population and a faster rate of population growth. They did, however, tolerate some family planning activity.

In 1972 a small family planning program was set up in the maternal/child health section of the Ministry of Health. Also, the Government had given support to the Association Khmere pour le Soutien de la Famille, an affiliate of the International Planned Parenthood Federation (IPPF). The hostilities of recent years, however, may have severely limited or even eliminated such activities. The current emphasis on expanding the rural labor force may not be favorable to family planning as such.

*See page 102 for North Korea.

External Assistance

The United Nations Fund for Population Activities (UNFPA), through the World Health Organization (WHO), supported a project to strengthen family health care, including maternity and family planning services in hospitals. The 1973-75 allocation was $71,000.

The IPPF provided financial assistance to the overall program of the national family planning association, which was the Republic's only facility for extending such services. Assistance by IPPF included an information and education campaign aimed at professionals and opinion leaders, the training of medical and paramedical personnel, and the improvement of clinical services—especially in refugee camps. Expenditures by IPPF for 1974 were an estimated $70,000.

Korea (South)*

The population of South Korea numbered 34.1 million at mid-1975 and was over one-fourth greater than the 1965 level. The rate of increase was estimated at 2 percent per year. The birth rate was 29 per 1,000 population in 1974, or significantly below the 1965 rate of 35 per 1,000. Deaths had declined from 11 per 1,000 people per year in 1965 to 9 per 1,000.

Economically, Korea has developed since 1950 from an agricultural country with a per capita income slightly over $50 to a substantially industrialized country with per capita GNP of about $600 according to Government estimates. Although not yet self-sufficient in food, it has bettered its agricultural production at twice the rate of population increase. Korea has made such substantial progress that the United States, which has provided large-scale economic assistance for many years, expects to be able to end its Korean aid program in fiscal 1976.

But although the Republic of Korea has made important advances during the past decade in slowing population growth and speeding its economic development, it is also widely recognized that prolongation of the present rate of growth would present overwhelming difficulties for Korea's continuing progress.

Therefore, Korea's national target calls for further reduction in its population growth rate to 1.5 percent by 1976 and to 1 percent in the 1980's. These goals will be difficult to meet. The recent decline in population growth has leveled off and a number of problems exist as Korea tries to lower its birth rates further. Among them are the following:
• The post-Korean War "baby boom" created an unusually large young population now coming into reproductive age.
• Koreans continue to view the "ideal" family size as not two children but three or four.
• Continuation rates for women who try out the pill or an IUD are not satisfactory.
• The Korean Government has failed to expand its national family planning expenditures at a rate that keeps up with expansions in the national budget.

Some steps, however, have been taken that should help program effectiveness. A longtime emphasis on IUD's has shifted to include strong support for sterilization, oral pills, and condoms. Legal restrictions on abortion and menstrual regulation have been eased. The Government program has adopted the slogan "Daughter-son without distinction; stop at two, and raise them well." This reflects an effort to overcome the traditional preference of Korean parents for boys and the desire to have two sons.

Population Programs

Korea's national census of 1960 and its revelation that the population was growing faster than was generally realized brought an awakening to the need for a population program. A voluntary organization,

the Planned Parenthood Federation of Korea (PPFK) was organized in 1961. The Government set up a national family planning program in 1962.

The national program incorporated family planning into the nation's First Five-Year Economic Development Plan, allocated funds for family planning, and repealed a long-standing law prohibiting the importation of contraceptives. (Very recently, a ban on the advertising of oral contraceptives in the mass media was lifted; this action should help the sale of contraceptive pills.)

Today the Government and the PPFK cooperate in administering an extensive program that covers the entire country and reaches down to the village level. The Government's leadership is extended through the Family Planning Section of the Bureau of Maternal and Child Health in the Ministry of Health and Social Affairs. Two cities, Seoul and Pusan, and each of the nine Provinces has a Bureau of Public Health and Social Affairs with a family planning section.

The health delivery system consists of 196 health centers, one for each country or city district, and 1,342 health subcenters. Family planning services are offered at some, but the main avenue is through a certified cooperating physicians program. A number of physicians are certified for IUD insertions and/or vasectomy operations and tubal ligations. A new law also allows trained nurses and midwives to insert IUD's.

Participation statistics for 1972 indicate that probably nearly half of Korea's mid-1975 estimated 8.6 million fertile women are participating in family planning. Of the participators, about two-thirds are acceptors through the national program, and one-third are acceptors through private services.

The PPFK offers family planning services in 14 demonstration maternal/child health clinics and—through a Population Council grant—in a number of public and private hospitals. Mobile clinics add to the availability of services.

The PPFK carries the major load of public communication on family planning. Its activities in information, education, and communication reach the general public, Government employees, military reserve forces, and even the residents of remote islands.

External Assistance

Financing from the U.S. Agency for International Development (AID), along with help from other external donors, has played a major part in Korea's family planning efforts since their beginning more than a dozen years ago.

*Korean women from 20 villages come to utilize the services of the family planning
mobile unit. Korea's birthrate has fallen from 35 per 1,000 population in 1965 to 29 in 1974.*

AID's cumulative obligations to the Korean program through fiscal 1974 totaled $5.9 million. This was for advisory services, equipment, contraceptives, training, institutions and research.

The United Nations Fund for Population Activities (UNFPA) more recently has become an active supporter of the program. In 1973, UNFPA signed an agreement with the Korean Government to provide $6 million over a 5-year period. The funds are for improvement of family planning services, communications, and population education. The various projects are being carried out by the World Health Organization (WHO), the United Nations Development Program, the United Nations Educational, Scientific, and Cultural Organization (UNESCO), and the United Nations Children's Fund (UNICEF).

The International Planned Parenthood Federation has provided major assistance for the Korean program, including funds and commodities. Its assistance since 1973 totals over $4.2 million.

Canada's International Development Research Center has made grants of more than $100,000 for research on the satisfactions and costs of having children and the motivations for childbearing in such countries as Korea.

The Swedish International Development Authority made disbursements to the Korean program in 1973, 1974, and 1975 totaling nearly $4 million. Funds supplied contraceptive pills, materials, and personnel assistance.

The Asia Foundation made grants totaling nearly $200,000 for 1973 and 1974 for supporting a number of projects having to do with family planning information and education. One innovation was assistance to the Korean Federation of Housewives Clubs to stage a 9-month "No Pregnancy Year" campaign.

The Association for Voluntary Sterilization has made grants of more than $50,000 to a hospital and college of medicine for laparoscopic andculdoscopic sterilization projects. CARE has implemented a feeding program through the Korean Day Care Centers, which also provide family planning information for mothers. Family Planning International Assistance has made grants for training staff personnel designed to stimulate family planning programs in a number of Korean Christian hospitals.

The Japanese Organization for International Cooperation in Family Planning has made grants totaling more than $300,000, including the provision of a family planning guidance bus with audiovisual aids. Oxfam has made grants of nearly $80,000.

The Population Council has made grants, which in 1973 were more than $500,000, for a wide variety of family planning assistance projects. And the Rockefeller Foundation has made grants for research, including a grant to the Korean Institute for Research in Behavioral Sciences, for studies concerning boy preference among Korean families. Grants in 1973 were $48,000.

The Ford Foundation and The Pathfinder Fund have given assistance to the program.

Laos

The population of Laos at mid-1975 was tentatively estimated at 3.3 million. Based on a high birth rate of 45 per 1,000 population and a high death rate of 23 per 1,000, this indicates an annual growth rate of over 2 percent. All rates are thought to be about the same as in 1965. The Laotian population in 1965 was 2.5 million.

These estimates do not take into account the now-unknown effects of hostilities in Laos in recent years nor the effects of the changes in government. Certainly, however, along with its growth in population, Laos has been beset with disruptions of food production in areas of armed conflict, the problem of war refugees, and a continuing movement of people from country to city. The generally low income of the people is reflected in the country's low GNP per person of $100 per year.

Prior to the recent government reorganization, the Royal Laotian Government had indicated an awareness of the need to slow population growth and thereby help ease the strain on the country's resources.

In 1972 the Government established a Committee for the Promotion of Family Well-Being. It assigned responsibility for implementing a nationwide voluntary family planning program to reduce the annual growth rate to 1.8 percent by the year 2000 to the Ministry of Public Health, which offers services in a number of centers and subcenters.

The Government program emphasized the relationship between maternal and child health and family planning—an approach based on the belief that a reduction in high levels of infant mortality would encourage increased practice of family planning and a reduction in pregnancies.

The program operated Government-wide, coordinated by the Commission for Family Well-Being composed of high-ranking civil servants from eight Government ministries.

While the future activities of the program are not clear at this time, it had already begun to break away from a hospital-based, physician-centered approach to one delegating more responsibility to nurses and midwives. The program had also begun the spread of services beyond the traditional population centers and was committed to integrating family planning into basic health services throughout the country within the next 10 to 15 years.

Some progress had been made. District maternal/child health centers were being renovated and equipped. A family planning manpower training program was underway. The number of family planning acceptors, though relatively small, was growing.

In 1974, about 20,000 users of contraceptives were recorded; oral contraceptives were the most popular.

The Lao Family Welfare Association worked closely with the Government program. An affiliate of the International Planned Parenthood Federation (IPPF), it was founded in 1968 by a group of the country's leading women. It operated family planning clinics and provided training.

External Assistance

Before termination of U.S. population assistance in 1975, the U.S. Agency for International Development (AID) had been the principal external supplier of assistance to the Laotian family planning program. From fiscal 1969 through fiscal 1975, AID assistance totaled $5.2 million. Other principal contributors during the same period included: the United Nations Children's Fund (UNICEF), $439,000; the United Nations Fund for Population Activities (UNFPA), $571,000; and the International Planned Parenthood Federation (IPPF), $182,000.

AID support was directed toward the improvement of health care for mothers and infants and the introduction of family planning techniques. The goal was to help Laos make maternal and child health/family planning services available to 70 percent of the accessible population and to enlist 95,000 couples in the practice of family planning by the end of fiscal 1979.

UNFPA was assisting two projects. One was the development of maternal and child health/family planning activities that was being executed by the World Health Organization (WHO). The second, the planning and conduct of a population census, was being executed by the United Nations. The maternal and child health/family planning project, funded at $123,000 in 1973, included services and training. The census project, funded at $150,000 in 1973, was helping the Government to plan and conduct a census of the Vientiane Plain and the major cities. The census was to provide data on the size and characteristics of the population, including data on refugees.

The Asia Foundation has made travel grants enabling participation in a youth leadership training conference in Korea with emphasis on population aspects.

The Thomas A. Dooley Foundation distributed family planning information and supplies with a medical program for refugee families.

The IPPF has given funds to the Lao Family Welfare Association for its overall program, including public information, training, and operation of clinics. Expenditures for 1974 were estimated at $194,000.

Malaysia

Malaysia's 12 million population at mid-1975 was believed to be increasing at a rate of about 2.9 percent a year. The birth rate for 1974 was estimated at 39 per 1,000 population and the death rate at 10 per 1,000—both reduced from the 1965 birth rate of 42 per 1,000 and the death rate of 13 per 1,000. The lowering of these rates, however, did not reduce the overall rate of population increase.

The Government of Malaysia has been concerned for some years that the country's rapidly expanding population will diminish the success of its aggressive economic development program, and since 1966 the Government has encouraged family planning as an integral part of its national development plan. Although Malaysia has been successful in expanding production of export commodities (rubber, tin, timber and palm oil) and in increasing its investments in domestic industry, the need for more and more public services to accommodate the growing population is a drain upon capital formation which the Government would like to ease.

Adding to the overall problem is the high dependency ratio; about 44 percent of Malaysia's population is less than 15 years old. The Government also has registered concern about the adverse effects of rapid population growth and large families on the health of mothers and children and on the general welfare of families.

Population Programs

Private family planning activities in Malaysia go back to 1953 when an organization was set up in one State. Others followed until by 1963 there were associations in all 11 peninsular States coordinated by a new Federation of Family Planning Associations (FFPA).

The Government of Malaysia made its beginning in national family planning in 1964 when it set up the Cabinet Sub-Committee on Family Planning to formulate a national program. The following year a National Family Planning Board was set up with the establishment of family planning goals as part of its mandate. The national program went into operation in 1966 and since then has been working toward a goal of reducing the population growth rate from its present 2.9 percent a year to 2 percent by 1985.

In its Second Five-Year Plan (1971-75), Malaysia identified the annual family planning acceptor rates needed to achieve this goal. They were targeted at levels increasing from 80,000 new acceptors per year in 1971 to 160,000 in 1975. Achievement has

been substantial though not complete.

Responsibility for carrying out the Government program lies with the National Family Planning Board, which coordinates its activities with those of several private groups. Among the latter is the FFPA, which receives grants from the Government and operates more than 300 clinics.

The Government program includes more than 100 private medical practitioners dispensing services through some 700 clinics, substations, and mobile units. As with the FFPA, these efforts are concentrated in West Malaysia—the home of 85 percent of the country's population. The other two States, Sarawak and Sabah, on the island of Borneo, are considered by the Government to be underpopulated; they are served by voluntary associations.

Pills are the chief form of contraceptive used in the program although many other types are also offered. Contraceptives are readily available.

In 1973 the Government inaugurated a 5-year action program, known as the Population Project, that calls for strengthening the national and State programs, integrating family planning into rural health services, incorporating population education into school curriculums, and setting up a university population research program.

The Government of Malaysia has been a major supporter of the Intergovernmental Coordinating Committee (IGCC) of the South East Asia Regional Cooperation in Family Planning and Population—established in 1971 and headquartered in Kuala Lumpur. The Committee provides population and family planning services to Malaysia and eight other countries. The services include field work, training, research, education, and mass communication.

External Assistance

Important help is being provided to the Malaysian family planning program by a joint effort of the United Nations Fund for Population Activities (UNFPA) and the World Bank. Under the terms of a 5-year agreement signed in 1973, UNFPA is providing a grant of $4.3 million and the World Bank a loan of $5 million.

These funds, along with matching funds from the Malaysian Government, are financing projects that include training, provision of equipment and supplies, communications development, health education, family planning services development, and building and equipping of family planning clinics. Additionally, a population study program is being developed at the University of Malaysia. Executing agencies are the United Nations Children's Fund, the World Health Organization, the United Nations Development Program, the United Nations Educational, Scientific, and Cultural Organization, and the World Bank.

The Swedish International Development Authority has supplied quantities of contraceptives to the national program. Disbursements through 1974-75 totaled an estimated $1¾ million.

The Ford Foundation's assistance through 1975 totals $681,000.

The U.S. Agency for International Development (AID) does not give direct assistance to the Malaysian program but does support other assisting organizations. An AID contract of $234,000 with the University of Michigan is financing an evaluation of the family planning program and its use of traditional village midwives. Approximately $60,000 has been expended in training and equipping six Malaysian physicians under the Advanced Technology Fertility Management Program. Also, AID has a 2-year, $194,000 contract with the Rand Corporation to assist the Government with a Malaysian fertility survey.

The International Development Research Center of Canada has made grants totaling $112,000 to the program to finance studies on abortion among Malaysian women and its health effects.

The International Planned Parenthood Federation (IPPF), which has been assisting private family planning efforts in Malaysia since 1961, continues to support the FFPA of West Malaysia as well as the Sabah and Sarawak family planning associations of East Malaysia. This support, estimated for 1974 at about half a million dollars, assists overall programs—including information and education, training, work with industrial and union leaders, and operation of clinics.

The Asia Foundation has made grants to Malaysian family planning associations and to the Government program for the following objectives: to assess the potential of Malaysian voluntary organizations as program participants; to foster information, education, and communication activities; and to obtain equipment. Fiscal year 1974 expenditures were $57,000.

The Association for Voluntary Sterilization made a grant of $6,000 to the University of Malaysia for training and for extending vasectomy services to rural areas.

The Population Council helped to finance a Government-sponsored meeting on sterilization and abortion.

The Interdisciplinary Communications Program of the Smithsonian Institution advanced $14,600 to finance analytical research into the 1970 Malaysian Post Enumeration Survey to measure correlations between fertility and various economic and social levels of subjects studied.

The World Assembly of Youth has helped to sponsor conferences and seminars for making the young people of Malaysia more conscious of rapid population growth and its consequences.

World Education has assisted the Government in the training of village leaders in family planning.

Mongolian People's Republic

The population of the Mongolian People's Republic was estimated at 1.4 million in mid-1975, compared to under 1.1 million in 1965. The birth rate (1974) of 40 per 1,000 population combined with a death rate of 10 per 1,000 result in a growth rate of 3 percent annually. Approximately 44 percent of the present population is under 15 years of age. The per capita GNP is estimated at $550 per year.

Mongolia's 600,000 square mile area is sparsely settled with about 70 percent of the population living in scattered rural settlements or following a nomadic existence. However, urbanization is reported increasing. In recent years the Government has expanded spending for education and for public services. No information is available as to the existence or extent of family planning or maternal/child health programs.

Nepal

Nepal, a small sub-Himalayan kingdom, had a 1975 population of 12.6 million, or 2.5 million more than in 1965. Its current rate of increase is estimated at 2.3 percent annually. The birth rate is 43 per 1,000 population, and the death rate is 20 per 1,000. Without a sharp drop in the rate of reproduction, Nepal could have twice its present population in 30 years.

It has a potential for the development of mining, hydroelectric power, and industry, but these are not near realization. Per capita income is only about $90 a year. The literacy rate is estimated at 13 percent, and life expectancy is 44 years.

With little doubt, Nepal's most urgent social problem is keeping its population from expanding faster than the development of its agriculture and industry. At present, most of the labor force is engaged in agriculture; but only about 30 percent of Nepal's total area is cultivable.

Population Programs

Nepal's first organized population program activity began in 1965 with the founding of the Family Planning Association of Nepal (FPAN), a private organization affiliated with the International Planned Parenthood Federation (IPPF). FPAN, apart from the family planning services it offered, was helpful in alerting the Government to the nation's growing population pressures and the need for a national family planning effort.

Although there were earlier public activities, the national program can be said to have begun only in 1968 with the establishment of a Family Planning and Maternal Child Health Board. The Government of Nepal has continued to support the program and to give population planning high priority in its national development plans. The major portion of family planning work is carried out as a semiautonomous activity within the Ministry of Health. FPAN continues to serve in a supporting role.

The national program aspires to reduce the crude birth rate from 43 per 1,000 to 38 per 1,000 between 1975 and 1980 with further reductions to follow. (At the same time, it seeks to reduce infant mortality from an estimated 200 per 1,000 live births to 150 per 1,000.)

Through its expanding services, the program's ultimate goal is to offer contraceptives and maternal/

child health services to virtually all of Nepal's estimated 2.3 million fertile couples and to induce an increasingly large portion of them to practice contraception.

The Government of Nepal has given increasing budgetary support to family planning through the past decade; its 1975 input is somewhat more than $1 million, and even larger funds are planned for 1976.

But despite Government determination, Nepal's family planning program operates under a number of handicaps. Transportation is difficult because of the rugged terrain; high illiteracy rates hamper getting the message to potential family planning acceptors; and the scarcity of doctors and other trained personnel may make family planning techniques unavailable in certain areas. Nevertheless, organizational progress is being made.

The program now has approximately 250 family planning and maternal/child health centers operating in 73 of the country's 75 districts. Together, they are capable of providing services to an estimated 15 percent of the people. A wide variety of contraceptive choices are offered including pills, condoms, IUD's, foams, vasectomy, and laparoscopic sterilization.

In addition, FPAN operates six family planning clinics, distributes contraceptives, and carries out motivation and education activities through press, radio, exhibits, and films. The distribution program is clinic oriented, but several pilot projects are underway to expand outlets through commercial sales and the use of home visitors.

An estimated 60,000 Nepalese are practicing contraception. Male sterilization is a leading method with the use of pills by women the next most practiced. Nepal has had good initial success in introducing the laparoscopic technique for the sterilization of women who desire the operation.

To improve family planning coverage and quality in Nepal, the Government has established the National Planning Commission Task Force on Population Policy with a broad mandate to examine present activities and problems and to recommend policies and programs for the next 5-year development plan period (1975-80). The Task Force's findings and recommendations are to be acted upon through a National Population Policy Coordinating Council, established in August 1975 as part of the National Planning Commission.

A Nepali Muslim is proud of having a planned family. Nepal has approximately 250 family planning and maternal and child health centers operating in 73 of the country's 75 districts.

External Assistance

The U.S. Agency for International Development (AID) is the major donor to Nepal's family planning program. Its 8 years of financial support have provided funds totaling $4.5 million, or more than 80 percent of all external assistance the program has received.

AID assistance began informally in 1966 and was formalized with budgeted funds in fiscal 1968. AID has supplied contraceptives and other commodities as well as funds for the training and development of low-cost family planning delivery systems. This assistance is being continued. At the same time, new efforts are being made to help the Government formulate a population policy, improve its demographic information, and assess the effectiveness of its family planning program. Part of AID's help to Nepal is carried out through a contract with the University of California (Berkeley).

The United Nations Fund for Population Activities (UNFPA) is sponsoring several projects. One is to analyze Nepal's 1971 census data; another is to undertake a demographic survey to estimate population growth, fertility, mortality, and migration; a third sets up a pilot registration leading to a civil registration plan. In 1974, UNFPA agreed to assist with a fourth project—the integration of family planning into health facilities at a cost of about $608,000 for 2 years.

In two country-to-country agreements, the British Ministry of Overseas Development helped to finance a training course for auxiliary health workers, and the Japanese Organization for International Cooperation in Family Planning supplied contraceptives and equipment.

Among voluntary organizations, Family Planning International Assistance made a grant to the Nepal Women's Organization for a pilot village-oriented contraceptive distribution project. The International Planned Parenthood Federation (IPPF) has given $363,000 since 1972 to the Family Planning Association of Nepal (FPAN) in support of its overall program—including education and motivation. The World Assembly of Youth has helped the Nepal Youth Organization to hold meetings making young people more aware of population problems and needs. The Pathfinder Fund has provided contraceptives. The Population Council has provided funds for fellowships for graduate study in demography.

Pakistan

The population of Pakistan in mid-1975 was estimated at 70.3 million, an increase of 17.5 million since 1965 within the present boundaries of the country. The 1974 rate of population increase was 2.9 percent annually with the birth rate estimated at 44 per 1,000 population and the death rate at 15 per 1,000. Unless such a growth rate is abated, it would double the country's population before the year 2000. Rampant growth, in turn, would cancel out the benefits of increased food production and would make it extremely difficult to meet the costs of creating new jobs and providing social services for the additional population.

In recent years, even though the country has many of the resources needed to develop a viable economy, Pakistan has had a difficult struggle. In 1971, East Pakistan broke away and became Bangladesh. There were basic governmental changes in 1972. In 1973 a disastrous flood struck followed by a near drought in 1974. All this has put additional strain on an economy in which 46 percent of the population is under 15 years of age and more apt to be consumers than producers. At present, the GNP per capita is about $130.

Population Programs

The Government of Pakistan first became concerned about the country's population growth some 20 years ago, and this concern—and the response to it—have continued to increase. Pakistan's current program to slow population growth is strongly supported and financed (including large inputs from foreign donors). It has high priority in the Government's national development plans.

The program aims at reducing the birth rate from 44 to 35 per 1,000 by 1978. It has a goal of making birth control information and supplies available to three-fourths of all fertile couples across the nation. (The size of the task is indicated by the estimate that only about 6 percent of eligible couples currently are practicing contraception.)

Pakistan's first organized family planning movement began in 1953 with the formation of a private Family Planning Association of Pakistan (FPAP), an affiliate of the International Planned Parenthood Federation (IPPF). Some clinics were opened, and a modest family planning publicity and education campaign was undertaken.

The Government recognized the impending threat of overpopulation in formulating its First Five-Year Plan (1956-60) and provided for preliminary family

I decided to plan my family!

Top to bottom: Family planning poster used at Islamabad, Pakistan; buying contraceptives at family planning stall; a midwife explains use of contraceptives in a Pakistani home. Family planning became a national policy in 1961.

planning work. Under the Second Five-Year Plan (1961-65), family planning was made a national policy, and a program for bringing family planning to the people was set up under the Ministry of Health to operate through existing health services. Increased emphasis to operations was given in the Third Five-Year Plan (1966-70), including expanded budget, more personnel, and improved administration. Much was done to improve all aspects of the population program. By 1970, reports indicated that 19 percent of Pakistan's urban wives of reproductive age and 4 percent of rural wives had practiced contraception at one time or another.

During the early part of the Fourth Five-Year Plan (1971-75), family planning lost impetus because of hostilities with India, the secession of East Pakistan, and internal changes in Government. The program rebounded, however, and beginning in 1973 has undergone rapid expansion and increased budgetary outlay. Pakistan's leaders are giving it their strong and continuing support.

Pakistan's increasing allocation to its population program is significant. Commitments have increased from about $2 million in fiscal 1973 to $4 million in fiscal 1974 to $8 million as Pakistan's share of the $24 million program in fiscal 1976. (In addition to Pakistan's own funding, substantial assistance is coming from outside sources.)

Any current appraisal of Pakistan's population planning program can best be based not so much on past results—which have been slow in coming—as on today's new approaches and expanding activity

An important feature of this expanding activity—one that will be watched with interest by other concerned countries—is a new "contraceptive inundation scheme." The scheme grew out of the Government's increasing awareness that family planning based on services provided by clinics and physicians was not enough; local nonclinical ways for married couples to obtain materials for family planning also were needed.

Basically a subsidized sales program, the "inundation scheme" aims at making oral contraceptives and condoms easily and cheaply available in most of Pakistan through retail shops and door-to-door distributions. Because of the subsidies, the program is able to offer the two contraceptives at prices within the reach of most Pakistanis—2½ cents for either a monthly cycle of pills or a dozen condoms.

One key part of the "inundation scheme" is the work of door-to-door man-and-woman distribution teams, which are an important part of Pakistan's continuous motivation system—a concept devised as an operational guide for the 1970-75 Population Planning Program and reaching about 74 percent of the country's population. Ideally, both team members are high school graduates and both are recruited from the area where they will serve. Usually, they are assigned a population of about 10,000 with 1,200 to 1,500 fertile couples. The teams, in turn, are backed up by three tiers of supervisory, inspection, and training officers.

As the teams make home visits, they sell pills and condoms at the low subsidized prices, refer couples to the nearest clinic or hospital if they are interested in the IUD or sterilization, educate couples in family planning, and obtain demographic data through registration of all married couples in the area. Regular repeat visits to households are made for followup. The male member of the team also handles contacts with and sales of contraceptives to participating local shops.

Pakistan's many small shops are the second ingredient of the "inundation scheme." Their enlistment is based on the recognition that the number of retail outlets in the country far exceeds the actual or even potential number of family planning clinics. Some 35,000 shops—pharmacies, tea stalls, general provision stores, and others—have been enlisted to sell pills and condoms. No prescription for pills is required of customers. As a sales incentive, the shopkeepers keep 40 percent of the price of the contraceptives. It has been anticipated that by early 1976 there will be at least one commercial sales outlet for contraceptives in each of Pakistan's more than 40,000 villages.

Pakistan's population planning program for the 5-year period 1974-78 is expected to expand the program's outreach and effectiveness to new high levels. The program is working through some 700 family welfare clinics, which employ female high school graduates to insert IUD's and provide other contraceptives and simple medicine. Program employees also do educational work and distribute contraceptive supplies at approximately 400 Government hospitals and at the 40 hospitals that operate postpartum family planning programs. In addition, some 2,000 cooperating physicians distribute orals and condoms provided free by the Government.

All this effort is accompanied by radio, television, and newspaper advertising telling where contraceptives may be obtained and urging their use. A simple how-to-use pamphlet in Urdu and Sindhi is distributed wherever pills are available.

The value of using multiple distribution methods is reflected in these early statistics from the Pakistan program. In July 1974, 146,000 monthly cycles of pills and 2.9 million condoms were sold. In October 1975, monthly sales had reached 458,000 monthly cycles of orals and 16.7 million condoms.

The Government is actively considering additional features to make the program more effective. One is offering incentives to grassroots workers (distribution teams and population officers) in which compensation would be directly related to any decrease in fertility rates. Another is providing small-family incentives through old age insurance. Still another is a proposal for bonus payments to female employees who do not take maternity leave for 5 consecutive years.

The Government also hopes to more than double the present number of family welfare clinics over the next 2 years and to provide some 250 additional jeeps for clinics to use in outreach work.

The sterilization program is being given a boost with the introduction of the laparoscopic method and the increased number of postpartum clinics, while IUD use will be helped as the number of rural clinics is expanded.

To accommodate expanded training of family planning workers, additional training centers are being constructed. To assure greater supplies of contraceptives, the Government plans that eventually Pakistan will manufacture its own pills and condoms.

To obtain more plentiful population data, the Government is funding two new demographic research organizations—the Population Section within the Pakistan Institute of Development Economics, and the Demographic Policies and Action Research Center within the Population Planning Division of the Ministry of Health.

In addition, a "surveillance" system is being set up under which detailed information on contraceptive delivery to outlets and acceptors will be collected routinely by field staff. This information will be reported, tabulated, and fed into a computer system in Islamabad. Analyzed data will permit a constant evaluation of program operation and ultimately of its impact on fertility.

To optimize other efforts, an extensive family planning publicity campaign has been undertaken, in which the program symbol is based on the "ideal" four-person family (husband, wife, and two children). A special attempt is being made to reach rural illiterate couples.

Within the private sector, family planning efforts continue to be spearheaded by the Family Planning Association of Pakistan (FPAP). It receives some funds from the Government, but most support comes from the International Planned Parenthood Federation (IPPF). FPAP has 14 district branches, mostly in urbanized high-density areas. Its activities include communication and education, training, research, and contraceptive services.

The All Pakistan Women's Association also maintains a few family planning centers and, in cooperation with FPAP, has organized a midwifery training course.

External Assistance

External assistance is highly important to Pakistan's population programs. In the 1974-75 fiscal year, such assistance provided more than 70 percent of the budget.

The U.S. Agency for International Development (AID) is the foremost supporter. AID's financing in fiscal 1975 was $7.1 million and, cumulatively since 1967, totals over $24 million. U.S. grant assistance in fiscal 1976 is expected to total about $9.1 million (plus an additional $3.5-million equivalent of excess Public Law 480-generated rupees as a contribution toward local costs).

U.S. support is directed mainly toward contraceptive commodity support. (In fiscal 1976, $8.5 million is scheduled for subsidizing the distribution of contraceptives.) The United States also provides, upon request, advisors in commodity supply, information feedback, vehicle maintenance and repair, training and manpower development, and communication and publicity.

In addition, AID is helping to develop, within the Pakistan Institute of Development Economics, a population section with the capability for demographic research aimed at improving population program planning and evaluation.

The United Nations Fund for Population Activities (UNFPA) is another active supporter of Pakistan's program. It has a commitment to contribute $3 million annually for 5 years. The work is carried out through the World Health Organization (WHO) and the United Nations Children's Fund (UNICEF) and includes the supply of contraceptives and equipment, transport, salaries of fieldworkers, training, and development of maternal/child health services.

Among private organizations, the Association for Voluntary Sterilization has made grants totaling $37,500 to the Lady Dufferin Hospital to establish a laparoscopic sterilization program and to the Lady Willingdon Hospital to establish a pilot laparoscopic program.

The Ford Foundation has supported Pakistan's population program for a number of years. Grants through 1975 to support research and training in the population field total $4.2 million. The International Association of Schools of Social Work has a pilot project to develop qualified manpower for population and family planning activities.

The International Planned Parenthood Federation (IPPF) gives financial assistance to the Family Planning Association of Pakistan for its overall work. This includes seminars, conferences, and meetings; information, education, and communication projects; and training. Special projects include work with rural and urban welfare centers, industry, and hospitals. Expenditures were $179,000 in 1972; $370,200 in 1973; and an estimated at $450,000 for 1974.

The Population Council gives grants for population fellowships, demographic staff support, and research on reproductive biology. Support in 1973 was $11,800.

Several other countries besides the United States assist Pakistan's population programs. The Norwegian Agency for International Development is helping to cover the current expenses of the family welfare clinic component of the population program. Planning figures for 1975-78 total $4.3 million. The United Kingdom has offered condom supplies and may provide a number of vehicles. Australia has promised $510,000 in audiovisual training equipment. Japan has offered to supply condoms, and Sweden has offered to supply latex for condom manufacture. Germany has expressed interest in offering assistance in the domestic manufacture of condoms. Denmark, Canada, and the Netherlands are considering possible aid to the program.

The Pathfinder Fund has also assisted the program.

Philippines

The population of the Philippines has grown from 27.4 million in 1960 to an estimated 42.8 million in mid-1975—an increase of 56 percent. The birth rate, as of 1974, was 41 per 1,000 population (down from 44 in 1965), and the death rate was 11 per 1,000 compared with 13 in 1965. The rate of increase is around 3 percent per year. At this present rate, the population of the Philippines would double by the end of this century. This growth rate is one of the highest for any country in Asia and one of the highest in the world.

The Republic of the Philippines has reversed its

population policy in recent years and has shifted from encouraging population growth to supporting comprehensive programs to lower fertility rates.

At one time Government leaders thought that a growing population would be beneficial because it would provide people to populate and develop uninhabited, outlying lands. But in the late 1960's a closer look was taken at how population growth was affecting the economic and social aspirations of the country. The findings led to new policies and programs to slow down the rapid expansion in numbers.

The degree of concern of the Philippine Government over population growth is indicated by the increasing funds devoted to family planning. Prior to 1971, population programs had no national budget. During the years 1971-73, $1.3 million were allocated annually. In 1974 the family planning budget was increased to $4.2 million, and in 1975 it was raised to $6.3 million. At the same time, these amounts were augmented by substantial additional funds that the Government welcomed from external sources.

Some examples of the results of headlong population expansion that influenced the change of attitude of the Philippine Government are listed below.

One is in the field of education. The Philippine people are education conscious and have one of the highest literacy rates in the South East Asian and Pacific areas—about 83 percent of the population 10 years and above. About 39,000 public schools have an enrollment of 7.6 million students, and about 3,000 private schools teach an additional 1 million pupils. Approximately 500,000 students are attending institutes of higher education.

But there is a double strain upon the educational system because of the rapidly expanding population. First a large proportion of the population is young and of school age (about 43 percent). Second, the number of boys and girls who should be attending school continues to increase. Although the Government devotes about 22 percent of the national budget to education, it has been unable to supply enough classrooms and teachers to meet its educational goals; many youngsters are not educated beyond the fifth grade.

Another example of population pressure has to do with food supply. Despite past and current improvements in agriculture, food production has not been able to keep up with the expanding population. Many children are malnourished. Despite abundant natural resources and the potential for becoming self-sufficient in such basic foods as rice and corn, indigenous production must be supplemented with substantial food imports.

In the area of health, too, services are inadequate. Drinking water often is unsafe and proper sanitation lacking.

Population Programs

Official Philippine concern over the runaway growth of population was preceded by private action. Family planning efforts began in 1965 with the founding of the Family Planning Association of the Philippines, an affiliate of the International Planned Parenthood Federation (IPPF). This was followed by the formation of the Planned Parenthood Movement of the Philippines and other private groups. In 1969 these merged into a new Family Planning Organization of the Philippines, Inc. A number of pioneering family planning clinics and centers were initiated as well as population and family planning training. Another pioneering private organization, the Institute for Maternal and Child Health, opened family planning clinics in child care centers throughout the Philippines between 1967 and 1970. Also, the City of Manila and Laguna Province preceded the National Government in adopting strong support for family planning service centers within their jurisdictions.

The Government's new position on family planning began to take form when—early in 1969—the President of the Philippines appointed a Commission to study the population situation. Late in the year, he approved its conclusions—which was that a reduction in population growth was vital to the nation.

In 1970, the President called for new legislation making national family planning the Government's official policy and expanding family planning services nationwide—especially to poor families and those in rural areas. Also, in 1970 the Commission on Population (POPCOM) was established and was made the overall coordinating body of the national program. All agencies of Government were instructed to support POPCOM's national effort.

Since 1970, certain legal changes have been made to reinforce the program. The Population Act of 1971 declares a national policy of making available to all citizens all medically acceptable means of contraception (except sterilization and abortion). The Constitution was amended in 1973 to include state responsibility to "achieve and maintain population levels most conducive to the national welfare." The population law was amended to legalize sterilization and to expand the scope of family planning services that may be legally provided by paramedics. The Labor Code now requires certain employers to provide free family planning services to their employees. New income tax laws favor small families (in contrast to earlier laws which provided special Governmental benefits to large families). An official instruction to all mayors requires marriage license applicants to present certificates showing that they have received family planning counseling.

The official goal of the Philippine population program is to reduce the national birth rate from the estimated 43 per 1,000 in 1970 to 35.9 per 1,000 in 1977. This would slow the population growth rate from its present higher level to 2.5 percent. To succeed, 3.5 million married women (58 percent of those of child-bearing age) would have to practice contraception.

The Philippine family planning program has made a good start in working toward its targets. Numerous public and private agencies are cooperating in the clinical, research, evaluative, informational, training, planning, and management aspects of the program. More than 2,300 fully staffed clinics are providing family planning services. More than 2 million couples are practicing some form of family planning, and approximately 750,000 new acceptors were recorded in 1974. On the other hand, despite increased emphasis being given to reaching them, family planning services and motivation still need to be extended to many people who live in the more remote and isolated areas.

External Assistance

The Philippine family planning program receives substantial financial assistance from external sources. Since 1965, a total of $59 million has gone into public and private efforts, of which $14.3 million was provided by the Philippine Government and the remainder by outside sources.

The U.S. Agency for International Development (AID) helped to pioneer the Philippine population program, starting in fiscal year 1968 with funds for private organizations that were providing services to a small but increasing number of acceptors. AID's role has grown along with growth of the program. AID's funds have helped to finance the opening of thousands of new family planning clinics; to train thousands of doctors, nurses, midwives, and motivators to operate the clinics; and to develop information and education programs. Also, AID funds have helped to buy and ship large quantities of contraceptives and equipment.

Through fiscal 1975, AID inputs into the Philippine program have totaled $36 million—with the prospect of an additional $7.3 million for fiscal 1976.

Another contributor, of growing importance, is the United Nations Fund for Population Activities (UNFPA). UNFPA signed a 5-year, $5 million agree-

ment with the Philippines in 1972 to assist projects in electronic data processing of census results; in strengthening management-information systems in POPCOM; in obtaining motorcycles for use in rural areas; in strengthening and expanding of population education; in educating nurses in family planning; in the improvement of family planning communication and motivation; in the compilation of laws affecting population programs; and in developing maternal/ child health services linked to family planning. The executing agencies are UNFPA, the United Nations Educational, Scientific, and Cultural Organization (UNESCO); the United Nations Development Program; the United Nations Children's Fund (UNICEF); and the United Nations central organization.

Among private organizations, the American Public Health Association is giving technical assistance to the Philippine Public Health Association (another private organization) to help improve its national health, population, and nutrition programs.

The Asia Foundation has made a number of grants to help improve the national program's work in information, education, and communication. Expenditures were $20,000 in fiscal 1973 and $60,000 in fiscal 1974.

The Association for Voluntary Sterilization has made grants totaling $212,000 to a number of institutions, including the Philippine General Hospital and the Jose Fabella Memorial Hospital, in further-ance of voluntary sterilization.

Family Planning International Assistance (FPIA) has made grants totaling $602,000 for family

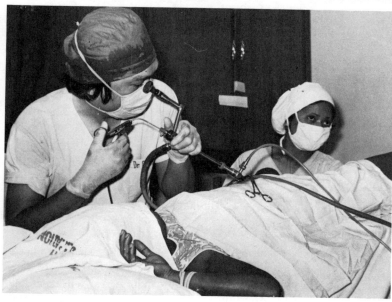

In the Philippines, a family planning worker, top left, goes into the country to talk to mothers and at the clinic, above, men and women hear about the benefits of limiting family size. Left a Philippine doctor carries out a tubal ligation. Since 1965, $59 million has gone into public and private services.

planning projects, including special church-related efforts to reach families living in outlying areas. Support has gone to mobile clinics, centers for family planning outreach, radio programs, literature for Catholic radio stations, and comic books and flip-charts explaining family planning. FPIA also supported the first sterilization clinic (at Mary Johnson Hospital) in the Philippines.

The Ford Foundation made a number of early grants in support of Philippine family planning efforts—particularly supporting population research and education and management of population programs.

The International Planned Parenthood Federation (IPPF), an early supporter of Philippine family planning efforts, gives its assistance to the Family Planning Organization of the Philippines for its overall program, which includes publications, radio and TV programs, community education, training, and operation of clinics. IPPF expenditures through 1975 totaled $3.5 million.

Oxfam has made grants to the Family Life Advisory Center of Mindanao and has supported motivation projects of the Responsible Parenthood Council.

The Pathfinder Fund has made a number of

grants over the years in support of the Philippine program, including assistance to the first family planning clinic to provide services in Manila. Recent projects sponsored have included the introduction of fertility regulation into leper colonies, work with the mass media to enlist its help in better informing the public of the causes and consequences of uncontrolled fertility, the introduction of community-centered promotion of both male and female sterilization, and the pioneering of clinical services that were later incorporated into the Government's program. Assistance from 1969 through 1975 totaled $863,000.

The Population Council has also supported the program for a number of years. Grants have included assistance in setting up the manufacture of IUD's in the Philippines, in expanding postpartum programs at hospitals, and in research and training in population and family planning. Assistance from 1968 through 1975 totaled $418,000.

The Rockefeller Foundation has made grants to institutions to support a study of midwives as family planning motivators, the construction of a population program headquarters, and a study of rural population structures in the Philippines.

The World Assembly of Youth has co-sponsored conferences and seminars to help make young people aware of the consequences of rapid population growth.

World Education has assisted several population-oriented groups, including the Philippine Rural Reconstruction Movement, to introduce population and family planning education concepts into adult literacy classes.

The Japanese Organization for International Cooperation in Family Planning has provided some assistance to the Commission on Population through the provision of audiovisual and other equipment.

Singapore

The island city-state of Singapore has a basic problem—crowding. It has only 225 square miles to accommodate its 2.3 million people as of mid-1975. Furthermore, two-thirds of the population are concentrated in the 37 square miles of the city of Singapore and its environs. It is one of the most densely populated areas of the world.

The 1974 birth rate was 20 per 1,000 population and the death rate 5 per 1,000; the result is an annual increase in population of 1.5 percent. Singapore has had a strong and active family planning program for several years; this succeeded in reducing the 1964 rate

of 31 births per 1,000 population to the current level. But the Government is concerned that the 1.5 percent annual increase is still too high. It views as excessive the country's present population, its growth rate, and its fertility rate. It has set a goal of a two-child family as the national norm, and the Singapore Family Planning and Population Board has an extensive program to reach this goal. The Government has initiated a series of disincentives for large families, limiting income tax relief, maternity benefits, and other benefits. Although Singapore has made great progress in development and the annual per capita GNP of about $1,930 is second only to Japan in Asia, a price is being paid. Pollution is prevalent. The water supply is insufficient. Though much building is taking place, there is little space for further thousands.

Population Programs

As early as 1949 the Singapore Family Planning Association was formed. The Government approved and provided financial aid and clinics were opened.

The Government brought its direct support to family planning in 1965 when it established the Singapore Family Planning and Population Board and gave it the responsibility for conducting an expanded and intensified program. A target was set up of reducing the national birth rate to 20 per 1,000 population by 1971.

The Board operates 35 clinics as part of the Government's maternal and child health service. A successful postpartum program is carried out at Kandang Kerbau Maternity Hospital; it is in this hospital that a majority of Singapore's births take place.

Singapore encourages family planning in a number of ways. No anti-contraceptive legislation exists. IUD's, orals, and condoms are available at low cost. Abortion laws have been liberalized, and sterilization is free of charge. Information and education programs concentrate on schools, places of work, and the community at large. Childless couples find public housing readily available. On the other hand, employed women with more than three children find it hard to get maternity privileges.

An estimated two-thirds of all married women between 15 and 44 years of age practice family planning. Oral contraceptives are the most frequently used method of family planning with condoms next.

External Assistance

The Singapore family planning program is largely self-supporting, though it has welcomed specialized types of assistance from outside sources.

The International Planned Parenthood Federation (IPPF) has assisted its affiliate, the Singapore Family Planning Association, since 1952. IPPF supports the Association in its overall information and education work, including marriage guidance courses, family life forums, and research into why some families reject family planning. Grants for 1974 were estimated at $55,000.

The United Nations Fund for Population Activities (UNFPA) is helping several Singapore projects in providing contraceptive supplies, establishing a family planning training center, and reviewing and compiling laws bearing on population and family planning. Executing agencies are the United Nations Children's Fund (UNICEF), the World Health Organization (WHO), and the United Nations Fund for Population Activities (UNFPA). Allocations in 1971-75 totaled $923,000.

The U.S. Agency for International Development (AID) provides indirect support to the Singapore program through its grants to various international organizations. In addition, AID has granted $475,000 for research at the University of Singapore to investigate the use of prostaglandins as a means of fertility control.

The British Ministry of Overseas Development has made grants to investigate the effects of oral contraceptives. Assistance for 1973 and 1974 totaled $64,000.

The Asia Foundation has supported a mass communication campaign directed at males and encouraging both the practice of family planning and male sterilization. Grants for 1973 and 1974 totaled $41,000.

The Ford Foundation awarded grants totaling $90,000 during the 1968-70 period for expansion of national family planning activities.

The Population Council gave financial aid to the University of Singapore to help organize an Asian seminar on population overgrowth.

The Pathfinder Fund has also rendered assistance.

Sri Lanka

Sri Lanka's or Ceylon's population (13.8 million as of mid-1975) almost doubled during the last 25 years and will double from its present level in 35 years unless its current rate of increase of 2 percent a year is slowed. The 1974 birth rate was estimated at 28 per 1,000 population, and the mortality rate was estimated at 8 per 1,000.

If population growth continues to dilute the benefits of economic development, the Sri Lanka per capita GNP of $200 per year may stagnate rather than increase. Most of Sri Lanka's people live on the land and agricultural production is the mainspring of domestic economy and foreign trade. During 1975, Sri Lanka experienced economic difficulties because 90 percent of its foreign exchange earnings come from tea, rubber, and coconuts—and the moderate price increases in these export crops failed to keep pace with rising prices for imported food, petroleum, and fertilizer. Poor weather added to the problem by necessitating additional food imports. The sharp decline in export earnings met the persistent costs of caring for an everexpanding population head-on, had a depressing effect on internal commercial life, and contributed to unemployment—now estimated to be about 20 percent of the work force.

These economic and population growth problems have left Sri Lanka in the vulnerable position of having to rely heavily on foreign economic aid to ease its foreign exchange shortage and to support its internal investment aspirations. A number of Western nations and Japan, under the leadership of the International Bank for Reconstruction and Development and the International Monetary Fund, have contributed extensively. The Asian Development Bank has contributed also, as well as the Soviet Union and the People's Republic of China.

The Government of Sri Lanka recognizes the problems facing the nation. In its current 5-year development plan (1972-76), the Government has outlined the grave implications for the future if the country's annual population growth continues at its existing rate. It has called for renewed emphasis on family planning as an integral part of the Health Department's system of health clinics and related maternal and child health facilities. In addition, it is seeking wider coverage by existing facilities, less than half of them providing family planning services.

Sri Lanka has had a family planning program since 1953, when the private Family Planning Association (FPA), an affiliate of the International Planned Parenthood Federation (IPPF), was founded. The Government program was initiated in 1965. About 500 Government clinics and 25 FPA clinics dispense family planning information and services. The optimistic targets set up early in the program have not been reached, but some reduction has occurred in the island's birth rate as a result of the more than two decades of effort.

Pills and IUD's are the most popular contraceptives in Sri Lanka. Abortion is legal on medical grounds. In addition to public information and education on family planning, sex education has been introduced into school curriculums.

External Assistance

The United Nations Fund for Population Activities (UNFPA) signed an agreement with Sri Lanka in 1973 providing for $6 million of assistance over a 4-year period. These funds support an effort to make family planning services available to all persons by the end of 1976. Major expenditures are budgeted for information, education, and communication work—including family health education, nursing and midwifery education, demographic training and research at the university level, and family planning education for workers. The World Health Organization (WHO), the International Labor Organization (ILO), and the United Nations Children's Emergency Fund (UNICEF) are all involved in carrying out the projects.

The Swedish International Development Authority has supported family planning work in Sri Lanka since 1958. Aid is in the form of personnel assistance and supply of contraceptives, clinical equipment, and audiovisual aids. Disbursements through 1974 totaled about $2.3 million.

The United States Government does not provide direct assistance to Sri Lanka's family planning program, but it does give considerable indirect help through intermediary family planning organizations that carry out projects there—such as the International Planned Parenthood Federation (IPPF), The Pathfinder Fund, Family Planning International Assistance, and U.S. universities. In addition, the U.S. Agency for International Development sponsors participant training for study abroad in improved fertility-control technology and management. It also extends economic assistance to other of Sri Lanka's programs in the form of food aid and development loans.

The Ford Foundation has supplied support totaling $271,000 through 1975.

The Population Council also has assisted the program.

The IPPF has helped Sri Lanka's Family Planning Association for a number of years and continues financial support of its overall program, including efforts to awaken key leaders and public workers to the need for family planning, training in family planning for Government medical personnel, mass media education and information programs, and operation of clinics. IPPF expenditures in 1974 were an estimated $260,000.

The Association for Voluntary Sterilization has given a grant of $3,100 to the University of Sri Lanka for a pilot program in sterilization and for an information project.

The International Association of Schools of Social Work has a pilot project to develop qualified manpower for population and family planning activities.

Population Services International implemented an IPPF-financed nationwide project to market non-clinical contraceptives through a retail network of some 3,500 general stores, pharmacies, tea houses, and neighborhood shops. Usual marketing techniques were employed. Initially the project has focused on Preethi-brand condoms with the expectation of later including oral contraceptives.

Thailand

Thailand's population, increasing by 2.5 percent a year, totaled over 42 million in mid-1975 compared with 31.3 million in 1965. The birth rate in 1964 was estimated at 36 per 1,000 people compared with 44 per 1,000 in 1965. The death rate of 11 per 1,000 was also down from the 1965 level of 14 per 1,000.

Thailand is experiencing a diminishing availability of unoccupied productive land to absorb its swelling population. This is causing rural underemployment and migration to cities—particularly Bangkok although urban unemployment is already a problem.

Population pressures are also affecting education. Rapid growth is making schooling a major concern as almost 20 percent of the national budget goes for education.

In March 1970, the Royal Thai Government approved voluntary family planning as a national policy. The policy announcement had been preceded by a 3-year (1968-70) family health project to train physicians, nurses, midwives, and paramedical personnel in contraceptive techniques. Primary operational responsibility was given to the Minister of Public Health, which made family planning services available through 4,500 clinics and hospitals of its health services network. By late 1975 over 2 million couples had accepted some form of planning service through the Government program and birth rates had definitely lowered.

Even at this lower rate, however, Thailand's population would double in 28 years. Such growth would make improvements in per capita GNP (now $230 per year) extremely difficult and would work economic hardship, especially on the poorer segment of the population. Through continuing its population program, the Thai Government hopes to slow population growth to a rate of 2.1 percent by the end of the Fourth Five-Year Plan period of 1977-81. This means contacting a large proportion of the nation's over 9 million women of reproductive age (15 through 49).

Population Programs

Specific responsibility for Thailand's family

A Thai mother shares food with her four children. With available land diminishing, rural families are migrating to the cities in ever increasing numbers. Urban unemployment makes it very difficult to find work. Family planning became a national policy in 1970, and the Government hopes to slow population growth to 2.1 percent by 1981.

planning effort lies with the Minister of Health, whose Undersecretary acts as the director of the National Family Planning Project. The Government's overall commitment to family planning is also indicated by the participation of other Government ministries and agencies, such as Education, Interior, and the Department of Local Administration.

The Thai Government's financing of family planning has been rising steadily—from the equivalent of $486,000 in 1969 to $2.7 million in 1975. Total expenditures during the period were $11.2 million.

A noteworthy aspect of the program has been its successful use of the national health infrastructure without having to set up a separate organization and facilities and train personnel for family planning work only. This approach has helped to speed up program accomplishments. Family planning services are now available through a network of 5,000 rural clinics and provincial hospitals.

The program makes available all modern means of fertility control except abortion. One innovation permits trained paramedical personnel, usually auxiliary midwives, to dispense oral contraceptives. This is considered important in reaching acceptors from rural areas where physicians are scarce. As a result of this liberalized feature, orals are by far the most commonly used type of contraceptive, and 85 per-

cent of all acceptors are from rural areas.

In northern Thailand an experimental program is being carried out by a private organization called Community Based Family Planning Services (CBFPS). It is supported by the International Planned Parenthood Federation (IPPF). Initiated in mid-1974 and covering some 25 districts, it enlists teachers and community leaders, who in turn work with local people to encourage them in family planning and to supply them with oral contraceptives and condoms at low, subsidized prices. The program is being evaluated by the Government with expansion in mind if it proves to be successful.

External Assistance

From 1967 through 1975, approximately $15 million was contributed to Thailand's population program from other countries and organizations. The major source of external support was the U.S. Agency for International Development (AID). AID began helping in 1967 when it assisted the work of a voluntary family planning association. With the entry of the Thai Government into family planning, AID's contributions were expanded. From 1967 through 1975, AID support totaled $11 million.

AID's assistance to the Thai program is mainly in the supply of contraceptives and clinical equipment (medical kits for IUD insertions or for sterilizations). AID also supports training, programmatic research, and tests of complimentary (Government and commercial) channels for contraceptive distribution.

The International Planned Parenthood Federation (IPPF) is an important donor to nongovernmental aspects of the overall effort. Its support goes partly to the IPPF-affiliated Planned Parenthood Association of Thailand—mainly for information, education, and communication projects—and partly to the CBFPS (mentioned above). IPPF support during the 1973-75 period totaled approximately $2 million.

The United Nations Fund for Population Activities (UNFPA) is another major supporter. UNFPA assistance to the program began in 1971 when it signed a 5-year agreement with Thailand providing $3.4 million in funds during the first 3 years. Projects in progress include the training of medical and paramedical personnel in family planning, the accelerated development of maternal/child health services and their integration with family planning, the improvement of family planning communication through motivational and informational material, and research. United Nations agencies carrying out the projects are the World Health Organization (WHO), the United Nations Children's Fund (UNICEF), the United Nations Economic and Social Council (UNESCO), the United Nations Development Program, and UNFPA.

The International Development Research Center of Canada has made university grants. One is for testing alternative methods of training midwives so that they can play a part in the national family planning program. Another is for surveying the satisfactions and costs of having children and the motivation for child-bearing.

The Danish International Development Agency has donated $460,000 to construct a family planning headquarters building.

The Ford Foundation has supplied assistance totaling over $433,000.

The American Public Health Association helped to set up a project to plan, develop, and continuously evaluate a low-cost, integrated delivery system to provide health services, family planning, and nutrition aid to a selected rural area.

The Asia Foundation has made a number of grants to aid information and education for family planning. Expenditures for fiscal years 1973 and 1974 were about $100,000.

The Association for Voluntary Sterilization has made grants totaling $272,000 for training and for equipment used in voluntary male and female sterilization programs.

Other private organizations have contributed special efforts. Family Planning International Assistance has made grants to churches to help them set up and promote the use of family planning services. The Population Council has made grants totaling $634,000 in support of program statistics reporting, the postpartum program, and population research, studies, and seminars. The Rockefeller Foundation has made university grants totaling $156,000 for research in reproductive biology and reproductive immunology. The World Assembly of Youth has worked with national, regional, and local groups to help make young people more aware of population problems and the need to cope with them. World Education has provided $117,000 to the Thai Government Ministry of Education for a functional education and a family life planning course for adults.

Korea (North)

North Korea's mid-1975 population was estimated at 15.9 million compared with 11.7 million in 1965. The 1974 birth rate was probably about 36 per 1,000 population, or, down slightly from 39 in 1965. The 1974 death rate was estimated at 9 per 1,000 population compared with 12 in 1965. The annual GNP in 1973 was estimated at $340 per capita—a gain of $80 a person since 1965.

Industrial development in the north of the Korean peninsula up to about 1940 had attracted large numbers of people from the south. This trend was reversed after 1945 when 2 million refugees fled south to the Republic of Korea when the peninsula was wracked by war. Refugees continued to migrate to South Korea for some years.

With large amounts of aid from the Communist countries, North Korea experienced high rates of economic growth immediately following the Korean conflict, but growth has subsided since about 1960. The country grows enough food to meet its low levels of consumption. Food rationing continues.

Information on Government policies and activities relating to population growth and fertility are not available at this time.

Viet-Nam (South)

The population of South Viet-Nam at mid-1975 was estimated at 21 million, compared with 16.3 million in 1965. With the birth rate at 42 per 1,000 population in 1974 and the mortality rate 16 per 1,000, the population is estimated to be increasing by

2.6 percent annually. If this growth rate were maintained, the population total would double in 27 years. With average annual GNP per person already low ($160), such continued growth would act to depress living levels still further.

The Republic of Viet-Nam has the background, facilities, and potential for carrying out a successful family planning program if its new Government so chooses. The Ministry of Health has more than 130 facilities, including provincial hospitals and some district clinics, through which family planning services can be or are being offered to the public. A substantial number of public health workers have had family planning training.

The future of the program, however, will depend on the new Government's interest and financial support. During the war years, the program was financed largely by external aid (especially aid from the United States, which ceased in April 1975).

The country has had some family planning activity since 1967 when the voluntary Family Happiness Protective Association, an affiliate of the International Planned Parenthood Federation was formed. It has promoted family planning educational work, conducted training, and operated a referral clinic.

A major handicap to this earlier work, and to more recent efforts, has been the existence of a long-standing law—imposed under French rule—that restricts dissemination of contraceptive materials and information.

Although the present Government does not have an announced national population policy, there was a certain degree of Government involvement under the preceding regime. After years of delay caused by the war, political and religious opposition to family planning, the archaic laws, by 1973 some progress was being made. In that year, the Government signed the World Leaders' Declaration on Population and created a National Population Council of Ministers. Another significant development was the change in name of the Ministry of Health's national family planning committee from the Committee for Research in Family Planning to the Committee for Family Health. This change reflected a new emphasis on family planning; not only was the health of the woman of concern but also the health of the children and the family as a unit.

The family planning program under the former Government was being implemented through facilities of the Ministry of Health. The Ministry reported in 1974 that there had been 40,396 acceptors of contraceptive service from the beginning of the program in 1968.

External Assistance

The major supplier of assistance to the population program before the 1974 change in Government was the U.S. Agency for International Development (AID). From fiscal 1970 through fiscal 1975, AID assistance totaled $3.7 million. Support included helping the Ministry of Health to extend family planning services to all districts, working with Vietnamese officials to demonstrate the economic and health benefits of fertility reduction, training of personnel, the development of public information, the improvement of population growth projects, and supplying commodities including contraceptives.

The United Nations Fund for Population Activities (UNFPA), in conjunction with the World Health Organization (WHO), assisted a Vietnamese maternal and child health/family welfare project initiated in 1971 and financed with $129,000. The project stressed the importance of family planning in securing a higher standard of living for the family as a whole.

The United Nations Children's Fund (UNICEF), helped the development of national maternal/child health services that directly or indirectly supported family planning.

The Swedish International Development Authority made grants to the program in 1971 and 1972 totaling $681,000.

The Asia Foundation made grants to help the national program's work in family planning information, education, and communication. Support also went toward the production and purchase of family planning films.

The International Planned Parenthood Federation assisted its affiliated planned parenthood association in the latter's overall program. This included work with opinion leaders, publications, training of social workers and motivators, clinical services, and distribution of contraceptives. Expenditures for 1974 were estimated at $140,400.

The Mennonite Central Committee assisted a Protestant church in operating two hospital clinics providing family planning information and supplies.

The Population Council made grants totaling $141,000 to the Ministry of Health for training physicians and other professionals in family planning.

Viet-Nam (North)

North Viet-Nam suffered great loss of life during the recent years of conflict. The true size of the country's present population is not known; estimates indicate a total of over 24 million. The annual rate of population growth is estimated at 1.8 percent.

The Government regards its population growth and fertility rates as undesirably high. Family planning services are made readily available to the populace as part of the nation's public health services.

External Assistance

At the request of the North Vietnamese Government, the Swedish International Development Authority (SIDA) began providing family planning assistance in 1971-72. Such aid was about $1 million a year during the succeeding 2 years and twice that much in 1973-74. SIDA's assistance has included the supply of contraceptives, of medical, nursing, and audiovisual equipment, and of scientific literature.

In South Viet-Nam, a long-standing law restricts dissemination of contraceptive materials and information. The population is growing at the rate of 2.6 percent annually.

Europe

The population of Europe—comprising 35 countries and slightly more than one-sixth of the world total—increased nearly 8 percent during the 1965-75 decade. As of mid-1975, the European population totaled 727.7 million (including all U.S.S.R.), an increase of 52.6 million over the 1965 level of 675 million. (Totals include Greece, shown in Near East section of the World Population Data table on page 269.)

The rate of population gain was down, however. The 1965-75 increase was only three-fourths the increment of the previous decade, when the population rose by nearly 70.3 million over the 1955 level.

The annual rate of natural increase for Europe dropped by one-third during the 1965-74 period, declining from a level of 0.9 percent in 1965 to 0.6 percent in 1974. The drop stemmed from the combination of a somewhat lower birth rate and a slightly higher mortality rate. The birth rate in 1974 was 16 per 1,000 population, down from 18 per 1,000 in 1965. The death rate in 1974 was 10 per 1,000 people, up from 9 per 1,000 in 1965. Europe has the lowest population growth rate of any continent.

The population of Europe is that of an economically developed region, and problems are expressed more in terms of urbanization and pollution of the environment than in terms of effects on national development. The predominant migratory flow during the decade was to northern and western Europe, drawing from the southern and eastern regions. A large share of such migration was of a temporary nature, however, responding to work opportunities in labor-short areas.

Per capita gross national product in the European area increased during the decade from a level of $1,900 per capita in 1965 to $3,010 per capita in 1973—an increase of 58 percent.

Regional contrasts prevailed over much of Europe during the decade with respect to population-related matters. A number of countries—primarily in northern and western Europe—moved to expand family planning services and to liberalize abortion. A number of others—primarily in southern Europe—continued active opposition to proposals for fertility limitation. Yet other countries where legalized abortion has been widely practiced—primarily in Eastern Europe—moved to discourage abortion in favor of more reliance on contraception. In most countries, abortion has been an important factor in reducing birth rates.

Family planning facilities in Europe vary considerably. Whereas some of the first family planning centers in the world were established in Europe, the sale and advertising of contraceptives are still illegal in some countries. Family planning associations have been developed in 18 countries with the assistance of the International Planned Parenthood Federation (IPPF).

Government participation in family planning varies considerably. In some countries it is integrated with public health services, and in others governments provide support for the activities of family planning associations. An increasing number of governments in Europe have made grants to family planning activities both in their own and in developing countries.

Assistance to developing countries for population programs was forthcoming from 16 European countries, totaling $70 million through 1974. Countries contributing in multimillion-dollar amounts were Denmark, West Germany, the Netherlands, Norway, Sweden and the United Kingdom.

Population developments in 26 of the largest countries of Europe are presented here in brief for the past decade. These countries account for 99.9 percent of the total European population. See "World Population Data" for most others.

Albania

The population of Albania in mid-1975 is estimated at about 2.4 million, an increase of approximately 550,000, or 30 percent over the 1965 level of about 1.87 million. The rate of increase was somewhat smaller than that of the previous decade, however, when the population grew by 35 percent.

Albania has the highest birth rate and one of the lowest death rates in Europe, both of which, however, declined during the 1965-74 period. The birth rate in 1974 was about 30 per 1,000 population as compared with 35 per 1,000 in 1965. The death rate in 1974 was 8 per 1,000 people as compared with 9 in 1965. The rate of natural increase for 1974 was 2.2 percent annually.

The per capita gross national product of Albania increased by about 28 percent between 1965 and 1973. In 1965 it was $360 per capita and in 1973, $460 per capita.

According to the report of the Swedish demographer Erland Hofsten, both abortion and sterilization are banned in Albania, and the attitude toward contraceptives is, if not hostile, as least one of

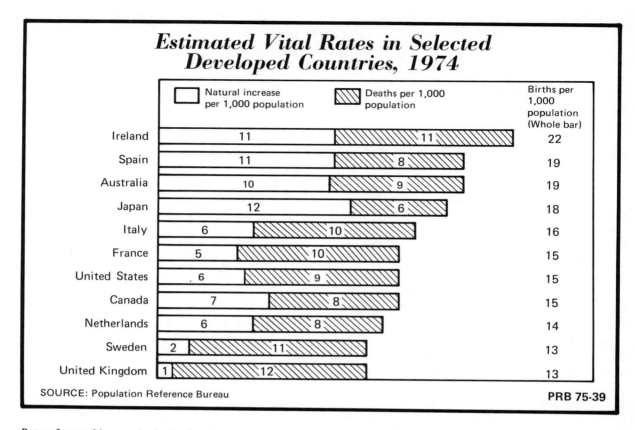

Estimated Vital Rates in Selected Developed Countries, 1974

	Natural increase per 1,000 population	Deaths per 1,000 population	Births per 1,000 population (Whole bar)
Ireland	11	11	22
Spain	11	8	19
Australia	10	9	19
Japan	12	6	18
Italy	6	10	16
France	5	10	15
United States	6	9	15
Canada	7	8	15
Netherlands	6	8	14
Sweden	2	11	13
United Kingdom	1	12	13

SOURCE: Population Reference Bureau

PRB 75-39

Rates of natural increase in the developed countries are far below the world average of 1.8 percent. Rates for Northern America and Europe averaged 0.6 percent in 1974. Low birth rates in some European countries have given rise to recurring official concern and measures aimed at increasing birth rates above what they regard as undesirably low levels.

suspicion. Imported condoms are said, however, to be available in pharmacies. The falling birth rate indicates that birth control must be practiced, but it is not clear what methods are used. Moslem traditions are believed to be still relatively strong in most of the country.

Austria

The population of Austria is approaching stabilization following a decade of steady decline in the rate of population growth and increasing activity in the field of family planning.

The population in mid-1975 was 7.5 million, an increase of 4 percent, or about 300,000 over the 1965 level of 7.2 million. The annual rate of natural increase during the period declined, however, from a level of 0.5 percent in 1965 to 0.1 percent in 1974. The decline stemmed from a drop of nearly one-third in the rate of births. Births in 1965 oc-

curred at a rate of 18 per 1,000 people, but in 1974 they were down to 13. Meanwhile, the death rate in 1974 was 12 deaths per 1,000 population, down slightly from the 1965 level of 13.

The per capita gross national product of Austria increased by 47 percent between 1965 and 1973. In 1965 it was $2,520 per capita and in 1973, $3,710.

Government officials attribute the decline in the rate of population growth to two causes. First, the age structure of the population has changed to include a relatively smaller group of women in their childbearing years. And second, increased use of effective contraceptives has enabled more couples to determine the number of children they want to have.

Austria has pursued a policy of supporting expanded family planning activities and wide distribution of information on contraceptives. It has done so in order to avoid unwanted pregnancies, as well as the abortions often resulting therefrom, and to enable couples to plan the number and spacing of their children. It seeks in all this to propagate the idea of responsible parenthood and the idea of the wanted child.

In this connection, an association of family planning groups was formed in 1966 and became a member of the International Planned Parenthood Federation in 1971. The association in 1974 ran 23 clinics, 14 of which were financed by the Austrian Government. Illustrative of the growing support for family planning activities, a 1953 prohibition against the use of IUD's was lifted in 1973. Also, abortion in the first trimester of pregnancy was legalized in 1974 to become effective in 1975. In addition, sex education has been made compulsory in schools, with the family planning association providing materials.

With its rate of natural increase at the present level, however, the Government opposes a further decrease of the birth rate as such. Its economic and social policy aims to combine a maximum of economic growth and price stability, taking into consideration the preservation of the environment, and to achieve as far as possible a state of social harmony between the different groups of the population.

The excess of the female population which had reached a total of half a million as a result of World War II casualties has decreased markedly during the past two decades. In 1951 an approximately normal sex ratio existed only for people under 25 years of age. By 1971, however, such a ratio existed for groups up to 45 years.

Belgium

Belgium is one of the most densely populated countries in the world (318 per square kilometer). A relatively low rate of population growth coupled with linguistic and related divisions in its society have tended to limit official attention to population growth matters. Changes are underway, however, which may alter this situation.

The population of Belgium in mid-1975 was 9.8 million—an increase of 3.4 percent, or about 300,000 over the 1965 population of about 9.4 million. Approximately three-fourths of the increase can be attributed to the natural rate of increase, with the remainder stemming from immigration.

The per capita gross national product of Belgium increased by 41 percent between 1965 and 1973; in 1965 it was $3,320 per capita and in 1973, $4,690.

The annual rate of natural increase declined during the 1965-74 period, dropping from 0.4 percent in 1965 to 0.1 percent in 1974. The birth rate in this period declined from a level of 16 births per 1,000 population to 13 while the mortality rate remained largely unchanged at 12 deaths per 1,000.

Regional variations, however, have occurred within the country which are thought to bear important implications for the sensitive balance between Dutch-speaking Flemings and the French-speaking Walloons, the country's two principal linguistic groups. Historically the northern Flemish part of the country has registered relatively higher natality and lower mortality than the southern Walloon area. In recent decades, however, the differential has been diminishing. The high natality rates in Flanders have been generally falling while the low rates in Wallonia have been generally rising. In Flanders, the pre-World War II birth rate of 20 per 1,000 population had fallen by 1968 to 15.6. In Wallonia, it had risen from 12 per 1,000 to 13.8. Most recent reports from the Belgian Government indicate that the size of families in the two areas has become practically identical.

Nevertheless, successive Belgian Governments have avoided consistent demographic policies although they have taken a number of measures that are population-related. On the one hand, relatively generous family allowances and childbirth allowances have been provided on the grounds of "family policy" rather than as an encouragement to have children. On the other hand, they have provided modest subsidies to privately operated family planning clinics on the same grounds.

A 1923 law prohibiting the display and advertising of contraceptives was repealed in July 1973. Contraceptives may now be sold in planned parenthood centers. The IPPF-affiliated Belgian Federation for Family Planning, founded in 1963, coordinates 19 Flemish and Walloon centers, including three university hospitals in Brussels, Ghent, and Liège. In 1970 it was estimated that about 12 percent of women aged 15-44 took oral contraceptives despite the restricted availability then in force. Abortions remain illegal in all cases, but a National Commission on Ethical Problems, appointed in December 1974, is to consider revision of the penal legislation on abortion, in response to growing public demand for *de jure* recognition of *de facto* circumstances. Annual numbers of abortions actually being performed have been estimated as high as 200,000, or 140 for every 100 live births. The Belgian demographer Louis Lohlé-Tart judged 50,000, or 35 per 100 live births, as probably closer to the truth in 1973. Random testimony from rural physicians suggests that the number of abortions is now declining, and probably can be expected to drop further with increasing availability of modern contraception.

Concern with the growing population density of the country has not been so great as to discourage immigration. The Belgian Government regards the immigration levels of the 1966-75 period as a positive element in the country's development.

Not only has in-migration helped offset a general shortage of labor throughout much of the decade, but many immigrants have gone into the mining, metalurgical, and household occupations which Belgians are increasingly reluctant to perform. About 80 percent of the total male immigrants are in the extractive industries. Of the total immigration, abut 54 percent is from the Mediterranean area, with 44 percent coming from Italy alone.

Bulgaria

Bulgaria's population increased from 8.2 million in 1965 to an estimated 8.7 million in mid-1975. Death and birth rates have also risen, deaths from 8 per 1,000 population in 1965 to 10 per 1,000 in 1974; births from 15 to 17 per 1,000. The 1974 rate of natural increase was 0.7 percent annually, the same as for 1965.

The per capita gross national product of Bulgaria increased by about 67 percent between 1965 and 1973. In 1965 it was $950 per capita and in 1973, $1,590 per capita.

The proportionate rise in deaths in Bulgaria stems from the present near-universal European phenomenon of an aging population. The overall birth rate rise, with intervening fluctuations, reflects in part increasingly generous pronatalist incentives and some recent restrictions on formerly permissive abortion, as in Romania, Czechoslovakia, and Hungary.

Legal abortion at a low cost—in effect, abortion on demand—was made available in 1956. In the decade that followed, legal abortions climbed sharply, reaching 82 per 100 births in 1966. The birth rate fell to a record low of 14.9 per 1,000 population in that year.

The Government reacted in February 1968 with some restrictions on abortion and a series of measures aimed at encouraging three-child families in particular. Lump-sum payments per birth were greatly increased, and like the generous monthly child allowances and paid maternity leaves, were highest for third-order births. Taxes were raised 5 to 10 percent for unmarried persons over 30 and for married couples who were childless after 5 years of marriage.

In the following 2 years, legal abortions fell and the birth rate rose, especially in urban areas where reduced availability of abortion and increased fertility

benefits (including preferential access to housing, jobs, and higher education for families with three or more children) might be expected to have impact. However, births again fell to 15.3 per 1,000 population in 1972. New restrictions adopted in 1973 limit abortion on demand to unmarried girls under 18 and women over 40 with one living child. Contraceptives are available but their use is not encouraged.

Like most East European countries, Bulgaria is faced with the dilemma of needing every able-bodied woman in the work force in order to achieve current development goals, and, at the same time, desiring to encourage family sizes sufficiently large to ensure adequate labor supplies among future generations.

Czechoslovakia

The population of Czechoslovakia was an estimated 14.8 million as of mid-1975, compared with 14.1 million in 1965. Concerned by the sinking birth rates of the mid-1960's, the Government since then has adopted broad and evidently effective measures to stimulate more births per family. From a low of 14.9 births per 1,000 population in 1968, the birth rate was up to 20 in 1974, one of Europe's highest. The annual rate of natural increase in 1974 had risen to 0.8 percent from 0.6 percent in 1965. The death rate increased from 10 to 12 per 1,000 population.

The per capita gross national product of Czechoslovakia increased about 79 percent between 1965 and 1973. In 1965 it was $1,600 per capita and in 1973, $2,870.

Pronatalist incentives include various maternity and family benefits which can exceed the average annual wage during the 2 years following a second and higher order birth if mothers choose to stay home; rebates on income tax, children's clothing and rents for families with children; and low-interest loans for newlyweds, on which the principal is progressively reduced at each subsequent birth.

The liberal abortion law of 1957 was tightened in 1973 in a further effort to promote family-building. Although theoretically never available on demand, broad interpretation by abortion boards of the law's permissible "reasons deserving special consideration" had encouraged increasing resort to abortion, to a high of nearly half the number of births in 1969.

Contraceptive advice after abortion and childbirth is obligatory and must be provided by public health gynecologists to all women who request it. All methods are available, including IUD insertions for 200 crowns, and pills on prescription at 9 crowns for a monthly cycle. However, it is estimated that currently only 2 percent of women of fertile age use pills and 8 percent IUD's. Condoms are preferred by 20 percent of couples, but coitus interruptus remains the leading method at 25 to 30 percent.

In place of the advisory State Population Committee dating from 1957, a high-level Government Population Committee was created in 1972 to initiate, coordinate, and implement population policy.

Denmark

The population growth of Denmark is sufficiently moderate—less than one-half of 1 percent per year—that the Government sees little point in pursuing policies aimed explicitly at changing the rate of growth, upward or downward. It does see the need, however, for qualitative or welfare-oriented population policies in the fields of health, education, and territorial distribution.

In mid-1975 the population (excluding Greenland and the Faroe Islands) totaled about 5 million—an increase of approximately 100,000 over the 1965 total of about 4.9 million. The annual rate of natural increase during the period declined from a level of 0.8 percent in 1965 to 0.4 percent in 1974. Births in 1965 occurred at a rate of 18 per 1,000 people but in 1974 were down to 14. Meanwhile, mortality remained largely unchanged at about 10 deaths per 1,000.

The per capita gross national product of Denmark increased about 31 percent between 1965 and 1973. In 1965 it was $4,070 per capita and in 1973, $5,340.

Since World War II, migration to and from Denmark has been fairly modest, the number of emigrants almost balancing the number of immigrants. The annual number of emigrants and immigrants each has represented about one-half of 1 percent of the population.

With the fertility down to around the replacement level—and assuming no change in present conditions—officials expect the Danish population to peak at a level of about 5.5 million people in the year 2020. Thereafter a slight decline would be expected to commence of about 0.2 percent per year. At the same time, the proportion of inhabitants over the age of 65 years would increase from the present level of 13 percent to 17 percent, while the under-15 age group would diminish from 23 percent to 19 percent.

A long tradition of birth control in Danish history may have served to facilitate today's wide acceptance of family planning. For centuries (as noted by P.C. Matthiessen in "Population of Denmark") it had

been common practice for prospective husbands and wives to live in sexual union prior to marriage. But under contemporary norms, such experiences were not intended to result in pregnancy. For this reason some contraceptive methods—chiefly coitus interruptus—had been widely employed for many generations which, in turn, served to accustom couples to regulate births according to economic and social conditions.

Since the end of World War II, however, contraceptive practices among the Danish population have altered radically. Today, in marriages where contraception is practiced and the woman is between 20 and 30, half use the pill and one-fourth the condom. The diaphragm and other devices such as the IUD are thus in relatively limited use.

During the 1966-75 decade new avenues of family planning have opened up. A law enacted in 1966 makes it obligatory for physicians to give free advice on contraception to all women upon termination of pregnancy, by childbirth or otherwise. In 1971, sex education, which had long been practiced in many schools, was made obligatory at all school levels. This teaching is intended to be adapted to the children's development at the different levels and is integrated with other subjects.

Since 1973, sterilization has been available upon request for all women and men of 25 years and over. Beginning in the same year, abortion also has been available upon request and is free of charge within the first 12 weeks of pregnancy.

Recent years have seen an upswing in political interest in reversing local trends toward depopulation so as to achieve a more even geographic spread of the population. The metropolitan area and the three eastern counties of the island of Zeeland contain altogether 35 percent of the total Danish population but only 7 percent of the country's land area. New legislation has therefore brought areas adjacent to the towns under the purview of urban planning, and authorities have been called upon to prepare plans for urban, rural and recreational zones.

A national development plan designed to encourage a balanced geographical spread of the entire population—on economic, social, and environmental grounds is thought by many officials to be one of the crucial future aims of Danish population policy.

Finland

The population of Finland in mid-1975 is estimated at 4.7 million, 3 percent above the 1965 level of about 4.5 million. This increase was less than half the increment of the previous decade when the population increased by more than 7 percent.

The annual rate of natural increase dropped sharply during the 1965-74 period from a level of 0.7 percent in 1965 to 0.4 percent in 1974. The decline stemmed largely from a reduction in the birth rate from 17 per 1,000 people in 1965 to 13 in 1974. Mortality rates during the decade fluctuated moderately at about 10 deaths per 1,000 population.

The per capita gross national product of Finland increased about 46 percent between 1965 and 1973. In 1965 it was $2,510 per capita and in 1973, $3,660 per capita.

Like the lower birth rate, out-migration has been an important factor in Finnish population growth. In 1969 and 1970 there was a marked drop in the total population due to extensive emigration to Sweden. In 1969 emigration is believed to have exceeded the natural population growth by about 15,000 persons. According to the Finnish demographer, Kauko Sipponen, the Government has taken no concerted measures to influence either the birth rate or emigration. The change in recent years resulting in a slight moderation in population growth, he states, has not been considered a threat. This is partly due, he concludes, to Finland's awareness that overpopulation is threatening the world, and that the environment is being polluted because of overconsumption of natural resources and population growth.

The Finnish Government, however, has long been sensitive to family welfare and has established a well-developed social security and health benefits system, including assistance to family planning. The social security system covers maternity and child allowances, and health insurance covers the majority of the cost of medical services. Education is free and compulsory for ages 7 to 15. Planned parenthood is integrated with the public health services. Family planning advice and services are therefore available throughout the country and from clinics operated by the Family Planning Association (Vaestoliitto). Generally speaking, family policies of the Government are intended to assist families in establishing and maintaining a home and to support the financial, physical, and mental well-being of the family.

The Government supports contraception as a means of preventing abortion. Public health centers distribute pills and insert IUD's and provide advice on contraception to women after abortion. Condoms, however, are regarded as the most widely used contraceptive method and are readily available at retail outlets.

Under the new abortion law of 1970, abortion may be induced at a woman's request under prescribed conditions. Previously, doctors who examined women and issued a certificate for an abortion were appointed by the State Medical Council. Now every doctor in the service of the local authorities or the state is automatically authorized to issue the certificate. According to the new law, a decision is generally made by two doctors jointly. The new law permitted 16,000 legal abortions in 1971.

In 1973 the Finnish Government granted $100,000 to the International Planned Parenthood Federation (IPPF). Its multilateral assistance to U.N. population programs totaled $920,000 through 1974.

France

The population of France grew by 8 percent during the 1965-75 decade to reach a total of nearly 52.7 million as of mid-1975. This is an increase of about 4.5 million over the 1965 level of 48.7 million. About one-half of the increase was from net migration. The increase for the period was less than for the previous decade, when it was 5.3 million, or about 12 percent.

Both the birth rate and mortality rate declined during the 1965-74 period. The birth rate dropped from 18 per 1,000 population in 1965 to 15 per 1,000 in 1974. The death rate in the same period declined from 11 per 1,000 people to 10. New legislation in the field of family planning, including the 1975 legislation of abortion under prescribed conditions, may contribute to a further decline in the rate of population growth.

The per capita gross national product of France increased between 1965 and 1973 by about 44 percent. In 1965 it was $3,370 per capita and in 1973, $4,850 per capita.

With an average density of 95 people per square kilometer as compared with 318 in Belgium, 248 in West Germany, and 180 in Italy, France manifests the characteristics of a relatively stable, long-term growth pattern.

Among the more salient of these characteristics is the progressive aging of the French population over the past century. Because of the increasing ratio of elderly people to economically active adults, the size of the economically active population in France is only marginally larger today than in 1901, although the population as a whole has grown by about 12.3 million, or 30 percent. Indeed, as recently as 1968 the economically active population of France was slightly smaller than in 1901, registering 20.44

million in 1968 as compared with 20.55 million in 1901 (Population Council, May 1972).

Several population-related movements active in France during the past century help to account for the current situation. The first of these was an active movement in favor of birth control which started in the last quarter of the 19th century and which has remained active to the present day. Advocated primarily as a means of liberating women, the movement contributed materially to the early reduction in the French birth rate. In the 1870's, the birth rate in France was 25 per 1,000 population, a rate far below the 35 per 1,000 of neighboring European countries. By the eve of World War II, France had a birth rate of 16.

A second movement developed during the same period, largely as a reaction to the first. Noting the continued decrease in the French birth rate, some people became alarmed about the demographic future of France and formed the National Alliance against Depopulation. It was this movement which championed a restrictive law against abortion, enacted in 1920.

A third movement, motivated by a sense of social justice, became active after World War I to defend the rights of the family. Joining forces with the pronatalists of the second movement, this movement helped to enact a set of laws and decrees providing various allowances to be paid to families. So extensive have these payments become as to represent, during the past decade, about 4.5 percent of the gross national product.

For much of the 20th century, therefore, the social policy of France, from a demographic point of view, has been molded primarily by the pronatalists and the advocates of social justice to families. From their efforts emerged a series of basic family allowances, paid by the Government, intended to enhance family welfare and insure a growing population. Since 1945 they have included allowances for families with two or more children and for families supported by a single income, prenatal allowances for pregnant women, and maternity benefits for the mothers of newborn children, and housing allowances.

In a French family planning clinic, young couples attend a lecture on the regulation of fertility. Recent developments in France favor family planning. Among these are changes in the family allowance system and the nullification of the prohibitions against abortion and contraceptive devices.

In addition, measures were provided to alleviate the costs of raising children. These included social welfare payments for the neediest, scholarships, social security benefits to children and mothers not engaged in the labor force, sick leave for pregnant working women before and after birth, and income tax calculated on family size.

During the 1966-75 decade, however, a shift in emphasis occurred. Additional family allowance measures were enacted, but according to the French demographer, Jean Bourgeois-Pichat, the measures were not entirely to the liking of the pronatalists and advocates of justice to families (in B. Berelson, ed., *Population Policy in Developed Countries,* McGraw Hill, 1974). Meanwhile, significant new measures were enacted which favor the practice of contraception and family planning.

Three new allowances were granted in the fields of specialized education, orphan care, and day care for children. But the new allowances, for the most part, were allowed only if certain conditions of income were fulfilled. Similarly, the single income allowance has also been made subject to limitations. Because the allowance is not paid above a certain income limit, an estimated 300,000 families have been excluded from its benefits.

Equally significant, however, were steps taken during the past decade to nullify the 1920 law prohibiting the promotion and practice of induced abortion and the distribution of contraceptive devices.

A new law passed in December of 1967 nullified the articles of the 1920 law prohibiting birth control information and the distribution and sale of contraceptives. Henceforth, the manufacture, import, and sale of contraceptives (earlier available only in terms of health measures) were freely authorized for distribution through pharmacies, family planning clinics, and state health centers. Social security funds are allowed to cover much of the costs. The use of IUD's is permitted if insertion is made by a doctor in a specialized hospital establishment or office. Commercial contraceptive information is forbidden, however, except in publications intended solely for doctors and pharmacists.

Most recent of the new developments favoring family planning—and one which bears significant implications for future demographic trends in France —has been the law of January 1975, legalizing induced abortion under prescribed conditions. An abortion may now be performed on a woman up to 10 weeks of gestation after she has been informed of the medical risks, referred to social agencies, and waits 1 week from the date of her first visit with a doctor. After 10 weeks gestation, an abortion

can be performed following certification of two doctors that the woman's life is seriously endangered by the pregnancy or that the child probably will be born with a serious incurable malady.

Each year, some 350,000 permanent and seasonal workers entering France (including workers from Algeria and lower Africa) are added to the economically active population of about 20 million compared to about 800,000 French citizens.

It is estimated that a net annual immigration of about 200,000, plus higher birth rates among the foreign-born, currently account for 50 percent of France's annual population increase of about 530,000.

Population forecasts have been made by the National Institute of Statistics and Economic Studies using hypotheses of both stable and decreasing fertility. Assuming a steady, unchanging rate of fertility (about 1.25 daughters per woman) and disregarding the factor of immigration the population of France would be expected to reach 63.4 million by the year 2000. Assuming a declining rate of fertility which would stabilize at a level of 1.04, the population would reach 59.2 million.

The impact of the new family planning measures upon the fertility rate is difficult to assess. It may be safely assumed, however, that the influences of these measures will be in the direction of lower fertility. The impact of immigration on the population projections for the year 2000 is also difficult to assess inasmuch as immigration rates are strongly affected by economic conditions both within France and the various source countries of Western Europe and Africa. It is likely, however, that immigration will continue at significant rates.

Federal Republic of Germany

After increasing sharply in the early part of the 1965-75 decade, population growth in Germany's Republic (West Germany) slowed dramatically during the latter part and showed a net decrease in the year 1974. Because of the overall increase for the period, the total of 62 million in mid-1975 was 3.4 million above 1965 (58.6 million). But the high point of West German population came at the beginning of 1974 when the total reached 62.1 million. The 1975 figure represented a drop of upwards of 100,000 from that peak.

The per capita gross national product of West Germany increased between 1965 and 1973 by about 34 percent. In 1965 it was $4,200 per capita and in

1973, it was $5,620 per capita.

The major variables in the population shifts of the decade were the birth rates and immigration rates. The immigration rate was erratic, including a net outflow of more than 100,000 in 1967 and a peak in-movement of more than 500,000 in 1969 before falling off to about 400,000 in 1974. However, the birth rate declined progressively throughout the decade to a point well below the replacement rate.

The birth rate in 1965 was 18 per 1,000 people, a level that had been generally maintained for a decade or more. During the 1965-74 period, however, it declined steadily so that by 1972 it had fallen below the mortality rate of 11.8 per 1,000, reaching a low of 10 per 1,000 in 1974. The mortality rate had begun the decade at a level of 11 per 1,000 people and had increased to 12 per 1,000 in 1974.

Whereas, the Federal Republic recorded 995,000 births in 1965, the number in 1974 had dropped to 626,000, of which one in six were born to foreigners residing in West Germany. This decline is only to a slight extent attributable to shifts in the age structure of women and of married couples. The major factor is the changing attitudes of married couples regarding the desirable number of children. There is an unmistakable trend to the two-children family, and about 10 percent of all marriages have remained childless for medical reasons. Thus the annual rate of natural increase which had been 0.7 percent in 1965 sank to -0.2 percent in 1974.

Whereas the birth rate represents the dominant factor in the population trend, changes in the immigration rate give rise to important yearly fluctuations. These fluctuations, in turn, have stemmed in part from political developments as between West and East Germany and, to a more decisive extent, from different economic conditions in the European countries.

Through the 1950's, movements between the two German states were the key factors in the immigration picture. When the borders between the Western sectors and the Eastern sector of Berlin were closed by the East German Government in 1961, however, the migration stream into West Germany was practically stopped. Since that time, exit permits from East Germany generally have been given only to persons beyond working age. As a consequence the immigration surplus from East Germany during the decade has remained at a low level of about 18,000 people a year.

The sharp rise and fall of the immigration rate from year to year therefore stemmed from economic developments, the most pronounced of which was the German boom beginning in 1960. Unlike the immigrants coming from East Germany, however, these workers from other countries did not come for permanent residence. As a rule they returned home in large numbers in periods when employment in West Germany declined. It was an economic recession which led to the net out-migration in 1967 and the economic boom in 1969 which brought the peak in-movement of more than half a million in that year. In the 1970's, however, the economic activity slackened, bringing a fall-off in net immigration to about 400,000. Since 1973, it has been Government policy that, generally speaking, recruitment for foreign workers will be conducted only in countries of the European Community.

Inasmuch as there has been no sign of stabilization in the declining German birth rate, population projections which do not take immigration into account indicate that the present population will decrease by 2.2 million by 1985 and by a further 2.7 million between 1985 and 2000. If these projections are borne out, the German population in the year 2000 will be only 57 million, about the same level as in 1962.

Meanwhile, life in West Germany, as in many other countries, is progressively determined by urban forms of living. In 1973 approximately 75 percent of the population lived in cities of more than 5,000 inhabitants while one-third was concentrated in 60 cities of more than 100,000. This high degree of urbanization and the unequal distribution of these cities within the nation as a whole led to a concentration of 45 percent of the population in so-called agglomeration areas comprising only 7 percent of the total area. This urbanization has doubtless contributed, as elsewhere, to reductions in the birth rate.

Owing to a variety of factors, West Germany has no Government-backed family planning program. But advisory services mainly by private organizations are available for individual contraceptive consultation and these receive financial subsidy from the Government. Under present laws, hormonal contraceptives may be issued only on medical prescription. All other non-hormonal contraceptives can be purchased without limitation or can be obtained by mail order.

The Federal Government recognizes the significance of demographic processes and continues to closely observe both the fluctuations in the immigration rate and the decreased birth rate. Although action has been taken to limit immigration to workers largely from other European Community nations, it is not at the present time the intention of the Government to initiate direct population policy measures for the purpose of influencing procreative behavior and the birth rate. Given the conditions of West Germany, the Government believes that a constant population level is more appropriate than the increases characterizing population trends of most other countries.

In its international relations, Germany has established a policy of assisting family planning activities in developing countries if requested to do so by their governments. A 1971 cabinet decision established that German assistance should be given primarily on a multilateral basis, although not to the exclusion of bilateral aid. It therefore has supported the United Nations Fund for Population Activities, contributing $24.6 million for the 1970-75 period. Other financial support has gone to the United Nations Development Program and to the Development Center of the Organization for Economic Cooperation and Development.

The first foreign contribution on a project basis was given in 1971 in support of a multifunctional training and research center in Tunis. German allocations to this project, which is executed in cooperation with the World Health Organization and with the Tunisian and German affiliates of the International Planned Parenthood Federation, amount to $369,400 for 1971-74.

German Democratic Republic

The German Democratic Republic (East Germany) registered a small decline in population from 1965 to 1975. The decrease was from an estimated 17 million in 1965 to 16.9 million at mid-1975. This followed a drop of 0.8 million during the preceding decade when large numbers departed East Germany prior to erection of the Berlin wall in 1961. With emigration virtually stopped since then, the 1965-75 decline can be attributed to the downturn in the birth rate, from 16 per 1,000 population in 1965 to 11 in 1974. The death rate meanwhile rose slightly to 14 per 1,000 due to the increasing proportion of aged persons. Except for 1971, deaths have exceeded births each year since 1969. The annual rate of natural decrease in 1974 is estimated at -0.3 percent.

The per capita gross national product of East Germany increased between 1965 and 1973 by about 82 percent. In 1965 it was $1,650 per capita and in 1973, $3,000 per capita.

The birth rate drop results from many factors. For example, the Government has strongly encouraged women to work outside their homes, and by 1970 women comprised nearly half of the country's labor force. Labor shortages are severe because of heavy male losses during World War II and subsequent emigration. Over 40 percent of the labor force was in industry by 1971 and nearly three-quarters of the country's population lived in urban areas.

Family allowances, birth grants, paid maternity leave, interest-free loans for newlyweds, and other measures have been instituted in an effort to encourage women both to work and bear children. However, these incentives have been less generous than elsewhere in East Europe.

Low birth rates have not inhibited the Government from providing the full spectrum of family planning services, which are seen primarily as guaranteeing women's rights to control their fertility. Founded by Karl-Heinrich Mehlan at Rostock University in 1963, the IPPF-affiliated Germany Family Planning Association joined with the Ministry of Health in 1966 to integrate family planning into the public health system. There are now some 200 Government planned parenthood centers and 200 Family Planning Association centers combining contraceptive services with marriage and sexual counselling. Pills and IUD's have been available since the mid-1960's. Contraceptive sterilization of women (but not men) is permitted if other methods are unsuccessful or inadvisable.

Concurrently, abortion has been increasingly liberalized. Unlike most countries of the area, East Germany did not immediately follow the 1955 lead of Soviet Russia in lifting most abortion restrictions. Temporarily liberalized in 1947 to cope with a postwar flood of illegal abortions, abortion was again restricted to medical and eugenic indications in 1950. Some easing of the law in 1965 was followed in March 1972 by complete liberalization of abortion. Largely replacing formerly illegal abortions, registered legal abortions jumped from about 17,500 in 1971 to 124,000 in the year after the law change, but dropped to some 111,000 in 1973. In this period, the Government began free distribution of pills on prescription and launched a massive campaign to encourage women to use them. Numbers of women using the pill consequently increased from an estimated 1 million in 1972 to 1.5 million in July 1973, about 40 percent of all women of childbearing age.

Greece

Population growth in Greece has been slowed in recent decades by emigration and a falling birth rate. The population in mid-1975 was estimated at

9 million—an increase of about 475,000 since 1966. In the previous decade, the increase was 519,000.

The rate of natural increase dropped during the 1965-1975 period from about 1 percent a year to 0.8 percent according to official data. The decline stemmed largely from a fall in the birth rate. Births in 1966 occurred at a rate of 18 per 1,000 people but by 1974 were down to 16 per 1,000. Mortality remained constant during the period at a level of 8 per 1,000 population.

Tending to offset the natural increase, emigration during the past decade has all but equaled natural population growth. International emigration has long been a significant factor in Greece. Since 1960, however, it has reached unprecedented dimensions. At the same time, large waves of migrants from rural areas have flooded Greek cities, increasing the urban population from 37 percent of the total in 1951 to 53 percent of the total in 1971.

The objectives of the official population policy in today's Greece are: a higher birth rate; higher immigration and lower emigration rates; and decentralization and redistribution of the population.

To combat subfertility, the Government provides monthly incentive allowances and tax benefits for families with three or more children. With respect to international emigration, no official action has been taken, but the short-term and long-term consequences are being studied intensively. Following the restoration of democracy in 1974 the Greek Government re-established the Ministry of Northern Greece as a means of promoting decentralization and regional development in that area.

Although there is strong religious opposition to contraception in Greece, there is no legislation concerning the importation and distribution of contraceptives. Condoms are sold freely. Diaphragms and spermicides have also been introduced. IUD's are rarely used except in private medical practice. Oral contraceptives have been available since 1963 and can be obtained without a physician's prescription.

Greece has no planned parenthood association. The modern aspects of control of conception are not included officially in the medical curriculum, and no legal fertility control services are provided in Governmental programs of public health. Abortion is illegal.

Hungary

The population of Hungary totaled some 10.5 million in mid-1975, an increase of nearly 400,000 since 1965. The death rate rose one point between these years from 11 to 12 per 1,000 population, while the birth rate increased from 13 to 18 per 1,000. The 1974 rate of natural increase per year was 0.6 percent.

The per capita gross national product of Hungary increased between 1965 and 1973 by about 62 percent. In 1965 it was $1,140 per capita and in 1973, $1,850 per capita.

Hungary's birth rate declined to a record low of 12.9 per 1,000 population in 1962, and continued below replacement levels through the 1960's. With legalization of abortion on request in 1956, legal abortions had outstripped births by 1959 and held at over 130 per 100 births until 1970.

Desiring increased births, the Government expanded an existing system of incentives, aimed at promoting two- to three-child families. Among the most successful of these measures was introduction in 1967 of a child care leave, permitting working women to stay at home until a child's third birthday at 25-percent salary, after 5 months maternity leave at full pay. Over two-thirds of eligible women initially availed themselves of this provision. The birth rate rose to over 15 in 1968, but dropped again slightly in the early 1970's.

Then, in October 1973, a Decision of the Council of Ministers on the Tasks of Population Policy introduced one of the world's most comprehensive population policies. Largely implemented in January 1974, the Decision explicitly aims at increasing fertility to avert long-term population decline, promoting the use of effective contraception and reducing the incidence of abortion.

The child care allowance is now progressive and can reach nearly 40 percent of average monthly earnings in the case of a third child. For each birth there is a maternity grant of 2,500 forints ($105), more than the average monthly wage in 1972. Monthly family allowances for workers are provided based on number of dependent children. Working mothers may take up to 60 days paid leave annually to care for a sick child under age 3 and 30 days for one aged 3 to 6. Further childbearing inducements include subsidized children's clothing, housing priority for larger families, and initial household assistance to newly wed couples.

To encourage responsible family planning, contraceptive supplies and services are being expanded, particularly for pills and IUD's. Pills may now be prescribed for women over 18 by any doctor of the National Health Service, with most of the cost covered by insurance. Couples under age 35 now cannot marry before presenting proof of having received contraceptive instruction and supplies from a physician. In September 1974, a beginning was made in introducing education in family life, sex, and contraception in the school and university system and as part of military training.

The 1973 decree restricted abortion for married women with less than three children, but it is still available on request for women over 35 (40, beginning in 1979), unmarried women, women with at least three living children, and on medical or grave social indications including lack of housing.

By the end of 1974, pill use was up to an estimated 17 percent among women of fertile age, from 11 percent in 1973. Legal abortions dropped 40 percent, from 170,000 in 1973 to 102,000 in 1974, well below the 1974 total of 186,000 live births.

Iceland

The population of Iceland in mid-1975 was 220,000, about 28,000 or 15 percent larger than the 1966 level of 192,000. The increase, however, was one-third smaller than the increment of the previous decade.

The rate of natural increase has declined from a level of 1.7 percent annually in 1965 to 1.3 percent in 1974. The decline has stemmed entirely from a fall in the birth rate, which dropped from a level of 24 births per 1,000 population in 1965 to 20 per 1,000 in 1974. The mortality rate remained unchanged at 7 deaths per 1,000.

The per capita gross national product of Iceland increased between 1965 and 1973 by about 22 percent. In 1965 it was $3,980 per capita and in 1973, $4,840 per capita.

The Government does not hinder the dissemination of contraceptives, but sponsors no organized family planning activities. The importation of contraceptives is permitted, subject to pharmaecutical requirements in the case of contraceptive pills and spermicides.

Abortion has been legal in Iceland since the 1930's if strong health and socio-economic considerations warrant. The incidence of abortion is relatively small, estimated at from 3 to 4 per 100 births.

Ireland

Ireland reversed a century of declining population during the 1965-75 decade, reaching a long-held objective of population increase. The rise during the decade was 233,000, or 8 percent.

Ireland's population has decreased over a period of more than 100 years due to a combination of adverse economic conditions, a high rate of emigration, and a low rate of marriage. The effect of each of these factors was moderated during the past decade, however, resulting in a total population of 3.1 million in mid-1975.

Along with the recent increase, however, has come a rapid shift in public concern with demographic matters. From a focus on achieving population growth, public attention has, in less than a decade, concentrated increasingly on other themes. These include correction of regional imbalances in population density and the possible need for changes in old laws and attitudes with respect to contraception and family size.

The per capita gross national product of Ireland increased between 1965 and 1973 by about 35 percent. In 1965 it was $1,600 per capita and in 1973, $2,160 per capita.

Offsetting its birth rate of around 22-23 per 1,000 and rate of natural increase of over 1 percent per year, emigration has long been the overriding population determinant. It has been the drop in emigration in recent years which has made the new growth in population possible.

Whereas more than 208,000 people emigrated from Ireland during the 1956-61 period, the number declined by nearly three-fourths to a total of about 54,000 in 1966-71. In more recent years, emigration has slowed even further chiefly because of high unemployment in the United Kingdom, falling at last below the rate of natural increase.

The annual rate of natural increase, in turn, rose by 0.1 per 1,000 during the 1965-74 period. In 1966 the rate was 1.0 percent and in 1975, 1.1 percent. With the birth rate remaining relatively stable at about 22 per 1,000 population the increase stemmed largely from a decline in the death rate. In 1966 the death rate was 12 per 1,000 population—in 1975, 11 per 1,000.

Another distinctive aspect of the Irish experience was the low rate of marriage and the high rate of fertility among women who did marry. Since World War II, however, marriage rates have been on the increase and by now have been virtually transformed. Between 1946 and 1969, the median age of bridegrooms fell from 32 to 26 and of brides from 27 to 24 years. The marriage rate per 1,000 unmarried population aged 15-64 rose from 18.5 in 1961 to 24.2 in 1969. And there has been a radical fall in the proportion of single persons in the age group 25-34. The Irish marriage rate is still one of the lowest in the world, and there is every likelihood that it will rise still further.

Along with the increase in marriages, marital fertility has fallen dramatically. In 1963 there began a downturn in the number of women with five or more children, and by 1970 the number of sixth or later births per family was almost 30 percent below the 1968 level. Even so, the Irish family remains very large by European standards. In 1970, 15 percent of Irish live births were to mothers who had five or more children compared with 2.9 percent in England and Wales.

Irish demographer Brendan M. Walsh has linked the increase in marriage rate to the decline in fertility on the basis that the traditional high fertility of Irish marriages acted as a deterrent to young people contemplating marriage. According to this argument, a reduction in family size implies a reduction in economic costs of the married state and, hence, tends to stimulate the marriage rate. Walsh noted, however, that with a birth rate of more than 21 per 1,000 people, Ireland's net reproduction rate is still the highest in Western Europe and is likely to remain high for a considerable time to come. The key determinant of future Irish fertility, he believes, will be the final family size of couples who are currently marrying at what is by Irish standards an early age.

The dramatic change in fertility patterns in the 1960's is generally attributed to the spread in use of oral contraceptives. Although the Irish desire for population growth had long been accompanied by bans on sale or importation of contraceptives, the pill became available in Ireland in the 1960's on medical prescription for menstrual cycle regulation. Following a Supreme Court decision in late 1973 that it was unconstitutional to prevent the importation of contraceptives, it has become possible to distribute contraceptives free of charge. Sales, however, remain illegal.

But not all is quiet on the subject. Birth control and relevant Irish laws have become more and more frequently a center of controversy in recent years. The public discussion that has centered on contraception, however, has rarely involved explicitly demographic arguments. Proponents of changing restrictive laws have stated their case in terms of the rights of individuals and the sectarian nature of existing legislation. Ecclesiastic conservatives form a large segment of the opposition to contraception.

There has been no significant public demand or pressure in Ireland for a change in the absolute prohibition on induced abortion. Nonetheless, evidence has become available that, since the 1968 Abortion Act in Britain, increasing numbers of Irish women have gone to Britain to procure abortion.

Despite lack of official support, family planning activities have achieved a beachhead in Ireland. In 1969, a private nonprofit company with a grant from the International Planned Parenthood Federation opened a family planning clinic in Dublin, and a second clinic was opened in 1971. By 1972, over 7,000 patients had passed through these clinics, but patients generally have to make their own arrangements to obtain the supplies necessary to implement the advice obtained. There are now 18 Roman Catholic Marriage Advisory Centers in Ireland, which deal with all aspects of marriage counseling, but advice is given only on church-approved methods of family planning.

Another area of public concern centers on correcting what is regarded as a regional imbalance of population development. Almost one-third of the country's population now lives in the Dublin region, and over 40 percent of the country's natural population increase occurs among Dublin residents. Accordingly, the Government has adopted the tactic of using incentive schemes "to send industry to depressed areas and as far as possible to keep the rural population where it is."

Italy

The population of Italy increased by about 7 percent during the 1965-75 decade to reach a total of 55.8 million in mid-1975. This was 3.8 million more than the 1965 level of 52 million.

The annual rate of natural increase slowed moderately during the period, dropping from 0.9 percent in 1965 to 0.6 percent in 1974. The decline stemmed entirely from a drop in the birth rate. Births during the period declined from 19 per 1,000 people to just below 16. Mortality held relatively steady at about 10 per 1,000 throughout the period.

The per capita gross national product of Italy increased between 1965 and 1973 by 40 percent. In 1965 it was $1,800 per capita and in 1973, $2,520 per capita.

For a century or more, Italy has been a country of net emigration with the outflow in some periods offsetting around 40 percent of the natural increase. During the 1965-75 decade, however, net emigration slowed to about 1 per 1,000 people, offsetting about 10 percent of the natural increase.

The most acute population problems for Italy have to do with marked regional differentials in fertility and an intense rate of internal migration. In the economically less developed southern part of the country, fertility traditionally has ranged from 30 to 50 percent above the replacement level since 1930, whereas it has been consistently below replacement in the northern and central sections. The southern sector has experienced extensive migration to the north and other countries. During the 1961-71 decade, net migration from the south amounted to 2.2 million, of which 1.2 million was to northern and central Italy.

Fueled by rural-urban migration, the 11 largest urban areas have grown from a population of 7.4 million in 1951 (15.6 percent of the total) to 10.4 million in 1971 (19.3 percent). Turin and Milan gained, through in-migration, more than 26,000 inhabitants per year from 1961 to 1971. Rome proper has gained more than 28,000 annually.

Although the country's birth rate is relatively low, there is no official family planning policy or program in Italy. Despite increasing public attention to population problems, religious and legislative factors have inhibited population action.

The Government under Mussolini advocated a fast increase of population as a means of increasing national power. From 1926 to World War II, a set of coordinated legislative and social measures were adopted in an effort to achieve a sustained population growth. Emigration was discouraged, nuptiality and fertility were stimulated through a broad range of economic incentives, and the unity of the family was sustained in an effort to prevent the kinds of changes which were leading in other countries to the emancipation of women. The system of family allowances continues to the present day, but because the amounts of the allowances have remained fixed for a long time, their value has been eroded by inflation and they offer little inducement for added births. In fact, the earlier objective of rapid increase is no longer pursued as a matter of national policy.

In 1971, the Constitutional Court struck down the law which made it a crime to distribute or sell contraceptives or to purvey information about them. Sterilization is strictly forbidden in all cases. More recently, a number of major political parties have introduced parliamentary bills aimed at changing the law restricting abortion. At present the Criminal Code calls for severe punishment of people who cause abortion for women who take recourse to it (except for cases in which a pregnant woman is in danger of losing her life). Some of the bills introduced are aimed at removing the punishments now prescribed, some are aimed at a thorough freedom for abortion, while others would allow abortion in more situations than is presently allowed.

A Planned Parenthood Association is active in Italy, offering advisory services through several city and suburban centers. A planned parenthood service also has been opened in the Institute of Obstetrics and Gynecology of the University of Rome. All methods of contraception are now considered to be available, and it is estimated about 2 percent of women between the ages of 15 and 44 take oral contraceptives, and 10-20 percent of the married women between ages 21 and 45 in the large towns.

Luxembourg

The population of Luxembourg in mid-1975 numbered 358,000, up 26,000 from 1965. The 1965-75 increase was about 1,000 less than in the previous decade, mostly reflecting a sharp decrease in the birth rate since about 1967.

The annual rate of natural increase in 1965 was 0.4 percent but by 1974 the birth rate had decreased to a level slightly below the death rate. The birth rate in 1974 was 11 per 1,000 population, down from 16 per 1,000 in 1965. The death rate in 1974 was 12 per 1,000 people, up from 1965. After many years of moderate population growth, the present negative rate of natural increase is a matter of considerable concern to many leaders and institutions in the country.

The per capita gross national product of Luxembourg increased between 1965 and 1973 by about 25 percent. In 1965 it was $4,170 per capita and in 1973, $5,230 per capita.

The penal code of Luxembourg strictly forbids abortion and propaganda about contraceptives, although the incidence of abortion is reported to be significant.

Support for the Luxembourg Family Planning Association is given by the Ministries of Family and Welfare, Education and Public Health and by the City Council.

Netherlands

The population of the Netherlands—one of the most densely inhabited countries in the world—increased by 11 percent during the 1965-75 decade. As of mid-July 1975, the population was estimated at 13.7 million, an increase of about 1.4 million over the 1965 level of approximately 12.3 million.

The increase, however, was 11 percent smaller than that for the previous decade, indicating a slowing of population growth. The annual rate of natural increase dropped by one-half during the 1965-74 period, declining from a level of 1.2 percent in 1965 to 0.6 percent in 1974. The decline stemmed entirely from a lower birth rate. Births in 1974 were 14 per 1,000 population as compared with 20 per 1,000 in 1965. The mortality rate was unchanged at about 8.

The per capita gross national product of the Netherlands increased between 1965 and 1973 by about 36 percent. In 1965 it was $3,260 per capita and in 1973, $4,440 per capita.

Population density as of 1971 was estimated at 323 people per square kilometer. Such high density derived in part from the fact that until shortly before the onset of the 1965-75 decade, the Netherlands had one of the highest birth rates in Europe. Delayed industrialization and a strong religious and family life contributed to highly pronatalist attitudes until that time. The year 1964, however, marked the beginning of a rapid decrease in fertility. By then, according to demographers Philip van Praag and Louis Lohlé-Tart, the Netherlands had become a modern industrialized country with changing attitudes and circumstances.

Oral contraceptives, introduced during 1963-64, were one factor influencing the change in fertility. Others included the rapid increase in levels of living, better education, increased resort to induced abortion, and infrastructural problems such as industrialization, urbanization, roads, spatial planning, and second residences.

Overcrowding is thus an important political concern. Among the measures being used to deal with overpopulation and unequal density are internal redistribution of population, territorial increase (by reclaiming land from the sea), and subsidized emigration. Nevertheless, during the 1960's, a policy of immigration was developed in order to cope with a shortage of unskilled manpower. With more than 50 percent of the Dutch working population occupied in the services sector, foreign workers have been needed to perform the jobs local workers are not prepared to assume. Approximately 1.8 percent of the Dutch salaried population is estimated to be made up of foreign workers.

Other measures to help deal with the demographic situation in the Netherlands include the liberalization of contraception. A 1969 law repealed the prohibition against display and sale of contraceptives to minors under the age of eighteen. Since then, most contraceptive devices have been freely available. Municipalities have the right to issue implementary bylaws but not to prohibit such devices. Parliament in 1971 issued a decree ordering the

inclusion of oral contraceptives, diaphragms, and IUD's under the public medical benefits scheme. As of mid-1972, all people under a specified income level are able to obtain, on medical advice, any such contraceptives free of charge.

Although abortion remains technically illegal, several abortion clinics are allowed to operate without interference and, about 1973, performed some 20,000 abortions annually. Increasing public and political pressure is expected to result shortly in official liberalization of abortion. In 1972 the Government established a Royal Commission on Population Problems to study the overall population situation and formulate a policy for future development.

The Dutch Planned Parenthood Association has over 60 contraceptive clinics. Family planning services are available through most of the clinics, university hospitals, and physicians.

Norway

The population of Norway in mid-1975 is estimated at 4 million, an increase of 8 percent from the 1965 level of 3.7 million. The 1965-75 increase was about 1 percent less than in the preceding decade.

The rate of natural increase per year was 0.4 percent in 1974, down sharply from the 1965 rate of 0.8 percent. Contributing to the decline were both a decrease in the birth rate and a small increase in mortality. The birth rate in 1974 was 15 per 1,000 population, compared with 17.5 in 1965. The death rate in 1974 was 10 per 1,000, up from 9.1 in 1965.

The per capita gross national product of Norway increased between 1965 and 1973 by about 34 percent. In 1965 it was $3,530 per capita and in 1973, $4,740 per capita.

The discovery of oil in Norwegian waters of the North Sea bears significant implications for Norway's future economic and social growth. Although the full effects of this new-found source of wealth have yet to become evident, the Government is taking steps to minimize the possibility of adverse ecological and social developments.

The social welfare system of Norway, like that of the other Scandinavian countries, is highly developed and supportive of family planning activities. The system includes health insurance and child and maternity allowances. Education is free and compulsory for ages 7-16.

The Government provides family planning services through its network of public health clinics and gives assistance to the Family Planning Association, founded in 1969. Assisting the Association are the Ministries of Social Affairs, Health, Family and Consumer Affairs, and Education and Ecclesiastic Affairs.

There is no law against contraception in Norway. Abortion is permitted on socio-medical indications before 12 weeks of gestation have elapsed. If a woman is married, her husband's consent is required. Male and female sterilization also are permitted on the basis of broad medical indications.

All methods of contraception are available and oral contraceptives are manufactured. In 1971, 8 percent of women aged 15-44 years were reported to be using oral contraceptives. The abortion ratio in the same year was reported to be 16 abortions per 100 live births.

Compulsory sex education is included in school curriculums. The Family Planning Association organizes sex education courses for teachers at all levels and is producing a program for teachers in cooperation with the University of Oslo. Meanwhile the health services of Norway have produced a film entitled "Family Planning and Contraception," which has been released in commercial cinemas.

Planned parenthood is included in the curriculums of the medical schools and in schools for nurses and physiotherapists. In addition, the Family Planning Association organizes training courses for teachers and pharmacists.

The Norwegian Government gives international assistance and grants to the International Planned Parenthood Federation (IPPF). In 1973, its grant to IPPF amounted to $1,180,000. Through 1974 its total multilateral assistance to U.N. population programs totaled $9,690,257.

Poland

The population of Poland reached about 34 million in mid-1975. This represented an increase of 8 percent, or 2.8 million, over the 1965 level of about 31.2 million. During the previous decade the increase had totaled about 3.9 million.

Moderately pronatalist policies were in effect in the 1965-75 period, adopted in response to a precipitous drop in birth rates during the previous decade. Whereas births in 1955 were at the level of about 30 per 1,000 population, they had fallen by 1968 to 16.2 per 1,000. Concerned at the possibility of a continuing decline, steps were taken which helped to raise the birth rate to 18 per 1,000 by 1974. Mortality during the decade was relatively stable at around 7 to 8 deaths per 1,000 population.

The per capita gross national product of Poland increased between 1965 and 1973 by about 83 percent. In 1965 it was $1,140 per capita and in 1973, $2,090 per capita.

Sharply fluctuating growth patterns and policies have characterized the population since World War II. The period from 1945 to the early 1950's was marked by population growth and an official pronatalist policy. This policy stemmed most importantly from Poland's need to compensate for the drastic population decrease caused by the war and its program to populate western territories acquired under the Potsdam Agreement of 1945.

The period from the late 1950's to the late 1960's, however, was marked by the introduction of measures to curb the "baby boom" which was thought to be a main cause of the economic difficulties of the mid-1950's. In this period an intensive campaign for family planning and contraception was conducted through mass media, hospitals, and clinics. Abortion also became widely available with the Abortion Act of 1956.

From the late 1960's to 1975 there has been widespread public discussion of population matters and the adoption of a more pronatalist policy. Measures in line with this policy include (1) efforts to improve housing for young couples, (2) extension of part-time employment for women, (3) improvement of maternity and child care, particularly for working women, (4) an appreciable increase in the family allowance for those who have more than two children, and (5) elevation of the social status of motherhood. Also, the social welfare system includes health insurance, child and maternity allowances, and paid maternity leave.

At the same time, the Government provides free family planning services to people covered by health insurance. Services are available from over 3,000 clinics throughout the country. A law of 1969 requires physicians to offer contraceptive advice after delivery and abortion.

The Government supports the Family Planning Association which is affiliated with the International Planned Parenthood Federation (IPPF). The Association has clinics of its own in Warsaw and Krakow and branches throughout the country. Through its own company, the Association manufactures cervical caps and spermicide. Diaphragms, IUD's, and oral contraceptives also are available. The Association also has its own publishing department, producing a quarterly journal, and literature on planned parenthood, sex education, infant care, hygiene and infertility.

Despite increasing availability of modern contraception, a country-wide survey of over 15,000 married women in 1972 revealed that while half were currently practicing contraception, coitus interruptus and rhythm remained by far the leading methods.

Portugal

The population of Portugal has decreased almost 6 percent since 1965, falling from 9 million in 1965 to 8.5 million in 1975. The decline more than offset a 5-percent increase in the previous decade. The rate of natural increase in 1974 was 0.8 percent per year, compared with 1.3 percent in 1965. The birth rate in 1974 was 19 per 1,000 population, down from 23 in 1965. The death rate in 1974 was 11 per 1,000 people, up from 10 in 1965.

The population decrease stemmed from net emigration to labor-short countries of Western Europe and to Brazil. Too recent to be included in the figures, however, has been the recent flow to Portugal of thousands of migrants from strife-torn Angola.

The per capita gross national product of Portugal increased between 1965 and 1973 by about 72 percent. In 1965 it was $760 per capita and in 1973, $1,310 per capita.

A new Government program provides family planning services within the 40 clinics of the Health Department Services. Such services are provided in cooperation with the Family Planning Association and are available primarily in the suburbs and some rural areas. All methods of contraception are available at the various clinics and at the Maternity and University Hospitals in Lisbon.

The advertising of contraceptives is illegal. Sterilization is prohibited except when life is in danger. Abortion also is illegal, even on medical indications.

The Government maintains a social welfare fund. Since January of 1974, education is free and compulsory for ages 6 to 14 years. The Government plans to expand higher education, doubling the number of universities from 4 to 8.

Romania

Between 1965 and 1975 the population of Romania rose some 11 percent, from 19 million to 21 million. While the death rate remained unchanged at 9 per 1,000 population (1965 to 1974), the birth rate climbed by a third, from 15 to 20 per 1,000, resulting in a 1.1 percent annual rate of natural increase in 1974.

Romania's population data fail to reveal the dramatic story of an abrupt, though short-lived, fertility change clearly wrought by Government policy—a change probably unique in demographic history. Following the example of Soviet Russia 2 years earlier, Romania adopted in 1957 what quickly became recognized as the world's most liberal abortion policy. Abortion solely at a woman's request in the first trimester of pregnancy became available on an outpatient basis at hospitals throughout the country. No bureaucratic procedures were involved, thus safeguarding secrecy, and costs were low. Despite some official efforts to encourage modern contraception, the number of abortions rose sharply, reaching a total of over 1 million in 1965, or four abortions per live birth.

Meanwhile, the birth rate dropped from 22.9 per 1,000 population in 1957 to 14.3 in 1966. Alarmed at the implications for the country's future population and women's health, the Government reversed its abortion policy in October 1966. Legal abortion was restricted to cases involving risk to the mother's life or of fetal defects, rape, women over 45 (lowered to 40 in 1972) or supporting four children, and to cases involving an explicitly defined set of physical and mental conditions. Also, family allowances were increased, and lump-sum payments equivalent to $85 (now $181) were instituted for each birth beginning with the third child. Further, a childlessness tax on persons aged over 25 was reintroduced, divorce was sharply curtailed, and official importation of pills and IUD's was discontinued.

The effect on the birth rate was immediate. From a low of 12.8 births per 1,000 population in December 1966 (1 month after the new law took effect), it tripled to 39.9 in September 1967. Thereafter, however, the rate receded slowly on an almost month-to-month basis, reaching 17.2 per 1,000 population in December 1973.

Legal abortions were reported to have dropped to 51,700 in 1967. Registered abortions then mounted again to 381,000 in 1972. Included in these totals is a disproportionate proportion of "spontaneous" abortions treated in hospitals. This and a striking rise in maternal deaths associated with abortion (from 19 per 1 million women aged 15 to 45 in 1966 to 69 per million in 1971) suggest that illegal abortions contributed to the resumption of falling birth rates after 1967. Pills and IUD's remain officially restricted to use only on medical indication and under gynecological supervision.

The official Government population policy has been to institute a wide mix of measures, including family incentive payments aimed at achieving reasonable population growth and ensuring the well-being of individuals. Also, there are monthly allowances for children of workers up to 16 years of age, state aid to families with four or more children, a 30-percent income tax reduction for families with three or more children, paid maternity leave of 112 days, and optional halftime work at half pay without loss of seniority for all employed women with children under age six.

In 1966, 73 percent of all Romanian women aged 15 to 49 were employed. The slight upturn in the birth rate from 18 in 1973 to 20 in 1974 suggests, however, that a relatively abundant labor supply and increasingly attractive incentives may be encouraging more women to opt for larger families over full-time employment.

Spain

The population of Spain in mid-1975 was 35.6 million, an increase of 3.5 million, or 11 percent, over the 1965 level of nearly 32.1 million. This growth was 24 percent greater than that of the previous decade when the increase was 2.8 million.

The rate of natural increase in 1974 is estimated at 1.1 percent per year, down slightly from a decade earlier. Whereas the birth rate in 1965 was about 21 per 1,000 population, it had dropped by 1974 to 19. The mortality rate in the same period declined from 9 per 1,000 people to 8.

The per capita gross national product of Spain increased between 1965 and 1973 by about 53 percent. In 1965 it was $1,130 per capita and in 1973, $1,730 per capita.

Spain traditionally has been a country of heavy emigration, in earlier years primarily to Latin America, the Philippines, and North Africa. Beginning in 1960, however, continental emigration has become a demographic, economic, social and political phenomenon of considerable consequence. Estimates indicate that between 1959 and 1970, 1.74 million Spaniards left their homeland and established themselves in other European countries. Some surveys show, however, that up to 80 percent of these returned to Spain within 3 years.

Spain also has been a traditionally pronatalist country, officially opposed to measures for fertility control. Equating population growth with national aspirations for "great power" status, the Government

for centuries has sought consistently to increase Spanish fertility levels.

In addition to the pronatalist policies, Spain also was, for many years, characterized by a strongly rural society, relatively low social mobility, and limited industrialization—factors which have tended to contribute to high fertility levels in other countries. However, Spanish marital fertility has not been markedly higher than that of other Western European populations, a puzzle which demographers find difficult to explain.

There are no organized family planning services in the country, although such services are available privately and to a limited extent in hospitals. The sale of contraceptives is illegal, but condoms are available as preventives against venereal disease. Oral contraceptives are available on prescription from private physicians as cycle regulators. No precise means of determining the usage of contraceptives in Spain is available, but one Spanish demographer—Salustiano del Campo—estimates that perhaps 12.2 percent of all women between the ages of 15 and 49 may be using pills. A 1973 survey of women about the methods they believe are most used for birth control indicates that the most well-known method is the pill but that the most used in Spain, in the opinion of those interviewed, are condoms and withdrawal.

Abortion is condemned in Spain as a crime deserving of harsh sanctions. Demographers such as Charles F. Gallagher suggest, however, that extensive resort to illegal induced abortion, together with the practice of coitus interruptus, may go far to explain the absence of a higher fertility rate in Spain.

Sweden

The population of Sweden in mid-1975 was 8.2 million—an increase of about 6 percent or nearly 460,000 over the 1965 total of 7.7 million. Upwards of one-half of the increase came from immigration.

The Swedish birth rate has been consistently among the world's lowest since the 1930's. Without the higher fertility of post-World War II immigrants and, until recently, a declining death rate, the surplus of births over deaths would be wiped out, leading eventually to a decreasing population.

The per capita gross national product of Sweden increased between 1965 and 1973 by about 22 percent. In 1965 it was $5,050 per capita and in 1973, $6,160 per capita.

Family planning is regarded as of great importance in Sweden, although for reasons other than that of avoiding a population increase. Here the basic assumption behind family planning is that every child should be wanted and taken care of properly. Also, family planning is widely regarded as a basic right, essential to personal freedom and dignity.

As an indication of the importance of immigration to the Swedish balance of population, it is estimated that during the post-World War II period, immigration has accounted for roughly 40 percent of the country's total population growth. In 1969 and 1970, the net gain from immigration was larger than the natural increase (roughly 60 percent of total increase). Today, one out of every 13 Swedish inhabitants is an immigrant. Of the more than 600,000 immigrants now living in Sweden, about 200,000 have become Swedish citizens.

Immigrants are important to the Swedish population balance for more than their initial numbers, however. Age-specific fertility rates are about 20 percent higher for the foreign-born than for the rest of the population.

The highest rate of net immigration was registered in 1970 when more than 48,000 foreign nationals entered Sweden. The greatest deficit in net immigration was reached in 1972 when emigration exceeded inflow by more than 11,000. The numbers in both cases were made up chiefly of foreign-born laborers. Immigration to Sweden is dominated by Finns, the proportion varying from 30 to 60 percent, and about half of all immigrants have been in the 20-34 age bracket, males being in the majority.

Meanwhile, the annual rate of natural increase declined during the 1965-74 period from a level of 0.6 percent to 0.2 percent. The decline stemmed in part from a decrease in the birth rate and in part from a small increase in the mortality rate. The birth rate declined from a level of 16 per 1,000 people to 13. The mortality rate increased from a level of 10 per 1,000 population to 11.

The Swedish Government provides family planning services through its extensive public health network. It also provides assistance to the Family Planning Association which runs two clinics. All methods of contraception are available. Gradually liberalized and increasingly broadly interpreted since 1938, the abortion law was changed in 1974 to permit abortion solely at a woman's request during the first trimester of pregnancy. Sterilization on request for any resident aged 25 or over was legalized in May 1975. Sex education was introduced in the school system in the 1940's and made compulsory in 1956. Such education contains information on human responsibility, basic physiology, and sexual life, and aims to counteract shortcomings arising from ignorance and thereby promote a harmonious relationship between individuals.

A recent investigation shows that there is widespread use of different contraceptive means and methods in the country. According to a 1969 study of legal aspects of abortion, some 350,000 children would have been born in Sweden had no form of birth control been practiced. The actual number born was 108,000.

Sweden has long been active in the international debate on the population issue and has advocated that the United Nations organization should play a leading role in this field. It also has been active in assisting developing countries with support for family planning activities.

The budget for population activities abroad has increased from some $200,000 annually in 1960 to approximately $15 million in 1972. Roughly half of the assistance has been provided on a bilateral basis. It has mainly consisted of contraceptives, clinical and printing equipment, vehicles, audiovisual materials, the provision of experts and, to a lesser extent, financial support to national family planning programs. The other half has consisted of resources channeled through international organizations and to applied research.

Switzerland

The population of Switzerland increased by 11 percent during the 1965-75 decade, totaling about 6.3 million (official estimates) at the end of 1975 as compared with nearly 5.9 million in January 1966. The 400,000 increase was about one-half the increment of the previous decade.

The Swiss Bureau of Statistics reports that the rate of natural increase dropped from a level of 0.9 percent per year in 1966 to 0.4 percent in 1974. It states that the birth rate in 1974 was 13 per 1,000 population, down from 19 in 1965, and that the death rate in 1974 was 9 per 1,000 people, the same as in 1965.

The per capita gross national product of Switzerland increased between 1965 and 1973 by about 27 percent. In 1965 it was $5,000 per capita and in 1973, $6,350 per capita.

The Public Health Department of the Canton de Vaud became an affiliate member of the International Planned Parenthood Federation (IPPF) in 1957. Family planning services therefore are available through this Department and the University Hospitals of Basel, Geneva, and Lausanne. The Federal Government has no official policy for planned parenthood.

The Schweizerische Gesellschaft fur Familienplanung (SGF) in Basel also promotes planned parenthood through general practitioners and other medical services. Pro Familia, a Federal family welfare organization, is a corporate member of SGF.

The Public Health Department in the Canton de Vaud encourages planned parenthood for the protection of the family and to combat abortion. It also publishes sex education literature. Lectures are given by physicians, family counsellors, nurses, and social workers cooperating with the Pro Familia center on various aspects of planned parenthood and sex education. Sex education also is included in the school curriculums in the Canton de Geneva.

There is no law against contraception in Switzerland although local religious influences sometimes make the obtaining of advice difficult. Abortion is available on broad medical indications in some Cantons, and a large number of women from neighboring countries avail themselves of it. Availability of contraceptive advice from physicians depends upon the attitudes of individual physicians.

Through 1975, Switzerland had pledged some $190,000 in assistance to the multilateral population programs of the United Nations.

United Kingdom

The 1965-75 decade in the United Kingdom was marked by a slow increase in population, an extension of immigration restrictions, and expansion of Government activities in the family planning field.

The population in mid-1975 was 56 million, an increase of 3 percent (1.7 million) over the 1965 level of 54.3 million. The annual rate of natural increase declined from a level of 0.6 percent per 1,000 population in 1965 to 0.1 percent in 1974. The decline stemmed almost entirely from a drop in the birth rate, the level of 18 births per 1,000 population in 1965 falling to about 13 in 1974. The mortality rate held relatively stable throughout the period at about 12 per 1,000 people.

The per capita gross national product of the United Kingdom increased between 1965 and 1973 by about 21 percent. In 1965 it was $2,580 per capita and in 1973, $3,120 per capita.

Although the United Kingdom is among the most densely populated countries (only Bangladesh, Japan, the Netherlands, Belgium, and a few island states

are more so), Government population measures have been more concerned with matters of distribution than with growth.

Since 1930, and more particularly since World War II, the Government has aided areas of high unemployment and encouraged the growth of industry there by means of tax, loan, and other fiscal inducements. Other means of encouraging and guiding effective movement of population and industry have included the founding of 33 new towns now housing more than 1.7 million people. In England and Wales, 11 of 23 new towns are designed to relieve housing problems in Greater London.

A large net immigration during the years 1960-62 (about 388,000 people) led in 1962 to the first act to control immigration from British Commonwealth countries and contributed, in part, to a growing concern during the 1960's with the problem of population increase as a whole. The Commonwealth Immigrant Act of 1968 extended the restrictions applying to Commonwealth citizens, including the requirement making entry of each person subject to possession of an employment voucher. European Community nationals, however, are now able to move freely between member states, including the United Kingdom and need only a residence permit. However, net migration has been outward since 1963. During the years 1970-72, for example, total immigration was 201,000 and emigration 240,000.

The Government has adopted no formal population policy, but a body of legislation was developed during the 1960's concerning family planning, abortion, and women's rights. These measures, while not enacted for demographic purposes, can be expected to have a demographic effect.

The Family Planning Act of 1967 empowered local health authorities to give contraceptive advice, without regard to marital status, for non-medical as well as medical reasons, and to use voluntary organizations such as the Family Planning Association as agents. Impetus for further expansion of Government activities in the family planning field stemmed, in part, from the recommendations of a Government-sponsored Population Panel which began an inquiry into national population problems in 1971 and issued a report in 1973.

General conclusions of the panel included the view that "the concept of optimum population is impossible to define in terms which provide any useful basis for policy making" but "a slower rate of increase is clearly preferable to a faster," and "the sooner we can approach the conditions necessary for a sustainable stationary population the better . . ." The panel indicated that drastic Government action might not be needed, but that efforts to reduce unplanned pregnancies would be desirable. Sterilization and abortion services, it held, should continue to be available.

The panel also made a number of recommendations on research and recommended the dissemination of information about family planning and about population size and growth. It suggested that the first positive step toward a population policy be development of comprehensive family planning services as an integral part of the National Health Service.

In 1974 family planning was made a normal part of health service arrangements, and the Government decided it would provide free family planning advice and make supplies of contraceptives available free of charge for both medical and nonmedical reasons.

In 1974 the Family Planning Association acted as the agency providing family planning services for 98 of the 113 new area health authorities. Of 160 programs offering free consultation and free supplies for medical reasons, 131 also gave free consultation for nonmedical reasons (and 38 of the 131 gave free supplies in addition).

Abortion on grounds other than the preservation of a woman's life was first legalized in the 1967 Abortion Act, effective in 1968. (The Act did not extend to Northern Ireland.) The Act states that a doctor may terminate a pregnancy if he and another doctor consider: (a) that the continuance of the pregnancy would involve risk to the life of the pregnant woman or injury to the physical or mental health of the pregnant woman or any existing children of her family greater than if the pregnancy were terminated; or (b) that there is a substantial risk that if the child were born it would suffer from such physical or mental abnormalities as to be seriously handicapped.

The number of legally induced abortions in the United Kingdom since the 1967 Act came into effect rose from 68,000 in 1968 to a peak of 176,000 in 1973, with abortions performed for nonresidents comprising almost a third of the total by 1972. However, abortions dropped in 1974. In England and Wales between 1973 and 1974, abortions declined from 110,600 to 109,400 among residents and from 56,600 to 53,700 among nonresidents.

A committee appointed by the Government in 1971 to review the effect of the 1967 Abortion Act reported in 1974 (Lane Committee, 1974). After receiving evidence from several hundred organizations and individuals, the committee recognized that responding to the demand had imposed considerable strain on the National Health Service and that there were inequalities in obtaining services. However, the committee's unanimous conclusion was that "the gains facilitated by the Act have much outweighed any disadvantages for which it has been criticized."

The 1973 report of the Population Panel made population projections to the year 2011 based on low, medium, and high population growth rates. The low model assumed a fertility rate that would decline by about 2.5 percent a year until 1977 to reach a gross reproduction rate of 1.02 and a net reproduction rate of 1.0 (approximately the replacement level). In such an eventuality, the population of the United Kingdom by 2001 would increase by about 12.2 percent, averaging 2.8-3.0 percent per decade and reach a total of 60.7 million.

Assuming a medium growth rate of 4.1-6.0 percent per decade, the population would increase by about 22.2 percent and reach a total of 66.1 million in 2011. With a high growth rate of about 5.6-10.7 percent per decade, the population would increase by about 37.7 percent, a 2011 total of 74.3 million.

The United Kingdom entered the field of population assistance to developing countries by providing bilateral (country-to-country) aid in 1964 and multilateral aid in 1967 (through international agencies).

A specialized unit, the Population Bureau, was established within the Ministry of Overseas Development to increase the capacity of the United Kingdom to give development assistance for population work by promoting training and research. In the fiscal year 1974-75, bilateral population assistance totaled an estimated $2.5 million and multilateral assistance totaled about $3.5 million. Together with other population assistance, the total for the United Kingdom in fiscal year 1974-75 came to more than $6.1 million, representing 1 percent of all British assistance programs abroad.

Assistance is also given by private agencies such as Oxfam and the British Family Planning Association.

Facilities for population training and research, directed mainly toward development assistance, have been increasing. The David Owen Centre for Population Growth Studies was set up at University College, Cardiff, in 1972 as an international and interdisciplinary training and research center. A Centre for Overseas Population Studies is being established at the London School of Hygiene and Tropical Medicine to provide training, research, and consultation services on population for developing countries.

U.S.S.R.

The population of the Soviet Union—the third most populous country in the world—increased just over 10 percent during the 1965-75 decade to reach an estimated total of 254.3 million in mid-1975. This was about 23.4 million over the mid-1965 level of 230.9 million—an increase nearly one-third less than in the previous decade.

The annual rate of natural increase declined moderately from a level of 1.1 percent in 1965 to about 0.9 percent in 1974. The decline stemmed almost entirely from a moderate increase in mortality. During the period the birth rate decreased from about 18 per 1,000 (1965) population to 17.0 in 1969, and then apparently rose again to about 18 in 1974. The mortality rate—still one of the lowest in the world—increased during the same period from about 7 per 1,000 population to 9, due primarily to the gradual aging of the population.

The per capita gross national product of the U.S.S.R. more than doubled between 1965 and 1973. In 1965 it was $1,020 per capita and in 1973, $2,300.

The Soviet Union has been a country of rapid demographic change. Official statistics indicate that as compared with 1913 levels, the birth rate by 1973 had been reduced by over half as had the mortality rate. Average life expectancy has more than doubled—from 32 to 70 years.* Most of this change occurred in the 35-year period ending in the late 1940's. The present-day pattern, characterized by a low overall level of births and a low mortality rate, has prevailed ever since.

Widespread differences in the pattern of growth exist between various parts of the country, however. Birth rates are relatively low in Latvia, Estonia, the Ukraine, the Russian Federation, Georgia, and Byelorussia—areas accounting for nearly 80 percent of the total population of the U.S.S.R.

Urbanization in the U.S.S.R. has been rapid for several decades. In 1974 the urban population accounted for 60 percent of the total, compared with 18 percent in 1913. This increase was mainly due to migration from rural areas, reflecting in part the rapid growth of industry in the Soviet Union. Between 1926 and 1971, 955 new towns and cities appeared. Cities with populations over 100,000 increased from 31 to 222, while the number of their dwellers increased from 9.5 million to 77.5 million.

Over the period between the censuses of 1959 and 1970, the urban population of the U.S.S.R.

had grown by 14.6 million due to natural increase, by 5 million due to conversion of rural settlements into urban ones because of their industrial development, and by more than 16 million on account of migration from country to town. There has been relatively little international migration for half a century.

The Soviet Union has no announced population policy, but a study issued by the Joint Economic Committee of the U.S. Congress ("Soviet Economic Prospects for the Seventies," issued June 27, 1973) comments upon growing Soviet concerns which might lead to such a policy. The study reports that the overall decrease and regional imbalances in the population growth rate have been often noted in the press and academic circles and are subjects of increasing discussion and analysis. In the mid-1960's, the serious study of demography was allowed to resume after a lapse of nearly 30 years, and a number of research institutes and academic centers are now engaged in population research.

Numerous studies have shown that the fertility of Soviet women is being increasingly affected by the desire for small families. Included in the factors responsible are urbanization, shortage of housing, industrialization, increased demands for education, and greater participation of women in political, economic, and cultural activities. The ready availability of abortion—available on demand since the early 1920's except for the period 1936-55—and the increasing availability of contraceptives have made it relatively easy for Soviet women to control numbers of births and accommodate to new patterns of life.

Surveys designed to determine desired and actual size of the family have been conducted in recent years by various institutions. In 1966 the Demographic Laboratory of the Scientific Research Institute, Central Statistical Administration, surveyed 1,462 women employed in several light industry enterprises in Moscow. The results indicated that well over one-third of the respondents wanted only one child or none while 95.5 percent wanted two or less.

The desired number of children in other areas, however, is significantly higher than that cited for the city of Moscow, particularly in the rural areas. A 1969 nationwide survey of some 36,000 married women under age 40 revealed the average ideal number of children to be 2.89. The average intended family size for the whole of U.S.S.R. was 2.42.

The total size of population reportedly is not of as much concern to researchers and officials as are the long-term implications for the numbers of potential

*Central Statistical Board, the Council of Ministers of the U.S.S.R. *The U.S.S.R. in Figures for 1973: Statistical Handbook.* Moscow: Statistinka Publishers, 1974.

mothers and of entrants into the work force. Since its earliest years, the Soviet Government has paid little attention to population policy, for until recently its labor supply was ample and at no time has there been a problem of overpopulation.

In 1955 a Government decree liberalized the 1936 prohibition against abortion, stipulating that abortions must be performed only by qualified personnel in medical installations.

Under current regulations, an abortion is not to be performed if the health of a woman is endangered or if a previous pregnancy was terminated within the preceding 6 months. Reportedly, it is now the usual practice that a gynecologist discusses with each woman the reasons for her application for abortion and warns her of possible adverse consequences. In cases of social difficulty a lawyer is consulted. If the pregnant woman persists in her request for abortion, her application must be approved. Termination is performed in a hospital at very low cost or free. Reliable data on the number of abortions performed annually are not available for the country as a whole, but the total is believed to be very large.

Reports on the extent of contraceptive practice in the Soviet Union vary widely. According to the Congressional study various types of contraceptives are available, including the pill and the IUD, although the condom reportedly is the most widely used.

Officially, demographic policy in the Soviet Union is regarded as one of the elements of the socioeconomic policy of the state. According to Soviet officials, the nation's population policy is designed to improve the conditions of life and work of the people. The social welfare system includes health insurance, paid maternity leave, birth allowances for third births and beyond, and other benefits relating to births.

There is no planned parenthood association in the Soviet Union. Advice is theoretically available within the public health service, at local health centers, and obstetrics and gynecology departments of hospitals. Planned parenthood training reportedly is included in the curriculums of physicians and midwives as a matter of routine. Many periodicals carry articles on various aspects of planned parenthood describing methods of contraception, clinical trials, and other activities. Two booklets have been produced by the Ministry of Health on abortion and methods of contraception.

According to a series of four population projections prepared by the U.S. Bureau of the Census, the population of the Soviet Union can be expected to number between 292 million and 348 million by the year 2000. If fertility remains at the 1971 level, as assumed by the second of the four projections, the total population is expected to be around 319.5 million by the year 2000. This figure would be about 65 million above the 1975 total of 254.3 million.

Yugoslavia

Yugoslavia experienced a 9.8 percent increase in population during the 1965-75 decade. The population in mid-1975 totaled about 21.4 million, an increase of 2 million over the mid-1965 level of 19.4 million. The increase was slightly smaller than the increment of the preceding decade, however, evidencing a slowing of population growth.

The rate of natural increase dropped from a level of 1.2 percent per year in 1965 to 0.9 percent in 1974. Affecting the decline was a decrease in both birth and death rates. The birth rate in 1974 was 18 per 1,000 population, down from 21 in 1965. The death rate in 1974 was 8 per 1,000, down from 9 in 1965.

The per capita gross national product of Yugoslavia increased between 1965 and 1973 by about 59 percent. In 1965 it was $690 per capita and in 1973, $1,100 per capita.

Marked differences among the eight major regions of Yugoslavia constitute the most distinguishing feature of the national population picture. In 1969, the birth rate in the multinational Vojvodina region was 13.1 per 1,000 population, among the lowest in Europe. At the same time, the birth rate in the Kosovo region, largely Albanian in makeup, was 37.9 per 1,000. Such regional diversity in fertility is affected by the differences in levels of economic and social development, social structures, history, religion, customs, literacy rates, and the quality and availability of health and social services.

The head of the Center for Demographic Research in Belgrade has summarized the overall picture as follows:

"The transitional demographic period, which is characterized by falling birth and death rates and by changes in the age distribution of the population, is virtually at an end in areas with a low birth rate, fully established in areas with a medium birth rate, and just beginning in areas with a high birth rate (Kosovo and some other smaller regions)."

The Center's projection of future population growth looks toward a continuation of present rate trends, with levelling off in low birth-rate regions partly balanced by the onset of the "transitional demographic period" in Kosovo and other high birth rate pockets. Given also the relatively youthful age structure of the present population, the nationwide total number of births per year is expected to rise slowly throughout the 1970's and then sink slowly in the early 1980's. According to the Center's projections, the total population can be expected to reach 23 million in 1981 and 23.5 million in 1986.

Family planning programs are supported by the Communist Party and the state. Contraceptives and contraceptive information are freely available in principle, the former through medical centers, some practitioners, and pharmacies and the latter through medical centers, through the work of the Councils for Family Planning, and more recently through courses in sex education and human relations being introduced in the schools of some areas. The Federal Council for Family Planning in 1969 reported about 500 health institutions concerned

exclusively or partially with contraception. Twelve contraceptives are now available on the market, including five oral, three mechanical, and four chemical methods. Distribution, however, is reportedly uneven. According to the first countrywide family planning survey conducted in 1970, abortion was then still the most common method of fertility control, used by 45 percent of the married respondents. Some 44 percent used no contraception, 38 percent relied on coitus interruptus, 3.6 percent the pill, and 1 percent the IUD.

Legislation to legalize abortion was enacted in 1952 and subsequently amended in 1960 and 1969. The effect of all these acts has been to make clinical abortion available to anyone desiring it. The 1969 law attempts to tighten the conditions, however, by requiring that the applicant be warned of the dangers and advised to desist, and that she be given information on contraceptive techniques and availability.

Latin America

Central and South America

The rate of population growth in Latin America in 1965-75 was highest of the world's regions. Mainland population increased 33 percent—rising from 219 million in 1965 to over 290 million in 1975.

Latin America's annual rate of natural increase—the excess of births over deaths per 1,000 people—was 2.9 percent in 1974, up slightly from 1965. Decreases in many countries, notably Chile, Colombia, Costa Rica, Nicaragua, Panama, and Venezuela, were more than offset by gains in populous Argentina, Mexico, and Peru.

Persons under age 15 accounted for 42 percent of the Latin American population in 1975, as compared with 36 percent for the world. This composition of the population points to continued expansion over a period of many years even if, as seems likely, there is significant progress in reducing rates of natural increase.

Latin America's net migration in the 1960-70 period has been placed by the United Nations at a net outflow of 1.9 million. Although complete statistics are not available, a continued outflow probably took place in 1970-74. In those years, legal migration from Latin America into the United States alone totaled 447,000 persons, of whom 300,000 were from Mexico. Other significant migration streams flowed to Canada and Europe. Illegal migration added still more to the out-movement.

Latin America's rapid population growth, only slightly dampened by migration, has hampered economic and social development generally. For individual Latin Americans it has adversely affected employment opportunities, health services, education, housing, the crime rate, and the overall quality of life.

One effect on individuals is revealed by statistics on gross national product (GNP). Total GNP in the region increased at an average annual rate of 7.2 percent between 1970 and 1974. This respectable rate of gain, however, was held by population increase to an average per capita GNP growth of 4.2 percent.

The high proportion of young people in Latin America's population mix helps to produce an unfavorable dependency ratio. This means that people of working age must support many others, not only most of those under age 15, but also some over age 64. The result is a low standard of living for workers and dependents alike.

The problems are most acute in the cities, some of which are expected to double in size within 10 years. The population of Mexico City is increasing at the rate of 11 percent annually and Mexico now has 35 other cities with more than 100,000 people. Brazil, Argentina, and several other countries are experiencing similar rapid urban growth, not only from high rates of natural increase but also from a heavy influx of people from rural areas. In most of the large cities, unemployment and underemployment rates are high. The increasing demand for goods, services, and facilities cannot be met completely, especially with regard to housing, education, and health.

Population pressures and the unavailability of contraceptives for a large portion of the population are largely responsible for the high incidence of illegal abortions in all countries of Latin America. Abortion has been especially prevalent in the countries at the southern "cone" of South America—Argentina, Chile, and Uruguay. Abortions, many of them crudely performed, are a principal source of maternal illnesses and deaths.

The impact of rapid population growth on economic and social development, and its relation to abortion, has increased Latin America's awareness of the need for family planning, which is often referred to in the region as "responsible parenthood." There also has developed in recent years a strong belief that individuals and couples have a basic human right to information and the means of determining freely and responsibly the spacing of their children.

Awareness of population problems has engendered official policy and statutory changes creating an increasingly favorable atmosphere for contraceptive use. In the past 10 years, family planning programs have come into operation in most countries. These developments in the formative years of 1965-75 show promise of significantly reducing Latin America's rate of population increase in the years ahead.

Some of the break-throughs have been substantial, especially in Mexico.

Mexico, long noted for its opposition to contraception, reversed its policy in the early 1970's. In 1975 family planning services were available in 431 Government clinics and 91 clinics of a private organization. A "Phase II" program was planned for establishment of some 2,000 new rural health posts to

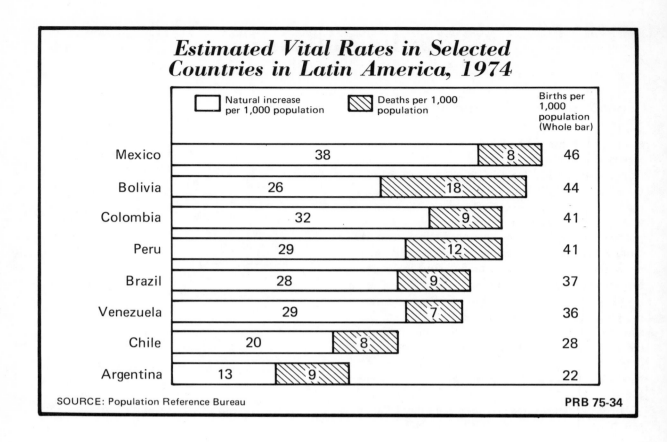

Estimated Vital Rates in Selected Countries in Latin America, 1974

	Natural increase per 1,000 population	Deaths per 1,000 population	Births per 1,000 population (Whole bar)
Mexico	38	8	46
Bolivia	26	18	44
Colombia	32	9	41
Peru	29	12	41
Brazil	28	9	37
Venezuela	29	7	36
Chile	20	8	28
Argentina	13	9	22

SOURCE: Population Reference Bureau

PRB 75-34

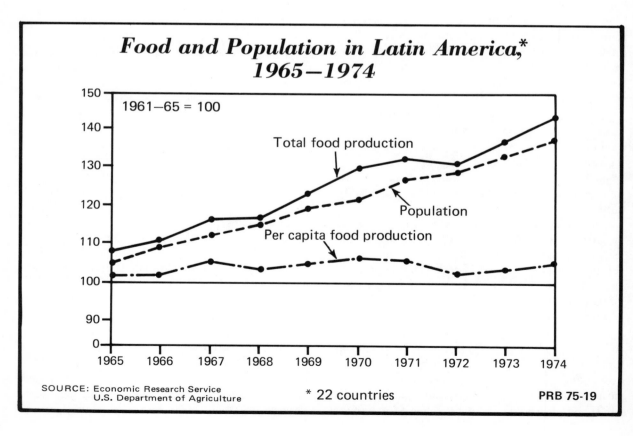

Food and Population in Latin America,* 1965—1974

1961—65 = 100

Total food production

Population

Per capita food production

SOURCE: Economic Research Service
U.S. Department of Agriculture

* 22 countries

PRB 75-19

Latin America's rate of natural population increase in 1974 was 2.9 percent, the highest of the world's major regions. But concern about population growth problems has led to the establishment of vigorous family planning programs in Mexico, Chile, Costa Rica, El Salvador, and Panama. Except for Argentina, family planning activities are being carried on in other Latin American countries, either with government support or through private and international agencies and organizations.

offer family planning to the 20 million Mexicans living in smaller towns and on farms.

Brazil, which also has taken the stance of a strong opponent of family planning, indicated in a formal statement to the 1974 World Population Conference in Bucharest that it may be in process of changing its earlier position. The Brazilian representative noted in his address to the assembly that the ability to resort to birth control measures should not be a privilege reserved for affluent families only. Instead, he stated that it is the responsibility of government to provide the family planning information and means that may be required by families of limited income. In 1975 the Brazilian Government had not implemented this stated policy; rather, as in other recent years it was remaining largely uninvolved in the efforts to establish an effective family planning program in the country. It was letting private organizations, state and local governments, and the regular commercial market do the necessary work. And these instrumentalities, it has developed, have been making substantial progress. For example, the major private organization, with the strong support of local officials, was carrying on in 1975 a pioneering community-based contraceptive distribution program in some areas; about 39 million cycles of oral contraceptives were produced locally and distributed in 1974 through commercial channels; demand for contraceptives in 1975 showed continued rapid growth.

Ecuador has officially announced availability of family planning services through its public health facilities. Chile, like Mexico, has taken steps to incorporate paramedical personnel into family planning programs. The President of Venezuela has emphasized his personal commitment to family planning and the Government's stated goal is to make family planning services available to every Venezuelan by the end of 1978. El Salvador in 1974 proclaimed an official population policy.

Although rates of natural increase have not declined in most countries, some very significant decreases have taken place in birth rates. Chile's birth rate declined from 32 per 1,000 population in 1965 to 28 in 1974; Costa Rica's from 41 to 28; El Salvador's from 44 to 40; Panama's from 38 to 31; and Venezuela's from 42 to 36. The only countries showing increases in birth rates, and those slight, were Argentina and Mexico.

Another factor in the family planning equation is the gain in contraceptive availability. In all Latin American countries, oral contraceptives are available—with or without prescription in pharmacies or through hospitals, health centers, family planning clinics, or authorized individuals. Condoms also are available in all Latin American countries, usually without prescription. Other "barrier" types of contraceptives—such as diaphragms, foams, and jellies—are available in many countries. IUD's are available in most countries through health centers, family planning clinics, private physicians, or paramedical personnel. Sterilization is generally legal. Abortion though often practiced as a family planning method is illegal in all of the countries of Latin America.

Proponents of family planning had setbacks in a few countries over the 1965-75 period, but they offset in only small degree the substantial gains made elsewhere in Latin America.

Argentina's population policy in the mid-1970's remained, as it had been for a number of years, pronatalist. In March 1974 the Government by executive decree forbade the dissemination of birth control information and closed existing family planning facilities. Domestic manufacture of contraceptives was permitted but their importation in finished form was forbidden. Provision of oral contraceptives was limited to medical prescription.

Argentina carried its opposition to family plan-

Total food production in Latin America increased rapidly in 1965-74, permitting the area as a whole to raise current per capita food output somewhat about the 1961-65 level. In some countries, however, a significant part of some food items is produced for export, reducing per capita availability. Food production per capita has been well above the base period in most Central American countries, Venezuela, Brazil, and Argentina. But a number of countries in 1974 had smaller per capita food production, notably Bolivia, Chile, Ecuador, Guyana, Paraguay, Peru, and Uruguay.

ning to the 1974 World Population Conference in Bucharest. There Argentina introduced scores of amendments to the Draft World Plan of Action that were designed to change the document from one expressing concern about population growth to one emphasizing recognition of the value of life and of human, familial, and natural rights. Also at Bucharest, Argentina argued that international migration should be considered as an alternative to family planning as a solution to the problem of unequal population growth.

Bolivia carries on some family planning activities but the "climate" for the program in that country has tended to be unfavorable.

In Uruguay, the Government has given low priority to development of population programs. In 1973 it put a 10-percent tax on all contraceptive sales to help finance a fertility center. In 1974 it substantially increased the birth allowance for the third-born child, a pronatalist action.

In many countries, programs for the delivery of family planning services underwent some changes in 1965-75. In the middle and late 1960's, family planning was carried on largely through private physicians, health centers, and family planning clinics. By the early 1970's, however, increased use was being made of paramedical personnel; in Chile, for example, family planning programs have relied heavily on the services of midwives. Also in the early 1970's there was a shift toward the distribution of oral contraceptives without medical prescription. In some countries where such distribution is permitted, retail sales have been made at low, controlled, subsidized prices; in other countries the distribution has been through local leaders or by satisfied users of pills.

Information and education continued to be provided potential acceptors of family planning over the 1965-75 period. Information is essential because it sets forth the importance of responsible parenthood in improving the quality of life and thereby motivates families to accept the service, apprises families of services available to them, and enhances social acceptability of the program. All methods of communication have been used: radio, television, press, publications, audio-visual materials, films, meetings and seminars. Radio, in recent years, has had increasing use, especially in Central America—radio having the virtue of permitting communication with people who are unable to read.

Training has been emphasized over the 1965-75 period. More and more paramedical personnel are being trained as one means of compensating for the shortage of physicians. A special project has been carried on since the middle 1960's for developing

and evaluating innovative family planning programs, especially in the field of information and education.

The need for data on which to base Latin American programs for health, family planning, housing, education, and employment called for continued activity in the field of population statistics. Much of this work came into focus through the Latin American Demographic Center (CELADE), an institution located in Santiago, Chile, which provides demographic training, information, and advisory services for its member countries. Latin America also benefitted from such global programs as the World Fertility Survey, administered by the International Statistical Institute at the Hague, and from U.S.-funded development of computerized population data systems. CIENES, an OAS sponsored training center in Santiago, and the Inter-American Statistical Institute also have had an important influence on the development of censuses and demographic statistics, including household surveys.

Statistics for 1965-75 show that host countries' inputs to population programs totaled $21.2 million, or 14 percent of total outlays, whereas assistance from external sources amounted to $114.9 million, or 84 percent of total expenditures.

External Assistance

U.S. AID assistance in Latin America is provided in large part through organizations that include the United Nations Fund for Population Activities (UNFPA), the Pan American Health Organization (PAHO), the Pan American Federation of Associations of Medical Schools (PAFAMS), the International Planned Parenthood Federation (IPPF), The Pathfinder Fund, the Population Council, the Association for Voluntary Sterilization (AVS), Family Planning International Assistance (FPIA), World Education (WEI), and the World Assembly of Youth (WAY). Other assistance has been provided by the Ford Foundation, the Rockefeller Foundation, the Tinker Foundation, and the Scaife Charitable Trust, Kellogg, and other organizations.

AID also provides support on a bilateral basis. In 1975 the agency was directly assisting 10 Latin American countries (and 3 Caribbean countries) the assistance including, but not limited to, supplying contraceptives and other commodities and equipment, training personnel, providing assistance of full-time advisors and short-term consultants, and funding local operating costs.

AID's outlays in the 1965-75 period were as follows:

AID Population Program Support, Latin America and the Caribbean Islands, Fiscal Years

Item	1965-71	1972	1973	1974	1975	1965-75
	1,000 dol.	1,000 dol.	1,000 dol.	1,000 dol.	1,000 dol.	1,000 dol.
Country projects	22,589	7,223	6,230	4,792	4,238	45,072
Regional projects	26,266	[1]3,811	7,383	2,655	1,430	41,655
Latin America Total . .	48,855	11,134	13,623	7,447	5,668	86,727

[1]Reduction reflects consolidation of some regional projects into worldwide projects.

UNFPA provides assistance both on a country and regional basis to population and family planning programs in Latin America. Requests for UNFPA assistance increased greatly in 1974 and 1975, especially for maternal and child health and family planning programs.

In Mexico, UNFPA is supporting, with outlays approaching $4.5 million, that country's expanding family planning program. In Colombia, the agency has financed assistance to maternal and child care programs, purchase of contraceptives, and a population census. UNFPA has provided funds of over $1,000,000 for programs in Chile, Costa Rica, and Ecuador. Substantial assistance has been extended to Argentina, Bolivia, El Salvador, Guatemala, Guyana, Honduras, Nicaragua, Panama, Paraguay, Peru, Uruguay, and Venezuela.

At the regional level UNFPA has supported, through the Economic Commission for Latin America, advisory services for census programs and research in basic population data and population dynamics. Support for CELADE was continued. Support also was provided to the Latin American Program for Social Sciences, which is working on guidelines for population policies in individual countries.

PAHO, the regional arm of the World Health Organization and a specialized agency of the Organization of American States, provides technical assistance related to population and family planning with funds from AID and UNFPA. PAHO seeks to incorporate population/family planning in existing health systems and organizations through education of professional staffs, provision of necessary supplies and commodities, and encouragement and support of related social and medical research through its advisory and consultative services. In Argentina, assistance has been given to the expansion of maternal and child care protection activities in the

northeastern and northwestern parts of the country. In Bolivia, Brazil, Ecuador, Guyana, Peru, Paraguay, and Uruguay, national maternal and child health units were strengthened.

PAFAMS carried on between 1969 and 1975 seminars in medical schools on demography (including family planning), the teaching of family planning in obstetrics and gynecology courses, and developing audiovisual materials for teaching population dynamics and family planning in medical schools.

The IPPF has provided financial and technical assistance to affiliates in most of the mainland Latin American countries. Over the 1965-75 period they have carried on three major types of action programs: information and education work, training, and medical and clinical operations. In many countries the IPPF has been the primary source of information on family planning—information which has reached the people through such means as press, radio, television, publications, meetings, and seminars. Training activities, often carried on in conjunction with Ministries of Health, have been aimed at a broad spectrum of personnel—physicians, nurses, midwives, and administrative assistants. IPPF clinics have been a trail that health officials of Latin America have followed. In a number of countries, the clinical activities pioneered by IPPF have been expanded greatly by Ministries of Health and other officials.

The Pathfinder Fund, with regional offices in Chile and Colombia, has furnished technical and financial assistance, contraceptive supplies, and literature to pioneering family planning groups in almost all Latin American countries. In 1975 Pathfinder continued to place major emphasis on seminars on population and family planning for decision makers; sterilization, clinical services, and research; use of mass communications to disseminate information on family planning to the general populace; introduction of clinical services in both urban and rural areas; and training programs.

The Population Council makes research, training, and institutional development grants, supplies IUD's and books, provides fellowships, and offers technical advisory services to institutions and individuals throughout Latin America. Such regional organizations as PAFAMS, CELADE, and the Regional Population Center have received Council assistance for multinational activities in addition to local institution support.

Activities receiving grant support in 1974 included research at various Latin American medical schools and institutions in contraceptives, reproductive physiology, and family planning. In 1974 the Council supported demographic research in Brazil, Chile (largely through CELADE), Colombia, Guatemala, and Mexico, and biomedical research studies in Argentina, Chile, and Peru. Grants were made to assist postpartum programs and other family planning services in Colombia and Venezuela.

The Council supports translation and distribution of population literature. Substantial grants for translation have been made to the Colombian Association for the Study of Population. Most Council publications are translated for broad distribution in Latin America, and basic books and research studies are made available to libraries of government agencies, universities, and other institutions.

The Ford Foundation's outlays for population activities in Latin America and the Caribbean area amounted to $14 million through 1974. Increasing emphasis was placed in the 1970's on research and training programs, improvements of systems for contraceptive delivery, and information and education, while outlays for reproductive science and contraceptive development were de-emphasized to some extent.

The Rockefeller Foundation, which has supported biomedical research in fertility control since the early 1930's, began to make major commitments in the late 1950's and early 1960's to the solution of population problems in Latin America. In 1972 support was provided for establishment of a Social Science Research Program on Population Problems Relevant to Population Policies in Latin America, a program to be conducted under supervision of the Commission for Population and Development of the Latin American Social Science Council. The program emphasizes institution building

Latin America's total GNP steadily moved up between 1970 and 1974 at an average annual rate of 7.2 percent. The per capita figure, however, was much lower—4.2 percent—because of the gains the region has been making in population.

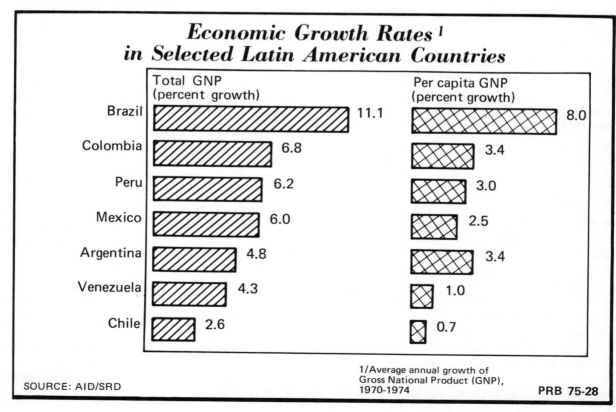

Economic Growth Rates [1]
in Selected Latin American Countries

	Total GNP (percent growth)	Per capita GNP (percent growth)
Brazil	11.1	8.0
Colombia	6.8	3.4
Peru	6.2	3.0
Mexico	6.0	2.5
Argentina	4.8	3.4
Venezuela	4.3	1.0
Chile	2.6	0.7

SOURCE: AID/SRD

1/Average annual growth of Gross National Product (GNP), 1970-1974

PRB 75-28

as well as population research by Latin American social scientists. Twelve Latin American population centers representing Argentina, Brazil, Colombia, Chile, Uruguay, Mexico. and Venezuela are now part of the program; additional centers in Peru and Central America are being considered for membership. Foundation grants to El Colegio de Mexico supporting its pioneer research and training program in the Center for Economics and Demography have made a contribution throughout Latin America.

The Association for Voluntary Sterilization (AVS) has, since 1972, stimulated, encouraged, and supported voluntary sterilization programs in Latin America through grants for the training of physicians, paraprofessionals, and auxiliary personnel and related information and education activities.

Family Planning International Assistance (FPIA) is the overseas arm of the Planned Parenthood Federation of America. It supports Latin American family planning programs in a variety of ways. It supplies contraceptives, medical equipment, audio-visual gear, and educational and motivational materials, such as movies, slides. booklets, pamphlets, radio spots, and posters. It supports three information and education programs in Central and South America—two in Costa Rica and one in Colombia. In Peru it carries on a special training program for medical students and doctors. It provides technical assistance. In Ecuador more than 10,000 women are receiving family planning services in an FPIA-sponsored program—the only one run by women physicians in Latin America. FPIA's cumulative funding of 17 individual projects over four program years was $1.8 million.

The Tinker Foundation's initial grant in the field of population was made in 1965 when it awarded $500 to the Population Reference Bureau to support that agency's Latin American publications. In a 10-year period from 1965 to 1975 a total of $1.2 million was awarded to various population projects, mostly in Latin America, to educate or inform national leaders about the serious economic and social implications of excessive population growth.

World Education, Inc., helps to incorporate family planning concepts into functional literacy programs and nonformal adult education. The scope of the work falls into definite categories: identifying learner needs, designing programs and curricula, developing learner-oriented materials, training teachers, and assessing program strengths and weaknesses. Projects were underway in 1975 in Colombia, Costa Rica, Ecuador, Honduras, and, in the Caribbean area, Jamaica.

The World Assembly of Youth (WAY), with regional headquarters in Managua, Nicaragua, has sponsored regional and national conferences in Latin America to increase among young people an awareness of the relationship between family planning and economic and social progress. WAY also issues a monthly bulletin, as well as handbooks, slides, charts, posters, graphs, and other materials for use in seminars and local meetings.

Argentina

The rate of population growth in Argentina is among the lowest in Latin America—1.3 percent a year as of 1974—or less than half the combined average for all countries of Central and South America. If this pace continues, 53 years will be needed for Argentina's population to double, or reach a level of about 50 million. The mid-1975 population was estimated at 25.4 million.

The Argentine Government views this slow growth with apprehension rather than approval. It argues that "to correct deficiencies and contribute to the occupation and integration of the national territory" a population of 50 million must be achieved within 25 years instead of 50, or by the year 2000 instead of 2025.

The Government's plan of action for more rapid population growth includes:
• Reducing mortality trends.
• Raising birth rates.
• Encouraging the flow of immigration.
• Reducing emigration.
The plan also is aimed at regulating internal migration to assure adequate populations in the outlying provinces.

Argentina's desire for an expanding population, a policy which is ordinarily designated pronatalist, is not new. The vision of a large and powerful Argentina was attractive to the late General Peron, who considered his country—with an area roughly the same as India's—to be underpopulated. In 1968, too, the Government took a strong stand against family planning and birth control when the President came out in opposition to what was interpreted as a suggestion that World Bank aid be tied to a nation's efforts to control population growth. Also, the Government supported the attitude of the Catholic hierarchy, which asserted obedience to the Pope's ruling on artificial birth control. (About 94 percent of Argentinians profess the Roman Catholic faith.) Pronatalism was further reinforced when a law introduced a wage policy of increasing subsidies and school allowances for each child.

Argentina has extended its pronatalist ideas into the international arena. The Population Council, in its *Report on Bucharest*—a summary of happenings at the August 1974 World Population Conference—notes that "Argentina introduced scores of amendments to the Draft Plan [World Population Plan of Action] that were carefully designed to change the weight of the document from one that essentially expressed concern lest the rate of population growth become an obstacle to socio-economic development into one that ". . . put main emphasis on the recognition of the value of life and of human, familial, and national rights." Argentina also argued at Bucharest, as it had at an earlier preparatory meeting, that international migration should be considered as an instrument of population policy that could provide countries with an alternative solution to problems of unequal population growth.

Earlier, in March 1974, the Argentine Government, by executive decree, forbade the dissemination of birth control information and closed existing family planning facilities. Domestic manufacture of contraceptives is permitted, but they must be officially tested and registered for sale. The importation of contraceptives in finished form is forbidden. Oral contraceptives may be provided only on stringent medical prescription.

The private Asociación Argentina de Protección Familiar (AAPF), an affiliate of the International Planned Parenthood Federation (IPPF), had provided services on a limited scale since 1966. Following the Government's decree in 1974, the organization closed its 56 clinics in Buenos Aires and the northwest provinces. The IPPF noted in its 1974 *Report to Donors* that "the Family Planning Association is currently engaged in promotional activities within Government circles, inculcating the concepts of responsible parenthood, of family planning as a human right, and of the need to eradicate the high incidence of induced abortion."

The abortion situation has been given considerable attention. A study early in the 1970's at Rawson Hospital, Buenos Aires, showed that one-third of the pregnancies of the 532 married women in the sample ended in abortion, of which 72 percent were said to be illegal. The inference from the study was that in urban areas at least one abortion occurred for each live birth.

External Assistance

External support, other than that from the IPPF, for population programs has come from the United Nations Fund for Population Activities, the Population Council, the Ford Foundation, the Rockefeller Foundation, and the Tinker Foundation. Funding has been largely for research in demography and reproductive biology.

Bolivia

The population of Bolivia had increased from 4.4 million in 1965 to 5.6 million by mid-1975, a gain of 28 percent. The birth rate over that period remained stable at 44 per 1,000 people, but the death rate declined from 20 to 18 per 1,000 per year. The annual rate of natural increase in 1974 was 2.6 percent; if continued, this would bring a doubling of the population in 27 years.

Bolivia is one of the poorest countries in Latin America. It has a per capita GNP of $200, a high level of illiteracy, and poor health services. Life expectancy at birth in 1975 was only 47 years in comparison with the Latin American average of 62 years and was the lowest for any country in the Western Hemisphere. Ironically, activities aimed at improving health in Bolivia tend to intensify population growth and its attendant problems.

Prior to 1973 there were several Bolivian attempts to create a family planning organization and initiate activities. In 1973, however, following some initiatives from both the public and private sectors, more specifically, promotional activities by the National Family Center (CENAFA) and some health officials, high Government officials seemed to come to the view that Bolivia's high population growth rate, if left unchecked, would drastically hamper its economic and social development. Subsequently, several important steps were taken.

Notable was the establishment in 1973 of the Asociacion Boliviana de Proteccion a La Familia (PROFAM), an affiliate of the International Planned Parenthood Federation (IPPF). The Ministry of Health (MOH) entered into an agreement with PROFAM for assistance in providing family planning services plus the management of some official MOH responsible parenthood clinics.

PROFAM opened a demonstration clinic in a slum area of La Paz in July 1974. Open 6 hours a day, it is staffed by two doctors, a nurse, an auxiliary nurse, and a social worker. PROFAM also provided family planning services for 6 hours daily in a Ministry of Health hospital in La Paz, but there are plans to extend services in facilities of its own and other Bolivian government organizations in Santa Cruz, Cochabamba, Potosi, and Oruro and to begin a pilot rural project in the village of Sapaqui.

PROFAM's training activities are carried out in coordination with the Ministry of Health. Training for physicians, nurses, and paramedical personnel is conducted in PROFAM's model clinic in La Paz. Information and communication activities of PROFAM are aimed at enlisting support of family planning through meetings with union and business leaders, civic organizations, and other groups plus parallel publication of a bulletin and monographs directed toward the influential people of Bolivia. These activities are coordinated with and supported by the activities of the Asociacion Boliviana de Educacion Sexual (ABES), which receives financial support from U.S. AID. The National Family Center (CENAFA) was established by Presidential Decree in 1968 as an autonomous agency under the Ministry of Health. Its purpose is to develop and implement seminars, demographic research, and publications designed to motivate Bolivian government officials and the general population to accept family planning. It has been influential in the creation of PROFAM and ABES and in greatly improving the local ambiance relative to the dissemination of family planning and sex education information.

Despite these favorable steps a "climate" favorable to family planning has not developed firmly in Bolivia. In March 1975 the Bolivian Catholic Church initiated an anti-birth-control campaign through a hard-hitting pastoral letter "condemning" as "modern genocide" the international support that has been given to family planning activities in Bolivia. The Government responded vigorously that it supported programs of "responsible parenthood" but not birth control—the latter term carrying a connotation throughout Latin America of Government determination of fertility. The Church eased tensions to a degree by giving approval in public for responsible parenthood programs—the stated objective of the Bolivian Government.

External Assistance

Inputs to family planning programs by AID have amounted to $2,003,000 in the fiscal year period 1969-75. UNFPA approved in 1976 a contribution of $1,520,000 for Bolivia's coordinated maternal and child health program. In earlier years, UNFPA had budgeted $463,000 for a population and housing census, maternal and child health services, and a regional development seminar. Other agencies contributing to Bolivia's overall family planning program include The Pathfinder Fund, the Population Council, the Mennonite Central Committee, the World Assembly of Youth, and World Neighbors.

Brazil

Brazil's population has risen from 81 million in 1965 to 107 million by mid-1975. The annual rate of natural increase in 1974 was 2.8 percent, or about equal to the Latin American average. This would bring a doubling of the population in 25 years. Births in 1974 occurred at the rate of 37 per 1,000 people and deaths at 9 per 1,000. A high proportion of Brazilians—about 42 percent—are under the 15-year-old age level.

Brazil's economy has been strong in recent years. The 1970-74 average annual rate of economic growth was about 10 percent, while the per capita average rate of growth for the same period was 8 percent—both well above the Latin American average. But Brazil's economic growth dropped to 5 percent in 1975, largely due to the burden of higher petroleum prices. Income distribution, meanwhile, continues to be an aggravating problem in rural and urban areas throughout the country as a whole.

Up to mid-1975, Brazil's reaction to its high population growth has been ambivalent. On the one hand, Brazilian officials have argued that the nation needs more people. The added population would occupy the sparsely inhabited north and west regions, create a strong internal market for trade and industry, and provide the minimum population required to become a major world power. On the other hand, the Brazilian representative to the World Population Conference in Bucharest in 1974 stated at that time that "Being able to resort to birth control measures should not be a privilege reserved for families that are well off, and therefore it is the responsibility of the State to provide the information and the means that may be required of families of limited income." The central Government has not actively implemented this policy. Instead, it has allowed States and municipalities to carry on family planning services or enter into agreements with private organizations to conduct such services and has permitted increasingly large sales of oral contraceptives and condoms.

One private organization, BEMFAM—the Sociedade Civil de Bem-Estar Familiar no Brasil, or the Brazilian Civil Society for Family Welfare—has been active in family welfare in Brazil since 1965. BEMFAM has, in the past, provided full financial support for as many as 102 clinics, but is reducing its outlays as quickly as possible for financial and policy reasons. It seeks to have communities or States pay the operating costs of clinics with BEMFAM providing mainly technical assistance. BEMFAM is expected by the end of 1975 to be supporting fully only 25 demonstration clinics in major cities and partially supporting 67 other clinics that receive operating expenses from communities. As the only organization educating and informing the Brazilian public about family welfare matters, BEMFAM devoted $400,000 in 1975 to information, education, and communication activities and plans to apply $720,000 to such operations in 1976.

BEMFAM is also, with the strong support of local officials, pioneering a community-based program in rural areas of the State of Rio Grande do Norte utilizing voluntary community leaders such as teachers, nurses, and midwives who have daily contact with many women. The distributors receive 3 days of training, with emphasis on problems women may encounter in taking oral contraceptives, and also attend occasional refresher courses held by regional administrators.

The program started in August 1973 and by December 1974 had an estimated 22,000 continuing acceptors—or about 6 percent of Rio Grande do Norte's approximately 370,000 fertile women. BEMFAM considers this program important because it shows that community members can do much to deliver a valuable service at little cost.

BEMFAM's information and education program is designed to reach leadership groups at the federal, state and local levels. A core program to convince top leaders that family planning is an essential service continues to center around seminars in which leaders from diverse fields participate and wide press coverage results. Meetings with student and university groups are scheduled as are seminars with professional groups. In addition there is participation in numerous professional congresses and meetings.

The mass media program is built around radio spots, films and slides for use in seminars, training courses and within clinics.

Abortion, though illegal, is widely practiced in Brazil. Estimates of its frequency range up to several million abortions annually.

Oral contraceptives are well accepted and their use is growing rapidly. According to a recent, internationally sponsored study, about 39 million cycles of oral contraceptives were produced and distributed within Brazil in 1974. During 1973 and 1974, sales increased 4 times as much as the increase in the number of women of reproductive age. Various estimates suggest that between 8 percent and 13 percent of women aged 15 through 49 years are now using the pill. Use is relatively high in the urban areas and among middle and higher income groups.

Local output of condoms has been running about 48 million pieces annually, with an estimated 3 million to 5 million additional pieces per year entering the country from abroad. Brazil's condom production is expected to double by 1978. The product line has been upgraded in recent years with the addition of colored and lubricated condoms. It is surmised that these higher priced items are used largely for contraceptive purposes while the less expensive, non-lubricated condoms are used primarily for protection against veneral disease. Distribution is not limited to pharmacies; supermarkets openly display and sell condoms in most major cities.

External Assistance

Major external assistance to Brazil's family planning program comes from nongovernmental organizations. The International Planned Parenthood Federation contributed $3.3 million to BEMFAM in 1975. The Ford Foundation, the Population Council, and the Rockefeller Foundation have provided grants primarily to Brazilian universities for demographic and medical research projects. The United Nations Fund for Population Activities and the International Development Research Center (Canada) are aiding demographic research projects. Other organizations providing assistance in recent years are the Association for Voluntary Sterilization, Church World Service, the Danish International Development Agency, International Education Development, The Pathfinder Fund, the Population Reference Bureau, the Tinker Foundation, and World Neighbors.

Chile

The population of Chile rose from 8.7 million in 1965 to 10.6 million by mid-1975—an increase of 21 percent. The current rate of natural increase of 1.9 percent is one of the lowest in Latin America. Contributing factors may be an active family planning program in recent years and a general improvement in the quality of medical care. While birth rates fell from 32 per 1,000 population in 1965 to 28 per 1,000 in 1974, death rates also declined from 11 to 8 per 1,000 per year, and decreases in infant mortality were especially marked.

Chile's family planning activities, unlike programs in many other countries, are aimed primarily at reducing abortions. By the early 1960's in Chile, these had reached large totals. Abortion traditionally has been a much more important phenomenon in the countries of the heavily urbanized southern wedge of South America—Chile, Argentina, and Uruguay—than elsewhere in the Western Hemisphere.

An issue of the American Universities Fieldstaff

Reports, *Family Planning in Chile, Part I: The Public Program* and *Part II: The Catholic Position,* notes that "In 1937 the National Health Service of Chile registered 8.4 abortions for each 100 births; by 1960 this had increased to 22.3 and the number of women involved had risen from 12,963 to 57,268. These figures represent only those abortions that came under hospital attention because of health complications. It is currently (1967) estimated that Chile has about 150,000 abortions a year, as compared to 300,000 live births. Abortions cause two-fifths of all maternal deaths, and in 1960 their treatment accounted for 184,000 bed-days and cost over a million dollars. They are responsible for 8.1 percent of all hospital admissions ... 35 percent of the surgery in obstetric services, and 26.7 percent of the blood used in all emergency services."

The article further stated, "Although both hospitalizations and maternal deaths caused by abortion have been reduced greatly...the ratio of abortions to total pregnancies seems to have remained constant and may even have risen, according to some specialists. Most Chilean women face a choice between effective contraception and an unremitting series of pregnancies, often ending in abortion..."

Chile's family planning information and services are provided within the Maternal and Child Health Service of the National Health Service (NHS) and in other semipublic and private institutions. The private Asociación Chilena de Protección de la Familias (APROFA), an affiliate of the International Planned Parenthood Federation (IPPF), provides vital support to the NHS, and other external organizations have funded various segments of the overall population program. Population/family planning activities apparently were not adversely affected by events following the change of government in 1973.

In 1973 APROFA signed an agreement with NHS under which APROFA will provide support for activities in the northern region of the country not covered by the United Nations Fund for Population Activities (UNFPA). Eighteen health areas in the north are included. APROFA's goal for 1975 was to cover 85,000 of the 432,000 women of fertile age in the north, and they expected to provide 180,000 consultations—145,000 by midwives and 36,000 by physicians.

In the south, APROFA hoped to cover 62,000 of the area's fertile-age women. Midwives were to provide most of the services.

External Assistance

Outside support for the Chilean family planning program in the past decade came largely from the IPPF (almost $2.8 million), UNFPA ($3.2 million including unexpended funds), and the U.S. Agency for International Development (AID) in the fiscal years 1967-72 (almost $2 million). Other organizations that provided help include the United Nations, the United Nations Children's Fund, the World Health Organization, the Pan American Health Organization, the Swedish International Development Authority, the Association for Voluntary Sterilization, The Pathfinder Fund, the Population Council, the Ford Foundation, and the Rockefeller Foundation.

The financial assistance budgeted for by the UNFPA will extend through the period 1973-76. Family planning services are to be increased to cover 40 percent of the women in rural and urban areas over the 4-year period. The program will be carried out in 600 hospitals, health centers, and health posts in 24 of Chile's 55 health areas. UNFPA financing, executed through various United Nations specialized agencies, also has made possible a variety of related teaching, training, reserach, demographic, and other population activities.

The Latin American Demographic Center (CELADE) in Chile, which is supported by the United Nations, has helped the Chilean Government improve the collection and processing of statistics.

Colombia

Colombia's population as of mid-1975 was 22.3 million compared with the 1965 total of 16.1 million —an increase of 39 percent for the decade and somewhat more than the 32 percent decade gain for all countries of Central and South America.

As of 1974, the rate of natural increase of population was about 3.2 percent per year, resulting from an annual birth rate of 41 per 1,000 population and a death rate of 9 per 1,000. Colombia's relatively high population growth rate of 3.2 percent a year has accentuated a number of social and economic problems by increasing pressures on health services, schools, housing, and food supplies. Unemployment and underemployment are high. Movement of people from rural to urban areas has also been heavy, and city dwellers now account for about 60 percent of total population.

The Government of Colombia, increasingly aware of the unfavorable implications of excessive population growth, has stated that "It is indispensable to...make available objective and sufficient information on family and sex life so that couples make a free decision [and] make available the necessary

Part of a family of 16—soon to be 17—poses in rural Paraguay. Through-out Latin America, there is a growing complex of national and interna-tional assistance, designed to make available to families like this many types of programs for planning family size and protecting maternal and child welfare. In Paraguay, a relatively weak economy high-lights the parallel problems of high population growth. Population activities began there in 1966; by 1975 the country's expenditures on family planning totaled about $4.5 million.

Right, a representative of Colombia's PROFAMILIA, a private family planning agency, explains the use of the monthly cycle of oral contraceptives. PRO-FAMILIA operates urban clinics, nonclinical con-traceptive services in urban and rural areas, and a wide range of information and education services. Below, a nurse in one of the 150 clinics operated by the Salvadoran Ministry of Health shows a mother a variety of contraceptive devices. El Salvador has had family planning programs since 1963; in 1974 its President announced a broadly based national population policy.

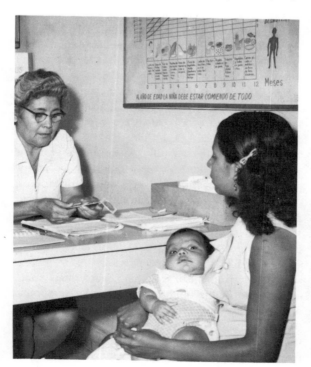

medical services which will both assure medical care and guarantee respect for conscience..." The overall program developed to deal with population problems in Colombia has consisted largely of education and the provision of family planning services by independent groups operating within and through integrated health agencies. Leaders of the groups involved have sought "to deal with a Colombian problem in a Colombian fashion." Specifically, they have sought to minimize political or religious conflict and have avoided offending social and cultural traditions.

Population program work got under way in a meaningful manner in 1967 when the International Planned Parenthood Federation (IPPF) began assisting a local private family planning agency called the Asociación Pro-Bienestar de la Familia Colombiana (PROFAMILIA). The aim of the new agency was to assist Colombians with their problems of excessive population growth and high abortion rates. That year, the U.S. Agency for International Development (AID) arranged for a $320,000 grant to the Colombian Medical Schools Association (ASCOFAME) for training doctors, nurses, and other population workers in all methods of family planning and to perform research and analyses of such factors as internal migration, housing, and family structure. The Pathfinder Fund, the Population Council, and the Ford Foundation provided various kinds of program assistance through interested organizations.

From this beginning, the program has continued to expand. Momentum picked up sharply after October 1970, when Colombia's President announced the extending of "social and medical assistance to all classes of the country in order that every family may have the liberty and responsibility to determine the number of its children." The following month, Colombia's National Council of Social and Economic Policy adopted guidelines indicating support for making family life and sex education, plus necessary medical services, available to families.

The Ministry of Health has continued to increase its emphasis on the family planning content of the maternal/child care program within the constraints of the sociocultural, religious-political milieu in which it operates. With a minimum of publicity, it has expanded its maternal/child care and family planning program to provide some service in essentially all population areas of the country. In 1975, family planning services were available in 928 public health clinics. The Ministry of Health has also assumed responsibility for the postpartum program in 35 nonuniversity regional hospitals. This work will be expanded by 1978 to 105 hospitals—or complete coverage for this type of facility.

In addition to continuing its in-service training program for physicians, coordinators, and nurses, the Ministry emphasizes training for professors of schools of practical (auxiliary) nursing. It has made changes in curriculums that have meant increased attention to maternal/child care and family planning.

The Ministry also has embarked on an ambitious program to train 10,000 rural health promoters. About 2,600 are now in service, functioning as a link with the health post and providing health education, motivation to use health services, and information on family planning.

PROFAMILIA has played a key role in Colombia's family planning program since 1967. In 1975 it operated 42 clinics in 31 major cities, as well as six cytology laboratories. The increase in new acceptors in 1975 totaled about 85,000, and control visits for the year were 300,000. The clinics provide specialized, high-quality family planning service to a substantial part of the urban population. The program encompasses a full spectrum of traditional and advanced concepts of fertility control.

A well-trained professional medical staff is maintained, but increasing attention is being given to the use of paramedical personnel and nonclinical programs of contraception. These nonclinical activities are operating both in urban and rural areas. In 1975 they included about 660 distribution points and provided service to more than 56,000 women. Although the bulk of the distribution points are in rural areas, over 200 eventually will be established in the urban slums of 15 cities.

A commercial marketing unit is aimed at reducing the price of contraceptives as well as expanding their usage through traditional commercial channels. The commercial unit also employs newer distribution techniques, including coupon campaigns utilizing the mail, newspapers, and radio and a special campaign aimed exclusively at drugstores.

PROFAMILIA's information and education program is aimed primarily at changing community attitudes and attracting new acceptors to the organization's clinics and distribution posts. In 1975 PROFAMILIA reinitiated—with locally contributed time—a radio campaign in 26 cities; the development of folders, posters, stickers, slides, and calendars for publicizing contraceptive distribution and other family planning services; regular courses and meetings; and the use of motivators, mostly in collaboration with the community-based distribution program.

The Population Reference Bureau, through its Bogotá office, conducted a wide range of information activities in Colombia and other Latin American countries between 1967 and 1974.

ASCOFAME has restructured its teaching and postpartum program, making it an integrated maternal/child care teaching and service activity that provides all medical graduates with academic and practical experience in family planning. New acceptors in 1974 totaled 21,120.

An outgrowth of previous work by ASCOFAME was the formation of the Regional Population Center with a charter permitting population activities by nonmedical institutions. The major thrust of the Center's program is in training and research, but it has shown an interest and ability to move into areas not covered by other programs.

A potentially important service organization, the Cruz Verde, has been formed by a group of influential citizens with the support of the Coffee Growers Association. The Cruz Verde wants to promote distribution of contraceptives in the rural areas.

Another organization, the Association of Physicians and Pharmacists (SOMEFA), provides incentives for physicians and pharmacists to extend information and services through private channels.

The national skills training program, SENA, proposes to give 200 of its own leaders short courses in population matters.

The Foundation for Family Life Orientation (FUNOF) has focused on training and community seminars outside Bogotá. Its activity is being taken over in part by the Colombian Welfare Institute, however, and FUNOF will be reduced to reaching 31,500 persons between 1976 and 1978.

The Association for the Study of Population (ACEP) has excelled in leadership training and family life education. Its program is targeted primarily toward women's leadership groups that have significant multiplier potential. It also has provided training for such diverse elements as pharmacists, military leaders, agrarian reform institutions, employees, union leaders, family welfare institute leaders, and hospital "gray lady" volunteers. ACEP has also translated, published, and distributed regionally—to a list of some 8,000 individuals and institutions—a large body of family planning material originally published by the Population Council and George Washington University.

All these activities by the Ministry of Health and the private organizations are paying off in family planning terms. In 1975 an estimated 18 percent of Colombian women in the 15-to-49 age group were taking part in the population program. About a million women, including those obtaining contraceptives from private sources, were participating in family planning. Of new acceptors, about 50 percent were choosing IUD's as a contraceptive method, 35 percent pills, 3 percent sterilization, and 12 percent other methods—condoms, diaphragms, foam, jelly, cream, and injectibles. Abortion is illegal in Colombia.

External Assistance

Substantial funds have been applied to Colombia's population program since 1967. From all sources, the total was $29.8 million, of which the Colombian Government supplied just over $9 million, the IPPF almost $7.3 million, the U.S. Agency for International Development over $3.1 million, the Population Council $3.1 million, and The Pathfinder Fund $1.2 million and UNFPA $3.8 million.

Other donors which provided diverse forms of assistance included Family Planning International Assistance, the Association for Voluntary Sterilization, the International Development Research Corporation, the University of North Carolina, the Pan American Health Organization, Development Associates Incorporated, CARE, the Ford Foundation, the Rockefeller Foundation, Oxfam, Population Services International, the World Assembly of Youth, World Education, World Neighbors, Canada, and Sweden.

Costa Rica

Costa Rica's population in mid-1975 totaled 2 million compared with the 1965 number of 1.5 million. The yearly rate of increase, however, has been declining over the decade. Although the rate for 1974 was still high at 2.3 percent per year, it was down sharply from the 3.9 percent in 1965 and substantially below the Latin American average of 2.9 percent. Moreover, with the help of a comprehensive family program, further reduction in the rate of increase is expected.

Costa Rica's population program traces to early perception by the nation's leaders that too many people vying for available resources was magnifying existing social and economic problems. The private Costa Rican Demographic Association (CRDA), an affiliate of the International Planned Parenthood Federation (IPPF), began in 1967 to provide family planning services. In 1968 the Ministry of Health initiated services, and it was joined in 1970 by the Social Security Institute (CCSS).

Costa Rica has a national family planning policy set forth by executive decree. The Government's highly successful program is coordinated at the national level by the central population committee (CONAPO) consisting of representatives of the

Ministry of Health, the Ministry of Education, the CCSS, the private family planning association, the university, and two family orientation centers.

In the first 6 months of 1975, the Ministry of Health handled 59 percent of the total 105,610 family planning visits, the CCSS almost 37 percent, CRDA 4 percent, and a small Catholic Church-sponsored Center for Family Integration (CIF), 0.1 percent.

In 1975 an estimated 25 percent of women in the reproductive age group (15 through 49) were using contraceptives obtained through organized programs or from private sources. Of methods used, oral contraceptives accounted for 78 percent, IUD's 11 percent, and other methods—largely condoms and sterilizations—11 percent.

The Ministry of Health offers family planning services in all of its health facilities, and the CCSS offers family planning services in 12 facilities. Under existing law, however, CCSS will eventually take over all the Ministry of Health hospitals with the Ministry determining policy and the CCSS providing services. The CCSS also has established an excellent center for training graduate and auxiliary nurses as women health care specialists. Over 70 students were graduated in 1975. This training center is the only one of its kind in Latin America, and will do much to promote the use of paramedical personnel for providing family planning services; the center is now being used as a show place and example for many Latin American countries interested in establishing similar training centers.

CRDA was one of the early promoters of non-clinical distribution of contraceptives—a system through which women who visit public health clinics receive coupons enabling them to buy oral contraceptives from participating pharmacies at a price substantially below the going retail price. CRDA's main role in national family planning work, however, has been to create favorable public opinion for the Government's program. This has been done through conferences, seminars, sex education, releases to the mass media and the distribution of other printed material on population and sex education. In addition, CRDA assists in the administration of a grant to Costa Rica for family planning work provided by the United Nations Fund for Population Activities (UNFPA).

The CIF in 1975 offered 175 courses of 15 sessions each for over 29,000 couples and pre-matrimonials. The Catholic Church of Costa Rica now requires each couple planning to marry to attend such a course, where all family planning methods are discussed. If a couple does not like a method such as rhythm, CIF may refer them to CCSS.

External Assistance

In relation to Costa Rica's size, outside financial inputs to the program have been substantial—almost $9.4 million between 1965 and 1975. Major donors include the U.S. Agency for International Development, just under $2.9 million; IPPF, over $1.9 million; UNFPA, over $1.5 million in assistance; the Ford Foundation $829,000; and Sweden $881,000. Other organizations and governments assisting have been Family Planning International Assistance, the Pan American Health Organization, the Association for Voluntary Sterilization, the Population Council, The Pathfinder Fund, World Educational International, the Government of Canada, the Tinker Foundation, the American Public Health Association, and Church World Service. Inputs of the Costa Rican Government totaled $1.6 million over the decade.

Ecuador

Ecuador had a mid-1975 population of 6.7 million compared with 4.9 million in 1965. The yearly rate of natural increase in 1974 was 3.2 percent, or above the average for Latin America. Though not yet a crowded country by Asian standards, Ecuador has the highest ratio of people per unit of arable land in South America. The great majority of Ecuadoreans are farmers. In addition to crops for local consumption, they raise bananas, the leading agricultural export commodity, and coffee, cocoa beans, and sugar for export.

Despite reduced levels of petroleum production and exports during the first half of 1975, the Ecuadorian economy generally continued to boom throughout the year with the per capita GNP rising significantly. While 1976 is generally expected to bring additional growth, that growth nevertheless will be tempered by the fact that almost half of the population is under 15 years of age and by the fact that a high ratio of dependency continues to exist together with high rates of unemployment and underemployment. Such problems tend to be intensified by the nation's continuing rate of rapid population growth.

Recent demographic projections indicate that, even with a moderate and gradual decline in the birth rate to replacement level, the population would reach about 30 million before stabilizing in the next century. This projected total, about 5 times larger than the present population, would very seriously overload resource availabilities.

The level of official and public awareness of the "population problem" is fairly high among educated citizens. Frequent articles appear about demographic matters in the daily press and in weekly journals, and there is some public discussion of the issues involved. However, there is no general concern about population imbalances, nor is there strong pressure to push family planning programs. As a result, family planning has been rather slow to develop.

Aside from private medical practice, the first limited urban family planning services were started in 1965 by the private Asociación Pro Familia Ecuadoriana (APROFE), affiliated with the International Planned Parenthood Federation (IPPF). Government-provided services, encouraged and largely financed by the U.S. Agency for International Development (AID), began in a modest way in 1969, were organized at the national level by 1972, and were given official sanction in 1973. This sanction, reaffirmed in 1974, does not give Ecuador a policy based on a demographic rationale; it does give it a policy based on health and human rights. However, family planning services are available in most public clinics as well as in several private facilities.

On an overall basis, active users of family planning services in public and private programs exceeded 70,000 in 1975, up from 53,000 in 1974. Over 300 public and private clinics were providing family planning services compared with 267 in 1974. An estimated 4.7 percent of women in the 15 through 49 age group were covered by the program in 1975. IUD's have been the most popular contraceptive method, followed closely by pills.

The Government's new policy of promoting family planning through the public media is expected to stimulate activity by making poor families aware of services and supplies that can reduce fertility.

External Assistance

Program inputs since 1967 have totaled almost $8.4 million. Of that total, AID contributed $5.3 million, of which $481,000 was in fiscal 1974 and $446,000 in fiscal 1975. Financing of the United Nations Fund for Population Activities will be, starting in 1976, $1,346,000. IPPF funding has been $888,000. Other sources include The Pathfinder Fund, the Population Council, Family Planning International Assistance, the University of North Carolina, Columbia University, the Ford Foundation, and the United Kingdom.

El Salvador

The population of El Salvador rose from 2.9 million in 1965 to 4.1 million in 1975, a gain of 41 percent. The rate of annual natural increase in 1974 was 3.2 percent, which, if continued, would mean a doubling of the nation's people in only 22 years.

Population pressures on limited resources have created numerous social and economic problems. For example, El Salvador's literacy rate and per capita GNP are well below the average for mainland Latin America. The country has high seasonal unemployment and a very uneven distribution of income.

Concern about the effects of excessive population growth was shown as early as 1963, when the Salvadoran Demographic Association (SDA), now an affiliate of the International Planned Parenthood Federation (IPPF), was formed. In 1964 the first family planning clinic was opened with the assistance of The Pathfinder Fund. In 1965 the Government requested support from the U.S. Agency for International Development (AID). In 1966, AID response made possible the opening of 11 family planning clinics, and, in 1967, 10 more. In 1968 the Ministry of Health initiated a 5-year program of family planning expansion including additional clinics, and in 1969 the Institute of Social Security inaugurated a program calling for still more clinics. In July 1974 the President of El Salvador announced and defined a national population policy, which sets very broad goals: population growth reduction, nutritional improvement, skills development, employment generation, balanced population distribution, and other health and welfare benefits. Official support for family planning activities is based not only on demographic factors but also on factors of health and human rights.

In 1974 current users of contraceptives in the public sector numbered 101,000.

SDA has complemented the activities carried on through the nationwide network of some 150 clinics operated by the Ministry of Health and the Institute of Social Security. SDA has succeeded in repopularizing the intrauterine device (IUD). One of SDA's clinics has become a center for male and female sterilization, and SDA uses that facility to train physicians in sterilization techniques. SDA also carries on numerous information and education activities. They include a motivational radio campaign, direct promotion by social workers in urban slums and rural villages, the training of agricultural extension and rural colonization personnel and of young people for family planning and sex education activities, and coordinating the work of women volunteers. In 1975 almost 20,000 group discussions and talks were given by the SDA to private and Governmental audiences.

External Assistance

Foreign financial support to family planning in El Salvador totaled $8.1 million between fiscal 1966 and 1975. AID assistance totaled $3.3 million, of which $312,000 was in 1974 and $316,000 in 1975. Other major donors over the 10-year period and their contributions included the IPPF with $1.1 million, the United Nations Fund for Population Activities for $868,000, the Ford Foundation with $540,000, and the Population Council with $134,000. Also assisting were The Pathfinder Fund, World Education, the Association for Voluntary Sterilization, Oxfam, the United Nations Children's Fund, the Pan American Health Organization, the Smithsonian Institution, the World Assembly of Youth, and Sweden.

Guatemala

The population of Guatemala, a basically rural country, had increased from the 4.2 million of 1965 to 5.5 million by mid-1975. The natural rate of increase in 1974 was 2.8 percent which, if continued, would mean a doubling of the population by the year 2000. The birth rate is a high 43 per 1,000 people a year, and only the relatively high annual death rate—15 per 1,000—precludes an even more rapid rate of natural increase.

The present rate of population growth has accentuated several basic problems. For example, there are not enough classrooms and teachers to permit all school-age children to attend school through the first six grades; and at the secondary level, nationwide, 88 percent of young people in the 15 to 20 age group are not in school. Less than 11 percent of the rural population has ready access to potable water, and sewage systems are available to only 6 percent of the people—mostly city dwellers. The per capita GNP in 1973 was $450, far below the average for the Latin American mainland which was $770.

Concern about these and other problems engendered by rapid population increase led to the organization in 1964 of the Guatemala Association for Family Welfare (APROFAM), an affiliate of the International Planned Parenthood Federation (IPPF). In 1965, APROFAM opened its first family planning clinic. During its first year of operation it provided 5,200 clinic consultations and services for 1,700 new acceptors.

Family planning began to make significant strides in 1967 with the signing of an agreement between the Ministry of Public Health and the U.S. Agency for International Development (AID), which provided funding for APROFAM's services in 20 Ministry of Public Health centers and 10 mobile health units. Progress slackened in 1970, but by 1974, the number of clinics had grown to 129, through which the Ministry and APROFAM provided family planning services to almost 21,000 new acceptors and close to 30,000 active users. Over the years the program had been strengthened through the training of medical and paramedical personnel, the initiation of a sex education project in public and private schools, the expansion of information and communication activities, and the installation of a computerized statistical system.

But this progress must be measured against the magnitude of Guatemala's growing population problem. The nation has some 1.3 million women of reproductive age. Acceptors under the APROFAM program, plus some users obtaining contraceptives through private sources, make up only 4.5 percent of the nation's fertile women. A special problem in Guatemala is the difficulty of reaching the rural population with the family planning message. About 44 percent of the people are Indians, speaking a wide diversity of dialects.

Furthermore, some opposition to family planning had surfaced as early as 1965, when a Pastoral Letter came out against the use of contraceptives not sanctioned by the Catholic Church. In 1968 the major university took a position against contraception. In October 1974 several newspapers, supported by some university students, started a campaign against family planning that ran until March 1975. In view of such opposition, and in the absence of a clear population policy on the part of the Government, organized activities have proceeded cautiously. Acceptance of family planning has tended to stabilize at relatively low levels.

In 1975, however, the Minister of Public Health took a strong positive stand in favor of family planning and in support of APROFAM. In March 1975, in a speech to the United Nations Second Meeting on Population in Mexico, the Minister clearly indicated his Government's concern with rapid population growth and added, in part, "The Government...recognizes the fundamental freedom of the individual and the couple to decide on the size of the family and spacing of pregnancy, and therefore makes available to all inhabitants (without discrimination with respect to creed, education, location, employment) the information, education and services indispensable for such determination to be made with good judgment, consciousness, and freedom."

The Government appears to be close to defining a specific policy. It has formed a top-level group consisting of members from the National Planning Council, the Ministry of Public Health, APROFAM, and other selected agencies to develop and present the policy. In July 1975 an 11-man working committee finished the first draft of a comprehensive "Population Policy" and submitted it, informally, to the Minister of Public Health.

External Assistance

From fiscal 1967 through fiscal 1975, a total of $8 million was channeled into family planning activities in Guatemala. Of that total, AID provided over $4.8 million, of which $673,000 was in fiscal 1974 and $500,000 in fiscal 1975. Funding from the IPPF over the 1967-75 period totaled $1.8 million, the United Nations Fund for Population Activities gave $720,000, The Pathfinder Fund provided $167,000, the Swedish International Development Authority allocated $85,000, the Population Council contributed $82,000, and the Pan American Health Organization gave $25,000. The inputs of the Government totaled $143,000.

Guyana

Guyana's population rose from 631,000 in 1965 to 786,000 in 1975. The annual rate of natural increase in 1974 was 3.0, which, were it to continue, would bring about a doubling of the nation's population in 23 years.

The Responsible Parenthood Association of Guyana was established in March 1974 with a grant from the International Planned Parenthood Association. Priorities for the new organization were stated to be: first, an education-public relations program utilizing local media; second, cooperation with the Ministry of Health to provide family planning services in existing facilities; third, cooperation with such organizations as trade unions and youth clubs to stress the need for following responsible parenthood practices; and, fourth, operation of clinics in both urban and rural areas. The Association planned to open its first clinic in 1975. The United Nations Fund for Population Activities has financed a fertility survey.

Honduras

Honduras had a population of 2.7 million as of mid-1975 compared with 1.8 million in 1965. The annual rate of natural increase was 3.5 percent in 1974 and the second highest in Latin America. Components of this situation are a birth rate (as of 1974) of 49 per 1,000 people per year—the highest in Latin America—and an annual death rate of 14 per 1,000.

Honduras has not felt the pressure of population on land resources to the same acute degree as some of its neighbors. But there is a growing awareness that the land/population ratio is not as much a problem as is the limited ability of the nation to develop economically and socially. Honduras had one of the lowest per capita GNP figures in Latin America—$290 in 1973. The nation's rapid population growth is also beginning to tax health and educational services.

Population program work in Honduras began on a small scale in 1964 when the private Honduras Family Planning Association, an affiliate of the International Planned Parenthood Federation (IPPF), opened a clinic in Tegucigalpa. In 1966 the Government opened a clinic and also offered family planning services through a rural mobile health program, known as PUMAR. Between 1966 and 1973 a total of 33 additional Government clinics were opened, with expanded services. During this period the private association opened a second clinic to provide postpartum service and an enlarged training program.

In 1973 the Government officially announced a "voluntary demographic policy" including three main principles: provision of adequate education about responsible parenthood; utilization of natural and technical resources that lead to a well-nourished, creative population; and application of the principle of voluntary participation in family planning programs. Family planning is supported not only for health reasons but also because it is deemed to be a human right.

In 1974 the Government, as part of its national development plan, announced a policy of providing family planning information and services to all who desired them. The Government implemented this policy with increased financial support for its 34 maternal/child health clinics, which were being used by 40,000 regular acceptors in 1975. At the same time, the private association started an outreach program using present family planning acceptors to motivate others.

In 1975 training in family planning techniques was begun for all of the Ministry of Health staff. In the earlier years, the medical profession required that all family planning be provided by doctors; but because of the small number of doctors available in the country, it is becoming apparent that services should and will be offered through other means. The private association has extended its outreach program and courses to student groups.

A major program target for the future is the complete integration of family planning into all services of the Ministry of Health—a move that will eventually make family planning easily accessible to 90 percent of the total fertile population, both urban and rural.

Of the acceptors now using the services of the 36 clinics in Honduras, about three-fourths have chosen oral contraceptives as a method, and one-fourth intrauterine devices (IUD's).

External Assistance

Between fiscal 1966 and 1975, the U.S. Agency for International Development (AID) provided over $4.6 million in budget support to the Honduras population/family planning program, of which $788,000 was in fiscal 1974 and $619,000 in fiscal 1975. AID is supporting the Honduras National Development Plan, which stresses agrarian reform, efficient use of agricultural resources, and expansion of basic health and other social services in the rural areas.

The IPPF has contributed $958,000 to the population/family planning program, and the United Nations Fund for Population Activities $653,000 Other sources of assistance include the Population Council, The Pathfinder Fund, World Education, and the United Kingdom. Honduras contributed $1.5 million through fiscal 1975.

Mexico

Mexico has one of the fastest-growing populations in the world; the annual rate of natural increase was 3.8 percent in 1974. The mid-1975 population was 60.1 million compared with 42.9 million in 1965. Mexico's numbers have doubled more than twice since the first modern census in 1895 enumerated 12.6 million people. Mexico's "responsible parenthood" program, initiated in 1973, is aimed at developing an eventual solution for the many exceptionally grave problems which, in one way or another, can be traced to this very high rate of overall population growth.

Mexico's population, overwhelmingly Roman Catholic, is marked by wide disparities in culture, degree of urbanization, and standard of living. At one end of the spectrum are the cultural descendants of Mexico's original inhabitants—those who live in "indigenous" communities (mostly in the central and southern parts of the country) and speak an indigenous language—and who are almost universally poor. At the other end of the economic scale are those city dwellers who have accumulated capital and become business entrepreneurs of various types or who have become skilled in one or more of a variety of professions.

Mexico's population has also been particularly mobile in recent years. For example, the movement of people from rural areas to cities has been rapid since 1960. The largest streams have moved toward Mexico City, whose population has been increasing by approximately 11 percent annually during this decade. As of 1974, Mexico City had 9 million inhabitants and was one of the largest urban conglomerations in the world. Other cities of rapid growth have been Guadalajara, Monterrey, and the cities along the U.S. border—Tijuana, Mexicali, Nogales, Juárez, Nuevo Laredo, Reynosa, and Matamoros. Smaller migratory movements have increased the size of State capitals and smaller industrial and commercial centers such as Chihuahua, Cuernavaca, Pueblo, Leon, and Acapulco. There also has been a substantial degree of migration to new agricultural areas along the coast of the Gulf of Mexico, to the southern and southeastern tropical areas, and to a number of irrigated areas which are devoted in large part to large-scale agricultural practices, particularly those that are located in the Pacific Coast States of Sonora and Sinaloa. The adoption of further farm mechanization in such areas can be expected to increase the need for skilled labor which, to some degree, will be drawn from other areas and add to the migratory flow.

Large numbers of Mexicans have moved to the United States; in 1974 they were the major group of U.S. immigrants. In addition to the Mexicans who entered the United States as permanent residents, many Mexicans who reside along the border commute to work daily in the United States. This south-to-north emigration, including the movement of daily workers, has tended to ease some of Mexico's population pressures—but many problems remain.

Problems also persist despite the nation's really substantial economic development. Growth of the Mexican economy in recent years has averaged out at about 6 percent. During this period Mexico has changed from a clearly developing country to a nation of middle-range growth. Gains have occurred particularly in construction, petrochemicals, manufacturing, and the output of electrical energy. The discovery of additional petroleum resources is expected to give the economy a further boost.

The per capita GNP in 1973 was $870—well above the average for 22 Latin American countries. But wealth is poorly distributed.

Although the highest earnings groups have accumulated and invested appreciable capital, and although a substantial middle class has appeared, population growth has accentuated the many problems of disadvantaged urban and rural inhabitants. The 1970 census found that over a third of the dwellings in use in Mexico had only one room. Medical care is concentrated in cities, and about 100,000 locales had no doctors. Almost 24 percent of the population was judged to be illiterate. Meanwhile, underemployment in the metropolitan area of Mexico City is estimated to be over 30 percent.

Such problems led to the beginning of a new population policy in 1959, when a small group of concerned people founded the Association for the Welfare of the Family, which was aimed at determining the receptivity of Mexicans to family planning through research and contraceptive services. The Association had much opposition and was forced by the Government to close its clinic for 3 months in 1961. It changed its name in 1963 to Association for Maternal Health. In 1975 the Association operated a large private clinic in Mexico City with 50,000 active users. The patients are middle, lower middle, and upper lower class, and their fees depend on ability to pay. The clinic also provides orientation programs for medical students and potential clients.

In 1965 the Foundation for Population Studies (FEPAC), an affiliate of the International Planned Parenthood Federation (IPPF), was established. Subsequently it carried out investigations of population characteristics and of attitudes toward contraception, trained medical and paramedical personnel, and became the leading private family planning institute. FEPAC's primary activity is offering family planning services through a national network of 91 clinics with 26 located at Government facilities.

Although Mexican women in the late 1960's expressed a growing interest in limiting the number of their children, the momentum toward family planning seemed sidetracked in 1969 when the Presidential candidate of the dominant political party, Luis Echeverria, came out for increased rather than decreased population. The position of Echeverria, who became President postponed a plan by the Ministry of Health, the Social Security Institute, other Governmental divisions, and FEPAC to include family planning within an expanded national program of maternal/infant health care.

By mid-1971, however, signs of a change in the President's position began to appear following key advisers' consistent and vigorous emphasis on population problems. In April 1972, the Mexican Government announced that family planning would be integrated with existing health centers and services started in January 1973. In September 1973, the President announced that he would submit additions and revisions to population legislation, and said, by way of justification:

Large sectors of our population are worried about the problem of the growth of the family. Mexican women by the thousands go to health centers, to Government and private clinics in search of orientation on the possibilities of regulating their fertility. We reject the idea that a purely demographic criterion to reduce births can replace the complex task of development. But we would be committing a grave error if we did not realize the seriousness of the increase of the population and the needs this increase generates.

In November 1973, a new General Population Law was passed, which included the following provision (Article 3, Part II):

To carry out programs of family planning through the educational and public health services of the public sector and to take care that these programs and those of private organisms be carried out with absolute respect for the fundamental rights of man and that they preserve the dignity of families, with the object of regulating rationally and stabilizing the growth of the population, so as to achieve the best utilization of the human and natural resources of the country.

The new law provides for a National Population Council to implement its provisions. The Council, inaugurated in 1974, gives Mexico a new orientation toward responsible parenthood—a national population policy deemed consistent with Mexican culture and political interest. The Council is a branch of the Secretary of Government and is composed of the titular heads of eight secretariats.

Emphasis has been placed by both the Government and the Catholic Church on the rights of the family and the role of responsibile parenthood in the strengthening of the family institution. Simultaneous to the Mexican Government policy reversal regarding the desirability of family planning, the bishops of Mexico made the statement that the decision on this matter (responsible parenthood) corresponds to the couple. The role of the authorities lies in urging responsibility, informing, and facilitating access to medical and supporting services. On occasion, since this 1972 statement, the Church has offered light criticism of Government policy through pronouncements advocating the treatment of family planning matters with discretion. That is, the Church has disapproved of the extensive use of public media for promoting artificial contraception. However, Government population officials continue to recognize the necessity of using all forms of communication to promote the concept of responsible parenthood

La Victoria is a morning day-care center operated by the Colombian Institute for Family Wellbeing. In afternoons and evenings, as a community center for other family members, it offers assistance on family planning along with a variety of other services including nutrition supplements for children and pregnant mothers.

Below left, typical migrant housing in San Jose. Rural migrants, who have Costa Rica's largest families, are a primary target for the nation's highly successful population program; for on a family as well as a national basis, it is clear to the program's leaders that when too many people vie for available resources, many will be left out.
Below right, graduates of a Guatemalan "granny midwife" training program talk with the Minister of Health and the U.S. official assisting the program. In several Latin American countries, family planning programs depend heavily on midwives to reach the rural population with the family planning message and with the necessary services.

among Mexico's citizens. Moreover, the generally low level of Church involvement in Mexican policies, which has prevailed throughout Mexican post-revolutionary history, shows no signs of change.

Mexican leadership has insisted that population planning will not substitute for economic development. And it views its program as one that did not come from outside pressure but rather one that grew out of Mexico's own awareness of the effects of population change on national problems. Mexico, which makes its own population decisions, is sensitive to the necessity for implementing a program fitted to Mexican situations.

In 1975 Mexico had one of the most comprehensive population policies in the Western Hemisphere. The increase in the provision of family planning services through the Ministry of Health, the Social Security Institute, and other Government and private groups is commensurate with the comprehensiveness of the official policy.

The program remains strongly viable. Demographic increase was the principal topic at the Mexican Government's 4th National Health Meeting in September 1975. At the meeting, Secretary-General Luisa Maria Leal, of the Mexican Population Council, called for greater dedication to family planning among Mexico's medical profession and termed the nation's population growth "irrational behavior of human reproduction" and added that, although the individual's rights are to be respected, Mexico's progress also must be considered.

FEPAC by 1973 had expanded its clinics to 91 and had received a 4-year, $2 million grant from the United Nations Fund for Population Activities (UNFPA), with the IPPF as the executing agent. This, the first UNFPA grant to a private agency, was for the expansion of clinical services. However, the Government now appears to be bypassing FEPAC, though allowing it to maintain existing programs. The IPPF noted in its 1974 report to donors that it had no plans to increase the number of its clinics, 91, of which 26 are located at Government facilities.

The new national program of the Ministry of Health offered family planning at 298 clinics in 1974—a "Phase I" program covering most of the population residing in communities of over 10,000. A "Phase II" program is planned for the establishment of some 2,000 new rural health posts to offer family planning to the 20 million Mexicans living in smaller towns and on farms. "Phase II" also is to include 11,000 "health houses" to be visited on a rotational basis by medical interns completing their required year of social service.

The Mexican Social Security Institute offers family planning services in 133 of its health clinics and plans to expand its facilities, paralleling those of the Ministry of Health, to the point of providing 40 percent of the total family planning services in the country by 1977.

The small, private Association for Maternal Health in the capital city also provides services, conducts training and undertakes some research. The Mexican Social Security Institute for Government Employees and the medical services of the military provide services for their personnel.

In 1974 a total of 250,000 new acceptors was reported. The clinics offer three contraceptive methods: orals, IUD's, and injections. The general target was to make family planning available to 306,000 women in 1975, gradually increasing to 717,000 by 1979; 20 percent of all institutionalized obstetric cases would have access to a postpartum program.

External Assistance

Considerable external assistance has been forthcoming to supplement inputs of the Mexican Government over the 1969-1975 period. The contribution of the UNFPA alone in this period has amounted to $4,470,000

Nicaragua

Nicaragua's population increased from 1.6 million in 1965 to 2.2 million by mid-1975. The rate of natural increase in 1974 was 3.4 percent annually, well above the 2.9 average for the Latin American mainland. At the 1974 rate, Nicaragua's population would double in 20 years. The annual births per 1,000 population were 48 (second only to the rate in Honduras), and deaths were 14 per 1,000 people.

Although the Government has generally indicated that Nicaragua's anticipated population size, the levels and trends of its population growth, and the country's fertility rates are acceptable, it has nevertheless sponsored family planning programs.

Family planning, as a Government program, was initiated in 1967 when the Ministry of Public Health established the Office of Family Welfare. By 1970 the family planning program of the Ministry of Health was expanded to include 60 health centers throughout the country and became the National Family Planning Program. By January 1975, this activity encompassed 77 clinics providing family planning services, including 62 Ministry of Health clinics, 7 Social Security clinics, 2 Moravian Missionary Group clinics, and 6 clinics operated by the Nicaraguan Demographic Association, an affiliate of the International Planned Parenthood Federation (IPPF). Official support for family planning is based on a health and human rights rationale rather than on demographic factors. Active users of contraceptives rose from 1,600 in 1968 to 25,400 in 1974. The Ministry of Health's target is to reduce the birth rate of 48 per 1,000 people in 1974 to 40 per 1,000 by 1977. Family planning will be integrated with health services wherever possible, with the Government assuming an increasing share of annual program costs.

External Assistance

Combined inputs to Nicaragua's family planning program totaled $8,681,000 from fiscal 1967 through fiscal 1975. The contribution of the U.S. Agency for International Development totaled $3,228,000 over the 1967-75 period, including $494,000 in fiscal 1974 and $400,000 in fiscal 1975. Assistance of The Pathfinder Fund totaled $2,379,000, and of the IPPF $2,298,000. Other organizations providing assistance included the United Nations Fund for Population Activities, the Pan American Health Organization, World Assembly of Youth, the Moravian Mission Group, the Ford Foundation, the Population Council, and the Rockefeller Foundation.

Panama

Panama's population rose from 1.3 million in 1965 to 1.7 million in mid-1975. The rate of natural increase—2.6 percent annually in 1974—would mean a doubling of the population in 27 years.

Rapid population increase is placing great burdens on education, health, security, and other. public services. There is much unemployment and under-employment.

Awareness of the many populated-related problems engendered led to the organization in 1966 of a voluntary Asociacion Panamena para el Plane-miento de la Familia (APLAFA), the voluntary Panamanian Association for Family Planning, which is an affiliate of the International Planned Parenthood Federation (IPPF). In the years that followed, the Panamanian Government took an increasing interest in family planning activities, leading to initiation in 1973 of an integrated health services program which by 1975, spread to five of the nine Provinces.

In 1975, 39 percent of the nation's fertile female population was reported using some form of contra-ception. The goal of the Panama program is to deliver family planning services to 50 percent of fertile women by the end of 1978. Eighty-eight of 106 hospitals, integrated medical centers, and health centers were providing services in 1974 and plans were under way to extend coverage to an added 105 sub-centers in 1975-76.

The medical profession has required all family planning services to be provided by doctors or medical personnel under supervision of doctors. Services provided include pills, IUD's, condoms, and tubal ligations.

External Assistance

Assistance from the U.S. Agency for International Development (AID), begun in fiscal 1967, totaled $3,840,000 through fiscal 1975, of which $638,000 was in 1974 and $360,000 in 1975. AID has provided assistance for clinical supplies and other services as well as the rural mobile health program, which is making it possible for the Government to reach areas that would otherwise not have planning services.

Over the 1969-75 period the IPPF has provided a total of $390,000 in help to APLAFA. In 1975 APLAFA undertook a comprehensive information and education program with press, television, and radio coverage; a community action program for teachers, schools, private groups, and parent associa-tions; and private sector coverage for industrial areas and university groups. Public information and discussions have helped to establish family planning as a socially and politically acceptable program. Earlier in 1973, the IPPF affiliate signed an agree-ment with the Ministry of Public Health under which the APLAFA will provide support and information and education to the family planning component of the maternal/child health program, provide sup-port for training medical and paramedical personnel within the Ministry, and reinforce the family planning services in the Government health centers.

The United Nations Fund for Population Activi-ties in fiscal years 1971-75 contributed assistance funds amounting to $285,000. This financing was for support of the Office of National Population Studies, for a national sex education program, and for train-ing of demographic personnel.

The Population Council and The Pathfinder Fund have also given assistance.

Paraguay

The population of Paraguay increased from 2.0 million in 1965 to 2.5 million in mid-1975. The rate of natural increase in 1975 was about 3.1 percent annually, slightly above the Latin American average of 2.9 percent. Life expectancy at birth is 62 years, equal to the average for other countries of Central and South America but well below the 71 years estimated for Northern America and Europe.

Paraguay is among the least developed countries of Latin America. Its per capita GNP of $400 is far below the average of $773 for Latin America. The nation's relatively weak economy highlights the parallel problems of high population growth. The Government cannot afford the infrastructure needed to stimulate development, nor can it provide adequate education, medical care, and other social services for the people.

Population activities began in 1966 when the Paraguayan Center for Population Studies (CEPEP) was established by a group of physicians, demographers, economists, and sociologists. In 1968 CEPEP established a planned parenthood clinic in the University Hospital at the National University of Asunción, and the following year the Center became an affiliate of the International Planned Parenthood Federation (IPPF). That same year the Institute for the Study of Human Reproduction (IERH) was created through an agreement between the Faculty of Medical Sciences of the National University of Asunción, the Ministry of Health (MOH), and the U.S. Agency for International Development (AID) to assist the Faculty of Medical Sciences to include family planning/population subjects in the medical students' curriculum, and to carry out demographic and social research activities.

In 1970 an AID project was begun with the MOH for the establishment of the first six public family planning clinics in Paraguay; the following year six additional clinics were established.

In May 1972 the Department of Family Protection (DEPROFA) was created through an AID/MOH project agreement. It was to be responsible for the implementation of all the governmental family planning programs and for supervision of those carried out by private and decentralized institutions such as CEPEP and the Social Security Institute.

In 1973 DEPROFA took several steps to improve services. Cancer detection was included as a standard test in all family planning clinics and regular follow-up procedures were initiated. Patients in the program reached a total of 4,969, and 7,300 Papanicolao tests were performed. Three refresher courses for paramedical personnel were given by DEPROFA with a total of 60 participants. About 7,000 copies of family planning/population publications were distributed throughout the country. Information, education, and communications activities of DEPROFA reached a total of 57,000 people.

In 1974 DEPROFA inaugurated seven new family planning clinics, bringing the agency's clinic total to 19. By the end of 1974 some 18,000 were using the facilities.

In the meantime, operations of CEPEP were expanding. In 1974 this IPPF affiliate was operating 25 family planning clinics throughout the country, including two new model clinics in Asunción. It also operates two clinics within military compounds, and has instituted a training program for officers and men within the armed forces. Training seminars for postgraduate medical students have been conducted at the National University.

CEPEP has done much in the area of information and education. In 1974 it organized four special meetings for over 120 community leaders to discuss population and family planning as it affects their communities. CEPEP planned 1975 seminars for 40 to 50 social security leaders; for about 50 educators; and another for 50 trade union leaders. Work was going forward to organize youth seminars for adolescents and university students. Hundreds of talks have been given in the clinics, strengthened with film presentations.

Users of contraceptives in Paraguay increased from 12,100 in 1972 to 43,000 in 1974. The 1974 total represented 14.6 percent of women between the ages of 15 and 49. Oral contraceptives were most popular with users, followed by IUD's and condoms.

External Assistance

Combined inputs to family planning work between 1967 and 1975 aggregated $4,478,000, of which the Paraguayan Government contributed $248,000.

Assistance from the U.S. Agency for International Development (AID) has amounted to $2,508,000, including funds for contraceptives obligated by AID's Washington office. AID assistance in 1974 amounted to $190,000 and in 1975 to $370,000.

IPPF outlays since 1967 totaled $1,596,000. Other agencies providing assistance have included the United Nations Fund for Population Activities, The Pathfinder Fund, the Population Council, the Mennonite Central Committee, and World Neighbors.

Peru

Peru's population rose from 11.5 million in 1965 to 15.5 million in mid-1975. The rate of natural increase was 2.9 percent annually in 1975—equal to the Latin American regional average, and a rate that would mean a doubling of the population in 24 years.

With an estimated 170,000 new entrants moving

into the labor force annually, population is acting as a drag on employment and labor productivity. High population growth has put strong pressures also on food, housing, schools, medical services, and other basic needs.

Substantial numbers of Peruvians have been concerned in recent years about the nation's spiraling population. Official anxiety first became evident in 1964 when, by Presidential Decree, the Center for Studies of Population and Development (CEPD) was established. CEPD's functions at first were to promote studies of population growth and economic and social development and publish them, to organize seminars and conferences on population, and to promote family planning and research. CEPD early in 1968 initiated a clinic-based family planning program supported by the Ministry of Health. Government policies changed with a new military government in 1968, and CEPD dropped the family planning phases. The Ministry of Health then struck out CEPD's family planning activities in Government-owned or -supported hospitals, prohibiting them beyond March 31, 1969.

In 1967 the church-sponsored Christian Family Movement (CFM) began a family life education program, including services to women to enable them to space their children, 2 years postpartum. Later, the church-sponsored Lay Apostle Responsible Parenthood Federation was formed, which offered an extensive program on marriage and responsible parenthood. These two organizations have continued to maintain several clinics in the poorer sections of Lima and Callao.

The Peruvian Association for Family Planning (APPF), a private organization founded in 1967, was reorganized in 1969 and became an affiliate of the International Planned Parenthood Federation (IPPF). From 1969 through 1973 APPF's clinics, two of them in rural areas, provided a total of 113,000 consultations for planned parenthood. In addition the organization placed much emphasis on information activities, such as distributing literature, conducting seminars, arranging exhibits, publishing a newsletter, and producing teaching materials, as well as carrying on education, training, and research operations. But in February 1974, the Government ordered the closing of APPF's clinics offering maternal/child health and planned parenthood services, although it allowed the organization to continue its education programs. In April 1975 the Government ordered APPF to cease all activities.

In early 1972 a new organization with maternal/child health responsibilities was instituted by the Ministry of Health. The organization, the Instituto Nacional de Neonatologia y Proteccion Materno Infantil (INPROMI), began operation in Lima but was later extended nationally. In June 1974 INPROMI began a study of medium- and high-risk mothers and in-country and foreign training of public health professionals. By decree, the Government in August 1974 made available to all women maternal and child care services free of charge.

An agreement between INPROMI and the U.S. Agency for International Development (AID), approved in June 1975 will provide during the 1976-77 period research to identify medium- and high-risk mothers all over the country, to develop means of reducing the risks, and to provide the Ministry of Health a program of maternal and child health, including education on family welfare, sex, nutrition, and other factors.

The program is expected to reach close to 284,000 mothers (about 3 percent of fertile-age Peruvian women) of whom 95,000 and especially the "gran multiparas" ("the highly fertile women") are expected to be the main recipients of the program. Responsible parenthood education will be included among other medical services to prevent and control risk as approved by the Government. The above program includes, also, training on maternal and child health and family welfare for Peruvian health personnel and especially for nurses aids, auxiliary and nonprofessional personnel.

One important factor must be noted, however: Peru's responsible parenthood program is being undertaken not for demographic reasons but largely in the interests of maternal and child welfare. Peru's position on population growth, as indicated by replies to a questionnaire at the Bucharest World Population Conference and other public pronouncements, assumes that general economic and social development will eventually dispose of the nation's population problem.

It should also be noted that the official position, even on this point, is not completely rigid. The Government has enunciated the "right of the family to choose the number of children it desires"— a position in line with that of the Catholic Church as set forth in the Episcopal Statement issued in 1974. The Government does not interfere in the teaching of medical courses whose content includes contraceptive technology for medically indicated reasons. The Government does not prohibit the commercial sale of contraceptives, although, legally, prescriptions are required. Responsible parenthood programs are carried on in military hospitals and hospitals owned and managed by cooperatives.

As this chronology indicates, a graph of Peru's policies since 1964 would be shaped roughly like a capital "U". Early interest in population activities was brought to a virtual halt in 1968. Very low-key operations were not opposed from 1969 through 1973. Increased interest in population matters in 1974 and 1975 has been followed by initiation of a responsible parenthood program limited to mothers who would endanger their health by having additional children.

External Assistance

Should Peru decide to relax its current position against family planning programs or, at least, not oppose them, substantial assistance undoubtedly would be forthcoming. Assistance relating to population matters, e.g., demographic and other research, limited education, and family education programs, including services for medically indicated reasons, from fiscal 1966 through 1975, totaling $5,024,000 has come from a number of sources.

Major donors include AID, $1,889,000, (with obligations of $92,000 in fiscal 1975); the United Nations Fund for Population Activities, $68,000, plus $2.8 million proposed over a 4-year period; Family Planning International Assistance, $918,000; and the International Planned Parenthood Federation, $636,000. Other donors include The Pathfinder Fund, Ford Foundation, and Rockefeller Foundation.

Surinam

Surinam's population increased from 336,000 in 1965 to 416,000 in mid-1975.

Stichting Lobi, the family planning organization affiliated with the International Planned Parenthood Federation, operates one clinic in Paramaribo. Visits to this clinic numbered 11,138 in 1973. Plans were under way in 1974 to introduce community-based distribution of contraceptives. A sex education program for secondary schools and an advertising campaign directed primarily at rural areas were being planned in 1974.

Uruguay

Uruguay's population increased from 2.5 million in 1965 to 2.8 million in mid-1975. The birth rate of 21 per 1,000 annually in 1974 was the lowest of any country in Central and South America. At the 1974 rate of natural increase—1.1 percent annually— it would take 63 years for Uruguay's population to double.

Uruguay's economic growth has been one of the slowest in the world. Over the 1970-74 period, gain in gross national product averaged, in total, minus 0.7 percent and, per capita, minus 1.8 percent. The average growth of GNP for all of Latin America over this period was 7.2 percent total and 4.2 percent per capita. Population pressure obviously does not explain Uruguay's situation, nor does lack of resources. Rather, it seems to trace to high consumption and inadequate investment. Also, Uruguay was hit hard in 1974 by increased world oil prices, which tripled oil import costs at the same time traditional export markets for beef were being reduced. In 1974-75, however, the Government of Uruguay embarked on a comprehensive economic reform program intended to reverse the impact of two decades of economic deterioration. In 1975 it succeeded in raising the GNP by approximately 3.7 percent.

Uruguay has had substantial emigration in recent years, which has relieved population pressures, especially in urban areas. Abortion is a major problem; there are an estimated three abortions to each birth.

The family planning program in Uruguay began in 1962 when the Ministry of Health (MOH) created the Association for Family Planning and Research on Human Reproduction (AUPFIRH). This association, now an affiliate of the International Planned Parenthood Federation (IPPF), offers family planning services and sex education plus treatment of genital diseases and sterility. It operates 21 clinics in Government health centers throughout the country. (The Government operates one clinic in Montevideo.)

In 1971 the Government entered into an agreement with AID under which the latter provided funds to equip and support maternal/child care clinics in suburban Montevideo. This 3-year project was undertaken to (1) reduce the high abortion rate by encouraging use of modern birth control methods, (2) decrease child mortality in Montevideo, (3) reduce child disease in Montevideo by 20 percent during the first year of operation, and (4) improve the quality of medical services available in low income sectors.

Prior to the 1974 World Population Conference in Bucharest, the Government issued the following statement on population matters:

1. Each nation has the unrestricted right to determine its own demographic policy.

2. The decision on the number of children will depend on the parents' free choice, and cannot be subject to official criteria.

3. Responsible parenthood will be promoted and stimulated so that in exercising the freedom of choice, parents will attend to their own good, that of their children, their families, and their society.

4. The international community's priority will be to raise the standard of living of the peoples so as to create conditions which will permit parents to reach the necessary level of responsibility.

5. Population programs should be at the service of the human being, and should guarantee family dignity and stability.

6. Contraceptive methods which imply an attempt on human life, debasement of human dignity, or depravation of marriage will be excluded.

In 1975 the Government named an interministerial commission. This commission was established for the purpose of studying the country's population problems and of preparing a population policy for Uruguay in furtherance of the action plan approved in Bucharest.

The private Family Planning Studies and Research Center (CIEF), affiliated with the Catholic Church, provides sex education services, conducts population seminars, and carries out research projects.

External Assistance

Financial inputs to the program total $1,422,000 over the fiscal 1969-75 period. The largest donor has been the IPPF, with $539,000. The Ford Foundation has contributed $460,000. AID contributed $191,000, virtually all of it in fiscal 1971. The United Nations Fund for Population Activities has applied $292,000 to the program. Others providing assistance include the Population Council and The Pathfinder Fund.

Venezuela

Venezuela's population increased from 8.6 million in 1965 to 12.0 million in mid-1975. This gain of 40 percent contrasts with an average gain of 32 percent for mainland Latin America. The increase in total population over the 1965-75 period reflects in part the influx of several hundred thousand illegal immigrant workers, mostly from Colombia and the Caribbean Islands, Venezuela's rate of natural increase in 1974 was 2.9 percent annually, equal to the Latin American average.

Venezuela's strong economy, based on petroleum, mining, agriculture, and manufacturing, gives its people one of the highest per capita gross national products in Latin America—$1,360 in 1973. This burgeoning economy has absorbed much of the population increase. Nevertheless, the nation's leaders have recognized that population growth is excessive and should be slowed down. There is particular concern about the high rates of illegitimacy and abortion,

especially in the slums of the large cities.

Venezuela faced up to its population problems in 1968 when a nationwide program of family planning was initiated by the Venezuela Family Planning Association (AVPF), an affiliate of the International Planned Parenthood Federation (IPPF), with the assistance of the National Government and several external donors. By 1973 AVPF had 137 family planning centers in operation, most of them in Government health facilities; by 1974 the number had risen to 142. In 1974 the Venezuelan Government created an Office of Family Planning within the Ministry of Health and Social Assistance, which assumed in 1975 administrative and funding responsibilities for the delivery of a nationwide family planning service, including the clinics of the AVPF.

Although the Venezuelan Government has no stated population policy, it has a de facto policy of furnishing family planning assistance to all who request it. This pro-family-planning attitude of the Government dates from the March 1974 inauguration of President Carlos Andres Perez.

President Perez, in a series of speeches in 1975, emphasized his personal commitment to family planning. The Government's goal is to make family planning services available to every Venezuelan by the end of 1978. Early in 1975 the Health Ministry announced that 90 new clinics will be opened during the following year and that pilot programs will be launched in rural areas in two States.

A collective Pastoral Letter issued by the Catholic bishops of Venezuela in 1969 recognized that the state should oppose extra-familial fertility. The Letter spoke out against abortion, female sterilization, and compulsory birth control, but recognized that, in a modern society containing many non-Catholics, family planning information should be made available to persons requesting it.

Although the Government and the Church endorse responsible parenthood, it should be noted that some policies would seem to encourage increased fertility. For example, all working women are allowed 12 weeks of paid maternity leave, tax deductions are allowed according to the number of dependents, and in certain industries bonuses are given for each child born to the worker.

One of Venezuela's big population problems is the high incidence of abortion. Abortion is illegal in Venezuela, except when it is deemed necessary to save the life of the mother. Data from hospitals that admit and treat a large proportion of women suffering from the complications of illegal abortion, however, show that many abortions are performed each year. In 1960 and 1970 complications from abortion were the

No. 1 cause of maternal mortality in Venezuela.

At the Concepcion Palacios Maternity Hospital (MCP) in Caracas, nearly 50,000 babies are delivered each year, and approximately 12,000 hospital admissions occur due to spontaneous and illegally induced abortion—a ratio of one abortion to about every four births. The Armando Castillo Plaza Maternity Hospital in Maracaibo reports similar figures.

To help deal with the problem of illegal abortion, as well as with the need to provide family planning services, MCP instituted a postpartum program in 1963. To make it easier for recently delivered women to receive contraceptive services, a referral system has been instituted. When a woman on the postpartum wards requests consultation on family planning and then decides she would like a family planning clinic appointment, she is given a choice of the MCP clinic or a clinic close to her residence.

The family planning services offered at MCP include educational meetings with the women during the pre- and postnatal periods and provision of IUD's or oral contraceptives on request to those who qualify medically. From 1963 to 1973 the hospital had served 48,022 new acceptors. Almost 91 percent of the women have accepted the IUD, as compared with 8 percent requesting the pill and 1 percent requesting other methods, including sterilization.

In clinics, medical personnel provide counseling and instructions on contraceptive use. Methods of contraception offered include the pill and the IUD, the two most often accepted. But the preference changes. In 1969, 63 percent of those accepting any method chose the IUD and 32 percent chose the pill. By 1973 the pill had become the most popular method with 52 percent of acceptors, while IUD acceptance dropped to 44 percent. Clients who visit the family planning clinics receive a physical checkup, which includes a breast examination, a pelvic examination, and a Papanicolaou smear test. Any problems that are detected are referred to specialized clinics. The regular clinics also offer their services to infertile couples.

Family planning and maternal training programs are carried out for the medical personnel who staff the clinics and the out-reach workers. Educational and motivational efforts to reach potential family planning acceptors are carried out by full-time health educators, both in rural and urban areas of the country. Educational meetings are also held for such community groups as factory workers and trade unions and others who use national health service clinics about the family planning services available to them.

Private family planning institutions now view their role in Venezuela as one of technical support for the Government family planning effort and maintenance of an independent voice dedicated to promotion of family planning. The AVPF continues to furnish advice and technical assistance to the Health Ministry on a contract basis and will be responsible for training and monitoring personnel for the new clinics.

External Assistance

In recent years four major international sources have given financial and material support to Venezuela's family planning program. These include, in addition to the IPPF, the Population Council, The Pathfinder Fund, and the United Nations Fund for Population Activities. The Ford Foundation has supported training programs.

Costa Rica's Family Orientation Center conducts programs on sex education and family life.

Caribbean Islands

Population of the Caribbean islands rose from 22.1 million in 1965 to 26.8 million in 1975—an increase of 21 percent. This percentage increase was slightly above that of the world's population, but was far below the 32 percent expansion since 1965 in Latin America.

The increase in total population of the West Indies, although large, has been moderated by two major factors: Declining birth rates plus rather heavy emigration. Birth rates dropped from 36 per 1,000 people in 1965 to 31 in 1974. The 1974 death rate was 9 per 1,000 people, down from 10 per 1,000 in 1965. The 1974 rate of natural increase was 2.2 percent annually.

Caribbean statistics on migration are fragmentary but U.S. immigration figures show that over 600,000 people from the West Indies were admitted to the United States alone between 1966 and 1974, mostly from Cuba (refugees), the Dominican Republic, Jamaica, and Haiti. According to the United Nations, the 1971 British census indicated that 152,000 persons born in the West Indies entered the United Kingdom in 1961 or later years. Other migrants from the Caribbean went to Canada and Latin America, notably to Venezuela.

The significant decline in birth rates over the 1965-74 period reflects to a considerable degree improved access to family planning services and contraceptives through family planning clinics, private physicians, and the commercial market.

Virtually all of the islands carry on activities designed to reduce fertility. Many of these programs are sponsored by private family planning associations affiliated with the International Planned Parenthood Federation (IPPF). Programs are similar in that they cover three principal areas: provision of family planning services and contraceptives, information and education activities aimed at "motivating" families to accept contraception, and training of physicians, nurses, nurse-midwives, as well as administrative personnel.

Available statistics from family planning associations indicate that oral contraceptives are most popular with acceptors, followed by condoms and intrauterine devices.

Family planning programs in the Caribbean have been adapted to a wide economic and social spectrum, for the islands vary greatly in living standards. The per capita gross national product averages high on islands with heavy tourism or having an abundance of exportable goods, such as sugar, coffee, bauxite, and other minerals, but it is low on others. As compared with a regional average of $780 per capita in 1973, per capita GNP of the U.S. Virgin Islands was $5,910, Puerto Rico $2,270, and the Bahamas $2,320, whereas populous Cuba had a per capita average GNP of $540 (up from $480 in 1965), St. Vincent $300 and Haiti $130 (lowest in the Western Hemisphere). Languages are about as varied as income; they include Spanish, English, French, Dutch, and Creole.

Excessive population growth has created problems in all countries. It seems likely, therefore, that family planning programs will continue, either for demographic reasons or because the spacing of children is perceived by governments to be a basic human right of parents that should not be infringed.

External Assistance

As in Latin America, the U.S. Agency for International Development (AID) has provided assistance to the Caribbean area generally through organizations that include, among others, the United Nations Fund for Population Activities (UNFPA) and related United Nations agencies, the Latin American Demographic Center (CELADE), Family Planning International Assistance (FPIA), the IPPF, and the Population Council. AID also provides population program support on a bilateral basis to Haiti and Jamaica.

The UNFPA has supported population and family planning programs in nine Caribbean countries, including work carried on under agreements with Cuba and the Dominican Republic. Regional UNFPA programs have strengthened activities in such areas as population statistics and dynamics, notably through assistance to CELADE, information and education, and training.

The IPPF has been a major factor in the family planning activities of the Caribbean since establishment of the Barbados and Jamaica association in the 1950's. The Trinidad and Tobago association was formed in 1961, and was followed by IPPF-affiliated associations in Guadeloupe and Grenada (1964), Curacao (1965), Montserrat and St. Kitts/Nevis (1966), Puerto Rico and St. Lucia (1967), Antigua and Aruba (1970), Dominica and St. Maarten (1973), and Bonaire (1974).

In 1974 IPPF organized the Caribbean Family Planning Affiliation (CFPA) as a unique means of bringing new but very small associations into the agency's framework, while continuing to allow them direct access to the regional office. Not included in

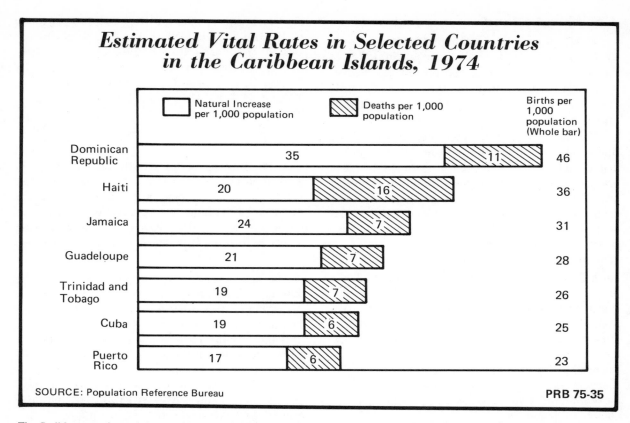

Estimated Vital Rates in Selected Countries in the Caribbean Islands, 1974

	Natural Increase per 1,000 population	Deaths per 1,000 population	Births per 1,000 population (Whole bar)
Dominican Republic	35	11	46
Haiti	20	16	36
Jamaica	24	7	31
Guadeloupe	21	7	28
Trinidad and Tobago	19	7	26
Cuba	19	6	25
Puerto Rico	17	6	23

SOURCE: Population Reference Bureau

PRB 75-35

The Caribbean area's rate of natural increase in 1974 was 2.2 percent, well below Latin America's 2.9 percent. The Caribbean is an area of sharp contrasts—extreme poverty in some countries, relative affluence in others. But population pressures are felt generally, and have engendered family planning programs, some of which started in the 1950's, and have stimulated heavy emigration from some islands.

the CFPA are associations in Spanish-speaking Caribbean countries and the older associations in Barbados, Jamaica, and Trinidad and Tobago.

FPIA cooperates on family planning activities with the Unitarian Universalist Service Committee in Haiti and with the Church World Service in the Dominican Republic. The Haitian program has become a model for the Government's national program. In addition to technical assistance, FPIA has furnished substantial quantities of contraceptives, audio-visual equipment, and information materials.

The International Bank for Reconstruction and Development (World Bank) has loaned a total of $5 million to Trinidad and Tobago and Jamaica, the bulk of it for construction of a hospital, health centers, and training facilities.

Other agencies providing assistance in the Caribbean area in the 1965-75 period included the Association for Voluntary Sterilization, the British Ministry of Overseas Development, the Ford Foundation, the International Association of Schools of Social Work, the International Development Research Center (Canada), International Education Development,

the Mennonite Central Committee, Oxfam, Oxfam-Canada, The Pathfinder Fund, the Population Council, the Smithsonian Institution, the Tinker Foundation, and the World Assembly of Youth.

Barbados

The population of Barbados, reversing the general pattern for Caribbean countries, decreased from 244,000 in 1965 to 239,000 in 1975. Two factors account in large part for the declining population: a low rate of natural growth—1.2 percent in 1974—and heavy emigration. The birth rate in 1974 was 21 per 1,000 people, the death rate 9 per 1,000.

The Barbados Family Planning Association has continued since 1955 its supplementary role to the Government as the only agency providing family planning on a national scale. Its activities have been funded by Government grants and grants from the IPPF and UNFPA.

In 1975 the Association introduced community-based distribution of orals and condoms and use of condom vending machines as well as an integrated health, welfare, and community project for the island's northern areas. The Association employed one full-time and five part-time physicians in addition to six nurse-midwives and two clinic attendants. First visits to the clinic in 1973 totaled 4,695, while 37,925 acceptors were served between 1955 and 1973. The Association planned to increase its referral service to the major hospital for male and female sterilization and pregnancy terminations conducted within existing law. The Association also consulted with the Government with respect to incorporation of family planning into health center service, and the first polyclinic was planned for 1975.

A mass information and education program was carried on through television, press, and display media. A special effort was made to obtain greater acceptance of family planning by Barbadian men.

Cuba

Cuba's population rose from 7.7 million in 1965 to 9.3 million in 1975. With the 1974 birth rate at 25 per 1,000 population and death rate at 6 per 1,000, Cuba's rate of natural increase was 2.0 percent per year.

Like other countries of the region, Cuba has a population picture that reflects efforts to reduce fertility through family planning plus rather substantial emigration. The U.S. Immigration and Naturalization Service reported in its 1974 annual summary that between 1965 and 1974 almost 285,000 Cubans were admitted to the United States alone.

Cuba's birth rate fluctuated between 27 and 30 per 1,000 persons during the 1950's, but reached a high point of about 35 per 1,000 during the early 1960's. Official concern about 'this trend led to initiation of family planning in 1966, a service offered free of charge through public health facilities. According to Thomas G. Sanders, writing in the American Universities Fieldstaff Report, "Cuba and the Bucharest Conference," Cuba's family planning services are offered within the framework of maternal/infant health care, although condoms are also for sale publicly. Sanders observes that the Cuban Government, while not giving priority or emphasis to contraception, holds the opinion that free access to efficient contraceptives and other means of fertility control ought to be guaranteed to all the population. The "contraceptives and other means" are primarily pills, intrauterine devices, and diaphragms.

Population Dynamics Quarterly (Vol. 2, No. 4, Fall 1974) states that Cuba's family planning program

is carried on not only to protect the health of mothers and children through child-spacing and discouraging illegal abortions but also to facilitate participation of women in the labor force. Reportedly, Cuban women now constitute over one-fifth of the state-employed civilian labor force. The International Planned Parenthood Federation (IPPF) estimated in 1972 that by 1975 close to half of Cuban women in the reproductive years of 15-44 would be employed in the nonagricultural sector.

Population Dynamics Quarterly also notes that the Cuban Government feels that economic development, rather than fertility reduction, will reduce the tension between national resources and population growth. This position was voiced by Cuba at the Bucharest World Population Conference. However, the *Quarterly* states that recent visitors to Cuba believe that Government officials are beginning to show concern about the social costs of providing for the rapidly increasing population.

External Assistance

Whatever its reason, the Government, beginning in January 1975, moved to strengthen its population program with the help of a 4-year, $3.9 million grant from the United Nations Fund for Population Activities (UNFPA).

The 4-year grant from UNFPA will be used for extension of maternal/child health services, equipment of family planning facilities, support for demographic research at the University of Havana's Centre for Demographic Studies, as well as training of demographers. UNFPA also has helped fund a course in demography at the University of Oriente.

Finland is providing assistance, through UNICEF, for improving 11 maternity wards in rural areas and constructing 3 central kitchens for day-care centers serving 50,000 children each. Finland's support for these projects reportedly totals $2,176,000.

The Swedish International Development Association (SIDA) has supplied the Government's maternal and child health program with contraceptives, medical equipment, audio-visual aids, and literature for sex education. Disbursements in 1974-75 were estimated by the UNFPA at $364,000.

The U.S. Agency for International Development provides no assistance to the Cuban program.

Dominican Republic

Population of the Dominican Republic rose from 3.5 million in 1965 to 4.7 million in 1975—an expansion of 34 percent. The 1974 birth rate of 46 per 1,000 people and death rate of 11 per 1,000 resulted in the natural increase rate of 3.5 percent annually. Both the birth rate and the pace of natural increase were the highest in the Caribbean area.

Overall economic growth has been vigorous. Gross national product over the 1970-74 period expanded at an average annual rate of 9.9 percent. Export commodities, including sugar, coffee, and minerals, have contributed to growth, as have Government and private investment financing.

But rapid population expansion has meant reduced shares of economic growth benefits for individuals. Gross national product per capita for 1973 was $510. There is much unemployment and underemployment, particulary in rural areas. Serious health problems exist: The death rate is high among children under 3 years of age; nutrition is subnormal for 60 percent of the people; the ratio of doctors and nurses to population is low.

Recognizing the unfavorable economic and social consequences of excessively high population growth, the Government in 1968 organized a National Council on Population and Family Planning (CONAPOFA), which has administered the nation's maternal/child health and family planning activities. CONAPOFA hopes to reduce the birth rate to 30 per 1,000 population by 1977 and to expand family planning services to provide coverage for 20 percent of fertile-age women. The major restricting factor has been the limited number of trained medical and paramedical personnel available for the program.

Family planning activities picked up momentum in mid-1974. By June 1975 active users of contraceptives had risen to 70,000, or 6.5 percent of fertile-age women as compared with only 30,000 in December 1973. In addition, the Government has developed a national community-based program that eventually will employ 4,000 health promoters who will sell and distribute contraceptives. Two pilot distribution projects were in operation in late 1975. The Government has taken other steps to increase contraceptive availability: Graduate nurses have been authorized to insert IUD's; and graduate and auxiliary nurses have authority to prescribe oral contraceptives. Orals are provided to acceptors without charge in health clinics, but there is a 25-cent charge for a month's supply of any contraceptive sold by the Government's distributors.

CONAPOFA is rapidly expanding the number of clinics that provide family planning services. In mid-1974 there were 71 clinics but by February 1975 there were 110, and the Government planned to have 200 in operation by the end of 1975.

Of an estimated 50,000 users of contraceptives in 1974, a total of 26,500 were using orals, 15,300 IUD's, and 8,200 condoms and other means.

The private Dominican Association for Family Welfare (DAFW), an affiliate of the International Planned Parenthood Federation; the National Institute for Sex Education; and the Pedro Henriquez Urena University have worked closely with CONAPOFA in research and evaluation, information and education, training of paramedical personnel, and development of expertise in social work and administration.

A lack of information and education is perceived by many officials as the most urgent need, and work in the these areas is being emphasized by DAFW. Its Radio School of the Air, started in 1972, has proved to be a major factor in increasing clinic attendance; daily listeners number about 125,000. The program was continued in 1975 on a national basis.

Two-week training courses primarily for medical and paramedical personnel are held jointly by DAFW and CONAPOFA four times a year. A demonstration clinic, operated by DAFW in collaboration with the government, serves as a training facility for doctors, nurses, and auxiliaries.

External Assistance

From the inception of the program through fiscal 1975 combined inputs to the Dominican Republic's family planning program have totaled $3,482,000. The largest contributors were the United Nations Fund for Population Activities, $1,330,000; the International Planned Parenthood Federation, $1,221,000; and the U.S. Agency for International Development, $869,000, which was provided in the fiscal year period 1967 to 1969. Other agencies providing assistance included the Population Council, Family Planning International Assistance, The Pathfinder Fund, Church World Service, and the Association for Voluntary Sterilization.

Haiti

Haiti's population rose from 3.8 million in 1965 to 4.6 million in 1975. The birth rate of 36 per 1,000 people is above the Caribbean average of 31, while the death rate of 16 per 1,000 is substantially higher than the regional average of 9. The rate of natural increase in 1974 was 2 percent per year. Life expectancy at birth—50 years—is the second lowest in the Western Hemisphere.

With a per capita gross national product estimated in 1974 at the very low level of $130, Haiti is the only Western Hemisphere state on the United Nation's list of 25 least developed countries.

Market day near Jacmel in southern Haiti. Cautious steps are being taken to lower Haiti's birth and death rates, both of which are above the Caribbean average.

About 70 percent of Haiti's people are farmers who live in densely populated areas poorly served by roads and other facilities. Farms are small; only 25 percent of the units have more than 10 acres. The World Bank estimates the per capita annual income of rural Haitians at about $80, and of the poorest 2.6 million of the rural population at no more than $40-$50.

Nutritional levels are generally poor. A 1974 study indicates that the people consume an average of only 1,850 calories per day, one of the lowest caloric intakes in the world. Disease, tracing in no small part to poor nutrition, is widespread. There are not enough medical and paramedical personnel, especially in rural areas, to meet the ordinary needs of the people; a 1974 report shows that there are 12,200 people per physician, and that the infant mortality toll is 150 per 1,000 live births—almost 10 times the U.S. rate. Nor is the medical situation improving. Most of the 100 or so physicians who graduate from Haiti's medical school each year emigrate in the hope of improving their incomes and living conditions. The exodus of nurses also has been heavy.

The educational level is low. Adult literacy is about 10 percent; and no more than 30 percent of school-age children, mostly from urban areas, attend classes. Only a few students finish college.

Haitian officials know that rapid population growth intensifies economic and social problems. In 1968 the President of Haiti requested technical assistance for family planning from the Pan American Health Organization (PAHO), but it was not until 1971 that a new law created a Division of Family Hygiene to coordinate public and private maternal and child health services, including family planning. A national family planning program within the maternal and child health system became official policy—as a basic human right and for promoting health rather than for demographic reasons.

The private Center for Family Hygiene has played a significant role in Haiti's family planning program. Established in 1969 as a nonprofit agency, the Haitian Government in 1972 recognized the Center as a "public utility," and that same year the Center inaugurated a family planning program in a rural zone between the capital city, Port-au-Prince, and the Dominican border. The program, sponsored by Family Planning International Assistance (FPIA) and the Unitarian Universalist Service Committee, included three family planning/maternal child health clinics and a broad complement of information and education activities.

In 1974, with financial assistance from the United Nations Fund for Population Activities (UNFPA), PAHO, the U.S. Agency for International Development (AID), and The Pathfinder Fund, the Division of Family Hygiene took charge of the national program. In May 1975, two of the Center's clinics were merged into the Government program. The third clinic operated by the Center was retained as a pilot demonstration facility.

Sixteen Government clinics were being operated in the urban areas and central towns in 1975 and it was planned that, by December 1975, 22 clinics would be providing services. It also was planned that another 18 clinics would be added by December 1977 to bring the total to 40.

Also, in 1975, 9 private clinics were authorized to provide family planning services, and requests for additional programs were awaiting review and authorization. All private family planning activities in Haiti must be sanctioned by the Division of Family Hygiene and are required to conform to the norms established by the Health Department. This policy is aimed at assuring coordination of programs and maximizing the use of valuable services.

FPIA continues to support an information, education, and communications program with the Center, which includes developing an educational curriculum for primary school students, development of slide series for family planning training, booklets for adults, elementary and secondary school text books, and a training program for teachers.

In 1975 the Center planned a "social marketing program", in cooperation with Population Services International. The objective is to reach an annual retail sales level by the end of the second year of 450,000 boxes of 3 condoms each, and 90,000 monthly cycles of oral contraceptives. The condoms are to be sold in units of 3 at 10 cents U.S. The same price is to be charged for monthly cycles of orals. The Center will market the contraceptives on a national scale through 2,500 or more small shops.

The subsidy program is deemed necessary because commercial sales volumes at "regular" prices are very low. Few people in Haiti can afford to pay full commercial prices for pills or condoms.

External Assistance

Total inputs to the program from fiscal 1971 through 1975 were $3,130,000, of which the Haitian Government contributed $214,000.

UNFPA has made available $2,020,000 for two major projects—one a population, housing, and agricultural census and demographic survey, the other a maternal and child health family planning program in two capital city hospitals as a first step to national coverage.

The U.S. Agency for International Development contributed $144,000, which was obligated in fiscal

1975 for a survey of the structure and organization of the Division of Family Hygiene; for a Haitian Community Help Organization project in northwest Haiti; technical assistance to the Government through the Johns Hopkins School of Hygiene and Public Health; and a study of fertility-nutrition relationships through Columbia University's International Institute for the Study of Human Reproduction.

Already noted are projects carried forward by FPIA, UUSC, and Population Services International. Other agencies providing assistance include The Pathfinder Fund, the Ford Foundation, the Rockefeller Foundation, the Mennonite Central Committee, Oxfam, and the Population Council.

Jamaica

Jamaica is a small densely populated country with limited natural resources. Jamaica's population rose from 1.8 million in 1965 to almost 2.1 million in 1975—an average annual increase of 1.7 percent—somewhat below the Caribbean average of 2.0 percent.

With the birth rate at 31 per 1,000 population in 1974 and death rate at 7 per 1,000, the annual rate of natural increase was 2.4 percent. However, the total population growth has been dampened by relatively heavy emigration, primarily to the United States and Canada. Nevertheless, the Government has indicated that it still considers the nation's overall population increase to be excessive and strengthened family planning programs a necessity.

The Government's position is unequivocal. Population growth, even on a moderate scale, has accentuated existing difficulties. Schools are overcrowded and there is a chronic shortage of qualified teachers. Unemployment and underemployment are high. Housing is in short supply in urban areas. The crime rate has risen sharply. Although emigration in 1975 dropped off sharply from what it was in the late 1960's, it was still substantial for a small country and consisted largely of the kind of people Jamaica could ill afford to lose—physicians and other professionals, nurses, paramedical personnel, and highly skilled workers. This "brain drain" has hampered Government efforts to find solutions to its serious economic and social problems.

The need for applying a brake to population growth was perceived a number of years ago. Family planning began in 1939 with small clinics operated by the Jamaica Birth Control League. In 1957 the Jamaica Family Planning Association (JFPA) was founded as an affiliate of the International Planned Parenthood Federation (IPPF).

Above, official at a Jamaican health center explains the use of the loop. Left, a mobile unit of the Jamaica Family Planning Association stops at the village of Philadelphia to explain family planning.

Government efforts began in 1963 with the first 5-year independence plan. In 1966, with 25 family planning clinics in operation, the Government created a National Family Planning Program as a unit within the Ministry of Health. In 1968, with 61 clinics offering services, the Government established a National Family Planning Board as a policy formation body appointed by the Minister of Health and responsible to him. The Board, working closely with JFPA, has continued to expand clinical services. By 1974 there were 170 health clinics, 26 hospitals, and 10 health centers offering family planning aid.

In 1974, a total of 50,700 individuals were using contraceptive methods, representing a participation through the organized Government program alone of 14 percent of Jamaican women in the 15-49 reproductive age group. Of total acceptors, about 26,000 were using oral contraceptives, 5,000 condoms, 4,000 IUD's, 7,000 sterilization, and 15,000 other methods, including foam, jellies, creams, and injectibles.

The Government is bolstering its contraceptive service program with comprehensive campaigns to extol the advantages of small families and to persuade couples to take the steps necessary to hold down family size. To help attain this broad objective, the Government provides sex education in schools and

Left, signs spread the family planning message in Jamaica—part of the country's intensive effort to slow its rate of natural increase.

stantial part of those funds—$8,796,000, increasing its contribution in every year since 1968.

External Assistance

AID assistance has amounted to $3,588,000. Other organizations assisting include the United Nations Fund for Population Activities, the IPPF, the Ford Foundation, the Smithsonian Institution, the World Bank, the Association for Voluntary Sterilization, the American Association for the Advancement of Science, The Pathfinder Fund, the Development Association, the International Association of Schools of Social Work, the World Assembly of Youth, the British Ministry of Overseas Development, and the International Development Research Centre (Canada).

Trinidad and Tobago

Population of these islands increased from 1 million in 1965 to 1.1 million in 1975. The rate of natural increase—2 percent in 1974—was a little below the Caribbean average. The birth rate in 1974 was 26 per 1,000 people, and the death rate 7 per 1,000.

The gross national product (GNP) per capita in 1973 was $1,200, one of the six highest in the region. About 40 percent of the population is under age 15, a high proportion of dependents.

The Family Planning Association of Trinidad and Tobago operates seven clinics. Medical goals for 1974 and 1975 were to locate and service the large number of dropouts, to provide fertility testing for couples, and to establish a sterilization service. In 1973 visits of acceptors to clinics totaled over 117,000.

External Assistance

Major external assistance has been provided through a $3 million World Bank loan. These funds are being used largely for construction of a family planning institute, a 100-bed maternity hospital, 7 health centers, a rural community health center, and extension of facilities of one nursing school.

The International Planned Parenthood Federation (IPPF) provided very substantial support to the private Family Planning Association of Trinidad and Tobago, with a budget of $349,300 in 1975. The Association operates seven clinics, and hoped, with funding by Oxfam, to provide a sterilization service

directs family planning publicity toward adult populations of working and childbearing age. In 1975 a commercial contraceptive program was launched (with assistance from the U.S. Agency for International Development) which makes oral contraceptives and condoms available through pharmacies and other retail outlets without prescription at a very nominal cost. About 35,000 cycles of orals were used in the first 6 weeks and reorders by pharmacies have been large.

A total of $14,174,000 has been spent in Jamaica since 1965 for population program assistance. The Government of Jamaica, underwriting its solid dedication to the program, has contributed a very subfor 600 acceptors in 1974-75. Information and education emphasis in 1975 was on the production of leaflets, booklets, pamphlets, and posters.

Other assistance was provided in 1965-75 by the Pan American Health Organization (PAHO), the United Nations Children's Fund (UNICEF), the Association for Voluntary Sterilization, the Population Council, and the Danish International Development Agency.

Other Caribbean Countries

Problems of population pressures and maternal and child health have long been of key concern in many of the small but densely populated Caribbean islands. Most of the family planning programs have been sponsored and assisted by outside agencies, primarily the International Planned Parenthood Federation (IPPF), always with Government permission and often with Government support. The descriptions given of the programs are based on a 1974 IPPF report.

The **Caribbean** Family Planning Affiliation (CFPA) is a body comprising the individual associations within the English, French, and Dutch-speaking islands. The membership in 1974 was comprised of Antigua, Aruba, Curacao, Dominica, Grenada, Guadeloupe, Martinique, Montserrat, St. Lucia, St. Kitts, Nevis, St. Vincent, and Surinam. The CFPA was accepted as a full member of the IPPF in 1973 and has headquarters in St. Kitts.

At a meeting in Barbados in May 1974 the membership considered a work program for 1975 as follows:

• Regional training: Interchange of personnel within CFPA and nonmember associations; working with academic bodies in developing specialized programs, observation tours, et cetera.

• Formalized training: Personnel training at recognized institutions in countries outside the Caribbean.

• Training center: Establishment of a permanent training unit in the Caribbean to cover all aspects of family planning.

Antigua—Antigua's population increased from 60,000 in 1965 to 73,000 in 1975. The rate of natural increase in 1974—1.1 percent—was one of the lowest in the Western Hemisphere. The birth rate was 18 per 1,000 population, the death rate 7 per 1,000. With 43 percent of the population under age 15, the per capita GNP in 1974 was $480. About 40 percent of the population is urban.

Services of the Antigua Planned Parenthood Asso-

ciation, an affiliate of the International Planned Parenthood Federation, began in 1970 and have expanded rapidly. A community-based program for distribution of contraceptives, launched late in 1973, has the following features: (1) removal of customs duties on contraceptives imported by the Association, and plans were going forward to remove duties on contraceptives for commercial sale; (2) distribution of contraceptives at subsidized prices through commercial outlets, such as bars, rum shops, and pharmacies plus free distribution to those who cannot afford to purchase them. The program is supported by an advertising and information campaign utilizing radio, television, the press, posters, exhibits, films, and public meetings.

The Association operates a postpartum program at the major hospital and the Government provides family planning services at three clinics. Visits to the clinics in 1973 totaled 2,693.

Grenada—Grenada's population rose from 92,000 in 1965 to 96,000 in 1975. The natural growth rate in 1974 was 1.9 percent, below the average for the Caribbean area. The birth rate was 26 per 1,000 population, the death rate 8 per 1,000.

Grenada's Planned Parenthood Association (GPPA) dates back to 1964 and is the only family planning agency in the country. In 1974 its position was strengthened when the Government declared the right of the individual to have access to knowledge and means of regulating family size.

Visits to the island's 13 clinics in 1973 totaled 35,598. Condoms were by far the most popular contraceptive methods, followed by pills.

The Association continued to accord priority to information and education and made special efforts to reach the country's leadership, business sector, and professionals. An advertising campaign, through radio, press, and posters, was supported by personal visits of field workers.

Montserrat—The population of Montserrat declined from 12,000 in 1965 to 11,000 in 1975. The island's natural rate of increase in 1974 was 1.6 percent. The birth rate was 25 per 1,000 population and the death rate 9 per 1,000.

The Montserrat Family Planning Association, founded in 1966, provides services at two centers staffed by nurse/midwives. The services are mainly referral; clients are sent to doctors willing, for fees, to insert IUD's or prescribe pills.

The Association intends to operate at least a part-time clinic. Because the rate of extramarital pregnancy is a source of concern, the Association will concentrate on educational activities among the young.

Netherlands Antilles—The population of the Netherlands Antilles increased from 205,000 in 1965 to 233,000 in 1975. The annual rate of natural increase was 1.8 percent in 1974: the birth rate being 25 per 1,000 people and the death rate 7 per 1,000. GNP per capita in 1973 was $1,650, among the highest in the region.

Aruba's Foundation for Responsible Parenthood, established in 1970 by a Catholic priest, has been operating with a limited annual grant from the Netherlands Antilles Government. The Association maintains two clinics, which refer potential acceptors to one of a panel of 13 doctors who are members of the Association. The Association plans to provide counselling and eventually to handle IUD insertions in one of its clinics, and hopes to increase awareness of the responsibilities of parenthood among Aruba's male population.

Curacao's Foundation for Responsible Parenthood conducts three part-time clinics. New acceptors are counselled by a paramedical staff and then referred to doctors for further counselling. In 1974 the Foundation began to provide counselling and other services to the island's many manufacturing companies, which are provided with pills and condoms for distribution to employees.

A communication program is divided into three components: (1) sex education; (2) lectures and seminars in cooperation with trade unions; and (3) a daily radio dramatic show, reportedly a widely popular radio production in Curacao.

St. Kitts/Nevis/Angilla—The combined population of these islands increased from 61,000 in 1965 to 68,000 in 1975. The rate of natural increase in 1974 was 1.5 percent annually, with the birth rate at 26 per 1,000 population and the death rate at 11 per 1,000. The per capita GNP was $450 in 1973.

The Family Planning Association was started in 1971 and has cooperated with the Government since that time in carrying on information and education activities. A postpartum program was made a part of maternal/child health coverage in 1974. At that time, it was estimated that more than half of the state's fertile women were using contraceptives.

The Association operates one clinic, and the Government makes contraceptives available to its six clinics. A special community-based contraceptive distribution project has been favorably considered by the Government. The IPPF and the UNFPA have provided assistance.

St. Lucia—Population rose from 94,000 in 1965 to 107,000 in 1975. The rate of natural increase in 1974 was 3.2 percent per year, one of the highest in the Caribbean area. This results from the high birth rate of 41 per 1,000 population and the death rate of 9 per 1,000.

Founded in 1967, the St. Lucia Planned Parenthood Association operates four clinics, three of which are in Government facilities. A project for female sterilization was developed for 1975. The Association saw a total of 14,452 acceptors in 1973, of whom 11,548 used oral contraceptives as their preferred method.

The Association has put emphasis on reaching potential acceptors through public meetings, film shows, house to house visits, and an advertising campaign.

St. Vincent—St. Vincent's population rose from 88,000 in 1965 to 94,000 in 1975. The rate of natural increase was 2.4 percent annually in 1974. The birth rate was 34 per 1,000 population and the death rate 10 per 1,000.

St. Vincent's Planned Parenthood Association was founded in 1965. It provides services from its clinic and 24 Government clinics. Special attention is being given to reaching the country's youth. The IPPF and the UNFPA have provided assistance.

Near East

The Near East, though large in land area, is relatively sparsely settled. Its population totals about 117.3 million (excluding Greece as European). However, because water and fertile land are at a premium, populations have tended to cluster in cities and villages in the more hospitable valleys and lowlands rather than trying to make a living in the more arid higher or desert areas. As a result, these settled areas may experience population pressures.

All the nations of the Near East have relatively young populations with high fertility and relatively high but decreasing mortality. Typical population growth rates range from close to 3 percent to well over 3 percent a year. Birth rates are among the highest in the world. Today's growth rates, if continued, would bring a doubling of the area's population around the turn of the century.

While economic improvement is taking place in some countries—particularly those fortunate enough to have income from oil—the Near East has far to go in catching up with more developed countries in terms of general well-being for citizens. Only about one-third of the people are literate. Per capita GNP averages about $710. Life expectancy is 54 years. And, because of high fertility, about 43 percent of the population is under 15 years of age and therefore dependent on others for sustenance, education, and general care.

With regard to population policies and family planning, Near Eastern nations tend to fall into one of three general categories: indifferent, tolerant, and supportive.

Indifferent. Some Near Eastern nations, especially the oil-rich countries of the Arabian Peninsula, regard themselves as underpopulated and encourage population growth. Saudi Arabia, as an extreme example, not only has no organized family planning activities but recently prohibited the importation of contraceptives. Others favoring a continuation of population growth include Israel, Kuwait, Oman, Qatar, the United Arab Emirates, and the Democratic Yemen.

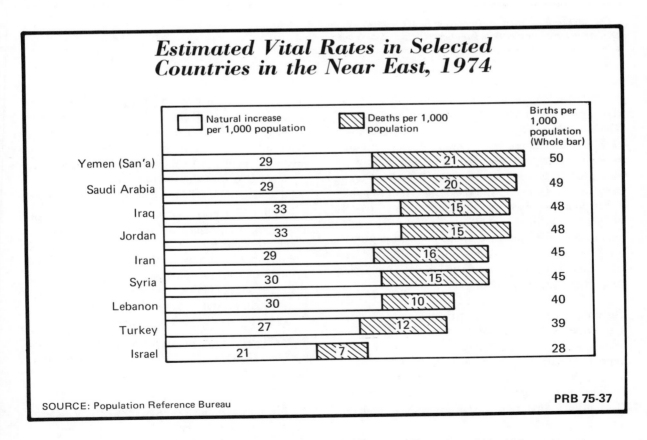

Estimated Vital Rates in Selected Countries in the Near East, 1974

Country	Natural increase per 1,000 population	Deaths per 1,000 population	Births per 1,000 population (Whole bar)
Yemen (San'a)	29	21	50
Saudi Arabia	29	20	49
Iraq	33	15	48
Jordan	33	15	48
Iran	29	16	45
Syria	30	15	45
Lebanon	30	10	40
Turkey	27	12	39
Israel	21	7	28

SOURCE: Population Reference Bureau

PRB 75-37

The Near East's rate of natural increase was 2.6 percent in 1974 as compared with the world average of 1.8 percent. The average birth rate of 41 per 1,000 is the second highest of any major world region.

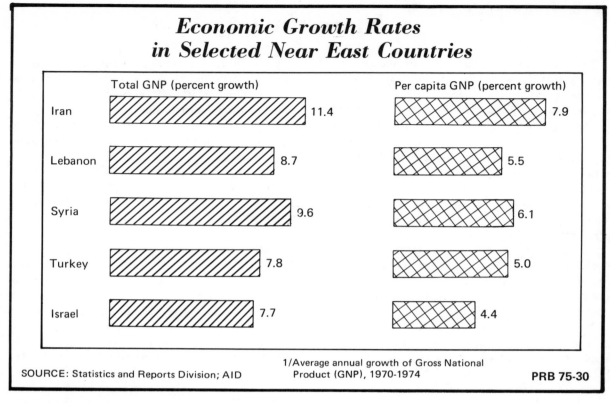

Economic Growth Rates in Selected Near East Countries

	Total GNP (percent growth)	Per capita GNP (percent growth)
Iran	11.4	7.9
Lebanon	8.7	5.5
Syria	9.6	6.1
Turkey	7.8	5.0
Israel	7.7	4.4

SOURCE: Statistics and Reports Division; AID

1/Average annual growth of Gross National Product (GNP), 1970-1974

PRB 75-30

As in other regions, satisfactory gains in total gross national product in the Near East are being eroded by population gains, which if continued, would bring a doubling of the population in 27 years.

Tolerant. Another group of Near Eastern countries appears to favor some slowing of growth rates. These tolerate or give limited support to private family planning activity and/or family planning services as part of national maternal/child health systems. Such countries include Bahrain, Cyprus, Iraq, Jordan, Lebanon, and the Syrian Arab Republic.

Supportive. Two of the largest Near Eastern countries—and these include nearly half of the area's population—are concerned about population growth, have explicit policies to slow such growth, and have both government-supported and private family planning programs. These are Iran and Turkey.

Summary Country Descriptions

Jordan is giving increasing attention to its population growth problems, seeing them as a major deterrent to its national development plans and its efforts to improve levels of living. A recent official paper spoke frankly of the Government's concern and may have been a first step toward eventual formulation of a population policy.

The Government of Lebanon, while not operating a national family planning program, has been favor-able to private efforts and has permitted the private Lebanon Family Planning Association to work through the Government's health centers. It has extended the Association special tax and custom privileges, as it has to the Middle East and African Regional Office of the International Planned Parenthood Federation (IPPF), which is located in Beirut.

Beirut was host in 1974 to the First Regional Population Conference for the United Nations Economic Commission for Western Asia. One of the Conference's recommendations was that "governments are urged to view family planning as a human right for every family, considering this as a basic human right in Arab society..."

The small country of Bahrain (population 240,000) has no organized family planning activities, but the Government is interested in incorporating family planning into its health services and expects to set up a pilot clinic.

In Cyprus (population 646,000), a private association offers family planning services through two clinics and has a program of sex education. The Government looks with favor on the work.

Israel (population 3.4 million) has an official pronatalist attitude and welcomes its population growth of 2.1 percent a year. A private family planning association has been active for 10 years.

Kuwait (population 1 million) permits family planning services to be offered within its maternal/child health program.

Oman (population 766,000) has no organized family planning program but expects to offer services within private hospitals.

Qatar (population 92,000) has no organized population program activities.

Saudi Arabia (population 6.2 million) is pronatalist. The country has no organized family planning services except those of the Arabian-American Oil Company, which in the past has provided such services to its employees.

The Syrian Arab Republic (population 7.4 million) has announced its intention of integrating family planning with its national health services. Syria has a national family planning association affiliated with the IPPF.

The United Arab Emirates (population 224,000) has no organized family planning services.

The Yemen Arab Republic, or Yemen (San'a), population 6.7 million, and the People's Democratic Republic of Yemen, or Yemen (Aden), population 1.7 million, do not have organized family planning services. Both, however, have requested the United Nations Fund for Population Activities (UNFPA) to help set up such services within their respective maternal/child health programs.

Iran

Iran has an active, expanding, well-financed national population program that aims to slow the nation's rapid population growth from its 1974 rate of 3 percent a year to 1.6 percent a year within the next two decades. The 1974 birth rate is estimated at 45 per 1,000 and the death rate 16 per 1,000.

The need for family planning action is indicated by the fact that Iran's 3 percent growth rate, if not reduced, would double today's 33 million population before the end of the century. Even though Iran's economy is benefitting from substantial oil exports, such population growth would be a severe handicap to the nation's program of industrialization and general economic modernization as well as to efforts to improve the health, welfare, and living conditions of the people generally.

The Government of Iran began to show interest in population matters and problems in the early 1960's when the first Iranian census showed that a rapid increase in population was taking place.

Ministry of Health officials were sent to study population problems in Egypt and Pakistan. By 1967, a special Population and Family Planning Division had been set up in the Ministry of Health. Family planning was made a part of Iran's successive 5-year development plans, and increasing funds have been made available in its support. For example, the 1973-74 family planning budget of $12.8 million was more than doubled to a proposed $28.8 million for 1975-76.

Since 1970 the number of Government clinics (both mobile and stationary) that offer family planning services is reported to have increased from about 900 to more than 2,200. These clinics usually integrate family planning services with general health care. As of early 1974, an estimated 700,000 Iranian couples were practicing family planning. Oral contraceptives (pills) are the preferred method. Contraceptives are widely available, both through program distributions and private commercial sales. Recent changes in Iranian laws will permit abortions and sterilizations.

Iran has expanded its family planning information and education programs and services to reach into rural areas where more than half the people live. Some 3,000 cooperative centers and 1,000 cultural centers, and their staffs, offer family planning motivation and supply contraceptives. Orientation and training programs for family planning workers are active. An estimated 1,200 radio and television programs on family planning were aired in 1974. Several films on the subject are being widely shown. Other publicity materials have been developed to keep the family planning message before the public.

A demographic survey of a number of villages is being prepared to ascertain the effect of the program on fertility.

A Model Family Planning Project to increase contraceptive use was initiated in Isfahan Province in 1972 and in 2 years more than doubled the use of contraceptives among fertile women. The project is being expanded to include 26 districts and cities with a total population of 3 million.

The Iranian family planning movement was pioneered by the Voluntary Family Planning Association founded in 1958. The Association supports the Government program by carrying out information and motivation activities as well as by operating a few clinics, mostly at community welfare centers.

Educational activities of the Association aim at reaching rural people, youth groups, and factory workers and at changing male attitudes toward family planning.

External Assistance

The two chief sources of assistance to Iran's population program are the United Nations Fund for Population Activities (UNFPA) and the World Bank.

In 1971, UNFPA and the Government of Iran signed an agreement providing financing of $1.6 million for a 17-month period preceding the 5-year plan for 1973-78, which called for additional UNFPA assistance to the Governemnt in the amount of $3,0 million. Under the agreement, UNFPA provides assistance for a variety of projects for which the United Nations, the International Labour Organisation, the World Health Organization, the United Nations Development Program, and the United Nations Children's Fund are acting as executing agencies. These projects cover a wide range of activities—demographic surveys, workers' education, curriculum development, sex and population education, rural education, vehicles, and research.

The World Bank has provided a loan of $16.5 million to assist the national population program in the 1973-76 period. The loan is principally for the provision of facilities, including building and equipping 78 countryside health centers, 9 regional family planning training centers, and 7 paramedical training schools and for purchasing 150 vehicles.

The U.S. Agency for International Development (AID) has provided support to the Iranian population program, through a contract with the Carolina Population Center, University of North Carolina. The assistance was given to Pahlavi University in Shiraz to set up a population center and reference unit. AID provides funding to several private organizations which are assisting the program. Also, through a contract with the Westinghouse Population Center, AID has supported a marketing analysis of the commercial distribution of contraceptive supplies in Iran.

The Association for Voluntary Sterilization is helping to set up an Iranian voluntary sterilization program, including provision of equipment and training of personnel.

The International Planned Parenthood Federation (IPPF) gives financial assistance to the affiliated Family Planning Association of Iran for its overall program, which includes information and education, training, and operation of clinics in urban areas and mobile clinics in rural areas. IPPF funding in 1974 was somewhat more than $400,000.

The Population Council has been supporting Iran's population work since the mid-1960's. Recent funding (1973 grants were $132,000) has helped the postpartum program, expanded family planning information and service activities in the Province of Isfahan, and supported the study of the socioeconomic implications of population growth.

The Rockefeller Foundation has made grants to Pahlavi University for courses in teaching population and family planning and to the University of Michigan for the study of rural population and family structure in Iran.

The Pathfinder Fund earlier helped to establish the Family Planning Association.

The national program also has been assisted by Sweden and the United Kingdom.

Iraq

In view of the nation's substantial income from oil and its sizable areas of underdeveloped land, the Government of Iraq does not look on the country's rapid population growth (3.3 percent a year) as excessive. It has indicated, in fact, that it would welcome the current growth rate of its population, now numbering 11 million, until at least 1980. The 1974 birth rate is estimated at 48 per 1,000 population and the death rate at 15 per 1,000.

Although the Government does not support family planning, it does accept the nation's relatively small family planning activity as a health measure. Therefore, the Iraqi voluntary family planning association has been able to integrate its activities with the national family health and welfare services. As a result, family planning clinical services are available in maternity and maternal/child health centers.

Family planning in Iraq was initiated in 1970 when a group of doctors set up a Family Planning Section in the Iraqi Medical Association. This section, funded by the International Planned Parenthood Federation (IPPF), a year later became the Iraqi Family Planning Association (IFPA).

No large-scale campaigns have been undertaken to gain acceptance of family planning. However, a small survey of mothers attending maternal/child health clinics in Baghdad showed that half of them favor the practice.

External Assistance

The International Planned Parenthood Federation (IPPF) gives financial aid to the Iraqi Family Planning Association (IFPA). This includes: support for the information and education program aimed at mothers attending maternity and child health clinics; training courses for doctors, nurses, and midwives; and operation of clinics. Budgeted funds in recent years have been: 1973, $71,500; 1974, $63,600; and 1975, $78,000.

The United Nations Fund for Population Activities (UNFPA) has granted a total of $472,000, mainly to strengthen the demographic capability of the country at Government and university levels. When a 3-year joint project between the World Health Organization (WHO) and UNFPA expired in 1974, the Government of Iraq did not request its renewal. The project's aim had been to further extend family planning services to maternity hospitals in urban and rural areas during 1975-80.

Israel

The population of Israel increased by one-third in the 1966-75 decade and totaled nearly 3.4 million in mid-1975. This is about 850,000 more than the 1965 level of slightly more than 2.5 million and represents an increase 8 percent greater than that for the previous decade.

The rate of natural increase rose slightly during the decade, registering 2.1 percent in 1974 as compared with 2.0 percent in 1965. Affecting the change were increases in both birth and death rates. The birth rate in 1974 was 28 births per 1,000 population a year and up from 26 per 1,000 in 1965. The death rate in 1974 was 7 per 1,000 people compared to 6 per 1,000 in 1965.

Although immigration in the early years of the Jewish State (1948-1951) ran at a rate of more than 20 percent of the total population per year, it had added rather less than 1 percent annually to the total during the 1966-68 period.

Both the Jewish and non-Jewish communities in Israel have experienced substantial population growth. But whereas the growth of the Jewish sector has depended mainly upon immigration, the growth of the non-Jewish groups has been a result of high natural increase. Because the volume of Jewish immigration has tended to decline over time, the non-Jewish population has been increasing more rapidly than the Jewish since the late 1950's.

An article* on Israel states that although abortion is technically illegal in most pregnancies, it nevertheless is cheaply and readily available privately from doctors and appears today to be "one of the most popular methods of family planning used." No public family planning services have been developed, Bachi reports, and modern contraception is relatively unpracticed. A family planning association was formed in 1966 and operates a small-scale information and education program. The Pathfinder Fund has assisted it.

---

*R. Bachi. "Induced Abortions in Israel," *In* R.E. Hall (ed.), *Abortion in a Changing World,* v. 1. New York, Columbia University Press, 1970.

Jordan

Jordan, while not yet committed to a national population policy, is showing increasing concern over its rapid population growth and the strain it is placing on efforts to improve the income, health, education, and food supply of its people. Its mid-1975 population (including the West Bank area) was estimated at somewhat more than 2.7 million with a growth rate of 3.3 percent. Unless this rate is reduced, the population will double in 21 years.

Jordan has several problems which add to its population concern. One is the small amount of agriculturally useful land—about 11 percent. Another has been the continuing conflict involving Jordan's richest area, the West Bank of the Jordan River. A third has been the influx of a large number of refugees from the 1967 war with Israel.

While Jordan is making progress in improving its agriculture, exports, general economy, and social services, the Government is beginning to look on rapid population growth as a deterrent to the development now taking place. In an official paper published in 1975, entitled *Country Statement Concerning Population Change and Development,* the Government stated that "Despite the marked increase in recent years in per capita Gross National Product and the ambitious goals of the 3-year program (1973-75), an important consideration is whether, in the face of the present and future prospects of population growth in Jordan, increases in per capita GNP may be continued to realize a decent level of living to the common man, and to achieve the high aspirations of the Three Year Plan." The Three Year Plan aspires to achieve an annual growth rate of 8 percent in the GNP.

Another part of the same paper noted that nearly 50 percent of Jordan's population was under 15 years of age, and therefore required considerable social, health, and educational services while diverting national income from much needed investments. It noted, too, that females in Jordan continued to marry at an early age so that 70 percent of married women had reproductive marriage spans of 25 to 35 years. The result was that women in the age group of 40 to 44 years have an average of 8.3 births during their fertile years.

That the Government of Jordan may be approaching the setting of a national population policy is indicated in this part of the 1975 statement:

The National Population Commission of Jordan (established in 1972) has been convinced of the interrelation between population growth, composition and distribution on the one hand and achievement of social and economic goals on the other. It realizes that the population element must be related to such goals as better education, full employment, and improvement of the general well-being of the population, including the health of mothers and children.

Although the Population Commission has not established a definite policy with respect to regulating the number of live births, yet it has been studying means and ways of recognizing the right of parents to determine freely and responsibly the number and spacing of children, and to assist those who so desire to enjoy this right by making available scientific information and advice on planned parenthood.

At present, the Government does not run family planning programs. However, it has been neutral with respect to the five private 'family planning clinics' established in the East Bank during the last 2 years. It observes the experiment with interest and for further knowledge of the desires of visitors.

The paper added that the Government was aware, from a National Fertility Survey, that two-thirds of Jordanian women either fully or conditionally approved of birth control and that half of those not opposed to family planning admitted their last pregnancy was not wanted.

Jordan's family planning services are maintained by the Jordan Family Planning and Protection Association (JFPPA), organized in 1963 and an affiliate of the International Planned Parenthood Federation (IPPF). The JFPPA has had many difficulties in operating its family planning centers because the 1967 war and its aftermath disrupted communication between East Bank and West Bank facilities. As of 1974, the JFPPA operated 13 family planning clinics on the West Bank and 10 on the East Bank in addition to house-to-house visits by social workers. The majority of acceptors favor the contraceptive pill. Plans called for extending home visits to rural areas in 1975.

External Assistance

The United Nations Fund for Population Activities (UNFPA) has provided $420,000 for demographic studies and projects, including fertility surveys and the development of a Statistical Training Center.

Much assistance to Jordan's private family planning effort has come from IPPF, whose expended or budgeted aid funds during 1973-75 totaled more than $300,000, and from Family Planning International Assistance, the International Division of Planned Parenthood of America, Inc. Such funds have been used for overall program work, including information and education and the operaton of clinics.

The U.S. Agency for International Development provides no direct assistance.

The Pathfinder Fund has supplied contraceptives, as have the Swedish International Development

Authority and the World Council of Churches. CARE has made donations and provided clinical equipment.

Lebanon

Although Lebanon has no official population policy it has laws to restrict contraception. The Government has permitted family planning activities. The rate of population increase is 3 percent per year; the birth rate is 40 per 1,000 population and death rate is 10 per 1,000 a year according to recent estimates.

Family planning services are extended to Lebanon's population (2.7 million) through the Lebanon Family Planning Association (LFPA), founded in 1969 and a member of the International Planned Parenthood Federation (IPPF). The LFPA runs 18 clinics in both rural and urban areas. Ten are in Government health centers, seven in voluntary clinics, and one in the LFPA Medical Center in Beirut.

Prior to the recent political disorders, public interest in family planning was high. A survey of 3,000 Lebanese wives showed that 74 percent wanted to use contraceptives and 15 percent were continual users of the pill. Further, family planning has received considerable mass media publicity—mostly sympathetic. And although the import of contraceptives is illegal, oral contraceptives are available (as period regulators) and so are condoms (for venereal disease prevention).

A Presidential Decree in 1971 proclaimed the LFPA a public utility. This status provides official support and tax exemption. The Government also has ratified an official agreement giving tax and custom exemption privileges to the IPPF regional office in Beirut. The Government has invited the LFPA to use public health centers as family planning clinics. Also, an LFPA representative is a member of a special committee convened to redraft existing restrictive laws affecting family planning.

The LFPA has been evaluating its impact during the past 5 years as a guide to the future. The LFPA's ultimate aim is to have family planning integrated into the nation's public health system.

External Assistance

IPPF grants to LFPA during 1972-74 totaled approximately $225,000. Support was for information seminars for educators, students, doctors, social workers, and midwives; for publications; for in-service training for medical staff and social workers; and for the operation of clinics.

The United Nations Fund for Population Activities (UNFPA) provided $486,000 for several projects—a survey of internal migration and fertility, training of family planning personnel, strengthening of social science studies at the Lebanese University, and compilation and review of laws bearing on population and family planning.

The Ford Foundation has made an $80,000 grant to the American University of Beirut for a population studies program. The Pathfinder Fund has sponsored an outpatient female sterilization clinic to introduce this approach and demonstrate its feasibility. Also, Pathfinder has assisted the American University Hospital, Beirut, to become a facility at which medical students can receive fertility regulation training.

Saudi Arabia

The population of Saudi Arabia increased by nearly one-third during the 1966-75 decade, reaching 6.2 million in mid-1975. This is an increase of 1.5 million over the 1965 level of 4.7 million and a 60 percent greater increase than that for the previous decade.

The rate of natural increase in 1974 was 2.9 percent, up from 2.6 percent in 1965. The birth rate in 1974 was estimated at 49 births per 1,000 population, or about the same as in 1965. The death rate was 20 per 1,000 compared with 24 per 1,000.

Saudi Arabia is a traditional Moslam country with a modernization process dating back only to World War II when oil in commercial quantities was discovered. Less than one-fifth of the population live in urban places. The balance of the population is engaged in the country's traditional occupation, agriculture—about one-third in settled agriculture and two-thirds in nomadic or semi-nomadic types. In no other country is such a large proportion of the population nomadic. This pattern creates difficult problems with respect to the promotion of health services and education.

The import and sale of contraceptive pills and devices were prohibited by the Saudi Arabian Government in April 1975—a decision consistent with the Government's view that Saudi Arabia can support a larger population and must increase its labor force if it is to carry out development plans.

Oil revenues have enabled the Government to provide free medicine and medical care for all citizens and foreign residents. A modern hospital has been built in Riyadh, and it provides special care and is a university teaching hospital.

Demographic information is deficient, but the United Nations Fund for Population Activities (UNFPA) has provided $128,000 for two demographic projects. One was a national census; the other the improvement of civil registration and collection of vital statistics.

Syria

The population of Syria increased by 38 percent during the 1966-75 decade. In mid-1975 the total was 7.4 million, an increase of 2 million over the 1965 level of 5.3 million.

In 1974 the rate of natural increase was 3 percent, compared with 3.2 percent in 1965. Contributing to the decline was a drop in the annual birth rate from a level of 48 births per 1,000 population in 1965 to 45 in 1974. In 1975 there were 15 deaths per 1,000 people a year, compared with 16 per 1,000 in 1965.

Syria has a relatively low population density. Large regions of the country are desert and sub-desert and capable of sustaining only small nomadic elements. The majority of the population is dispersed throughout the fertile areas of the river valleys, but the country's population is most dense along the Mediterranean coast where irrigation is widely practiced. Prospects are good for expanding arable land as a result of the newly opened Euphrates dam.

Prior to 1974 Syria had no formal family planning "program" of any kind—national, regional or voluntary. But very recently the Government has shown increasing interest in the concept of family planning as a component of family (particularly maternal and child) health care. A Center for Population Studies and Research was established in 1972, and a National Committee for Developing Population Awareness was set up under the chairmanship of the Minister of Planning. In cooperation with the Ministry of Health and several U.N. agencies, the Central Bureau of Statistics undertook surveys on infant mortality in Damascus and several studies on the relationship between family size, health, and economic structure. The Syrian Family Planning Association was formed in June 1974, and began operations with the Government's support. The Syrian Ministry of Health is moving to incorporate family planning services into the country's existing health structure.

The selling, prescription, and spreading of information about contraceptives are illegal in the Syrian Arab Republic, but conventional contraceptives are available in most pharmacies. Abortion is legal only for medical reasons.

Turkey

Turkey's population in mid-1975 was estimated at 39.2 million and increasing at 2.7 percent per year. The 1974 birth rate was 39 per 1,000 population and the death rate 12 per 1,000.

Turkey has had a national family planning policy and program since 1965. It operates through the Ministry of Health and Social Service facilities, which are located in each of the country's 67 provinces. Nominally, family planning services have been made available to all people. In practice, however, both Government support and program effectiveness have been variable. An estimated 2.5 percent of married women in Turkey in 1974 used the IUD, which, since the program's beginning, has been virtually the only contraceptive available through Government clinics. The number of new acceptors recorded in each of recent years has been somewhat more than 50,000.

Pro-natalist attitudes linger in this large and sparsely populated country. New progress may be emerging, however, as indicated by some of these recent developments:

• The Ministry of Health, in 1974, signed a comprehensive 5-year agreement with the United Nations Fund for Population Activities (UNFPA) under which UNFPA will provide up to $10 million to help expand family planning and maternal/child health services throughout the national health network.

• The annual quota for importation of condoms for commercial sale was doubled from $100,000 to $200,000. (As recently as 1972, the quota had been only $10,000.)

• The Ministry of Health has developed plans for a national contraceptive distribution program that would make adequate supplies of contraceptives available throughout all health facilities.

• The Government budgeted nearly $2 million for family planning in 1975—by far the largest annual amount to date.

Turkey's first family planning activity was that of a private organization, Türkiye Aile Planlamasi Denegi (TAPD), founded in 1963. It is a member of the International Planned Parenthood Federation (IPPF). TAPD played an important role in motivating the Government to set up its family planning services, and it continues to support the program today through information and education activities, training, and medical services carried out by its 5 mobile teams and 17 fixed clinics.

At present, the Ministry of Health is responsible for making family planning services available to the people. Some 578 clinics in the 67 provinces offer

family planning services, and educational teams (working from a fleet of 528 mobile units) go to villages to enlist acceptors and distribute contraceptives. Health personnel of the Ministry number more than 10,000 including about 7,000 midwives. And organizational changes are being made to give a stronger position to family planning in the Ministry's maternal/child health program.

Other organizations that support the national program include the Hacettepe University in Ankara and its Institute of Population Studies, which has been heavily assisted by the Ford Foundation. The Institute's social, demographic, and national fertility surveys are made available to Government policy-makers to assist in program determinations.

External Assistance

The largest provider of assistance to Turkey's population program has been the U.S. Agency for International Development (AID). Although AID is not currently helping finance the program, approximately $2.5 million has been made available since mid-1965—much of it to help establish the program. This assistance helped to purchase vehicles for use in the health program network, to perform marketing analysis of the commercial distribution of contraceptives, to train nurse/midwives in family planning,

Above left, a 5th-year
medical student conducts
a demographic study in
Turkey; the mother is 20
years old, has five
children, and is newly
arrived in the Istanbul
area where her husband
has not yet found a
regular job. Above,
men of a village gather
to hear Ministry of Health
educator instruct them
in contraceptive techniques.
Below, poster at a Turkish
food store says too many
children require too
expensive a load of food.

to study the impact of rapid population growth in Turkey, and to help the Ministry of Health make contraceptives available through health centers.

AID also has helped fund the Turkish Demographic Survey Center in the State Institute of Statistics, which the University of North Carolina has provided with technical assistance in demographic data collection and analysis.

The United Nations Fund for Population Activities (UNFPA), with its $10 million of funding for 1974-78, will enable 20 high-level Turkish officials to study family planning programs in South East Asia, establish a hormone laboratory at Ankara Maternity Hospital, provide current information on population trends in Turkey, compile and review existing laws affecting family planning, and facilitate the integration of family planning and maternal/child health services.

The International Planned Parenthood Federation (IPPF) gave financial support to the private Turkish association (TAPD) during the 1973-75 period that totaled somewhat more than $300,000. Among other helpful activities, the money financed a family planning seminar in 1974 (the first of its kind in Turkey). Earlier IPPF support enabled TAPD mobile teams to contact more than 1.1 million persons about family planning during the period 1966-73.

The Association for Voluntary Sterilization has made a grant of $17,750 to Hacettepe University to establish a female voluntary sterilization program. Ford Foundation grants to Hacettepe University have financed training and research in population and demography.

World Education funds totaling $77,500 during 1971-73 helped the Ministry of Education to establish adult education programs including family planning elements. The Population Council assisted Turkey's early family planning efforts, and the United Kingdom has provided consultants to the Ministry of Health for specific population/family planning projects. The Pathfinder Fund has also given some assistance.

This large area, which includes Cyprus, Iran, Iraq, Israel, Jordan, Lebanon, Syria and Turkey, has a rapidly expanding population. Maintaining adequate per capita food production is becoming increasingly difficult for some countries, notably Iraq, Jordan, and Syria.

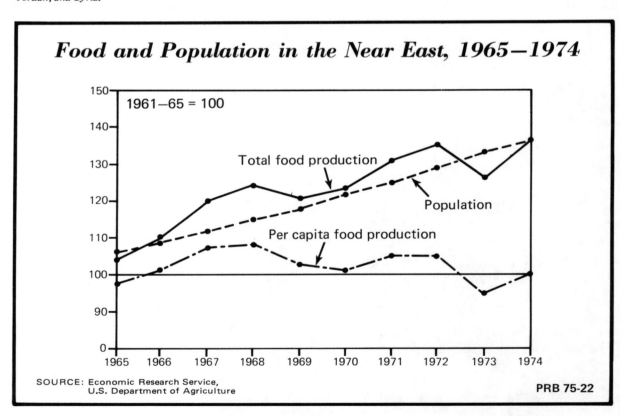

Food and Population in the Near East, 1965–1974

1961–65 = 100

Total food production

Population

Per capita food production

SOURCE: Economic Research Service,
U.S. Department of Agriculture

PRB 75-22

Northern America

The population of Northern America—comprising about 6 percent of the world total—increased by 10.5 percent during the 1965-75 decade. As of mid-1975, the Northern American population amounted to 236.6 million, or 22.6 million more than the 1965 level of 214 million.

This 10-year gain, however, was only two-thirds the increment of the previous decade, and indicates a slowing of population growth. Population growth during the 1955-65 period was 32 million over the 1955 level of 182 million.

The annual rate of natural increase for Northern America was 0.6 percent a year, based on 1974 statistics, compared with 1.1 percent in 1965. The drop stemmed entirely from a sharp decline in the birth rate. The birth rate in 1974 was 15 births per 1,000 population, down from 20 per 1,000 in 1965. The death rate held steady at about 9 deaths per 1,000.

Immigration, however, continued to play a significant role in the growth of both Canada and the United States, the countries with the largest populations. Immigration accounted for one-fourth of the population growth of the United States and more than half of that of Canada.

The per capita gross national product in Northern America increased between 1965 and 1973 by about 24 percent. In 1965 it was $4,950 per capita and in 1973, $6,130 per capita.

Both the United States and Canada have experienced, with some variations, the demographic history of Western civilization in general and the English-speaking "overseas" colonized countries in particular. In the 18th and early 19th centuries, mortality and fertility were very high and the rate of growth was rapid. Today the rate of natural increase is well under 1 percent for both countries—0.6 percent for the United States and 0.8 percent for Canada in 1974.

The legal situations in both countries have shifted in recent years from restrictions on contraception to the present official support for family planning by Federal and many State or Provincial governments. The shift has been stimulated especially by emphasis on responsible parenthood, women's rights, family well-being, and a recognition that growth, in itself, is not necessarily good.

U.S. and Canadian governmental assistance to developing countries for population programs totaled more than $740 million during the 1965-75 decade. Significant additional support also was forthcoming from private organizations.

The United States and Canada—with populations of approximately 213.6 million and 22.8 million, respectively—account for more than 99 percent of the Northern American total. Bermuda with 55,000, Greenland with 50,000, and the islands of St. Pierre and Miquelon with 5,000 comprise the remainder—less than 0.0006 percent of the total population of Northern America. The population developments of Canada and the United States are presented here in some detail.

Canada

The population of Canada in 1975 was approximately 22.8 million, or 3.1 million more than in 1965. The increase, however, was upward of a million less than during the preceding decade. The initiation of a Federal family planning program in 1970 is expected to contribute to this trend.

The smaller rate of increase came directly from a marked drop in the birth rate, since net immigration was larger in the 1965-74 period and mortality in the two decades held relatively steady at about 7 to 8 deaths per 1,000 population. In 1974 there were 15 births per 1,000 people, 21 percent below the 1965 figure of 21 per 1,000. Whereas women in the 15 to 49 age bracket produced 74.4 children per 1,000 in 1966, the figure dropped to 67.7 in 1971 and to 61.5 in 1974.

As another consequence of the lowered birth rate, immigration accounted for about two-thirds (1.5 million) of the 1965-75 population increase in Canada. For the previous 10-year period, it had represented one-third (1.1 million) of the population increase.

The Government of Canada recognizes that the country of tomorrow will be largely shaped by the decisions Canadians make about future immigration policies. The Government in 1975 issued a comprehensive "Green Paper" on the subject to stimulate a countrywide debate with a view toward developing a common perception of population goals for the nation as a whole. When he issued this "Green Paper," Canada's Minister of Manpower and Immigration stated:

To many Canadians, with our country's pioneering tradition, the "population question" may often have seemed remote. We think of ourselves as inhabiting a vast land mass; yet one-third is the granite crust on the Pre-Cambrian shield. We think of Canada as possessing virtually boundless farming potential and therefore a huge capacity to produce food for our own and the world's use; yet only 17 percent of Canada's territory is even potentially arable, and of this only about one-third is really good for agriculture. Moreover, metropolitan expansion is making perceptible inroads in high-quality farm land.

We have been accustomed to think of housing as cheap and easily available; yet everyone is well aware that, in urban centers, land prices have risen at staggering rates. We have always regarded ourselves as having almost infinite elbow room; and yet some of us have begun to feel crowded in our cities. The urgency of the question is now coming home to us. We are beginning to appreciate the importance of knowing where we are going in population terms and of taking deliberate decisions to choose our population future.

With over half of Canada's immigrants going to three major cities—Toronto, Vancouver, and Montreal—Government officials recognize that population policy must also be concerned with where people live and how they live. Since 1871 Canada has evolved from a rural to an urban-based society. In 1871, 18.3 percent of the population was considered urban compared with 76.1 percent in 1971. Since World War II, the most rapid increase in urban population has taken place in metropolitan regions with populations of 100,000 or more. If present trends continue, well over half of all Canadians will be living in 12 metropolitan areas by the end of the century, with one-third of the total population located in the two largest cities—Montreal and Toronto.

In line with the increase in population, the Canadian gross national product also followed an upward trend during the past decade. It increased between 1965 and 1973 by about 34 percent. In 1965 it was $4,010 per capita and in 1973, $5,370.

Federal and Provincial Programs

Federal support for family planning activities was made possible by legislation which in 1969 removed a longstanding legal prohibition against provision of contraceptive information and services.

A Federal family planning program was initiated in 1970 to make readily accessible to Canadians the knowledge and means enabling them to make informed decisions about the number and spacing of their children. It includes the administration of a grants program; the development and distribution of family planning, family life, and sex education materials; the provision of consultation on related matters to governmental and nongovernmental organizations; and assistance in the training of needed personnel. Family planning grants are available for the development and expansion of family planning services and for demonstration, training, and research projects. A limited number of university teaching and/or research fellowships are offered. Substantial support also has been provided to voluntary agencies.

The means of achieving the objectives of the Federal family planning program come largely under the jurisdiction of the provinces through their departments of health, education, and welfare. Federal aid to the provinces is provided by three important pieces of shared-cost legislation: The Medical Care Act of 1966, which makes possible comprehensive medical insurance for all Canadians; the Hospital Insurance and Diagnostic Services Act of 1957, which provides a Federal contribution of 50 percent of the costs of insured hospital services; and the Canadian Assistance Plan of 1966.

Under the two health measures, the costs of family planning consultations with physicians, of surgical sterilization, and of clinical services are publicly financed. The Canadian Assistance Plan shares the costs of contraceptives and of family planning counseling services provided through provincially approved programs to needy people. This means that family planning services are theoretically available to most Canadians. Their availability, however, is not yet universal.

Provincial programs are at various stages of development. Quebec has announced its intention of making family planning an integral part of a broad spectrum of health and welfare services. Ontario has appointed an interdepartmental committee, chaired by the Ministry of Health, to coordinate the development of family planning services and family life education. Saskatchewan's Health Department has a full-time coordinator of family planning, and the government is studying reports of citizen advisory committees on family planning and family life education. Alberta supports the growth of family planning services through its Preventive Social Services program. British Columbia is integrating into its health services a number of family planning clinics first established under volunteer auspices.

Sex Education

The place of sex education in the schools is a matter of controversy. A national public opinion poll in January 1974 indicated that 73.1 percent of Canadians approved sex education in the schools. Of those approving, 88.8 percent thought that such courses should include discussions of birth control. However, in some places a minority of parents opposed this on the grounds that such teaching encourages sexual promiscuity and constitutes an invasion of parental rights.

There is also conflict over the provision of contraceptive services to minors. This area is under provincial jurisdiction through laws which are not uniform across Canada governing the age at which young people may be given medical care without parental consent. Some argue that provision of contraceptive services will encourage immorality among teenagers. However, in the light of evidence that the majority of young unmarried people requesting contraceptives are already sexually active, others maintain that such services are a necessary preventive of teenage pregnancies leading to demands for abortions.

The Subject of Abortion

Canadian public opinion is sharply polarized on the subject of abortion. The 1969 amendments to the Criminal Code authorized the performance of an abortion by a medical practitioner in an approved or accredited hospital when that hospital's abortion committee, consisting of at least three other medical practitioners, certifies that the continuation of the pregnancy would or would be likely to endanger the woman's life or health. This provision does not operate evenly across the country because the establishment of hospital abortion committees is optional, and less than half of Canadian hospitals have established them. Since health is not defined for this purpose, interpretations by individual abortion committees vary widely. Hospitals which do perform abortions cannot meet the demand. Many women seeking abortions obtain them in the United States.

In 1973 the number of therapeutic abortions in Canadian hospitals for Canadian residents totalled 43,201, an increase of 4,348 over the 1972 level of 38,853. The abortion rate increased from 11.2 percent of live births in 1972 to 12.6 percent in 1973. However, the increase in numbers and the rate was the smallest year-to-year increase since the amendment of the Criminal Code in 1969 and was only about one-half the increase recorded between 1971 and 1972.

A public opinion poll taken in September 1974 indicated that 62 percent of Canadians believed that the decision about abortion should be made by the woman concerned and her physician. A number of influential organizations, including the Canadian Medical Association, are on record as favoring this principle through the removal of any reference to abortion from the Criminal Code. On the other side, a coalition of "pro-life" groups presented to Parliament, in June 1975, a petition signed by over 1 million Canadians requesting that the abortion law be tightened.

In October 1975, the Federal Minister of Justice announced the appointment of an Abortion Law Study Committee. It will conduct a study to determine whether the procedure provided in the Criminal Code for obtaining therapeutic abortions is operating equitably across Canada. Its report, due in 6 months, is expected to be essentially findings of fact. The report will be made public and will form the basis for further consideration of the law. In addition to the chairman, a medical sociologist, the Committee consists of a physician and a lawyer.

External Assistance

Most of Canada's population and family planning support to developing countries has been provided by the Canadian International Development Agency (CIDA) and channeled through multilateral organizations. In fiscal year 1975-76, multilateral assistance totaled $7.5 million, an increase of $1.7 million over the fiscal year 1974-75 level of $5.8 million. Primary recipients were the United Nations Fund for Population Activities, the International Planned Parenthood Federation, and the World Health Organization. Until fiscal year 1974-75, Canada also provided support for the OECD Social Development and Demographic Program.

Some bilateral assistance also has been given to a family planning program in India; vehicles and educational equipment have been provided for some Caribbean countries; a workshop in Montreal for personnel from French-speaking African countries has received support; funds have been provided for production of a family planning film in Ghana; and a contribution of $2 million has been made to a population program in Bangladesh supported jointly by the World Bank and several bilateral donors.

In addition, CIDA's nongovernmental organizations division has contributed more than $435,000 to 20 family planning projects in developing countries through such Canadian voluntary agencies as the Family Planning Federation of Canada, Canadian UNICEF Committee, Canadian Unitarian Service Committee, Oxfam (Canada), World Literacy, SERENA, and the Canadian Teacher's Federation.

The United States

The population of the United States at the beginning of July 1975 was 213.6 million, an increase of 19.3 million from the total a decade earlier of about 194.3 million. With population growth in the period slowing, this 10-year increase was 9 million less than in the preceding decade. Whereas population rose nearly 2.3 million in the first year of the 1965-1975 period, it climbed only 1.6 million in 1974. Significantly, about one-fifth of the increase in 1965 was from net immigration. In 1974 the proportion from immigration was somewhat higher.

The overall situation reflects a marked decline in the rate of natural population increase stemming from a sharply lower birth rate offset only slightly by a small decrease in mortality. The drop in mortality was from 10 per 1,000 population in 1965 to 9 in 1974. The overall birth rate for 1975 is estimated at about 15 per 1,000 or the same as in 1973 and 1974 but 26 percent lower than the rate of 1965. The 1973 and 1974 birth rates, and the rate for 1975 were the lowest in U.S. history. These birth rates are approaching those noted for the United Kingdom and Scandinavia.

However, the low U.S. rates of today are not necessarily the pattern of the future. For one thing, the large generation born after World War II and known as the "baby boom" is entering its most active childbearing period. This group—from 20 to 34 years of age—will do much to determine the future trend in population increases.

Although relatively large numbers of women are in the reproductive age group, they are likely to have fewer children per woman because the small family is becoming the ideal of most Americans. Many believe their own quality of life and that of their children will be easier to ensure with fewer children to maintain and educate.

A survey of 47,000 households by the Bureau of the Census in June 1974 showed that 72.7 percent of the younger wives (ages 18 to 24) expected to have two or fewer children and only 27.2 percent of them expected to have more than two.

The wives 18 to 24 years old interviewed in the Census survey expected, as a group, to have an average of 2.2 children. This figure implies an expectation for their future families to include about 2.1 children. If immigration were nonexistent, the rate of reproduction which, if adopted and maintained by the entire population, would result in eventual zero growth of the U.S. population. Meanwhile, however, because of the extra large proportion of people of childbearing age, the population would continue increasing substantially for about 50 years.

Three projections of the population of the United States for the year 2000 have been recently made by the Bureau of the Census on the basis of different fertility rates. They range from 245 million to 287 million. The low projection assumes that women between now and the year 2000 will have an average of 1.7 children, and the high projection assumes they will have an average of 2.7 children. Thus, a difference of one child per woman in the next 25 years means a difference of 42 million in the size of the population by the year 2000. An intermediate projection for an average of 2.1 children per woman would give a population of 262 million in the year 2000. All of these projections are based on the same assumptions regarding mortality and immigration with fertility as the only variable component. It is assumed that death rates will decline slightly and net legal immigration will remain at 400,000 a year.

The projection that appears likeliest to reflect actuality is the intermediate one that indicates a growth in population of about 50 million by the end of the century with approximately one-fourth of the increase resulting from legal immigration. The projections do not take into account illegal immigrants which some estimates put as high as a million annually. However, illegals are less likely than legal immigrants to stay permanently.

In keeping with the increase in population, the U.S. gross national product also followed an upward trend during the past decade. The per capita gross national product increased between 1965 and 1973 by about 23 percent. It was $5,050 per capita in 1965 and in 1973, $6,210 per capita.

It is not known to what extent the decline in economic activity since 1973, the accompanying inflation, and the rise in unemployment influenced the birth rate. However, uncertainties as to employment and income are significant factors in family decision making.

While U.S. population continued to increase, changes also occurred in its distribution. For example, during the past decade metropolitan areas no longer grew faster than nonmetropolitan ones. The South, historically an exporter of people to other parts of the Nation, experienced a net influx.

For the past century or longer, the cities, or metropolitan areas, of the United States have grown more rapidly than the country as a whole as a result of their attraction to migrants from rural areas and to immigrants from abroad. Until about 100 years ago, urban residents constituted only one-fourth of the U.S. population, and by 50 years ago they had passed the one-half mark. At present, approximately three-fourths of the Nation's people live in urban areas. But since about 1970 there is evidence that although immigration into the cities from abroad is continuing, the metropolitan areas, on balance, are no longer gaining population through migration from the nonmetropolitan countryside.

Several factors account for the change. For many years, the more rapid expansion of metropolitan, as compared with nonmetropolitan, areas has been associated with rising productivity and higher levels of living in metropolitan areas. However, such side effects as traffic congestion, air and water pollution, tensions arising from crowded conditions, and a rising incidence of crime have placed serious strains on the provision of public services. Such effects have tended to offset some of the lure of all metropolitan areas. In addition, there have been increases in the number of jobs available in nonmetropolitan areas. Retirement communities have developed in outlying areas and attracted older migrants from metropolitan territory. An increasing number of workers commute to metropolitan jobs from small-town or open-country residences. And some developments have occurred beyond the boundaries of metropolitan areas.

The above changes in population trends, however, do not represent a return by metropolitan dwellers to farm communities or pursuits. The farm population, after recording an average annual decrease of 4.8 percent during the 1960's, appears to have stabilized at nearly 9.0 million.

From a regional standpoint, the Northeast and North Central States, on balance, have continued to lose some people to other areas during the past decade while the West has continued to gain—but at a lower rate than in the 1960's.

The South, however, for the 1970-75 period, has reversed its longstanding role as a net exporter of people and become a net importer. More whites are moving to the South, fewer blacks are leaving, and significant numbers of Latin Americans have immigrated—primarily from Cuba. Many incoming residents have responded to new business opportunities in the South; but new retirement developments in Florida have also been a major attraction. For blacks, the decline in the volume of outmigration between 1970 and 1975 was so far reaching that the number of blacks moving to the South now nearly equals the number moving from the South. This change represents a significant departure from the large-scale outmigration of blacks from the South in the period between World War II and the late 1960's—a period when fully 4½ million more blacks left the South than returned to it.

Regionally, the most rapid population growth in 1970-75 occurred in the Mountain States of the West (an increase of 16.3 percent) and in the South Atlantic States (9.9 percent). At the other extreme, the population of the Middle Atlantic States was virtually the same in 1975 as in 1970.

Meanwhile, dramatic changes in attitude and behavior toward family planning have occurred within the United States during the 1965-75 decade. Public opinion and public policies have become increasingly favorable to measures for voluntary control of family size and spacing of births, including provision of clinical services.

The increased availability of family planning services and supplies has thus contributed, to some degree, to the declining birth rates of the past decade. But economic and social factors have also been an important part of the picture. Among such factors are increased urbanization and the changing status and independence of women in the society. Increasingly, public opinion and public policies have come to approve the principles of the United Nations Declaration of Human Rights, including the right of women to control their own bodies and reproduction.

Family Planning Practices of the General Population*

In the United States today, more than 9 out of 10 married couples have practiced—or expect to practice—some form of contraception to limit or space births. Couples are using contraception earlier in marriage than they used to, more are using the most effective methods, and couples are increasingly successful in assuring their desired family size.

The latest available data indicate that three in four Americans who are practicing contraception are using scientific methods. Of this group, 58 percent are using the most effective contraceptive methods: pill (oral contraceptive) 34.2 percent; sterilization 16.3 percent; and, IUD (intrauterine device) 7.4 percent. In addition, among couples who had borne all of the children they wanted, more than one in six had been voluntarily sterilized for contraceptive reasons. Among older couples (in which the wife is 30 to 44 years of age) sterilization—typically, tubal ligation for women and vasectomy for men—were among the most popular methods of contraception. Sterilizations were almost equally divided between men and women.

Significantly, individuals served by Federally supported family planning programs are using the most effective contraceptive methods to a far greater degree than the population at large. During 1974, 89 percent of female patients in subsidized programs were using the pill (75 percent) or the IUD (14

---

*From "Survey of Family Planning in the United States," by Ruth Galaid, Office of Population Affairs, Department of Health, Education, and Welfare, December 1974.

percent). Also, low-income couples—in part through the efforts of these programs—have almost reached the level of contraceptive usage of high-income couples.

While fertility rates have declined, especially for married and older single women—and this to some measure can be attributed to the greater effectiveness of their contraceptive practices—teenagers are a highly vulnerable group. A national sample of teenage females showed that less than one-half of those considered to be sexually experienced had used any method of contraception for the most recent exposure to the risk of conception and less than one-fifth always utilized a means of contraception. While a majority of Americans favor giving contraception to teenagers who are sexually active, controversy still exists about the rights and wrongs of premarital sex. There is no evidence that availability

of contraceptive services to unwed teenagers encourages sexual activity; but available data do suggest that if a minor requests contraception there is a definite need for it.

Although the contraceptive use rate of American couples is among the highest in the world and, although the United States is in the midst of an unprecedented low overall fertility, there remains a distinct and crucial gap between desired family size and the incidence of unwanted pregnancy. On the one hand, the average number of children American couples desire for themselves is trending downward, as noted above. On the other hand, according to the 1970 National Fertility Study, 44 percent of all births between 1966 and 1970 to currently married women were unplanned, and 15 percent of these births were reported by parents as never having been wanted. The survey indicates that unwanted births

The sharp decline in U.S. fertility rates began in the late 1920's. The continuing drop in the 1930's traces to the Depression, which brought postponement of many marriages and increased emphasis on contraception. The end of World War II brought a reversal of these factors; a sharp increase in fertility rates resulted in a post-war "Baby Boom." Since the mid-1950's more than nine out of ten married couples—for personal reasons or out of concern about U.S. and world population growth—have practiced or expect to practice some form of contraception to limit or space births. Couples are using contraception earlier in marriage than formerly and more are using highly effective contraceptive methods. The result has been a trend toward fewer births.

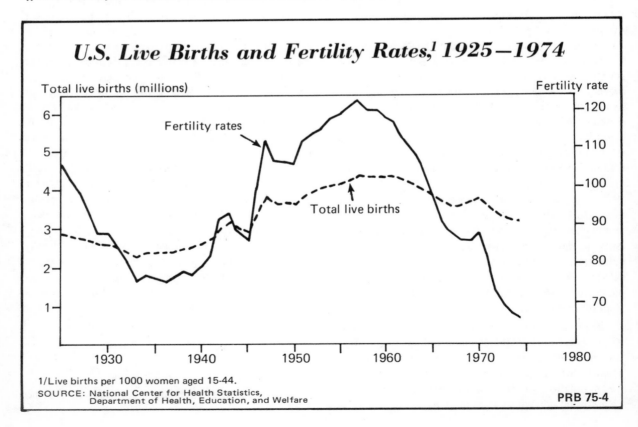

U.S. Live Births and Fertility Rates,[1] 1925—1974

Total live births (millions)

Fertility rate

Fertility rates

Total live births

1/Live births per 1000 women aged 15-44.

SOURCE: National Center for Health Statistics,
Department of Health, Education, and Welfare

PRB 75-4

are highest among those who have the lowest educational and income levels.

The oral contraceptive pill, considered one of the most effective methods, had the following failure rates according to the 1970 Fertility Study: after one year of use, 7 percent of all those American women who intended to delay their next pregnancy by using the pill were accidentally pregnant, and 4 percent of those who never intended to have more children were also pregnant. Twelve-month failure rates among users of the IUD, another effective contraceptive, were even higher: 15 percent for women who intended to delay their next child, and 5 percent for women who wished to end their childbearing.

When all methods of contraception were taken into account, the overall failure rates were very much higher. During 1970, one out of every four couples who practiced some form of contraception for spacing their family experienced an accidental pregnancy. And among those who practiced contraception to prevent all future births, unwanted pregnancies occurred in 14 out of every 100 couples. Those women who are relatively young at the beginning of exposure to risk (that is, younger than the national average for any specific pregnancy order) are much more likely to fail than those who are older. Sixty-six percent of those attempting to prevent pregnancy altogether are successful for at least 5 years, but this success proportion ranges from 44 percent for the youngest to 84 percent for the oldest relative age category.

Estimates indicate that about 900,000 legal abortions were performed in the United States in 1974 (as reported by Edward Weinstock, Christopher Teitze, Frederick S. Jaffe, and Joy C. Dryfoos in the January/February 1975 issue of *Family Planning Perspectives Magazine*). This represented an increase of 150,000 over 1973. It is estimated that about 50,000 legal abortions were performed in 1969.

The estimated 900,000 legal abortions in the United States in 1974 compares with the total of 3,166,000 births in that year. Thus, there were close to 3 legal abortions in the United States in 1974 for each 10 live births. The number of legal abortions has increased dramatically since the Supreme Court's decision liberalizing abortion restrictions in 1973. However, it is not known to what extent these merely replace abortions that would have occurred illegally had it not been for the Supreme Court's decision in 1973.

Organized Family Planning Services

Rapid expansion of organized family planning services in the United States during the 1965-75

decade stemmed largely from (1) repeal of statutory restrictions which previously had prohibited the dissemination of contraceptive materials and supplies, and (2) Congressional initiatives which translated public interest into concrete program authority.

Prior to 1965 most States had continued to operate on the basis of laws modeled after the famous Comstock Act of 1873—a Federal law that banned from the mails and from interstate and foreign commerce any and all materials relating to contraception. But such laws had become seriously outmoded in terms of public opinion. Studies in 1941, 1955, and 1960 showed that a large share of Americans of all religious, ethnic, and socioeconomic groups favored the use of contraception. The first major statutory changes at the State level thus came about with relatively little controversy in 1965 and 1966 when five States repealed restrictions on the dissemination of contraceptive information. In 12 other States, laws were adopted authorizing or encouraging public health departments or welfare agencies to provide family planning services to their clients at public expense. And the U.S. Supreme Court added its weight to the shift in attitude when it ruled in 1965 that married couples have a constitutional right to practice contraception free of legal interference—a right which the Court extended in 1972 to unmarried persons.

These developments were followed or accompanied by challenges to the abortion laws of many States, almost all of which prohibited abortion except to save the mother's life. Colorado liberalized its abortion law in 1967, and 17 other States did so subsequently. In January of 1973, the U.S. Supreme Court overturned many of the remaining restrictions on abortion throughout the Nation by its ruling that States could not interfere with a woman's decision to have an abortion during the first 3 months of pregnancy, so long as it was performed by a physician.*

It was against this background of sweeping statutory change that the 1966-75 expansion in organized family planning services developed in the United States. The Planned Parenthood Federation of

---

*The U.S. Supreme Court held that during the first trimester "the abortion decision and its effectuation must be left to the medical judgment of the pregnant woman's attending physician." After the first trimester "the State, in promoting its interest in the health of the mother, may, if it chooses, regulate the abortion procedure in ways that are reasonably related to maternal health." After the fetus has reached viability "The State. . . .may, if it chooses, regulate, and even proscribe, abortion except where necessary, in appropriate medical judgment, for the preservation of the life or health of the mother."

America reports that as late as 1960 no more than 150 public and private health agencies were operating family planning clinic programs serving persons of low or marginal income. Most of these were affiliates of Planned Parenthood and served about 150,000 women.

By 1974, however, family planning programs receiving Federal support were serving over 3.4 million women with a combination of medical, educational, informational, and social services necessary to enable them to freely determine the number and spacing of their children. (See the accompanying tables.) Over 70 percent of the women served were members of families with incomes below 150 percent of poverty ($7,557 for a nonfarm family of four in March 1974).

Federal family planning support in 1974 totaled $201 million, compared with $60 million as recently as 1971.

It should be noted, however, that not all of the new developments were accepted without organized challenge. One response during the past decade was the formation within the United States of a militant antiabortion movement. Known generally as the "Right to Life" movement, it has actively opposed abortion and further lifting of legal restrictions.

In less than a decade, however, U.S. law and policy had moved from deterring, or at least making difficult, effective voluntary regulation of fertility to permitting it and, indeed, using public resources to facilitate it and to remedy some of the deficits deriving from inequities in the distribution of medical care. Sharp differences in views over abortion continue to exist, however, as is evident in the continuing efforts of the "Right to Life" movement to rally increasing numbers of Americans to its cause.

Federal administrative policy began to shift toward support of family planning activities after 1965 with the active encouragement of Congress and President Lyndon Johnson. In 1966, the Department of Health, Education, and Welfare issued its first policy statement on family planning, and President Johnson stated the objectives of U.S. domestic policy in a message on health and education:

We have a growing concern to foster the integrity of the family and the opportunity for each child. It is essential that all families have access to information and services that will allow freedom to choose the number and spacing of their children within the dictates of individual conscience.

The first Federal agency to move actively into family planning was the Office of Economic Opportunity. As part of its antipoverty program, it began in 1965 to make grants to community action agencies to finance voluntary family planning projects. In the same year, Federal maternity care projects enabled some city health departments to start providing family planning services on a limited basis.

By 1967, however, Congress was pressing for expanded family planning programs. In a major development it brought the Department of Health, Education, and Welfare into the forefront of the

Women Served in Organized Family Planning Programs, in the United States, Fiscal Years 1968-1974

Fiscal year	Number of women served
1968	863,000
1969	1,070,000
1970	1,410,000
1971	1,889,000
1972	2,612,000
1973	3,120,000
1974	3,417,000

Source: Department of Health, Education, and Welfare Fourth Progress Report to the Congress, May 1975.

Estimated Number of Women Served in Organized Family Planning Programs in the United States, by Income Level, 1974

Income level	Number of women	Percent of all women in organized family planning programs
Below poverty level[1]	1,832,000	54
125 percent of poverty level or less[2]	2,194,000	64
150 percent of poverty level or less[3]	2,499,000	73

[1] Estimate for nonfarm family of four, March 1974, $5,038.

[2] Estimate for nonfarm family of four, March 1974, $6,297.

[3] Estimate for nonfarm family of four, March 1974, $7,557.

Source: Department of Health, Education, and Welfare Fourth Progress Report to the Congress, May 1975.

family planning effort by amending the Social Security Act to provide funding for family planning service projects within the maternal and child health programs. Congress at this time also amended the Foreign Assistance Act to designate funds for aid on family planning and population programs to other nations requesting it.

In 1968 President Johnson appointed a Committee on Population and Family Planning to assess the adequacy of the Federal program. In its report, the Committee recommended rapid increases in funding and strengthening of the administrative machinery for the three main parts of the Federal program: (1) voluntary family planning services at home, primarily for low-income persons; (2) biomedical and behavioral research to improve methods of contraception and the understanding of population dynamics; and, (3) assistance to family planning programs in developing countries.

A year later President Nixon issued a historic first presidential message to Congress on population problems calling for increased Federal support of each of these programs and asking for the establishment of a population commission. Legislation creating the Commission on Population Growth and the American Future was enacted in 1970. That same year Congress passed the Family Planning Services and Population Research Act, which embodied most of the recommendations of President Johnson's population committee. That act—the only major legislation in this field to be adopted by the U.S. Congress—authorized $382 million for a 3-year program of services and research.

In 1971, the Department of Health, Education, and Welfare submitted to Congress a 5-year plan outlining a program to provide services by 1975 to an estimated 6.6 million women of low or marginal income at risk of unwanted pregnancy. A year later the Commission on Population Growth and the American Future, in its final report, recommended a broad array of health, education, economic, and social programs to enable the United States to achieve a stabilized population in an orderly manner as rapidly as possible.

The change in public policy was thus expressed in numerous legislative and administrative actions at Federal, State, and local levels. And in addition to providing medical contraceptive services, the resulting organized family planning programs also became the largest providers in the Nation of preventive health screening service for low- or marginal-income women of childbearing age. A decade before, no public money was available for such screening services; in fiscal 1974 the Federal appropriation for overall family planning within the United States, as noted above, was $201 million.

Such a multilevel program requires multilevel decision making. Involved at different levels are National Government health and welfare officials; State, county, and community governments; State, county, and community health departments; associations of service providers; and hospital and clinic administrators.

The level of administrative responsibility varies with the type of administrative unit and its level of authority. The Federal level of government interprets national policy and establishes regulations and guidelines for the provision of services. Federal officials located in regional offices approve or disapprove specific grant applications and contracts from service providers.

State officials also review and approve or dis-

Types of Agencies Providing Family Planning Services in the United States, Number and Percent of Total Patients Served at Each, and Average Number of Patients Served Per Type of Agency in Calendar Year 1969 and in Fiscal Year 1974

Type of agency	Number of agencies		Percent of patients served		Average number of patients served per agency	
	CY 1969	FY 1974	CY 1969	FY 1974	CY 1969	FY 1974
Hospital.	505	755	26	18	612	799
Health department.	1,177	1,767	33	38	344	738
Planned parenthood	146	222	33	25	2,742	3,864
Other	155	639	8	19	599	1,011
Total	1,983	3,383	100	100	609	1,010

Source: Department of Health, Education, and Welfare Fourth Progress Report to the Congress, May 1975.

Origins of U.S. Immigrants, 1965 and 1974

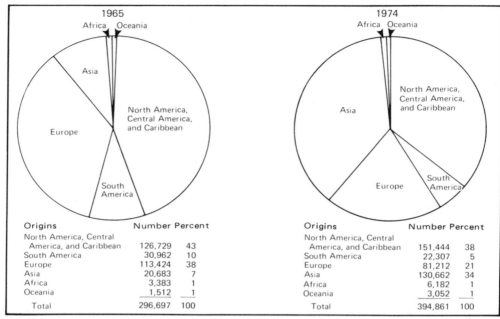

1965

Origins	Number	Percent
North America, Central America, and Caribbean	126,729	43
South America	30,962	10
Europe	113,424	38
Asia	20,683	7
Africa	3,383	1
Oceania	1,512	1
Total	296,697	100

1974

Origins	Number	Percent
North America, Central America, and Caribbean	151,444	38
South America	22,307	5
Europe	81,212	21
Asia	130,662	34
Africa	6,182	1
Oceania	3,052	1
Total	394,861	100

Source: U.S. Bureau of Immigration and
Naturalization 1974 Annual Report

Fiscal year data

PRB 75-14

Immigrants Admitted to the United States

Total	Annual average
1931-1940 528,431	52,843
1941-1950 1,035,039	103,504
1951-1960 2,515,479	251,548
1961-1965 1,450,312	290,062
1966-1970 1,871,365	374,273
1971-1974 1,550,087	387,522

SOURCE: U.S. Immigration and Naturalization Service
1974 Annual Report

PRB 75-33

Fewer Europeans sought new homes in the United States in 1965-74, but America has become highly attractive to migrants from Latin America, the Caribbean, and Asia as a result of a shift in U.S. immigration regulations.

approve grants under State control. State welfare officials are responsible for determining eligibility of low-income individuals for family planning services through welfare programs.

Health departments and association administrators have responsibility for obtaining funds and caring for the needs of the service providers they represent. Hospital and clinic administrators are responsible for scheduling and appointments, information, health personnel, facilities, equipment and supplies, and provision of quality medical services.

Federal regulations as set forth in Title X of the Public Health Service (PHS) Act require providers to offer a broad range of medically approved methods of family planning services, including the rhythm method, and to provide for diagnostic services and treatment for infertility. Abortion services are specifically excluded as a family planning service under the PHS Act Title X and the Social Security Act (SSA) Title V.

More than half of all patients served within organized programs are served in specialized family planning clinics while the remainder receive care through maternal health and general medical clinics. Nearly all patients in 1974 had low or marginal incomes. Half were 23 years of age or younger, and nearly 3 in 10 were still in their teens. More than two-fifths had not yet had any children, and an additional one-fifth had only one birth. Two patients out of every three were white. More than four out of five patients chose the most effective methods available—pills, IUD's, and voluntary sterilization. Before enrollment in the family planning clinic, half of the new patients used no method or one of the less effective methods. After the first visit, more than four out of five switched to the most effective methods.

In the field of population research, U.S. Government and private programs account for an estimated 90 percent of all funds expended worldwide. In 1974,

the combined U.S. programs provided approximately $61.7 million.

Among the major Federal research programs in the United States are those of the Department of Health, Education, and Welfare, which provided $54.9 million in 1974 and the Agency for International Development, which provided $3.9 million. Among the major private U.S. research organizations were the Ford Foundation (which in 1973 accounted for $10 million), the Rockefeller Foundation ($4 million), and the Population Council ($1 million).

Department of Health, Education, and Welfare

The U.S. agency responsible for administering the preponderant share of Federal support for domestic family planning services is the Department of Health, Education, and Welfare (HEW). In fiscal year 1975, HEW provided $201 million for organized family planning programs in the United States. This was nearly 3½ times the funds available to HEW in fiscal 1971 for family planning purposes when approximately $60 million was available.

As noted, the dominant role of HEW began with the Social Security Amendments of 1967 which authorized funding for family planning services grants and also required that not less than 6 percent of funds appropriated for Maternal and Child Health Service under Title V of the Social Security Act be made available for family planning services. Since that time HEW funds have provided a little over $1.1 billion for research and family planning services within the United States (fiscal years 1971 to 1975).

HEW population programs are almost entirely domestically oriented with more than 99 percent of available funds allocated for Stateside activities. The major thrust of these domestic programs, in turn, is in the fields of family planning services and population research.

Family planning services. HEW's domestic family planning activity falls largely within its public health programs, which are carried out chiefly with State departments of health, the private organization of Planned Parenthood/World Population, and other such health care agencies. It is this cooperative program which, as described above, has funded family planning services with some $201 million in fiscal

The United States accepts more immigrants than any other country. Public Law 89-236, enacted in 1965, provides that certain immediate relatives of U.S. citizens may be admitted without numerical limitation; that no more than 120,000 immigrant visas be issued annually to natives of independent Western Hemisphere countries; and that no more than 170,000 immigrant visas be issued annually to aliens from elsewhere, with further provisions that within the 170,000 limit no more than 20,000 be issued to any one country and no more than 200 to any one independent area.

1974, reaching more than 3.4 million women of whom more than 70 percent were from low-income families.

But further, by June 30, 1974, some form of organized, subsidized family planning services had been made available by this program to residents in more than 95 percent of the 3,074 counties in the United States. This was an increase of 295 counties over those reported with services available on June 30, 1973.

Of the 2,920 counties with services available, 2,386 counties had facilities or physician referral programs in adjacent counties. The percentage of counties considered to have some coverage increased from 85 percent of all counties in FY 1973 to 95 percent in FY 1974. Most counties still without coverage are sparsely settled and have few low-income women. Efforts are continuing, however, to provide some form of service to counties which do not have services available.

Former Secretary of HEW Caspar Weinberger noted the cost effectiveness of the program as follows:

In spite of a few sensitive issues, the federal family planning program has been remarkably successful. The goal of making family planning services available to all who need but cannot afford them is approaching fruition. By reducing unwanted births, the program has been cost-effective, saving more than two dollars for every dollar spent. I take pride that these results have been achieved on a voluntary basis without violating the rights of the people to choose freely the dimensions of their own fertility.

Such a cost-effectiveness estimate has been developed by Frederick S. Jaffe of the Planned Parenthood Federation of America, who has attempted conservative approximations of (1) the number of unwanted births averted due to tax-supported family planning programs, (2) the cost of these births, and (3) the medical care and public assistance during the first years of a child's life. An analysis of the short-term savings in Government expenditures is presented in the accompanying table. From fiscal 1967 through fiscal 1972, $402.8 million was expended with the cost/benefit ratio ranging from a low of $1.7 saved for every $1 spent to a high of $2.5 so saved.

Population research. The activities of the public and private agencies involved in population research may be divided into **biomedical research** and **behavioral science research**. Biomedical research involves targeted and basic investigations of human and animal reproductive processes, development of improved methods of fertility regulation, and evaluation of the safety and effectiveness of current contra-ceptives. Behavioral sciences research consists of directed and fundamental studies of the economic, social, and psychological determinants and effects of population size, composition, and distribution and the relation of various psychological and sociological factors to fertility.

HEW research activities in these fields totaled $54.9 million in 1975 compared with $11.5 million in fiscal 1969.

HEW research programs concentrate on methods of fertility regulation that are safe, effective, inexpensive, easy, and likely to be used with a minimum of medical supervision. Fundamental biomedical research in reproductive biology seeks greater knowledge of basic reproductive processes, essential for the development and improvement of contraceptive agents. The search continues for new and efficacious chemical contraceptives for women that will not have undesirable side effects. Research investigations also seek to discover effective contraceptives that men will find acceptable.

While many HEW biomedical research projects are worthy of note, three new initiatives are particularly significant:

• Male contraception. An initial clinical trial of a chemical contraceptive for men has been completed which has successfully decreased sperm counts to levels considered incompatible with fertility after 2 months of therapy. This work involved the daily oral administration of a weak synthetic male hormone combined with a once-a-month injection of a potent synthetic male hormone. Six weeks after the therapy ended, sperm numbers returned to normal levels with none of the men reporting reduced libido or other undesirable side effects.

• Long-acting injectible drugs. Injectible drugs that could provide contraceptive protection to women for from 3 to 6 months have undergone extensive laboratory and clinical testing. During fiscal 1975, one promising long-acting injectible contraceptive was the subject of a special evaluation.

• IUD study. During Fiscal 1975, HEW initiated a retrospective case-control study to delineate the risks of specific severe complications for all IUD's currently in use and to identify subpopulations of women at high risk of such complications.

Evaluation of the medical effects of oral contraceptives and of vasectomy is also of continuing interest to HEW biomedical research specialists.

The goals of the behavioral sciences research program of HEW are to ascertain the social, psychological, and economic determinants of fertility and to expand understanding of the causes and consequences of population growth and change so that the public

Short-Term Benefit/Cost Ratios of Federal Family Planning Expenditures in the United States, Fiscal Years 1967-72[1]

Fiscal year of expenditure	Estimated expenditure for family planning[2] in millions of dollars	Calendar year when births were averted	Benefit/cost ratio based on:	
			One birth averted per 10 woman-years	One birth averted per 7 woman-years
1967	$18.1	1968	2.6:1	3.7:1
1968	25.2	1969	2.4:1	3.5:1
1969	60.6	1970	1.4:1	2.0:1
1970	70.0	1971	1.6:1	2.3:1
1971	80.3	1972	2.1:1	3.0:1
1972	148.6	1973	1.5:1	2.2:1
Total	$402.8		1.7:1	2.5:1

[1] Developed by Frederick S. Jaffe, Planned Parenthood Federation.
[2] Derived from *Special Analyses, Budget of the United States* for FY 1969, 1972, 1973.

may be guided by adequate information.

The relation between social and psychological factors and premarital behavior is one area being explored. A research project is looking into the extent to which premarital sexual behavior is affected by such factors as sexual ideology, self-concept, peer and parental influence, sources of information about sex, social background, and opportunity for premarital sexual behavior.

Organizational structure. The HEW program is directed by the Deputy Assistant Secretary for Population Affairs. His office—the Office of Population Affairs—serves as the primary focus within the Department on family planning and population research matters relating to:

• services, making family planning information and services available and accessible;

• training, meeting the professional and lay manpower needs in health, social services, and education;

• research, promoting and supporting research, and research training in the biomedical and behavioral aspects of fertility, sterility, population dynamics, and program implementation; and

• population education, the study of the causes and consequences of population change.

Although program responsibilities are delegated to numerous agencies in the Department, the Office of Population Affairs coordinates the programs within the Department and works in close cooperation with other agencies of the Federal Government and private agencies to develop programs in this field. The following HEW agencies carry out the various delegated responsibilities within the Department.

The **Food and Drug Administration** approves contraceptive drugs for safety and effectiveness before they are marketed and maintains surveillance over them after their approval. Its involvement in population research and family planning services lies primarily in (1) sponsoring the research necessary to carry out its regulatory responsibility relating to oral contraceptive safety and (2) using its regulatory functions with regard to the safety and effectiveness of contraceptive drugs and devices.

The **Health Services Administration** is the major administrative support agency for Federal programs of subsidized family planning services. Within it, the **Bureau of Community Health Services** provides for (1) project grants to providers of family planning services, (2) grants and contracts for training family planning services personnel, (3) grants and contracts for services, delivery, improvement, and research, (4) grants and contracts for the development and distribution of family planning information, and (5) maternal and child health formula grants to assist States by extending and improving their services for promoting the health of mothers and children—especially in rural areas. Such project grants represent the major Federal source of direct funding for family planning services.

A second important organization within the Health Services Administration is the **Bureau of Medical Services,** which provides comprehensive family planning services to eligible Federal beneficiaries through Public Service hospitals and outpatient clinics. A third such organization is the **Indian Health Service,** which provides comprehensive health

The rapid growth of U.S. metropolitan areas has led to strain on the quality of city life, and hence to a lessening of its attraction for migrants. City people are more likely than rural people to suffer from noise, air pollution (which affects health and also makes it harder to keep clothes and homes clean), and crowding (which makes difficulties both for movement along the streets and for relationships within the family).

services, including family planning, to American Indians and Alaskan natives.

The **Health Resources Administration**, through its **National Center for Health Statistics**, collects and publishes vital statistics. It operates the National Reporting System for Family Planning Services, which provides monthly, quarterly, and annual reports essential for the efficient and effective development, operation, and evaluation of family planning programs throughout the Nation.

The **Center for Disease Control** assists State, local, and international health agencies in evaluating family planning programs. Epidemic Intelligence Service Officers and Public Health Advisors are assigned in a number of States to develop and maintain data systems for family planning service statistics and to conduct special studies relating to contraceptive use and effectiveness.

The **National Institute of Mental Health** under its broad mandate for research and training in the field of mental health, supports many activities related to family planning. An important responsibility is to determine the kinds of mental health services needed by families of differing sizes and forms, the adequacy of one-parent homes in providing crisis support to individual members, and the correlation between family size and the emotional characteristics of family members.

The **National Institute of Child Health and Human Development** supports research to develop new means of fertility regulation, to evaluate current contraceptive methods, and to analyze the social and behavioral factors involved in population growth, change, and distribution. It also supports fundamental research in reproductive biology and the social sciences upon which are based advances in contraceptive development and the solution to problems associated with population dynamics.

The **Community Services Administration** is responsible for the social services program authorized under the "Aid to Families with Dependent Children" section of the Social Security Act. Current recipients of public assistance under this program are eligible to receive family planning services, and Community Services assists States in developing plans and administering programs for such family planning services.

The **Medical Services Administration** administers the Federal-State medical assistance program known as Medicaid, under which participating States are required to provide medical assistance (including family planning) to all recipients of cash assistance.

The **Office of Education**, through its varied grant programs, enables educational institutions at all levels to include family life, sex education, and population education in their programs and gives limited Federal support to innovative projects. Plans are developed by State educational agencies, local school districts, and colleges and universities.

The **Office of International Health** serves as HEW's principal focal point for work relating to international health matters including work relating to overseas population and family planning programs. Among other services it provides consultative and other professional assistance to AID missions overseas and AID regional and technical bureaus in Washington, D.C.

Other Federal Programs

In addition to the Department of Health, Education, and Welfare, three other government agencies also conduct programs concerned with population and environmental matters. These include the Department of Labor, the Department of Agriculture, and the Department of Commerce.

U.S. Policy Situation

Despite the activities above, the U.S. Government has no explicit policy for curbing U.S. population growth. The stated objective of its assistance for family planning within the United States is to enable parents to achieve their own preferences in family size. It seeks to assure that people in all income groups—not just those with higher incomes—are able to obtain the knowledge, services, and supplies that are necessary for this purpose.

A simple "no population policy" label, however, does not adequately describe the situation since a number of key developments indicate that a broad policy consensus, adapted to U.S. needs, is in the course of development. Among the important indicators of this can be included the following:

• The first special presidential message to Congress on population problems in 1970 by President Nixon calling on the Congress, the American people, and all nations to recognize and meet the challenge of the world population crisis—a message which followed indications of concern relating to population growth by Presidents Truman, Eisenhower, Kennedy and Johnson.
• The 1972 report of the temporary Commission on Population Growth and the American Future which—although accorded little in the way of official follow-up—nevertheless calls for attack on a broad array of health, education, economic, and social problems to enable the United States to achieve a stabilized population in an orderly manner as rapidly as possible.

• Establishment of Federally financed research programs to provide better understanding of the problems of population growth and distribution and of means for coping with these problems.

• The establishment of the position of Deputy Assistant Secretary for Population Affairs in the Department of Health, Education, and Welfare, and of a Center for Population Research in the National Institutes of Health.

• Clear evidence in the legislative history, if not the statutory language, of the Family Planning Services and Population Research Act of 1970 that a tacit objective of that legislation—or at least of some of its supporters—was to lessen the pressure of excessive population growth by helping to avoid the birth of "unwanted" children.

• The inclusion in recent statutes of at least minimal authorizations for informational and educational efforts to provide the public with an understanding of the problems of population growth and its implica-

tions for the American future.

In the light of these developments, therefore, it might be more accurate to describe the present population policy—or at least the present population posture—of the U.S. Government as one that is openly confronting and exploring the problems of population growth in relation to the quality of life and the strength of social services and institutions.

External Assistance

The United States' support for the population and family planning programs in developing countries focuses in the U.S. Agency for International Development. The activities of AID are described as part of the section that follows, "Aid to Developing Countries."

The related activities of the Department of State and the Department of Health, Education, and Welfare are outlined elsewhere in special sections devoted to those agencies.

Right, a young woman picks up information material from a self-service station, under a sign that reads "Family Planning Is Altogetherhood." Below, a nurse gives counsel on family planning. The U.S. Government's objective in its various types of family planning assistance is to make sure that parents can obtain the information and services they need to achieve the family size they prefer.

192

Oceania

The population of the Oceania region is estimated at 21.2 million as of mid-1975. The population has increased 3.7 million, or one-fifth from the 1965 level of 17.6 million. Natural increase in Oceania as a whole was 1.2 percent annually in 1974, the regional birth rate being 22 per 1,000 people and the death rate 10 per 1,000. For individual areas, however, the natural increase rates varied widely, ranging from 1.1 percent in Australia and New Zealand to highs of 3 percent or more in American Samoa, Western Samoa, Guam, and the Pacific Islands.

Gross national product per person in 1973 averaged $3,300 for the region, but ranged from a low of $210 in Tonga to a high of $4,000 in Australia.

All but 1.8 million of the region's people live in Australia, New Zealand and Papua New Guinea. Australia alone accounts for nearly two-thirds of the region's total 1975 population and for 60 percent of the region's increase since 1965. Net immigration has contributed significantly to Australia's increase since 1965.

Australia

Australia's population as of mid-1975 is estimated at 13.6 million, an increase of 2.2 million from the 1965 level of 11.4 million. The 1974 birth rate is reported as 18 per 1,000 population, the death rate 9 per 1,000. The rate of natural increase is estimated at 1.0 percent annually, the same as in 1965.

The Government in 1970 commissioned a national population inquiry to consider the future size, composition, and distribution of the population. The survey report observed that Australia's period of rapid population growth has ended; that, considering natural increase alone, the total population in 2001 would be about 15.9 million, far below previous projections; that, with new immigration of 75,000 a year, the total by 2001 would be about 18.5 million. Earlier, economists and planners visualized a population of 20 million to 25 million by the turn of the century. Those estimates, however, had to be modified owing to the relatively low rate of natural increase coupled with growth of public opinion favoring more modest immigration than in the past.

Whereas some 3 million immigrants have entered the country in the past 30 years, many Australians advocate a future maximum of 75,000 a year or less. While Australia foresees no problem in meeting the needs of its population, it is widely felt that population levels should be balanced carefully with resources to enable improvements in the well-being of the people.

The survey report pointed out that the high birth rates of 15 to 20 years ago—which followed a period in the depression years when the rate of natural increase dropped below 1 percent—are responsible for the greater number of men and women now entering the labor market. This group is also entering its high reproductive period and its attitudes and actions will determine population growth for years to come.

The Government has been responding to changing national attitudes by increasing its support of family planning activities. In 1974 its contributions to family planning on the national and international level totaled almost $2 million (Australian). In addition, it has removed the sales tax on oral contraceptives.

The Family Planning Association of Australia, founded in 1926, has expanded its operations significantly since 1968. Its national program calls for setting up family planning clinics in all States, supporting contraceptive research, training medical and paramedical personnel for service in other countries as well as in Australia, and a broad program of public education.

Family planning activities were strengthened in 1974 by formation of the Australian Federation of Family Planning Associations (AFFPA), with Associations of all eight States as members. The Government has provided central financial support as have the various State Governments.

AFFPA is encouraging universities and other educational institutions to include demographic, medical, and sociological aspects of population in their curriculums. Several, including Macquarie University, have offered such courses.

A special family planning program is maintained for aborigines, at the Government's suggestion. Training has a high priority and the National Training and Research Unit will conduct advanced-level and innovative courses in family planning and also will coordinate and evaluate basic training courses throughout Australia in collaboration with member associations and special units such as the World Health Organization (WHO).

AFFPA has outlined a mass national communications program to be carried out in conjunction with the Government, and an advisory committee has been formed to establish communications policies and guidelines. Plans have been made for the Federation, with the cooperation of the postgraduate extension studies division of the University of New South Wales, to televise a series of 10 programs on youth projects and sex education.

The International Planned Parenthood Federation (IPPF) has supported individual family planning organizations and also the new Federation. Some 400 doctors and scientists from 40 countries attended an IPPF congress in Sydney in 1972. This meeting concentrated on the medical and biological aspects of family planning and stressed family planning as a part of social medicine.

New Zealand

The mid-1975 population of New Zealand is estimated at 3.1 million, 17 percent larger than the 1965 total of 2.6 million. About one-third of the increase was from net immigration. The annual rate of natural increase in 1974 was 1.1 percent, the birth rate being 19 per 1,000 population and the death rate 8 per 1,000.

The New Zealand Government is concerned for family health and well-being as well as for balance between population growth and the physical, economic, and social resources. Although there is no officially conducted family planning program, the Government announced grants to the International Planned Parenthood Federation (IPPF) and the United Nations Fund for Population Activities (UNFPA) of $2 million each for 1974 and has assisted the New Zealand Family Planning Association with grants and medical services.

The Department of Health recognizes family planning as part of its health program. It has subsidized and provided other assistance to the Family Planning Association.

Papua New Guinea

The population of Papua New Guinea was estimated at 2.8 million in 1975, an increase of 30 percent over the 1965 level of 2.1 million. The 1974 birth rate is estimated at 41 per 1,000 people, the death rate at 17. Both these rates are slightly below those in 1965. The rate of natural increase at 2.4

percent annually is down fractionally from 2.5 percent in 1965.

A Government-sponsored family planning program has been operating since 1968. The New Guinea Family Planning Association, founded in 1974, is an active element in the overall program. Family planning services are provided by Government and church hospitals and by mobile services.

External Assistance

Assistance for this program has been provided by the International Planned Parenthood Federation, the United Nations Fund for Population Activities, and Community Aid Abroad of Australia.

British Solomon Islands

The British Solomon Islands' population of 191,000 in 1975 would double by the year 2000 if the 1974 annual growth rate of 2.5 percent continues. The birth rate is estimated at 36 per 1,000 and the death rate at 11.

External Assistance

The Solomon Islands Planned Parenthood Association receives a share of the Pacific Islands grant made by the International Planned Parenthood Federation (IPPF) for information and education programs and for other services.

The British Ministry of Overseas Development provided grants in 1973 and 1974 for a computer program and analysis of birth data.

Fiji

Fiji, with a population of 570,000, has one of the lowest annual rates of growth among the Pacific Islands groups. The rate has been declining steadily from the 4.2 percent reported in 1959. By 1970 the rate was 2.9 percent and the 1974 figure is 2.3 percent. Over the same period, the birth rate has dropped from 42 per 1,000 to about 28. The death rate is 5 per 1,000.

The Government has a well-established family planning program which was started in 1962 and is encouraging a still further reduction in the birth rate. The Family Planning Association, a member of the International Planned Parenthood Federation (IPPF), has had an important part in the program especially in educational activities.

In April 1974 the regional resident representatives of the United Nations Development Program, stationed in Fiji, convened a meeting to determine interest of agencies engaged in family planning in the Pacific Islands in coordinating their activities and forming a federation. Plans are proceeding for such a federation with a representative of the United Nations Fund for Population Activities (UNFPA) serving as coordinator. A pilot survey for the World Fertility Survey was conducted in Fiji during 1974, entirely financed by the U.S. Agency for International Development under the auspices of the International Statistical Institute.

External Assistance

IPPF has given the Family Planning Association overall program support.

The United Nations Childrens Fund (UNICEF) has provided assistance in developing national maternal/child health services, training medical and paramedical personnel, supplying contraceptives, and developing teaching aids.

The Population Council, The Pathfinder Fund, Oxfam, and the British Ministry of Overseas Development also have contributed to family planning activities in Fiji.

Gilbert and Ellice Islands

The estimated population of Gilbert and Ellice Islands in 1975 is 63,000. A birth rate of 35 and a death rate of 8 per 1,000 population produces an annual growth rate of 2.7 percent. If this rate continues, the population would double in less than 27 years.

However, a family planning organization was established in the late 1960's. Family planning is part of the Government's 1970 development plan and is included in Government health services. Use of contraceptives is reported to be increasing.

External Assistance

The International Planned Parenthood Federation (IPPF) provides financial assistance to the Family Planning Association for its information, educational, and clinic activities.

Since 1970 UNFPA and the World Health Organization (WHO) have helped fund activities to make family planning services available to the entire population and to improve information and education programs.

The United Nations Childrens Fund (UNICEF) also has provided assistance.

The British Ministry of Overseas Development has provided funds in increasing amounts since 1972 ($176,000 in 1974) for training medical officers, operating clinics, and for expenses involved in a population survey.

Western Samoa

The population of Western Samoa in mid-1975 is estimated at 159,000, compared with 127,000 in 1965. The 1974 birth rate is 37 per 1,000 population and the death rate 7. The resulting rate of increase is 3 percent per year.

External Assistance

The Family Planning Association of Western Samoa (FPAWS) receives financial assistance from the International Planned Parenthood Federation (IPPF). A clinic has been established with a doctor in charge. Integration of family planning activities into the Government's maternal/child health services was initiated in 1971.

In 1973, IPPF stationed a consultant in Western Samoa to encourage formation of voluntary family planning organizations in the Pacific Islands and to work with island governments to develop favorable attitudes. In 1974 a regional resident representative of the U.N. Development Program spearheaded a meeting of representatives of the various agencies engaged in family planning in these islands with a view of coordinating their activities. It is anticipated that organizations from about 10 island groups may form a federation.

Also in 1974 a seminar was organized in Western Samoa with IPPF assistance to motivate the MATAIS of Samoa to accept family planning. A follow-up of the seminar indicated increasing awareness and changes in attitudes toward family planning in this influential group.

The United Nations Childrens Fund (UNICEF) has allocated funds to help the Family Planning Association make its services available to the general public, conduct training programs in fertility regulation for health personnel, make surveys, and try to increase citizen's awareness of the causes and consequences of rapid population growth.

World Health Organization (WHO) has funded advisory services by a medical officer, fellowships, supplies and equipment, and supporting services in connection with the UNICEF program. Assistance was provided in 1972 and 1973 for national seminars on health education in family planning.

The United Nations Fund for Population Activities (UNFPA) provided funds to establish a data preparation and processing unit for the population census of 1971.

The Peace Corps has given some assistance, primarily on the technical staff level.

Other Oceania

Guam—The population is estimated at 111,000 in mid-1975, an increase of 37,000 (50 percent) over the 1965 level of 74,000. The rate of natural increase (1974) is 3 percent per year. The birth rate in 1974 was 35 per 1,000 people, up from 33 in 1965. The mortality rate in 1974 was 5 per 1,000 population, compared with 4 in 1965. Per capita gross national product from 1965 to 1973 increased by a third to about $4,130.

American Samoa—The population totaled 29,000 in mid-1975, up 4,000 from 1965. The annual rate of natural increase in 1974 was 3.2 percent compared with 3.7 in 1965. The birth rate in 1974 was 37 per 1,000 population, down from 43 in 1965. The death rate in 1974 was 5 per 1,000, down from 6 in 1965. Per capita GNP in 1973 was $1,020 per capita, up 40 percent from the 1965 level of $660.

British Solomon Islands—Population increased by one-third during the 1966-75 decade, totaling 191,000 in mid-1975. The rate of natural increase in 1974 was 2.5 percent with the birth rate at 36 births per 1,000 population and the death rate at 11. The per capita gross national product in 1973 was $280 40 percent above the 1965 figure of $200.

Cook Islands—Population increased by about one-fifth from 1965 to 1975, totaling 23,000 in mid-1975. The rate of natural increase dropped during the period, falling from a level of 3.4 percent annually in 1965 to 2.7 percent in 1974. The decline stemmed from a steep drop in the birth rate—33 births per 1,000 population in 1974 compared with 41 in 1965. The death rate was 6 per 1,000 people in

1974, compared with 7 in 1965.

French Polynesia—Population increased by one-half from 1965 to 1975, reaching 128,000 in mid-1975. This was an increase of 43,000 over the 1965 level of 85,000. The annual rate of natural increase dropped during the period from a level of 3.5 percent in 1965 to 2.7 percent in 1974. The decline stemmed from a sharp drop in the birth rate—34 births per 1,000 population in 1974 compared with 46 in 1965. The death rate also dropped significantly during the period—7 deaths per 1,000 in 1974 as compared with 11 in 1965. The per capita gross national product increased moderately during the period from a level of $2,180 in 1965 to $2,680 in 1973.

New Caledonia—Population increased nearly one-half during the 1965-75 decade, totaling 134,000 in mid-1975. This was 43,000 above the 1965 level of 91,000. The birth rate in 1974 was 36 births per 1,000 population; the death rate 10. Per capita gross national product more than doubled between 1965 and 1973. In 1965 it was $2,200 per capita, but by 1973 it had increased to $5,010.

New Hebrides—The population here has increased by one-fourth since 1965, reaching 94,000 in mid-1975. The rate of natural increase was 2.5 percent in 1974. The birth rate continued at about 45 births per 1,000 population, the death rate at about 20. The per capita gross national product increased by only 9 percent between 1965 and 1973. In 1973 it was $480 per capita.

Pacific Islands—The inhabitants have increased by one-third since 1965, totaling 116,000 in July 1975. The rate of natural increase was 3 percent in 1974 with the birth rate at 35 births per 1,000 population and the death rate at 5. The per capita gross national product in 1973 was $450 per capita, compared with $340 in 1965.

Tonga—The population has risen 29 percent since 1965, reaching 97,000 in mid-1975. The rate of natural increase was 2.5 percent in 1974, and in that year there were 35 births per 1,000 people, with 10 deaths per 1,000. Gross national product in 1973 was $210 per capita.

The past decade has seen increasing assistance—both private and governmental, technical and financial—in helping developing countries cope with their population problems. This assistance is for programs based on the voluntary participation of individuals and is provided only at the request of the countries themselves and their institutions.

The United Nations and its Specialized Agencies have greatly expanded their assistance during the decade, as have numerous nongovernment private organizations and private foundations. The United States has been the major source of assistance to date, but other advanced countries have also provided significant help, both bilaterally and through international agencies and organizations.

Multilateral Agencies
United Nations System

The United Nations and U.N. Specialized Agencies, the principal means for multilateral action on world problems, have given increasing attention to population matters since 1966, including provision of assistance to the population programs of developing countries.

Prior to 1966, the U.N. system was restricted in the population field by limited mandates, lack of funds, and also by the fact that few governments had yet formulated national or foreign aid policies on population. However, an essential technical basis for the growth of an action program by the U.N. had been laid, beginning from the earliest days of the U.N. itself, beginning from the earliest days of the U.N. itself, by the pioneer demographic work of the Population Division of the parent U.N. organization. The basis for U.N. activity was laid in the early and mid-1960's, with the passage by the General Assembly and other U.N. bodies of resolutions that tied population growth to economic development and urged additional U.N. activity in the population field.

It was this rising tide of sentiment for U.N. work in population and the growing awareness and concern about the rapid increase in world population that led to Secretary-General U Thant's decision to establish a Trust Fund for Population Activities in 1967 that eventually became the United Nations Fund for Population Activities in 1969 and the active operational arm of the U.N. in the population field.

It was also this rising interest in world population problems that led the General Assembly in 1970 to designate 1974 as World Population Year and to call for the convening of a World Population Conference in the same year. The Conference was the first meeting of Governments ever to be held on the subject of population, and resulted in the adoption by consensus of the World Population Plan of Action, a kind of blueprint for Governments, multilateral, bilateral, and other organizations and agencies in the population field.

United Nations Fund for Population Activities

As the leading funding organization within the U.N. system for population activities, the United Nations Fund for Population Activities has seen its annual budget grow to $80 million in 1975 and its cumulative contributions from a total of 78 countries reaching more than $238.6 million by the end of 1975. The UNFPA has become the largest multilateral source of funding for action programs in the population field in developing countries. Currently, it is supporting more than 1,200 global, interregional, regional, and country projects in more than 100 countries.

UNFPA assistance is made possible by voluntary contributions. (The United States has contributed some $77 million to the work of the Fund.)

For an organization so important in the world population field, UNFPA's history is relatively short.

In its first 2 years as the Trust Fund for Population Activities, the Fund, with $5 million provided through member country contributions, assisted the United Nations in strengthening its statistical and demographic work. About the same time, several organizations in the U.N. system were authorized by their governing bodies to carry on population activities.

In 1969 the U.N. Trust Fund became the U.N. Fund for Population Activities (UNFPA). Its mandate involved it in the population activities of all U.N. organizations as well as those of appropriate non-government bodies. UNFPA's role was strengthened further in 1971 and 1972, and in 1973 it was placed under the authority of the General Assembly—specifically under the Governing Council of the U.N. Development Program (UNDP). Thus, UNFPA became, by stages, a separate entity in the U. N. system under the authority of an intergovernmental body.

In 1972 UNFPA formulated its first work plan based on an analysis of the outstanding population problems and needs of the developing countries. It outlined 4 years of population projects based on perceived needs of countries and was developed with the cooperation of recipient countries and U.N. organizations. Since then, the plan has been revised annually and it covers six categories: basic population data, population dynamics, population policy, family planning, communication and education, and program development.

UNFPA assistance is provided only upon request of Governments, and it is neutral as regards the types of assistance it provides and may fund activities to limit population growth as well as to stimulate growth.

In Latin America, where until the end of 1973 the majority of aid requests to UNFPA were for demographic research and training, requests for projects in maternal and child health and family planning have increased sevenfold. The new emphasis is particularly notable in Central America, the Caribbean area, and Mexico but also affects a growing number of South American countries.

In South West Asia, assistance requests have tripled since the beginning of 1973. Although emphasis is still strong on the development of basic population data required for economic and social development, interest in family health and family planning projects is increasing.

In the northern part of Africa, the bulk of assistance has been for support of family planning programs, such as those in Egypt and Tunisia. In Africa south of the Sahara, UNFPA funds have provided support chiefly for the African Census Program; but interest is growing in assistance to family planning services as part of national basic health services.

In Asia and the Pacific, funds provided for population activities in 1974 were double the 1973 amount, and most of the resulting projects were at an advanced stage of implementation in 1975. Over 95 percent of the requests for UNFPA support have been for family health and family planning programs. Many Asian countries have concluded agreements with UNFPA.

New country agreements were concluded by UNFPA in 1974 with Bangladesh, Kenya, India, the Republic of Korea, and Turkey, and a revised and extended agreement was made with Pakistan. Other country agreements were in an advanced state of preparation. Prior to 1974, country agreements had been concluded with Chile, Cuba, the Dominican Republic, Egypt, Indonesia, Iran, Malaysia, Mauritius, Pakistan, the Philippines, Sri Lanka, and Thailand.

The UNFPA also funds a number of interregional and global programs, such as the World Fertility Survey (see below).

UNFPA's contributions of $68,375,553 to population programs in 1974 went, in the following shares, to these geographic areas: Asia and the Pacific, 33 percent; Africa, 20 percent; Latin America and the Caribbean, 18 percent; interregional, 17 percent; global, 12 percent; and Europe, less than one-half of 1 percent.

The projects that UNFPA supports and funds are normally executed through the United Nations Secretariat, through the specialized agencies within their respective fields of competence, or through nongovernmental organizations. Among these are the United Nations Development Programme (UNDP), United Nations Children's Emergency Fund (UNICEF), International Labour Organisation (ILO), Food and Agriculture Organization (FAO), United Nations Educational, Scientific, and Cultural Organization (UNESCO), and the World Health Organization (WHO). It is also cooperating with the World Bank in two major country programs.

United Nations

As previously indicated, much of the basis for the U.N. action program in the population field had its origins in the demographic groundwork laid in the first two decades of the U.N.'s history.

Both the Population Division and the Statistical Office within the United Nations have made and continue to make important and valuable contributions to the work of the U.N. multilateral population assistance program.

The work of the United Nations itself includes important regional programs in Africa, Asia and the Far East, Western Asia, and Latin America, including regional demographic training and research centers. Its assistance is provided mainly through: the development and improvement of national systems of demographic statistics; the worldwide dissemination of national statistics in as comparable forms as possible; the development of international recommendations; the preparation of studies, reports, technical manuals, and handbooks, the convening of conferences, seminars, and training courses; the provision of advisory services; the development of regional training and research centers; and the provision of fellowships.

The Population Division has assisted developing countries with the improvement of their demographic statistics, with demographic training, and by the preparation of studies of the relationship between population trends.

The primary arm of the United Nations in providing assistance to developing countries' population programs is the Fund for Population Activities (UNFPA), an element of the U.N. Development Program (UNDP). The projects that UNFPA supports and funds are normally executed either through the United Nations or through the specialized agencies within their respective fields of competence. Among the more important of these organizations are the World Health Organization (WHO), the Children's Fund (UNICEF), the Educational, Scientific, and Cultural Organization (UNESCO), the Food and Agriculture Organization (FAO), the International Labour Organisation (ILO), and the Environment Program (UNEP).

An essential technical basis for the growth of U.N. population action was laid, beginning in 1946, by the pioneer demographic work of the Population Division of the parent U.N. organization. The Division since that time has assisted developing countries with the improvement of their demographic statistics, with demographic training, and by the preparation of studies of the relationship between population trends and social and economic factors. The Statistical Office of the United Nations also beginning in 1946, made a similarly valuable contribution through its work for improvement and dissemination of demographic data.

A continuing function of the U.N. system is the evaluation of the accuracy and the consequent adjustment of basic demographic data for each country—particularly on the age and sex structure of population and on fertility, mortality, and international migration. Much of this work is carried out by the Population Division in collaboration, insofar as possible, with the regional economic commissions and the U.N.-sponsored research and training centers. The adjusted data are made available for the use of organizations in the U.N. system. Attention is also given by the specialized agencies to the improvement of the adequacy and the international comparability of the statistics in their respective fields. The Population Division also does basic work in demographic projections, fertility analysis, family planning analysis, mortality analysis, urban studies, analyses of and international migration population policies.

An ancillary program in which the United Nations is participating is the World Fertility Survey, which will add considerably to fertility data. This survey is being undertaken by the International Statistical Institute, in cooperation with the International Union for the Scientific Study of Population and other organizations, with the collaboration of the United Nations. Financial support is provided by UNFPA of the United Nations and AID of the United States. The survey is planned for completion by June 30, 1977. Its aim is to provide scientific information that will enable each country to describe and interpret its situation with regard to human fertility and to help compare fertility levels and the factors that influence them in different countries and regions.

The most comprehensive sources of worldwide population statistics are the U.N. *Demographic Yearbook* and the *Statistical Yearbook*. More current population statistics are published in the U.N. *Monthly Bulletin of Statistics* and the quarterly *Population and Vital Statistics Report.*

United Nations Development Program

Established in 1966 through the merger of two earlier programs—the U.N. Special Fund and the Expanded Program of Technical Assistance—the United Nations Development Program (UNDP) assists developing countries around the world by providing technical assistance and preinvestment studies designed to provide public infrastructure for modernization and the necessary basis for the development of sound capital projects which can then be financed by either public or private investment capital.

In the population area, UNDP acts as executing agency for the UNFPA for UNFPA-funded projects in a variety of areas, such as support communications projects for census and family planning programs. In 1974, UNFPA contributions to projects executed by UNDP amounted to $8.8 million.

UNDP is currently playing an increasingly larger role as an executing agency for UNFPA projects implemented in countries. With the growing number of UNFPA projects funded directly, the role of the UNDP Resident Representatives in the field, assisted by UNFPA Field Coordinators, has increased considerably. UNFPA funds to Government agencies in recipient countries are channeled through the Resident Representative's offices for disbursement.

United Nations Children's Fund

The United Natons Children's Emergency Fund (UNICEF) supports responsible parenthood because children suffer when families exceed the size parents can adequately support. However, UNICEF works on the principle that only when parents and prospective parents—the ultimate decision makers—can see the chance of a better and a more assured life for their children will they be motivated to limit and plan family size. Improving prospects depends heavily on services that help the health, welfare, and development of children and the family.

Thus, when UNICEF's Executive Board launched assistance for family planning services in 1967, it was through extension of the existing basic assistance rather than as a separate activity.

Indonesia, for example, promotes responsible parenthood with UNICEF help through basic health services; this work is complemented by a family-life education program for out-of-school girls and mothers. More than 2,000 family planning clinics, established in health and maternal/child health centers, now reach 2 million of Java's 15 million fertile couples. The complementary education program offers nonformal courses in child care and nutrition, hygiene, family planning, sewing, cooking, and household budgeting.

UNICEF help takes the form of supplies, equipment, and vehicles as well as training and education materials. Specific aid depends on the requirements of the individual project. In Thailand, for instance, where family planning activities are similarly linked to the development of basic health services, more than 3,000 nurses and midwives are provided with UNICEF-supplied motorcycles to enable them to increase the number and frequency of visits to client's homes.

UNICEF's assistance to health services, nutrition, water supply for home use, and women's programs—valued at $80 million in 1974—all contributes to responsible parenthood by helping to build the conditions necessary for that effort. In addition $6.4 million in UNFPA funds went to assist family planning services in 14 countries in 1974.

UNFPA has also asked UNICEF to procure and stockpile supplies and equipment worth $4 million. This procedure is aimed at expediting UNFPA-financed projects, permitting reduced costs through bulk purchasing, and contributing to better coordination.

International Labour Organisation

The involvement of the International Labour Organisation (ILO) in the U.N.'s population activities stems from the impact of rapid population growth in developing countries on employment, training, and the welfare of workers. Research and action on population, employment, income distribution, and population policies are carried out under the ILO's World Employment Program.

Further, the ILO seeks to widen the involvement of workers and employers in population matters including family planning. The ILO's program in this respect (with UNFPA funding) seeks to: encourage and enable trade unions and labor education bodies to participate in family planning programs; help employers to appreciate the role that occupational health and welfare services can play in bringing family planning information and facilities to places of work; encourage the extension of family planning promotional, educational, and motivational activities through cooperatives; and promote family planning services through the medical care components of social security—especially in Latin America.

In 1971, UNFPA allocated $285,000 to ILO activities. In 1974, UNFPA contributions to ILO population programs totaled $3.6 million.

Food and Agriculture Organization

The Food and Agriculture Organization (FAO) was among the first of the specialized U.N. agencies to be seriously concerned with world population growth; this was because of the effect of population increase on the balance between food and people. In 1967, the FAO Conference recommended that the Organization should be increasingly involved in the study of the relationship between food supplies and population growth and the interaction between demographic and agricultural changes. The Conference also approved an integrated approach to reaching families, through existing national programs, with information about the relationships among family resources, needs, goals, and size. Most funding for FAO population activities comes from the UNFPA, whose support for such activities increased from $137,000 in 1970 to $2.8 million in 1974.

Furthermore, the U.N. World Food Conference held in Rome in November of 1974 passed a resolution recognizing the need for achieving a desirable balance between population and the supply of food. The resolution called on governments and people everywhere to make every possible effort to grow sufficient food and equitably distribute income so that all human beings could have an adequate diet and also "to support for a longer-term solution, rational population policies ensuring to couples the right to determine the number and spacing of births, freely and responsibly, in accordance with national needs within the context of an overall development strategy."

FAO and its institutions and services provide excellent channels of communication with rural people through measures for extension, education, home economics, agrarian reform, social security, agriculture credit, cooperatives, improved nutrition, and improvement in rural life.

U.N. Educational, Scientific, and Cultural Organization

The active role of the United Nations Educational, Scientific, and Cultural Organization (UNESCO) in the population field dates from 1968. Its mandate, established by successive sessions of its General Conferences, lies in the three areas of research, education and information, and technical and advisory support. It provides services in these areas upon request by members.

UNESCO's 1974-75 program has consisted mainly of global programs aimed at identifying and investigating, by means of expert meetings and research, the substantive fields of family sociology, the interrelations between population dynamics and the natural and cultural environment, and the techniques of population education. A handbook on population education curriculum development was finalized by the end of 1974. In the communication sector, UNESCO has concentrated mainly on the development of communication activities through mass media with special emphasis on film production, radio and TV programs, and development of audiovisual materials. As part of this effort, it established the International Audio-Visual Resource Service in collaboration with the International Planned Parenthood Federation (IPPF) funded by UNFDA.

Operationally, UNESCO is concerned with two main lines of endeavor: the introduction of population education in formal and nonformal school systems and helping member states take account of population dynamics in their educational planning. Increasing importance has been attached to the activities of field teams and to the quality of support services provided by headquarters staffs. Its 1974

allocation from UNFPA of $4.8 million is more than five times the 1971 allocation of $850,000.

In its population work, UNESCO is promoting research, training, evaluation, and materials development in family planning communications and has begun work on the development of a systems approach for integrating communications and family planning programs. Regional family planning communications advisors have been appointed for the Arab states, Africa, Asia, and Latin America to service and assist regional and national programs on request. Long-term assistance is being given with UNFPA financing to the communications components of a number of large-scale national programs, and training programs have been established for national personnel. UNESCO expects to assist some 25 national programs and train approximately 400 family planning communications personnel during the period 1973-78.

World Population Service, published by the U.S. National Commission for UNESCO in cooperation with the UNESCO Secretariat and the national commissions of the 38 member countries, has completed its second year of publication. Circulation is worldwide with English, French, and Arabic editions.

World Health Organization

The World Health Organization (WHO), as part of its mandate and in answer to requests from member Governments, works in three areas relating to human reproduction, family planning, and population dynamics. These are: the introduction of family planning into health services, the provision of appropriate education and training for health personnel at all levels, and research—both biomedical and operational—in human reproduction. The underlying strategy of the organization is to assist the strengthening of national health services, in which family planning is included as an integral part of health care through maternal and child health services supported by nutrition programs and health education.

To help administrations to meet the demands posed by the increased scope and multidisciplinary nature of family planning, WHO pays particular attention to the planning, administration, and evaluation of projects. It especially emphasizes the use of modern managerial techniques and the importance of operational research. In addition, WHO sponsors scientific and technical meetings in human reproduction, family planning, and population dynamics to provide an international forum for collaborative efforts and to emphasize the importance of national and international coordination of efforts and resources.

WHO's collaborative research program in human reproduction is concerned with the effectiveness, safety, and acceptability of existing fertility regulating methods, further contraceptive technological development, and other problems, such as infertility and subfertility.

As an intergovernmental organization serving its 145 member countries, WHO does not endorse any particular population policy. It does, however, fully recognize the health aspects of family planning in terms of appropriate timing and adequate spacing of pregnancies. It is also WHO's position that integrated family health services—which help to secure the survival of an already born child and to further promote its health—will, in all probability, facilitate the acceptance of overall family planning services in a manner that might not be achieved by family planning programs alone. At present, WHO is assisting more than 60 countries to integrate family planning services into maternal and child health care—and thus into general health services.

In 1970, WHO's budget included $1.8 million from UNFPA for activities in the above areas; by 1974 it had increased to $11.5 million. In addition $10.6 million was received from various donor governments for WHO's expanded program of research, development, and research training in human reproduction.

World Bank

The decision in 1968 for the World Bank and its soft-loan affiliate, the International Development Association (IDA), to enter the field of population assistance was based on the conviction that rapid population growth is a major barrier to the economic and social progress of many developing countries. The Bank uses a three-step program, which begins with an assessment of the implications of population growth on development as part of the Bank's periodic economic reviews; it then undertakes, on request, sectoral analyses; finally, it provides financial assistance to specific projects on conventional Bank terms or, to especially weak economies, on special soft-loan terms (no interest, 50-year repayment).

To date, World Bank or IDA loans for population programs have been extended to eleven developing countries—Bangladesh, Egypt, India, Indonesia, Iran, Jamaica, Kenya, Malaysia, the Philippines, Trinidad & Tobago, and Tunisia.

World Bank/IDA funding for population projects has covered a broad range of "hardware" items such as buildings, vehicles, furniture and equipment, and "software" items including training, demographic research, pilot projects, technical assistance, and recurrent costs in certain circumstances. By the end of 1975, the Bank had committed a total of $123 million for population projects in eleven countries though disbursements were only at the 10 percent level. In six of the eleven countries the Bank is co-financing population projects in cooperation with other donors.

Organization for Economic Cooperation and Development

The Organization for Economic Cooperation and Development (OECD) is actively concerned with population problems, primarily in relation to economic development.

Such interest first found expression at the high-level meeting of the OECD Development Assistance Committee held in 1966 in Washington, D.C., dealing with world food problems. It led, in 1968, to the creation of a special Population Unit within OECD's Development Center, a semi-autonomous body for research and liaison with developing countries. This unit, financed out of special contributions from interested member countries, was given a twofold mandate: to study the role of the population factor in economic development in order to provide guidance to developing countries; and to keep OECD member countries informed of population-development matters as a basis for the members' formulation of assistance policies.

Direct assistance by the OECD has thus been mainly of an informational nature and includes the dissemination of population aid statistics and the exchange of experience. Member governments channel their contributions for population assistance either directly to the national programs of the recipient countries or indirectly through multilateral organizations and private agencies, although a number have given their total contributions to intermediate agencies.

The OECD's future work in the population field is expected to emphasize increasingly the role of demographic factors in development. The Development Center will focus on the relationship between population dynamics and such subjects as development planning, rural development, migration movements, nutrition, and the economic status of women.

U.S. Agency for International Development

The United States through the Agency for International Development has been the foremost supporter of global action during the 1965-75 decade in response to the world crisis of runaway population growth. Of the $1,054 million total of international donor assistance provided for population programs in the developing nations of Asia, Latin America, and Africa-nations with over half the world's people—$732 million has been provided through AID.

At the same time, the continuing spread of world concern with population problems during the decade has been marked by rising assistance provided by the United Nations, by other countries and institutions, and by great increases in individual countries' funding of their own programs. Progress toward this wider assistance and action has been stimulated and encouraged by AID.

AID's assistance for the population programs of developing countries is guided by the following principles: (1) Assistance is extended at the request of the recipient country or institution and as a supplement to the country's own efforts; (2) help is given only for programs in which each individual is free to choose methods of family planning which are in keeping with his or her beliefs, culture, and personal wishes; and (3) the Agency does not advocate any specific population policy for another country nor any particular method of family planning. Its aim is to provide needed family planning assistance upon request so that the people of assisted countries may have freedom to control their reproduction as they desire.

The Agency's assistance program in this field is carried forward through six major types of activities aimed at specific goals for program advancement. These activities, described in the following sections, include improvements of demographic data collection and analysis, population policy development, biomedical and social research, family planning services programs, communication, and manpower and institutional development.

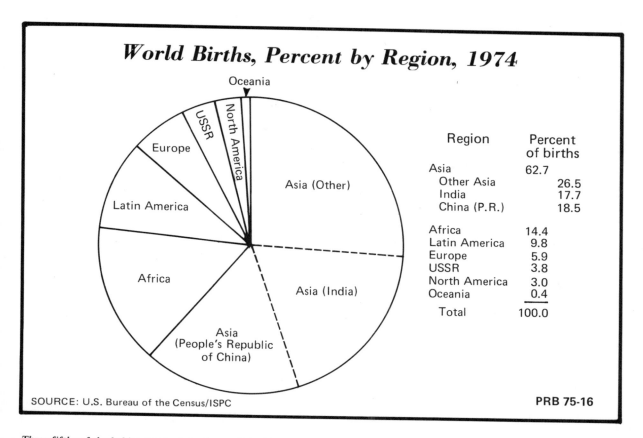

World Births, Percent by Region, 1974

Region	Percent of births	
Asia	62.7	
Other Asia		26.5
India		17.7
China (P.R.)		18.5
Africa	14.4	
Latin America	9.8	
Europe	5.9	
USSR	3.8	
North America	3.0	
Oceania	0.4	
Total	100.0	

SOURCE: U.S. Bureau of the Census/ISPC

PRB 75-16

Three-fifths of the babies coming into the world in 1974 were born in Asia. But this great region is making real progress in reducing fertility. Birth rates dropped from 39 per 1,000 people in 1965 to 31 in 1974.

Dependents Supported by Adults in Developed and Developing Countries, 1975

Developed countries

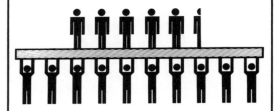

55 persons under age 15 and over age 64 are supported by each 100 aged 15 through 64

Developing countries

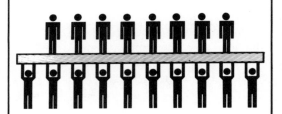

79 persons under age 15 and over age 64 are supported by each 100 aged 15 through 64

SOURCE: U.S. Bureau of the Census, based on United Nations data

PRB 75-23

Population Composition of Two Countries with Widely Differing Growth Rates

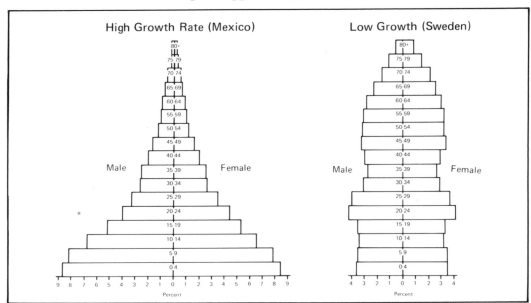

SOURCE: 1972 Demographic Yearbook, United Nations (1972 data)

PRB 75-24

The high proportion of young people in the populations of developing countries, plus people over age 64, puts a burden on working-age people and reduces living standards of all age groups. Also, countries with a high dependency ratio have difficulty in accumulating the savings required for investment and stimulation of economic growth.

Demographic Data Collection and Analysis

The U.S. Agency for International Development (AID) has supported the collection and analysis of population statistics for decades. This support, one of AID's oldest activities, traces to the need for an accurate "yardstick" to evaluate population problems and family planning performance, especially in developing countries where birth rates are high. Statistics measure the dimensions of the problem— the current population, rate of population growth, and the effects of that growth in total and per capita terms on employment opportunities, housing, food availability, health services, education, and other essentials of living. In countries that have established family planning programs, statistics measure progress made in reducing fertility.

The earlier AID studies were aimed at defining and describing the still little-understood relationship between population growth and economic development—studies which indicated that in many developed countries excessively high birth rates were reducing the overall quality of life for individuals. Over the years increasing emphasis has been placed on development of statistics that can be used in one way or another to improve family planning programs.

In 1975 the collection and analysis of population data have the objective of: (1) measuring the impact of AID-supported family planning programs; (2) helping to develop awareness and understanding of population problems in developing countries, and (3) helping family planning administrators improve program design and implementation.

AID's activities in some countries are hampered by a lack of good census data; a few countries have never taken a census of population and in some countries censuses have been inadequate. Therefore, an early AID project, in cooperation with the Department of Health, Education, and Welfare, was a search for techniques by which birth and death rates and population changes can be estimated from interview data where no detailed census information is available, or where there is no registration or incomplete registration. Progress was made in developing the new techniques.

In 1968 AID made the first of several grants to the University of North Carolina, which established laboratories in Colombia, Kenya, Morocco, and the Phillipines in cooperation with overseas academic and research institutions. These laboratories have improved the reliability and predictive value of data for population and family planning programs. The projects they administered included surveys, development of experimental data systems, and research on the effectiveness and validity of data collection techniques.

Support to Census Bureau

AID has strongly supported world population work of the U.S. Bureau of the Census. The Bureau maintains current estimates of total population for all countries and estimates of current levels of fertility, mortality, and population growth. Population projections by age and sex have been made for selected countries. To provide AID a broad overview of the demographic situation in each of the developing countries, the Bureau maintains a computer file containing data on a wide variety of demographic measures for both the most recent census year and the current year. A family planning program sub-model has been modified to take account of post-conception birth control methods in evaluating the effect of family planning programs on population growth.

The Bureau has provided advisory assistance to many countries on censuses and other surveys of population. In fiscal 1973, the Bureau's advisory and training resources were used extensively in support of the Africa Census Program of the United Nations Economic Commission for Africa under which 22 countries have been undertaking population enumerations.

Until the age structure of a population can be shifted away from one with many young people (as in Mexico) to one with many older people (as in Sweden) rapid population growth will continue. This "momentum" arises from the fact that there will be more young people forming families and having babies at a faster rate than older people are dying. Even if fertility rates were to drop to the replacement level of slightly over 2 babies per mother, it would take an estimated 60 years before populations of the developing countries would stabilize.

Technical assistance of the Census Bureau has led to development or improvement of methods of population measurement and the processing of demographic data. One example is the development of the Census Tabulating System (CENTS), a new method of rapidly tabulating data from censuses and surveys. This method, designed for the IBM 360 Model 25 computer, was an immediate success and was adopted by many countries. However, because not all countries have IBM 360 computers, a companion package called COCENTS, written in the COBOL language and adaptable to a number of computers, was developed later. COCENTS has been made operational on computers manufactured by several U.S. companies, as well as those of Japanese and British makers. CENTS/COCENTS is now operational in more than 40 countries and the demand is still strong because it can be used for virtually every type of data. Development of CENTS/COCENTS has saved much time previously spent preparing computer programs tailored to specific tasks, often by inexperienced programmers. Surveys have shown that the simplicity of the CENTS/COCENTS system results in substantially lower costs than those incurred when other systems are used.

In developing CENTS/COCENTS, AID and the Census Bureau concluded that regardless of the data types collected, the processing was essentially similar. Information relating to individual reporting units must be recorded on a preprinted form. The reporting unit may be persons, families, or households, as in a census or survey—or an event, such as a birth, death, or visit to a family planning clinic—or units, such as contraceptives. The completed forms must be transmitted to a central processing center where information is transferred to computer readable form, such as punch cards or key to tape. Computer readable form information must then be edited to identify and correct obvious errors (such as a pregnant male or 20-year-old grandmother). Edited data are then tabulated and printed in tabular formats for use.

AID made several sizable grants to support the population activities of the Latin American Demographic Center (CELADE), at Santiago, Chile. CELADE offers courses in demography and statistics, conducts demographic research, and makes technical and demographic assistance available to national governments. A subregional center of CELADE was established in 1967 in San Jose, Costa Rica, to assist in demographic training and research in Central America.

AID has financed regional demographic projects in Africa and has carried on country activities in Ethiopia, Ghana, Liberia, and Uganda.

U.S. AID in 1972 initiated a World Fertility Survey and has supported it through the International Statistical Institute along with the United Nations Fund for Population Activities. The Survey will provide information on fertility patterns in over 40 countries. The survey material to be obtained will be nationally representative but, also, internationally comparable.

AID, recognizing that family planning programs are new in many countries, has evolved the concept of the management information system (MIS), which can provide management the information needed for sound decision-making. The process of developing an MIS calls first for the identification of "decision points;" that is, the individuals who, within a certain period of time, must make the critical decisions. The next step is to determine what information is required at each decision point to enable the decision-maker to arrive at a sound management judgment. Then, an MIS can be designed and implemented. Systems have been established in about a dozen countries with varying levels of assistance from AID.

In fiscal 1975 highest priority was given to measurement of the impact of family planning programs on fertility in Indonesia, the Philippines, Korea, Thailand, Pakistan, Colombia, Bangladesh, Kenya, Nepal, and Mexico. The first four of these countries have vigorous family planning programs. The other six may be expected to develop strong national programs before 1980, but benchmark data must be gathered ahead of time.

High on AID's priority list is support work by the United Nations Fund for Population Activities (UNFPA) in developing demographic data to alert Government officials to the extent and consequences of rapid population growth within their borders. Controversy about national population policies, notably in Africa and to some extent in Latin America, traces in part to the fact that basic data on population size, age and sex distribution, and birth rates are incomplete or, often, grossly inaccurate.

Demographic data are required for the establishment and administration of family planning programs. Data are needed for "target definition"—to pinpoint geographic areas of greatest fertility, to chart the demographic and socioeconomic characteristics of potential acceptors, and to assess current knowledge and attitudes toward the practice of contraception. Data also are needed to measure the degree of "target attainment." Required data include numerator analysis of family planning acceptors, surveys of fertility change among acceptors as contrasted with nonacceptors, and controlled experiments to demonstrate the differential impact of alternate program mixes.

Some gaps remain.

Although many countries require that births and deaths be registered, there is great variability in registration. Some countries register most of their births and deaths, but have difficulty in processing the data and putting them into usable form. Other countries have spotty registration—good in some areas, poor in others. For countries where registration systems are weak, sample surveys, sample registrations, and dual record systems can provide valuable data on the general level of fertility. However, there is a need to document the specific impact of family planning programs, and AID is developing a project for this purpose for fiscal 1976.

A lack of census data is still a problem, although the United Nations has lent its strong encouragement to census-taking, which is often done once in a decade in the year ending with the digit zero. Censuses taken in 1980 will produce very valuable data on the accomplishments of family planning programs as well as data needed for many other purposes, including assessment of the impact of population on development. Some planning is under way now in many countries to devise training programs, to perfect methodology, and otherwise take steps to ensure complete and accurate enumerations of population.

Population Policy Development

Attitudes on population matters differ widely among countries. Some countries announce as official policy their determination to slow the population growth rate through certain types of family planning programs. Others, though espousing no official policy, permit both public and private population programs to function and may even support or encourage them. Within each of these two categories some programs are more advanced, more purposeful, and more goal-minded than others. Still other countries have adopted some form of population growth control but do not adequately implement the program. And still others have not yet developed any significant national policy of family planning. These differing attitudes stem from broadly varying historical, cultural, religious, philosophical, psychological, and economic factors.

The U.S. Agency for International Development (AID) has identified among countries experiencing serious population growth problems four stages of policy development—start-up, intermediate, maturing, and self-sustaining. AID, to support and speed policy development in countries in the start-up and intermediate stages, is disseminating information to decision-makers on the unfavorable impact of too rapid population growth on national development goals and on the need for measures to encourage reduced fertility. Also, AID is furnishing numerous countries periodic information on the social and economic determinants of fertility, and sponsoring studies of the status and implication of laws bearing on family planning activity. Through this assistance a country's decision-makers and its scientific community gain an understanding of population dynamics in that country—an understanding that is essential to establishing and implementing rational population policies.

AID's objective in the policy field consists primarily of enlisting and supporting indigenous leaders who will themselves determine and implement whatever measures are needed to promote policy development. In pursuing this objective, AID uses research and persuasion to discover and elaborate lines of informal national self-interest that, in turn, can buttress an adequate fertility control policy. AID, in a sense, is an "information broker," bringing together the experts who study the problem of population with the decision-makers of the developing countries—the latter the ones in a position to direct resources to deal with population problems.

Country studies and conferences have been AID's principal means of bringing together population experts and decision-makers.

Through fiscal 1974 a total of 50 subprojects supported by seven AID contracts were initiated to study population factors in countries experiencing serious population growth problems. A total of 32 of the 50 subprojects have been directed at the six countries with maturing population policies—India, Indonesia, Pakistan, Philippines, Thailand, and Kenya. Examples of these 50 subprojects include work agreements executed by the Interdisciplinary Communications Program (ICP) of the Smithsonian Institution with indigenous researchers to study social and economic determinants of fertility. The American Academy for the Advancement of Science (AAAS) has initiated studies of cultural factors in population dynamics, employing host country scientists. Tufts University, through the International Advisory Committee on Population and Law (IACPL), has compiled and analyzed national laws related to population and fertility control. GE-TEMPO, the Center for Advanced Study of the General Electric Company, has also sponsored a series of country studies that measure the consequences of rapid population growth and assist development planners in weighing the policy alternatives.

Workshops and seminars have reached decision-makers in five countries in the policy start-up stage and four countries having inadequate policies. The ICP has held nine conferences on the population problem and determinants of fertility. The AAAS held a seminar in Bucharest just prior to the World Population Conference (August 1974), to discuss studies on cultural consequences of population growth. The IACPL sponsored a seminar on law and population in Nairobi, while the National Academy of Sciences held five international seminars on population dynamics.

Officials of AID's Population Office took part in the 1974 World Population Conference, which focused global attention on population policies and their development. Wide-ranging debates at the Conference dramatically displayed the way myriad politi-

cal considerations influence population policies. Representatives of most developing countries insisted that population matters be integrated among other concerns, such as a more equitable distribution of income within and among countries. And countries were more willing to support family planning services from the standpoint of improving health of their populations than of reducing fertility for demographic reasons.

These and other attitudes evident at the Conference demonstrated once again that population policy is subject to endless change in nearly every country. In part, this condition derives from the continued evolution of the unique set of demographic, economic, and social factors that shape each country's current development prospects. Furthermore, population policies are often closely identified with forceful public figures whose own rise or fall in power greatly affects the state of policy commitments. Finally, public decisions typically rest on inadequate demographic data and rough-and-ready analysis. As improved data and improved studies come to light, future policies will be more finely tuned or yield to more relevant expressions of public commitment.

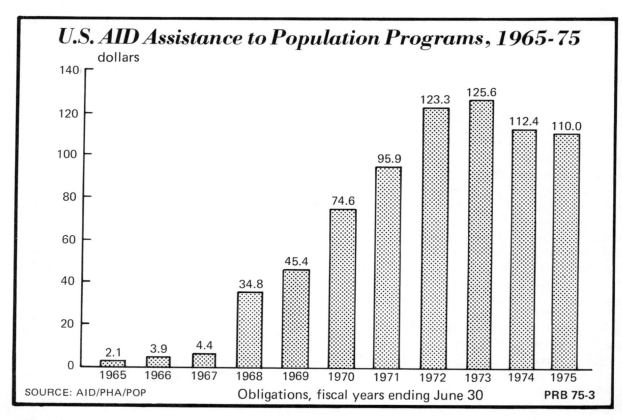

U.S. AID Assistance to Population Programs, 1965-75

dollars

SOURCE: AID/PHA/POP

Obligations, fiscal years ending June 30

PRB 75-3

AID support for population programs in developing countries is authorized by Title X, Foreign Assistance Act of 1968. Through fiscal 1975, cumulative obligations for this purpose totaled $732.4 million, all of which was for authorized Agency programs.

Insofar as the basic stock of population dynamics knowledge is inadequate to meet AID's program requirements, AID has developed a strategy to fill the critical knowledge gaps. Research is needed in four basic areas: (1) study of those consequences of rapid population growth that, in the view of a significant body of developing country policy-makers. are *favorable* to development, e.g., low-density countries that relate population growth to the effective occupation of national territory; (2) research on those socioeconomic determinants of fertility whose close association with fertility decline is known but where research findings are not specific enough to guide policy decisions, e.g., the kind of female education or type of student that is most likely to bring about reduced fertility; (3) cross-cultural studies designed to distill from country research more general findings and new or revised hypotheses to be rested in specific country research, e.g., a common education threshold beyond which further female education has little effect on fertility; and, (4) research to clarify the processes of policy formulation and development.

In carrying on its policy development work, AID has compiled a ranking of 92 developing countries. Variables used in measuring the urgency of relative assistance claims are: (1) projections of country population growth over the decade of the 1970's, (2) an index comparing country birth and death rates to average developed country vital rates; and (3) GNP per capita.

The top 20 countries—those having the most serious population problems—fall into the first three stages of policy development. One group, Ethiopia, Sudan, Mali, Afghanistan, Yemen Arab Republic, and Burma, represents the "policy start-up" stage. These countries have not yet developed a significant national policy to restrain fertility. Implicit population policy may be pronatalist. A national consensus to support the development of population policy is weak or absent; popular views may favor rapid population growth, rather than restraints on growth, as a path to national greatness.

Another group of countries are in an "intermediate policy" stage, Zaire, Tanzania, and Nepal. These have generally adopted some form of population growth control policy, but the public commitment has shallow roots in terms of demographic understanding and an inadequate pace and breadth of implementation. No high-level governmental body exists with the power to coordinate national policy. Many influential public officials pay lip service to it.

The remaining group of countries of the top 20, Indonesia, Thailand, and the Philippines, have "maturing policies." Policies have been adopted and a basic institutional framework has been established to promote the implementation of policy. However, policy decision is not translated into adequate support; policy tends to rely solely on family planning efforts to achieve lower fertility goals. There is need to orient development initiatives outside of the area of family planning toward support for lower fertility. Moreover, the national coordinating body occasionally needs expert consultation services and it lacks adequate staff training opportunities to ensure its continuing effectiveness.

None of the 20 countries are in the "self-sustaining policy" stage, where there are reasonably adequate national policies and institutional bases to carry them on.

Of the 72 other countries in the AID ranking, approximately a third do not receive AID support— for instance, Angola, Argentina, Cuba, Iraq, Libya, New Guinea, Saudi Arabia, and Uganda.

The next largest group of countries are in the "policy start-up" category—Upper Volta, Niger, Haiti, Malagasy Republic, Bolivia, Cameroon, and Senegal. All of these are in Latin America or Africa.

A smaller group of the 72 are considered to have "intermediate policies" at the present time—Ecuador, Guatemala, Liberia, and Zambia; again, all of these countries are in the developing world outside Asia.

A similar number of nations are classified as having achieved a "maturing policy"—Egypt, Ghana, Malaysia, Venezuela, and Costa Rica.

Finally, a few countries among the 72 have vigorous, "self-sustaining policies," such as South Korea, Taiwan, Chile, Hong Kong, and Singapore.

Looking toward the future, AID's highest policy development priority will be given to those lines of activity likely to result in relatively clear prescriptions by public decision-makers—in general, research on the social determinants of fertility and application of fundings to policy issues. This activity will focus on the situation of nations whose natural population increase poses the most serious problems for the world as a whole, including India, Indonesia, the Philippines, Pakistan, Bangladesh, Thailand, Zaire, Nepal, Kenya, Morocco, Egypt, Mexico, Iran, and Colombia. It is possible, however, that small-scale determinants research will continue to be supported in countries considered to have relatively weak population policies at present but which are demographically important—Nigeria, Ethiopia, and Afghanistan. Since only a few selected countries will be candidates for large-scale research on determinants of fertility in the near future, AID will closely coordinate its activities with those of other international agencies and organizations to minimize overlap of activities.

Research

Since the mid-1960's, AID has supported population research with the purpose of developing and implementing improved means of controlling fertility. This research falls into two major categories: (1) biomedical research to develop improved fertility control technology and (2) operational, or "action," research to improve implementation of family planning programs.

Both types of research are essential to improve effectiveness of family planning programs. Biomedical research is supported on the premise that the ready availability of means for fertility control is a prime determinant of fertility behavior and of the time and fiscal requirements for a fertility control program to achieve its objectives. The objective of operational research is to improve the effectiveness of family planning delivery systems.

Biomedical Research

Between 1967 and 1975 AID has provided about $46 million for biomedical research to develop improved means of fertility control. The high priority given this work has been based on the assumption that, if effective fertility control technology can be developed and delivered to countries with rapid population growth, the people of those countries tend to make use of that technology. AID's research program has been directed toward applied rather than basic research, and has pursued relatively few leads in depth rather than attempting to explore all possible approaches to the development of new technology. Relevance to the needs of developing countries has been a consideration of paramount importance in the selection of topics for research.

Funds for biomedical research have been applied in three areas:

1. Research on a once-a-month self-administered method.
2. Research to improve currently available means of fertility control.
3. Comparative clinical field trials of means of fertility control under use conditions in developing countries.

This biomedical research has been carried out through contracts with various universities, including, in the United States, Colorado, Harvard, Johns Hopkins, Minnesota, North Carolina, Northwestern, Pittsburgh, Washington (St. Louis), Wisconsin, and Yale, and, abroad, Makerere University (Uganda), Royal Veterinary College (Sweden), and the University of Singapore. Cooperating institutes and foundations have included the Battelle Memorial Institute, the International Fertility Research Program, the National Institute of Child Health and Human Development, The Pathfinder Fund, the Population Council, the Salk Institute, the Southwest Foundation for Research and Education, and the Worcester Foundation.

Once-a-month self-administered fertility control method. Research is being conducted to develop a self-administered means for controlling fertility after exposure to or recognition of pregnancy.

A "hindsight" means of fertility control would be a major technical advance in this field. Since fiscal 1965, AID has obligated about $15 million for research on a self-administered once-a-month means of fertility control.

The effort has been focused on four areas:
1. Research on regulation of ovarian corpus luteum (ovarian) function.
2. Studies on anti-progestins.
3. Research on gonadotropin-releasing factors.
4. Prostaglandin research.

AID has obligated $4.8 million for over 40 studies seeking new ways to control corpus luteum function and block progestational activity. This research is based on the premise that by altering the function of the corpus luteum—the part of the ovary that produces a hormone (progesterone) essential to reproduction—fertility can be regulated.

AID has obligated $4.4 million for research to develop inhibitors of gonadatropin-releasing factors as contraceptive agents. Releasing factors are chemical "messengers" that link the hypothalamus part of the brain with the pituitary gland. The pituitary, among other functions, produces gonadatropic hormones required for conception; it is theorized, therefore, that if the releasing factors can be inhibited from stimulating the pituitary, the hormonal "chain" would be broken and conception prevented. Some anti-releasing factor substances have been identified. Although their value for fertility control has not yet

AID's large-scale purchasing of oral contraceptives in bulk, with standardized ingredients and packaging, has reduced procurement costs. Costs of large purchases in 1973, 1974, and 1975 ranged from .1378 cent to .1498 cent per monthly cycle, as compared with costs of earlier smaller contracts ranging from .1675 cent to .3470 cent per cycle.

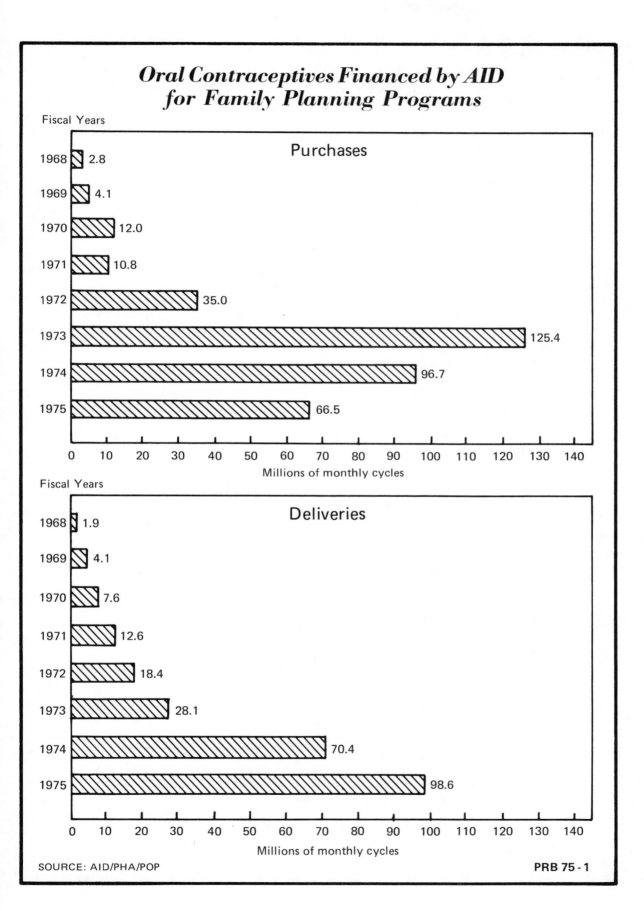

Oral Contraceptives Financed by AID
for Family Planning Programs

Fiscal Years

Purchases

1968	2.8
1969	4.1
1970	12.0
1971	10.8
1972	35.0
1973	125.4
1974	96.7
1975	66.5

0 10 20 30 40 50 60 70 80 90 100 110 120 130 140

Millions of monthly cycles

Fiscal Years

Deliveries

1968	1.9
1969	4.1
1970	7.6
1971	12.6
1972	18.4
1973	28.1
1974	70.4
1975	98.6

0 10 20 30 40 50 60 70 80 90 100 110 120 130 140

Millions of monthly cycles

SOURCE: AID/PHA/POP

PRB 75-1

been fully established, the compounds can be taken orally and seem to have no bad side effects.

Since fiscal 1968, AID has obligated about $7 million to support prostaglandin research, seeking "a nontoxic and completely effective substance or method which, when self-administered on a single occasion, would ensure the nonpregnant state at completion of a monthly cycle." Following early promising results, progress on developing a practical self-administered means of fertility control was stymied for several years because termination of pregnancy was not always complete and side effects remained troublesome.

But work to solve these problems with new prostaglandin analogs and delivery systems has continued. Recent findings have given rise to considerable optimism among researchers and others that many of the old difficulties are on the way to being solved. A report at the May 1975 International Conference on Prostaglandins at Florence, Italy, indicated that an excellent post-conceptive, self-administered means of fertility control based on prostaglandins is close to being a reality. The farthest along at present is the vaginally administered analog 15 (S)-15 Me PGF$_2$ methyl ester, which appears to offer virtually certain and complete induction of mensus with acceptable side effects in the first 4 weeks following missed menses.

Improving currently available control methods. Although important progress will come from research in new means of fertility control, many important gains have come from the less costly research aimed at improving existing technologies, for example oral contraceptives, condoms, sterilization, and pregnancy termination. Improvements in existing technologies are now exerting a powerful "multiplier effect" on the effectiveness of family planning programs wherever these technologies are being made available.

AID's research efforts to improve existing means of fertility control relate to such characteristics as improved convenience for the individual; simplicity of use; attractiveness and appeal of the product or method; safety and freedom from side effects; effectiveness (relatively few failures); a low cost— simple and cheap to manufacture and distribute; cultureal acceptibility; minimal reliance on highly skilled medical practitioners; and, overall adaptability in family planning programs.

Although often disparaged for their imperfections, *oral contraceptives* constitute a tremendous advance toward womankind's ancient goal of a completely effective and coitally independent means of preventing unwanted pregnancies. Use of oral contraceptives is increasing rapidly in developing countries. Because major improvement in steroidal contraception is unlikely, AID has confined its research to studies on safety and side effects in developing countries, devoting $2.1 million to that area since fiscal 1970.

Progress toward perfection of *intrauterine devices* has been slow. Although innumerable IUD's of plastic, metal, and fiber have been "invented" and tested, few, if any, have demonstrated decided advantages over the Lippes Loop. Earlier enthusiams for copper-bearing IUD's and a variety of plastic shapes have been tempered by increasing experience and awareness of practical limitations to their use. Although the loop continues to have an important place in family planning programs, limitations on its use include lack of complete contraceptive protection in some cases, lack of retention by some, and unavailability of adequate follow-up clinical services especially in many remote rural areas.

Introduction of attractively packaged, colored, and lubricated condoms has led to greatly increased demand for these as a means of fertility control. Wherever available, these are useful for family planning.

Important advances are being achieved in the technology of *female sterilization*. Previously considered a difficult and dangerous procedure requiring expensive hospitalization, female sterilization is now being done as a low-cost out-patient procedure by any of several methods.

One of these recent AID-supported developments includes single aperture laparoscopic sterilization with tubal (Hulka-Clemens) clips and (Yoon) Fallope rings; it avoids the two main hazards of laparoscopic female sterilization—general anesthesia and electro-cautery.

Clinical trials with improved tubal clips and rings and their applicators are now in progress in several countries—the United States, Britain, India, Thailand, Korea, and Singapore. As results of additional field trial experience become available, AID will apply knowledge gained to perfect specifications for laparoscopes; and then will purchase the instruments in considerable number for delivery to developing countries.

AID is also sponsoring experimental work on new techniques of female sterilization using cornual trauma, cryosurgery, tissue glues, plugs, transcervical methods—all would eliminate the need for an operation.

AID-sponsored studies are seeking a reversible means of *male sterilization* and simplified means of male sterilization for field use.

Termination of Pregnancy remains a controversial means of fertility control. Nevertheless, the proportion of the world's population living in countries where abortion is now legal has increased from one-third in 1971 to two-thirds in 1976. In 1973 the U.S. Congress adopted an amendment to the Foreign Assistance Act which prohibits assistance by AID for abortion services as a means of family planning. However, some abortion-related research and training are supported by AID for the purposes indicated below.

AID-supported research relating to termination of pregnancy has focused on development of methods and equipment which allow safe termination of pregnancy and effective treatment of illegal and spontaneous abortions and miscarriages suitable for use in developing countries.

AID also sponsors research in pregnancy testing. Early detection of pregnancy allows early initiation of prenatal care or, for those who choose it, early termination of pregnancy on a wholly voluntary basis and in accordance with prevailing local custom and medical practice. A new 5-minute test which can detect pregnancy as early as the time of the missed menses has been developed at Johns Hopkins University and is entering field studies.

Field studies. To improve currently used means of fertility control and to evaluate fertility control methods which may have differing efficacy and risks associated with them when used in the less developed countries, a major component of the AID research program is collaborative and comparative clinical trials of new methods. The focus of this effort is the epidemiologic evaluation of the success and the performance characteristics of each of these methods under use conditions in field programs. This type of evaluation studies is performed through a network of collaborating investigators. These field studies have also made it possible to carry out double blind trials of new methods in the same clinical setting.

Beginning in fiscal 1967, AID supported the development of the International IUD Program of The Pathfinder Fund. This $1.5 million field study of IUD characteristics has provided high-quality comparative data from 40 countries. Uniform records and centralized data processing have allowed the determination of which performance patterns are related to IUD user and clinic characteristics. For example, the highly important category of removals because of bleeding or pain has been shown to be greatly related to individual clinics providing contraceptive service.

To extend the availability of a clinical network for field trials, an International Fertility Research Program (IFRP) was initiated in fiscal 1971. Since that time a total of $9 million has been provided to the IFRP to support conduct of collaborative field trials of new IUD's, sterilization techniques, pregnancy termination techniques, prostaglandins, and pharmacologic contraceptives in many countries.

Biomedical research by others. Although AID's fertility research program is focused on the applied end of the spectrum, a great deal of basic research concerning human reproductive processes is being carried on by others. The major institutional sources of funds for both applied and basic research in reproductive biology and contraceptive development are governments, private foundations, international organizations, pharmaceutical firms, and universities. Research is being carried out in government laboratories, universities, private research laboratories, and at pharmaceutical firms. It was estimated in 1970 that at that time there were 145 major institutions carrying out research in the biomedical field.

Operational Research

In the fiscal period 1965-74 AID provided $20 million for over 70 technical assistance and operational research projects in 20 countries of Africa, Asia, and Latin America to improve delivery of family planning services.

In many developing countries, especially those in Asia, the family planning infrastructure is well established and the full spectrum of fertility regulation methods is available. There are, however, numerous economic, administrative, geographic, and cognitive barriers which restrict this availability. In many programs, people still must pay for contraceptives, wait in long lines, fill out lengthy forms, receive services only during certain hours, and travel long distances. In addition, many persons are not aware of the services that are available, or have inaccurate information about specific fertility regulation methods. The general objective of "action" research projects is to develop delivery systems that eliminate or minimize such barriers, therby making fertility regulation methods truly available. These systems must be cost-effective and have the potential for replication by the host countries.

Taiwan. The project's objective is to measure use and effects of contraceptives when made available to women in their homes. Twelve study townships and twelve control townships are used in the project. Each study area is matched with a control. A baseline survey of client characteristics has recently been concluded and a followup survey will be conducted at the end of the project in mid-1976.

Egypt. AID is providing the American University in Cairo with funds to demonstrate two contraceptive delivery systems in both urban and rural settings. The first system entailed a household canvass during which pills or condoms were offered free to residents. Under the second system, pills and condoms were distributed through group meetings of neighborhood women. This year-long demonstration has been adjudged highly successful and will be continued.

Korea. A new project provides for the "saturation" of a study area with pills and condoms through village-wide household canvasses. After an initial canvass/meeting, resupplies can be obtained from a village depot. The study area has a population of approximately 450,000 people. There will be a control area which will not receive the saturation, and an intensive cost analysis of the saturation area. Backup services offering other fertility regulation methods will be provided. In addition to this cost analysis, there will be three contraceptive prevalence surveys in each area—before, mid-point and after.

Bangladesh. This is a study of the acceptability of various contraceptive methods in rural Bangladesh. It involves assessing household delivery of contraceptives in rural areas by comparing acceptor data, periodic estimations of prevalence of contraceptive use, and age-specific fertility rates.

Research by others. The international effort supporting research to improve family planning delivery systems is much less extensive than that supporting biomedical research. Much support has come from the budgets of national programs. Other major sources of funding are the Ford and Rockefeller Foundations and the Population Council, although recent cutbacks in foundation funding have diminished the role of the foundations. The International Planned Parenthood Federation has recently launched some research and community-based distribution and demonstration projects.

Strengthening Family Planning Services

From the beginnings of assistance to family planning programs of developing countries, the U.S. Agency for International Development has emphasized types of aid aimed at the development and strengthening of field services of country programs. Through its Office of Population and country Missions, AID acts in this sphere to (1) provide and encourage adequate availability of contraceptives and program services, (2) promote the development of improved delivery systems for family planning supplies and services, and (3) provide technical consultation on program problems. Such services—available at the request of the host country—are essential to the growth and expansion of family planning programs in these countries.

Over the 10-year period AID has provided $99.3 million for purchase of contraceptives and other fertility control materials alone. The Agency is now, as it has been since 1966-67, the leading source of contraceptive supplies and other assistance for the family planning programs of developing countries. To date some 7 million IUD's have been purchased. Further, more than $9.5 million has been used for purchase of medical equipment and other commodities used in extending family planning services. For fiscal 1974, contraceptive purchases totaled $21.9 million and other equipment $6.0 million. In fiscal 1975 such purchases totaled $26 million and $1.5 million, respectively.

AID outlays for family planning services other than contraceptives for the 1966-75 period amounted to $229.2 million. In fiscal 1974 they amounted to $29.1 million and in fiscal 1975 to $27 million.

In Washington this type of assistance centers in the Family Planning Services Division. The Division arranges delivery of contraceptives and other medical supplies and equipment as requested by the AID Mission in individual countries, provides technical consultation to help resolve special problems arising in development of country prorams, and monitors grants to private organizations.

The strategy of providing family planning services is now focused directly on the delivery of contraceptives and on reaching that part of the population in greatest need of family planning services.

Postpartum Approach

A first step in this direction during the 10-year period was the postpartum approach—a technique pioneered by the Population Council in 1966 with AID assistance and since widely adopted as a basic part of family planning programs in countries throughout the world.

The postpartum program is based on the fact that in the period immediately following delivery (or abortion) many women are highly motivated for fertility control and are more than usually responsive to family planning information, education, and services. Furthermore, women clients in obstetrical wards represent the most fertile segment of society. They are readily reached by family planning educators, the aura of confidence in the hospital staff is favorable, and the setting for subsequent delivery of contraceptive services seems appropriate and logical to the potential clients.

The hypothesis that a program conducted in keeping with such a setting would be effective was first verified in demonstration projects conducted in large urban hospitals. On the basis of the success of these projects, the approach was then extended to smaller units in a wide array of countries.

Reports from large urban hospitals indicate that younger women tend to prefer different means of contraception than older women. Younger women having few or no children prefer oral contraceptives while sterilization acceptors were of a median age of over 32 years and had a median of 5 living children.

AID Commodity Support

In keeping with the growth in family planning programs throughout the world, AID during the past 10 years has dramatically expanded its program of providing contraceptive commodities to cooperating private and government organizations. It financed delivery of contraceptive supplies to more than 70 countries in fiscal 1975.

The provision of commodities authorized under Title X of the Foreign Assistance Act includes a wide range of supplies and equipment. In addition to oral contraceptives, intrauterine devices (IUD's), condoms, aerosol foam, diaphragms, creams and gels. AID has provided essential clinical equipment and supplies such as examining tables and sterilization equipment for both stationary and mobile clinics.

Expanded education and training activities have required increased amounts of training aids, audio-visual equipment, and a wide range of auxiliary supplies including films, booklets, and pamphlets.

As a reflection of expanded activity in family planning programs in developing countries and of increased demand for contraceptive supplies, expenditures for contraceptives increased from $21.9 million in fiscal 1974 to $26 million in fiscal 1975. Of the $99.3 million expenditure for contraceptives and other fertility control materials made in the last 10 years, $35.9 million was destined for countries

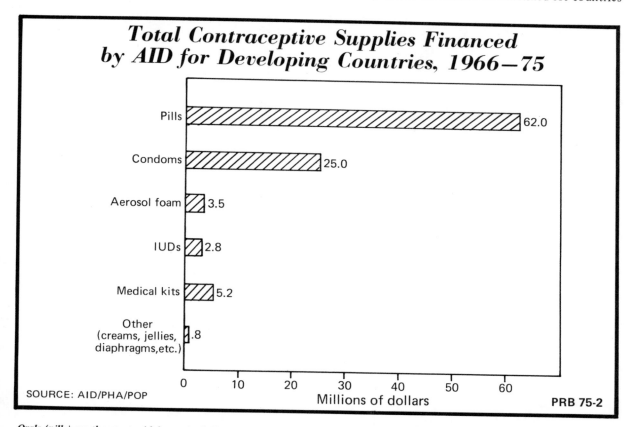

Total Contraceptive Supplies Financed by AID for Developing Countries, 1966—75

Category	Millions of dollars
Pills	62.0
Condoms	25.0
Aerosol foam	3.5
IUDs	2.8
Medical kits	5.2
Other (creams, jellies, diaphragms, etc.)	.8

SOURCE: AID/PHA/POP   Millions of dollars   PRB 75-2

Orals (pills) are the most widely used of all contraceptives in family planning programs of developing countries, but use of condoms is increasing. AID offers other safe and effective supplies and equipment, because a broad choice of methods increases program flexibility and effectiveness.

New Acceptors of Family Planning Services in Selected Countries: 1970 and 1974

(contraceptive methods)

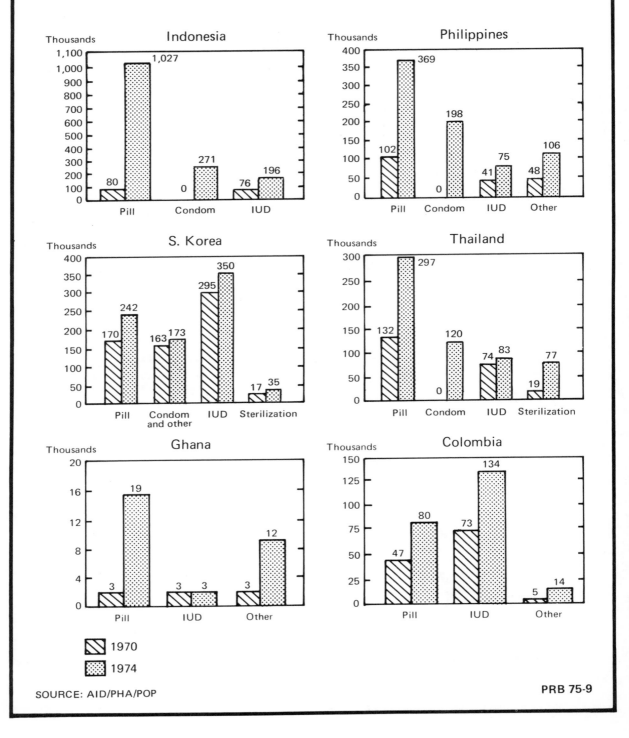

SOURCE: AID/PHA/POP

PRB 75-9

in Asia. For deliveries, $24.6 million has gone to Asia of a total of $76.9 million. Similar patterns were maintained in fiscal 1975.

Oral Contraceptives

In fiscal 1975, AID assistance amounted to 66.5 million cycles of oral contraceptives representing a value of $10.4 million. Cumulatively, through fiscal 1975, AID has furnished 355 million cycles of oral contraceptives at a cost of $62.0 million. AID supplies oral contraceptives on a bilateral basis to 20 countries at the present time and, by working through other participating organizations, makes contraceptives available to some 70 countries.

AID has procured contraceptives through contracts negotiated by the General Services Administration (GSA) using the competitive bid procedure which resulted in changes in the brand or type of oral contraceptives supplied from time to time. Brand changes in some cases brought complaints from users, with resultant detrimental program effects. In June of 1973, after a thorough review of procurement practices, AID initiated a policy of central procurement for oral contraceptives. This allows procurement under generic specifications rather than under brands that may change, thus enabling cost savings to the U.S. Government as well as aiding the continuing acceptance by the users.

Since June 1972, all AID-furnished oral contraceptives have been in a standard "Blue Lady" pack, each containing three monthly cycles. The Blue Lady pack, with a silhouette of a young woman, putting a pill in her mouth, has become familiar to women in the developing world and has facilitated education and communication concerning oral contraceptives as well as enhancing distribution.

Oral contraceptives are widely available to purchasers in many countries, including the Philippines, Jamaica, Bangladesh, Botswana, Chile, Egypt, El Salvador, Ethiopia, Gambia, Honduras, Iraq, Jordan, Nepal, Liberia, Paraguay, Sudan, Trinidad, Tunisia, Uruguay, and Pakistan. In several of these countries there are no prescription barriers. Others such as Thailand and Korea are considering a similar approach.

Since an estimated 60 percent of women of childbearing age in developing countries are less than 30 years of age and over half of all children are borne by women in their twenties, assistance for oral contraceptive distribution is being given priority by AID. To meet the rapidly growing demand, alter-

native methods of manufacture, procurement, and distribution are being explored. For example, AID is providing support for the distribution of oral contraceptives and/or condoms through retail outlets at subsidized prices in the following countries: Pakistan, Bangladesh, Jamaica, Sri Lanka, the Philippines, and Indonesia. These efforts complement existing family planning programs by greatly increasing the availability of contraceptives, especially for individuals who do not have easy access to family planning clinics.

Intrauterine Devices

Demand for IUD's has continued to grow over the past 10 years, with AID providing 830,000 IUD's in fiscal 1975. The types now being furnished are the Lippes Loop and the Saf-T-Coil. AID has supplied four sizes of Lippes Loops (A, B, C and D).

Until it came under question by the U.S. Food and Drug Administration, two sizes of Dalkon Shields (small and standard) were also provided. However, the Dalkon Shield is no longer provided and all outstanding supplies have been recalled. Cumulatively, AID has provided 7 million IUD's at a cost of $2.8 million during the past decade.

Condoms

Condom provision in fiscal 1975 showed a marked increase from previous years' purchases—346 million units as compared to 9.3 million in fiscal 1966. Renewed interest in this type of contraceptive has resulted from the introduction of multicolored lubricated condoms which are now available in red, green, black, blue, and pink. Cumulatively through the program, 950 million condoms have been provided at a total cost of $25 million.

Other Contraceptives

There is only a limited demand for other contraceptives of the conventional variety. Aerosol foam continues to be provided by AID to developing countries requesting it for their programs. Similarly, diaphragms, vaginal creams, and gels are also provided on request. Cumulatively, funds used to provide the latter commodities amounted to slightly more than $810,000.

In addition to supplying the above listed contraceptive devices, AID has acted to standardize the components supplied in medical kits so as to simplify procurement procedures and assure availability of the necessary equipment in the numerous special-purpose clinics in developing countries. Major activi-

Although reversible means of fertility control, such as pills, condoms, and IUDs, continue to be the most widely used methods in family planning programs generally, sterilization is rapidly assuming more importance in many countries.

ties have included development of specifications for a simplified mini-laparotomy kit.

To assure the availability of all the various commodities in adequate quantities to carry out the objectives of the family planning programs, AID has established a policy to maintain a 1-year supply in country and a 1-year supply on order.

Sterilization

Accompanying marked improvements in equipment and techniques for surgical sterilization, especially laparoscopic and minilaparotomy sterilization for women, greatly increasing numbers have chosen voluntary sterilization for control of fertility in recent years.

Sterilization is popular in many countries including the United States. Sterilization, especially tubal ligation, has long been widely used in Puerto Rico. India is also a leader in use of sterilizations, the number rising to a peak of more than 3 million in 1972, mainly vasectomies. With a decline in vasectomies since 1972, the growing availability and acceptance of advanced techniques of female sterilization lifted the 1975 total in India to more than 3 million sterilizations. It is estimated that some 17 million couples in India are currently dependent on this method of fertility control.

Increasing demand for female sterilization has also been manifest in other countries whenever quality services have been made available—in Bangladesh, Colombia, Costa Rica, Egypt, El Salvador, Jamacia, Korea, Nepal, Pakistan, Philippines, Thailand, Tunisia, among others.

Assisting country programs in use of advanced techniques of female sterilization, especially laparascopic sterilization, the Agency for International Development has supplied 455 laparascopes for programs in 53 countries since 1972, plus more than 10,000 minilaparotomy kits.

Monitoring of Grants

In providing assistance to strengthen field work by private organizations abroad, the Office of Population monitors four major grants.

The International Planned Parenthood Federation (IPPF) uses its amount from AID to help establish and support affiliate associations in 84 developing countries. These associations provide family planning information and services through over 3,000 clinics. IPPF also trains clinic personnel in basic contraceptive techniques and family planning education and it develops and distributes information/education materials to increase knowledge about family planning among prospective acceptors.

Family Planning International Assistance (FPIA), the international division of Planned Parenthood Federation of America, uses its grant to help provide financial, technical, and commodity assistance to family planning programs of church-related and other private service organizations in developing countries. Since the inception of its program, FPIA has provided grants to more than 80 projects in 22 countries, with the emphasis on low-cost/high benefit programs that are innovative and have the potential for replication elsewhere. In addition to direct project grants, FPIA has provided commodity assistance—contraceptives, medical equipment and supplies, educational materials—to a total of 75 countries to date.

The Pathfinder Fund uses its grant in dealing with a variety of groups which demonstrate a willingness and capacity to undertake innovative and pioneering family planning programs, particularly in areas where none have existed. Pathfinder has supported projects in a total of 56 developing countries.

The Association for Voluntary Sterilization (AVS), in turn, uses its grants in working with all the aforementioned groups, but limits its efforts to voluntary sterilization. It supports some 35 voluntary sterilization information and service projects in 25 developing countries. AVS also trains medical personnel in advanced techniques of sterilization and sponsors international and regional conferences on voluntary sterilization for leading medical and health professionals. In addition, AVS helped establish several national voluntary sterilization associations in developing countries and a World Federation of Associations for Voluntary Sterilization.

Data Collection for Management Purpose

In order to provide maximum support to national family planning programs, monitor the development of program progress, and gather information vital for the proper management of its large contraceptive commodity assistance, the Office of Population has instituted a quarterly and annual reporting system which measures the in-country flow of contraceptives and the development of family planning services.

The data requested from the field are limited to relatively few variables considered most important in providing support to programs and thought to be standard for almost all programs. Feedback reports are provided to all countries submitting data so that the data can be used for management purposes in the field as well as in the Office of Population.

By collecting these data quarterly, the Office of Population can adjust its contraceptive procurement and shipping procedures to reflect actual program realities and support programs by providing technical assistance when logistical and managerial problems are noted in the submitted information.

Technical Services

The Family Planning Services Division provides technical back-up to the Office of Population and to USAID Missions and responds to requests for help from overseas family planning organizations.

These functions are performed by two full-time physician/family planning specialists who provide technical services in several ways:

(1) Developing specifications for contraceptives commodities and medical instruments and providing medical guidelines to the field on use of these.

(2) Keeping field staff informed of medical developments related to family planning.

(3) Responding to written and cable requests for technical help from USAID Missions.

(4) Attending national and international family planning meetings to present AID's point of view.

(5) Visiting overseas family planning programs to assess progress and provide technical advice.

(6) Providing short-term highly specialized family planning consultant help to voluntary programs through the use of contracts with the American Public Health Association, the Family Planning Evaluation Branch of the Center for Disease Control in Atlanta, and Management Sciences for Health, a Boston-based firm.

(7) Expediting the acceptance of contraceptive and medical family planning techniques overseas by persuading physician colleagues in developing countries of their importance and benefits.

Communication

Just a decade ago, most of the world's people, particularly those in the developing nations, had never heard of family planning. Most did not realize that their countries had population problems or that many of their own family problems were directly related to the fact that they could not adequately care for the number of children who were being born.

Now, in country after country, people have become aware that rapid population growth is occurring and that family planning exists. What made the difference? New research from demographers, economists, and social scientists described the magnitude and seriousness of explosive population growth and its negative effects on development, the environment, and individual health and well-being. New inventions

and improved applications in contraceptive technology made family planning methods more effective and safer. However, the mere existence of new information and materials was not enough. To bring these findings out of scholarly literature, to grasp public attention and generate action, dozens of organizations mounted a broad range of information, education, and communication (IEC) programs through a variety of channels.

IEC activities over the past 10 years have greatly expanded public knowledge, and interest concerning the problems of high rates of population increase have stimulated needed program action and provided information on family planning methods and program services. Radio, television, posters, pamphlets, newspeper articles, and films have spread the word; health and family planning curriculums have been developed and introduced in thousands of schools; local, national, and regional meetings have brought people together for discussions and to initiate action.

The overall purpose of the U.S. Agency for International Development (AID) in this field is to assist developing nations create or improve their systems for the delivery of information and education in support of population and family planning programs. With so many differing conditions and settings involved, the importance of specific IEC programs for a developing country cannot be over-emphasized. Varying messages must be delivered in different ways depending on the resources available, the stage of policy acceptance and interest in a country, the social and cultural climate, the target audiences to be reached, the channels and media to be used, and a number of other factors.

Funding Channels

Approximately 11 percent of AID population resources over the past decade has gone into IEC activities, including those conducted by various organizations such as the United Nations Fund for Population Activities (UNFPA) and the International Planned Parenthood Federation (IPPF). AID funds for IEC projects reach developing nations though four major channels:

1. Bilateral or country-to-country financing in 27 nations is directed toward providing resources needed for IEC activities within a given country.

2. Financing through UNFPA-sponsored projects in more than 40 countries goes primarily for governmental population/family planning activities, such as health delivery systems and population education in the schools.

3. AID assistance to IEC programs of private voluntary organizations such as IPPF and The Path-

finder Fund supports private family planning associations, church-related health and community programs, private welfare agencies, and service projects in more than 80 countries.

4. Interregional projects funded through AID contracts and grants are carried out by institutions or private firms to support and supplement programs being conducted through the other channels.

Action Audiences

Despite the increase of knowledge and acceptance of family planning in many areas and despite the wide variety of projects already mounted, the IEC task is just beginning. The availability of services and supplies in an area often depends upon the level of local interest and demand stimulated by information and education. At the same time, the use of services/supplies depends on public knowledge of them and their availability.

In recent years, AID has sought to aim its IEC assistance toward five basic "action audiences" and encourage other contributors to do the same. These audiences are definable target groups who help determine the success or failure of a national family planning program.

The potential *reproducers* action audience is the primary target. These are the women of childbearing age and their partners who must be encouraged in appropriate ways to adopt and practice effective means of family planning.

IEC activities attempt to persuade the *controllers of policy* audience to adopt and support population policies applicable to their areas of influence. Policy controllers are the individuals or groups who make family planning programs possible and give them a respected stamp of approval.

On-coming reproducers are children below the age of marriage and childbearing. IEC projects both in and out of school aim to provide this key target group with full knowledge of the national and personal reasons for family planning.

Messages to the *general public* help develop knowledge of population problems in society, family, and individual—which fosters the concept of family planning and the introduction and widespread use of program services. The public is urged to adopt lower family size norms and determine to slow the rate of population growth in their countries.

Deliverers of information and services are those who staff clinics, serve as family planning field workers, have access to media channels, and are in other ways responsible for bringing reproducers together with services. IEC activities teach them effective methods for doing their work, provide continuing information on developments in family planning, and encourage them to treat clients in ways that promote sustained family planning practice.

Because resources are limited, AID is concentrating mainly on campaigns to reach the first three audiences—the reproducers, the controllers of policy, and the on-coming reproducers.

Program Strategies

Through its years of population/family planning experience, AID has adopted six major strategies as those most likely to result in the development of successful IEC support for population programs:

1. Through country-specific IEC programs taking into account the differing needs of the people to be reached, to encourage population/family planning groups within a country to design and implement IEC activities in the country which will greatly increase public knowledge of the need for fertility control and of the availability of commodities and services.

2. To organize AID's staff, skills, and resources, plus those of contractors and grantees, around a series of campaigns aimed toward action audience projects which are relevant to country plans and abilities.

3. To cooperate and coordinate with international organizations and major voluntary groups on activities to improve the quality of assistance provided and avoid duplication of effort.

4. To work with and through professional and broad-based special interest groups, such as home economics association and, labor unions, to reach their members and the people they influence, enlisting their educative support for family planning.

5. To encourage local production of IEC materials required by country programs and cooperate with other groups to improve the quality and usefulness of materials going to developing nations.

6. To utilize the mass media for wide dissemination of basic messages of population/family planning programs.

Grant/Contract IEC Support

By awarding grants and contracts to a number of organizations to carry out specific IEC activities, AID multiplies the skills and resources it has available in the IEC field, greatly expands the numbers of people reached, and is able to meet developing country needs more quickly and effectively than would otherwise be possible. Staff specialists within the Office of Population's IEC Division monitor grants covering far-reaching IEC programs. They also coordinate closely with other AID officers on AID-funded projects, such as those of Family Planning International Assistance, which have a major IEC component as part of their operations. Grants monitored directly by the IEC Division include:

East-West Communications Institute (EWCI). An AID grant to EWCI in 1970 assisted that organization to improve its capabilities to serve as an international resource for improving information-education support of population/family planning programs. EWCI is involved in IEC training service and research in the population field and other spheres of economic and social development activities.

More than 325 participants from 42 countries have taken part in the 19 conferences and workshops sponsored by the Institute through June 1975. EWCI staff members have collaborated on research and case studies with personnel of action programs and research institutions in 14 developing nations. Major surveys have been conducted of the abilities, magnitude, and needs of IEC programs in 25 selected countries. Numerous graduate students and short-term trainees have learned IEC methods and contributed to projects at the Institute.

One recent innovation is the development of a modular training system incorporating instructional materials for 15 different segments of IEC studies. With general guidance and tuitoring from the EWCI staff, a student selects modules according to his interests, professional needs, and time available.

EWCI's Resource Materials Collection Center serves as a clearinghouse of IEC materials which are made available to professionals on an exchange basis. The Institute has received more than 7,000 requests for materials, 1,325 in FY 1975 alone. EWCI publishes the bimonthly IEC newsletter which reaches approximately 4,000 people in more than 100 countries. EWCI staff members and consultants have provided technical assistance to a number of ongoing country IEC programs through short-term visits.

University of Chicago. The Community and Family Study Center (CFSC) of the University of Chicago has carried out a number of population research, training, publication and consultation activities for more than a decade. Funding for its fall program has been provided from both private and public sources.

Long-term, graduate-level IEC training, initiated in 1971 under an AID grant, emphasizes a combination of classroom training and practical laboratory experience to prepare graduates for posts as top-level administrators or technicians in IEC population programs in their own countries. Since it began, the degree program has granted 37 Master's degrees, 7 Ph.D.'s and 4 certificates to students from 23 countries. The program has a capacity of 25 students

annually and has 8 fellowships to award to professionals who will become key communication experts in their own countries.

Some 957 participants from 79 countries have attended CFSC's summer workshops on "Mass Communication and Motivation for Family Planning" since they began in 1962. The workshops, funded mainly by the Ford Foundation, were partially funded by AID in recent years.

Beginning in 1974 a parallel program in population education (which includes the training of family planning workers) for both long-term and short-term training was launched in collaboration with the Department of Education of the University.

The CFSC has established a Communications Laboratory with a materials production branch and a research branch, and a small population research library. The Center has produced a variety of monographs which serve an international teaching function and are of practical use to programs in developing nations. Staff members have undertaken a number of short-term consultation activities.

American Home Economics Association (AHEA). Helping young women and girls understand family needs and processes has long been a role of home economists in schools and through extension services. They are recognized as authorities in this field and their programs are growing in many developing nations. They reach both urban and rural women. Thus, home economists occupy a strategic position for teaching population concepts and motivating women to practice family planning. To add this new dimension to the home economist's activities, the AHEA has been conducting an international IEC program under an AID grant to involve home economists in active support of family planning programs underway in their own countries. Since July 1972, AHEA has conducted 33 seminars and workshops in 14 countries. Some 3,000 home economists have participated. Eleven summer institutes held at U.S. universities have provided specialized family planning training to 135 home economists from developing nations.

International Confederation of Midwives. Assisted by a 5-year grant from U.S.-AID, the International Confederation of Midwives has been conducting a project since 1972 emphasizing the family planning responsibilities of midwives throughout the world, especially in regions and areas where midwives are the usual source of assistance at child-birth.

Three regional programs for this purpose were conducted in fiscal year 1975–in Bogota, Colombia, for South American midwives and obstetricians; in Manila, the Philippines, for delegates from East Asia; and in Kuala Lampur, Malaysia, for those from West

Asia. Others were conducted in fiscal 1974 for the Caribbean area, in Bridgetown, Barbados; and for western Francophone Africa, in Dakar, Senegal. In the preceding year, they were held in San Jose, Costa Rica, for Central American delegates; in Nairobi, Kenya, for East African representatives; in Yaounde, Cameroon, for midwives and obstetricians from the Francophone countries of Central Africa; and in late 1972, the first of the programs was held in Accra, Ghana, for delegates from English-speaking countries of West Africa, with midwives and physicians attending from five countries.

Airlie Foundation. Under projects funded by U.S.-AID, the Airlie Foundation has received support for its continuing information-education services to population programs in developing countries, particularly in Latin America.

The AID funded projects include support for the Inter-American Dialogue Center at Airlie House and funding for production of training films and teaching materials relating to population problems and family planning. Since establishment of the Inter-American Dialogue Center in 1962, the Center has been host to approximately 50 dialogues on population matters in which more than 1,800 Latin American leaders took part. In 1975, Airlie completed a series of 63 population films in support of country family planning programs in 13 Latin American countries.

Asia Foundation. Working with a wide variety of Asian local and cultural groups, the Asia Foundation has assisted some 235 population projects, including law and policy projects, in 14 countries under an AID grant awarded in 1972. The Foundation has emphasized help to small-scale locally initiated projects, bringing many new people, new approaches, and new organizations into the family planning field for the first time.

The Foundation supports training and study tours to increase the competence of persons engaged in population/family planning work; the design, production, and distribution of IEC materials; purchase of IEC commodities, such as slide projectors; purchase and distribution of books on population for universities, organizations, and key individuals; family planning education programs in cooperation with unions, midwives and other groups.

World Assembly of Youth (WAY). A broad range of international, regional, national, and local youth organizations has been made aware of the need for action in the population field through the World Assembly of Youth. AID supported its program through grants from 1969 through fiscal year 1975.

The organization has sponsored a series of seminars, conferences, and workshops in many countries of Latin America, Asia, and Africa. It has initiated population essay contests, mass media programs, public meetings, speaking contests, house-to-house visits, and other events. WAY has cooperated with UNFPA, IPPF, and other groups and joined with several youth associations to organize an International Youth Population Conference in Bucharest in 1974. A "Population File" produced and distributed by WAY as a comprehensive kit for population information-education campaigns includes graphs, charts, articles, and suggestions for activities.

World Education, Inc. (WEI). Under AID grants first provided in 1969, WEI has performed a series of country analyses of functional literacy programs in 32 countries. In 16 nations, the organization created enthusiasm for incorporating family planning concepts and information into the curriculums of these nonformal education programs conducted by many different organizations. More than 300,000 acceptors have been recruited through this project.

WEI provides technical assistance to develop or redesign curriculums tailored to specific programs and countries, trains teachers, provides assistance in developing publications and teaching materials, and evaluates the effectiveness of materials used. The organization's major operations are in Colombia, Ecuador, Ethiopia, Ghana, Indonesia, and Thailand.

Country Programs

Assistance for the population IEC activities of specific countries is often extended by AID in collaboration with the UNFPA or other international organizations. Programs in Asia—most notably India, Indonesia, Korea, Pakistan and the Philippines—have been the major recipients over the past decade. Increased attention to and interest in information, education, and communication in the population/family planning field is now being seen in many areas of Latin America and Africa, with significant programs underway in Colombia, Costa Rica, Ghana, Kenya, and many others. Projects are too numerous to detail, but a selection of different types of country IEC activities supported by AID countries includes:

Philippines. With a strong national leadership dedicated to reducing population growth rates, the Philippines has created a dynamic program. AID provides assistance for the activities of the National Media Center, which produces a broad range of population information materials, including radio and television programs, films, pamphlets, and posters. Rapid strides are being made in incorporating population curriculums throughout the entire school system.

Colombia. Consultation and financial aid were

provided to help Javeriana University introduce population-related materials into the health curriculum and develop a graduate level program of population studies. Information on family life and responsible parenthood is disseminated through radio and newspapers.

Ghana. Funds were provided to operate IEC activities within the Danfa Rural Health/Family Planning Project, a comprehensive demonstration, teaching, and research program.

Indonesia. A cadre of health education specialists is being developed to act as a community catalyst in linking family planning services with community and individual needs. IEC materials development has been given support and now plays a role in many aspects of the population program.

Korea. The IEC program directed by the Planned Parenthood Federation of Korea (PPFK) for the Korean Government has developed a trained staff and professional IEC direction to serve as a model for Asia. The senior staff has been trained at the Universities of Chicago and North Carolina, the East West Communication Institute, and other AID-supported centers of population communication. Several years ago the Korean Government asked AID to assist in the design of the population IEC program and in its training efforts. The innovative promotional and informational techniques developed by the PPFK, and successfully applied, now serve as prototypes for other Asian countries and beyond.

Manpower and Institutional Development

Population and family planning activities in developing countries require the services of many skilled, dedicated people. To meet these needs, the U.S. Agency for International Development (AID) since 1965 has made it possible for over 4,000 trainees to study in the United States in programs lasting at least 1 week. An active manpower training effort, through contracts and grants to universities, public and private foundations, institutes, agencies, and other organizations for training both within the United States and abroad, has absorbed 10 percent of the resources allocated to population/family planning work.

Many different capabilities are needed for effective programs. Clinical personnel, including physicians, nurses, and midwives, accounted for about 67 percent of all U.S. AID-sponsored trainees, and social workers, outreach personnel, and training officers brought this total to over 75 percent. Also required are support personnel: Sociologists, economists, communication specialists, demographers, accountants, and a nonprofessional and clerical support staff. In addition, bio-medical researchers and instructors in universities and medical and nursing schools play an essential role in a nation's family planning program. Of those trained in the United States since 1966, 22 percent were support personnel.

To a maximum extent, the training and utilization of population manpower should take place within the countries where programs operate. The transfer of U.S. capabilities within the developing countries often takes place through (1) the training facilities of the agency operating family planning programs (such as the Ministry of Health or the International Planned Parenthood Federation affiliate in the country), and (2) through the training facilities of universities, medical and nursing schools, institutes of public health, and other institutions. Nevertheless, highly qualified individuals from developing countries still have a great interest in coming to the United States for training at an institution that has worldwide reputation in the field and the capacity to develop effective short-term training programs for individuals who already have expertise in a particular subject matter area.

The manpower training inventory reveals that fewer than 33 percent of all AID-funded participants were trained for a period of 15 weeks or more whereas approximately one-third of the participants received training of 2 to 5 weeks. The data are revealing, for rather than primarily seeking a degree, two-thirds of the participants received intensive "involvement" type seminars, clinical and nonclinical on-the-job training and organized occupational study. The training experiences provided these participants were "academic" programs—22 percent, seminar-workshops—40 percent, on-the-job training or organized occupational study—31 percent, and "observation" training programs—14 percent.

Within these short-term training programs, the problems brought by trainees from their own countries are given priority analysis and attention. Participants receive essential instruments, books, and documents to use when they return. Trainees are expected to apply their new knowledge to training programs in their own countries—the "multiplier effect"—and are expected to provide "feedback" to the U.S. training centers: the experience, knowledge and data they encounter in their own country, a reverse flow that improves the overall quality of training.

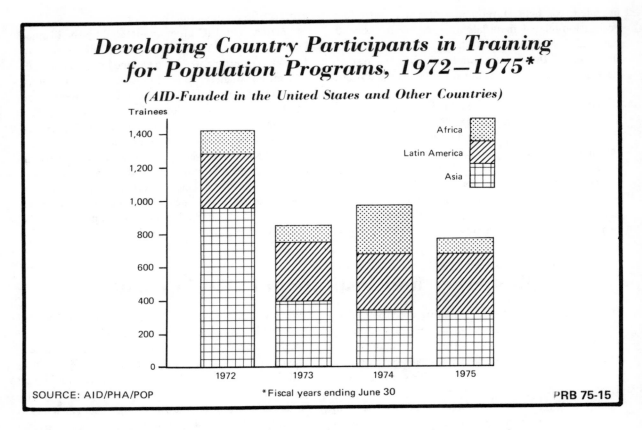

Developing Country Participants in Training for Population Programs, 1972–1975*

(AID-Funded in the United States and Other Countries)

SOURCE: AID/PHA/POP *Fiscal years ending June 30 PRB 75-15

AID-funded training for population programs covers a broad personnel spectrum. Training is carried on for physicians, nurses, midwives, economists, social workers, demographers, statisticians, communicators, administrators, and other personnel categories.

Nurse-Midwives

Training for nurse-midwives in the United States is based at the Downstate Medical Center of the University of New York in Brooklyn, where teams of nurse-midwives, leaders, and trainers from less developed countries take 8 to 10 weeks of intensive advanced training in all aspects of family planning relevant to services nurse-midwives provide. These teams then return to their home countries to strengthen or establish nurse-midwife family planning clinical training programs, and in the process are advised and assisted by the faculty of Downstate. Thus far Downstate has been instrumental in upgrading the quality of training for nurse-midwives in 10 developing countries. In addition, many individuals have been trained simply as practitioners and in some cases as trainers providing additional training outside their country.

Public Health and Community Nurses

Enrollees in this program are being trained at the Harbor General Hospital in Los Angeles, at Meharry Medical College in Nashville and its contracted sub-

training centers, and at the University of California at Santa Cruz.

Collectively, the need for increased involvement of obstetricians, gynecologists, nurse-midwives, and public health and community nurses is great. A 1970 survey of 37 program countries having a combined population of 1.2 billion found 300,000 physicians, 185,000 nurses, and 129,000 midwives providing medical services for this population. Significantly, only 3.0 percent of the doctors, 1.6 percent of the nurses, and 17.9 percent of the nurse-midwives in these countries were giving half or more of their time to family planning.

Managers and Executives

A twice-a-year training program for managers and executives is conducted by the Center for Population Activities at Washington, D.C. Top and middle management personnel are given training in all aspects of family planning program development and operation from the point of view of the managers at various levels from clinic to national. Transfer of this training to overseas locations is under consideration.

Social Workers

Training for social workers is conducted through the International Association of Schools of Social Work which has set up pilot programs in 30 schools within 15 developing countries. The schools provide pre-service professional training for social workers so that whether they enter full time work in family planning organizations or work in social welfare or social service capacities in other kinds of institutions, they can teach or handle counseling, referral, and other service necessary in the family planning field.

Under a related program operated by the University of Michigan's School of Social Work, selected young professors from less developed country schools of social work are given masters degrees in population and family planning.

Economists and Behavioral Scientists

Government representatives and scholars are being given advanced education at Harvard University in population economics, dynamics, and policy. The project over a 5-year period will have encompassed graduate level instruction for 56 students, 41 of whom are degree recipients or candidates. The program not only is helping highly qualified people from developing countries acquire a systematic overview of the character and consequences of rapid population growth, but also is giving them the status and capability needed to become influential voices in population matters in their own countries.

Trainers

A program aimed at improving the quality and effectiveness of trainers in developing countries is carried on at the University of Connecticut, in Hartford.

This program provides trainers 12 weeks of intensive work in how to design, manage, and teach all aspects of family planning through training programs operating in their home countries. These officers are responsible for the training of the very large number of para-professional personnel that make up the great bulk of family planning workers having direct contact with client families. Plans are now underway to increase the capacity of this program to provide training at overseas locations—a development that could markedly expand high-priority countries' capacity to meet training requirements.

Family Planning Orientation Training

A program of family planning orientation is targeted at influential people from developing countries who come to Washington as diplomats, development specialists, public administrators, and businessmen. The program also is aimed at Americans who go to developing countries in connection with assistance programs.

The program, through a wide variety of orientation visits, demonstrations, seminars, and printed materials, shows participants that the United States through public and private action is effectively providing its citizens with the knowledge and means to practice family planning. The program is conducted by the Planned Parenthood Association of Metropolitan Washington, and during its first 22½ years over 1,300 people have received from ½ day to 3 days of orientation, or have attended conducted seminars and conferences. Many participants have expressed surprise that the United States is practicing at home what it advocates for developing countries: family planning conducted on a voluntary basis.

Training Communicators, Home Economists

These activities are discussed in the section on information, education, and communication.

Training of Demographers and Statisticans

Training in this area is discussed in the section on demographic data collection and analysis.

Supportive Institutions

Since an overall AID objective is helping developing countries reach the point where they are able to conduct their affairs without outside assistance, one requirement in the area of population/family planning programs is "institution building." There must be effective institutions within the United States to help such development in the less developed countries. Similarly there must be institutional support within the developing countries themselves. Institutional development has absorbed 6 percent of total resources allocated to population programs.

AID's institutional development program consists of six projects. Three are conducted under the "university service agreements" with Johns Hopkins University, the University of Michigan, and the University of North Carolina. Through another project the University of North Carolina also provides technical assistance to development of a population center at the University of Ghana. Two other projects are carried out by the University of Hawaii and the Population Council. Three other projects are carried out by the University of Hawaii, the University of North Carolina, and the Population Council.

The prime objective has been to help U.S. universities gear up for research, training, and advisory services needed for population/family planning programs in the 1970's. A second objective has been to expand the number of knowledgeable U.S. and developing country students capable of staffing or assisting family planning/population programs in developing countries.

In 1971 AID negotiated follow-up agreements with grantee universities which involved activities in research, demonstration programs, pilot studies, and experiments—activities which were prototypical, innovative, and practical. But as these subprojects were implemented, it became obvious that, in the main, the developing countries had inadequate supportive functions and by and large were incapable of sustaining and promoting the self-sufficiency required for more extended programs.

On the basis of this evidence, AID revised its grant to the University of North Carolina to test the applicability and viability of long-range subprojects that would permit the United States and collaborating developing countries to participate in more sustained institutional building activities. University services agreements are being focused and structured to enable universities to respond to basic training and specialized problem needs, while every effort is being made to channel funds into subprojects closely

integrated with the needs of population/family planning programs in developing countries.

U.S. Participant Training

Each year between 400 and 500 participants have come to the United States under existing bilateral agreements and contracts to study in a variety of institutions and centers. As part of this worldwide training effort, AID provides professional guidance, funds, placement, and support to these individuals and is actively engaged in recruitment in those countries where AID missions exist. Many participants are recruited annually by U.S. universities under contract with AID. The majority, 56 percent, have been women. The developing countries and regions from which these participants come are generally those in which a pressing population problem has been recognized and in which a vigorous national family planning program is under way.

An AID inventory reveals that 50 percent of all participants trained in the United States since 1966 came from 10 developing countries, and 9 additional countries bring the total to over two-thirds. Regionally, 43 percent of the participants came from Asia,

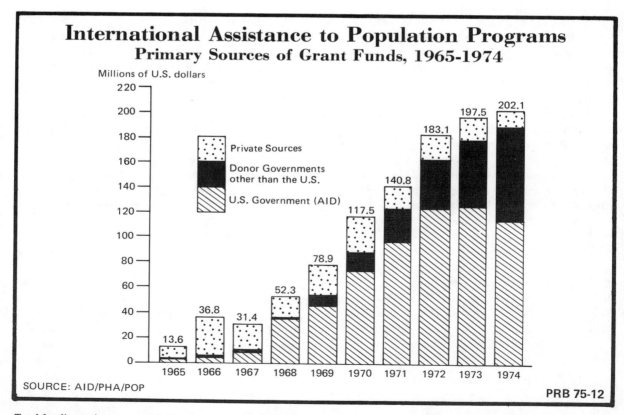

International Assistance to Population Programs
Primary Sources of Grant Funds, 1965-1974

Millions of U.S. dollars

Private Sources
Donor Governments other than the U.S.
U.S. Government (AID)

1965: 13.6
1966: 36.8
1967: 31.4
1968: 52.3
1969: 78.9
1970: 117.5
1971: 140.8
1972: 183.1
1973: 197.5
1974: 202.1

SOURCE: AID/PHA/POP

PRB 75-12

Total funding assistance provided by donors to population programs of developing countries continues to increase. A small decline in U.S. assistance in 1974 was more than offset by expanded aid from other governments and from private sources. This assistance supplements the increased total inputs of local currencies by the developing countries as a whole.

40 percent from Latin America, and 15 percent from Africa. A rank order of these countries is (1) the Philippines, (2) Colombia, (3) Pakistan (and Bangladesh), (4) India, (5) Thailand, (6) Indonesia, (7) Paraguay, (8) Bolivia, (9) Ghana and (10) Nigeria, while a sizable number of participants were also recruited from: (11) Nepal, (12) South Korea, (13) Peru, (14) Chile, (15) Ecuador, (16) Mexico, (17) Turkey, (18) Costa Rica and (19) Panama. More recently a greater emphasis has been placed on recruitment and training of African nationals.

In-Country Training

Notwithstanding the importance of U.S.-based training over the past decade, most of the training in population/family planning has been provided

A.I.D. Population Program Assistance, Financial Summary Fiscal Years 1965 – 1975

Program goals	1965-67	1968	1969	1970	1971	1972	1973	1974	1975	Total 1965-75	
	1,000 dol.	1,000 dol.	1,000 dol.	1,000 dol.	1,000 dol.	1,000 dol.	1,000 dol.	1,000 dol.	1,000 dol.	1,000 dol.	Per-cent
Goal 1 Development of adequate demographic data	900	2,632	4,082	4,480	7,720	9,778	9,121	11,601	11,906	62,220	8
Goal 2 Development of adequate population policies:											
Policy development.	665	620	1,259	2,844	950	2,134	1,430	654	999	11,555	2
Social science research	679	932	955	1,527	4,424	7,698	3,480	2,166	3,771	25,632	4
Goal 3 Development of adequate means of fertility control:											
Biomedical research.	204	173	5,963	8,163	6,820	11,520	5,550	3,356	4,227	45,976	6
Operational research	651	1,262	1,088	7,787	3,231	1,639	2,025	1,704	1,377	20,764	3
Goal 4 Development of adequate family planning services:											
Contraceptives (orals, condoms, IUD's, etc.)	—	1,059	4,130	4,105	3,686	7,049	36,067	21,857	26,009	[1]103,962	14
Service programs	4,258	17,828	16,555	30,307	33,031	45,368	25,771	29,129	26,966	229,213	31
Goal 5 Development of adequate information programs	225	2,002	3,873	4,204	10,766	17,277	16,335	13,999	12,976	81,657	11
Goal 6 Development of adequate manpower and institutions:											
Training	888	2,102	2,666	7,195	13,840	9,954	15,308	12,475	8,799	73,227	10
Institutional development	1,477	5,705	3,789	2,491	9,507	8,434	6,538	3,204	2,945	44,090	6
AID operational expense	524	435	1,084	1,469	1,893	2,414	3,929	12,300	10,000	34,048	5
Total	10,471	34,750	45,444	74,572	95,868	123,265	125,554	112,445	109,975	732,344	100

[1] Includes $99,336,000 of contraceptive supplies purchased directly by AID.

Prepared by Office of Population, 5 December 1975

within developing countries themselves.

Over the past decade many tens of thousands of people have participated in various in-country training programs. The largest number trained have been outreach workers, communicators, motivators, and home visitors. Many of these individuals have a background in health education, but increasingly they are specially recruited community workers residing in the area in which they work. In addition, short-term courses for clinical personnel have also been developed in several countries. Much of this training is specifically for service personnel, but increasingly the population and family planning content is being brought into medical, nursing, public health, and health auxiliary schools so that new graduate professionals are better prepared to render population/family planning services than was formerly

the case. Leading in this development of extensive in-country training have been the Philippines, Pakistan, Indonesia, Colombia, Thailand, Ghana, Costa Rica, South Korea, Kenya, and Egypt.

Physicians

Physicians play a key role in family planning programs. They provide clinical and surgical methods of fertility regulation, supervise paramedical and auxiliary personnel, and are active in administering nonclinical and contraceptive services. Of 4,673 AID-sponsored trainees who have studied in the United States 28 percent were physicians.

In 1975, training for obstetricians, gynecologists, and other surgically qualified physicians was carried on under the leadership of Johns Hopkins University's Program for International Education in Gynecology

Summary of 1965-75 AID Funding Allocations to Organizations for Population Activities and to Bilateral Programs

Organization or program	1965-68	1969	1970	1971	1972	1973	1974	1975	Total 1965-75	Share of total
Voluntary organizations:	*1,000 dol.*	*1,000 dol.*	*1,000 dol.*	*1,000 dol.*	*1,000 dol.*	*1,000 dol.*	*1,000 dol.*	*1,000 dol.*	*1,000 dol.*	*Percent*
International Planned Parenthood Federation	4,478	5,964	7,300	5,000	8,000	12,104	12,747	12,437	68,030	9
The Pathfinder Fund . . .	1,494	4,359	..	3,066	4,350	6,735	4,001	3,660	27,665	4
Population Council	3,104	7,487	2,435	4,247	5,525	7,280	—	750	30,828	4
Association for Voluntary Sterilization	—	—	—	—	876	1,000	1,250	1,850	4,976	1
Family Planning international Assistance—Church World Services.	—	—	—	3,800	4,000	—	3,730	4,424	15,954	2
Other private voluntary organizations	421	458	6,868	6,241	13,542	9,469	6,654	8,204	51.857	7
Voluntary subtotal	9,497	18,268	16,603	22,354	36,293	36,588	28,382	31,325	199,310	27
Universities	8,014	3,797	6,494	23,559	14,741	14,100	11,430	10,672	92,807	13
Participating Agency Service Agreements	419	2,585	1,301	1,883	2,911	3,767	3,667	3,772	20,305	3
Bilateral programs.	22,942	13,778	39,635	25,287	34,230	47,588	33,617	30,319	247,396	34
United Nations Fund for Population Activities. . .	500	2,500	4,000	14,000	29,040	9,000	18,000	20,000	97,040	13
Other[1]	2,890	3,432	5,070	6,892	3,636	10,582	5,049	3,887	41,438	6
AID operational expenses .	959	1,084	1,469	1,893	2,414	3,929	12,300	10,000	34,048	4
Total	45,221	45,444	74,572	95,868	123,265	125,554	112,445	109,975	732,344	100

Prepared by the Office of Population, U.S. AID.

[1] Includes primarily the Pan American Health Organization, the Salk Institute, the Latin American Demographic Center, the Latin American Center for Studies of Population and Family, Management Services for Health Incorporated, and the General Electric Company.

Summary of a Decade of AID Dollar Obligations for Population and Family Planning Projects, by Fiscal Years

Project	1965-67	1968	1969	1970	1971	1972	1973	1974	1975	Total 1965-75
Nonregional:	1,000 dol.	1,000 dol.	1,000 dol.	1,000 dol.	1,000 dol.	1,000 dol.	1,000 dol.	1,000 dol.	1,000 dol.	1,000 dol.
Office of Population	2,079	10,623	17,745	22,518	35,913	50,206	59,422	[1]57,547	[1]59,415	[1]315,468
Office of Health ...	---	—	---	---	978	1,355	438	750	667	4,188
Office of Science and Technology .	---	—	---	—	---	---	200	200	180	580
Office of International Training ..	132	38	40	304	546	503	430	531	399	2,923
AID operating expenses	524	435	1,084	1,469	1,893	2,414	3,929	12,300	10,000	34,048
U.N. Fund for Population Activities	---	500	2,500	4,000	14,000	29,040	9,000	18,000	20,000	97,040
Nonregional total	2,735	11,596	21,369	28,291	53,330	83,518	73,419	89,328	90,661	454,247
Africa:										
Country projects ..	23	404	983	2,484	2,084	9,008	7,596	4,071	3,862	30,515
Regional projects ..	30	259	457	179	5,699	2,259	3,556	334	1,262	14,035
Africa total	53	663	1,440	2,663	7,783	11,267	11,152	4,405	5,124	44,550
East Asia:										
Country projects ..	496	3,525	6,388	8,853	10,977	12,620	15,194	7,971	6,620	72,644
Regional projects ..	350	1,325	1,608	623	1,942	1,826	1,425	96	29	9,224
East Asia total	846	4,850	7,996	9,476	12,919	14,446	16,619	8,067	6,649	81,868
Latin America:										
Country projects ..	1,539	5,457	3,071	5,437	7,085	7,223	6,230	4,792	4,238	45,072
Regional projects ..	2,861	2,468	7,256	5,520	8,161	3,911	7,393	2,655	1,430	41,655
Latin America total ..	4,400	7,925	10,327	10,957	15,246	11,134	13,623	7,447	5,668	86,727
Near East and South Asia:										
Country projects ..	2,437	[2]29,061	3,349	[3]22,908	5,181	1,395	10,471	3,138	1,473	59,413
Regional projects ..	---	655	963	277	1,409	1,505	270	60	400	5,539
Near East and South Asia total	2,437	[2]29,716	4,312	[3]23,185	6,590	2,900	10,741	3,198	1,873	64,952
Country and regional total	7,736	23,154	24,075	46,281	42,538	39,747	52,135	23,117	19,314	278,097
Grand total	10,471	34,750	45,444	74,572	95,868	123,265	125,554	112,445	109,975	732,344

[1] Includes contraceptive commodities supplied to programs in developing countries.
[2] Includes $2.7 million loan to India for program vehicle parts.
[3] Incudes special $20 million grant to India.

and Obstetrics (PIEGO). Johns Hopkins PIEGO operates through associated institutions in the United States including Johns Hopkins, the University of Pittsburgh School of Graduate Public Health, and the Washington University (St. Louis) School of Medicine. Abroad, the School of Medicine at the Beirut (Lebanon) American University and several institutes in South Korea contribute to the program.

PIEGO training consists of intensive 4- to 6-week courses in advanced fertility techniques for obstetricians and gynecologists. It includes an extensive review of reproductive physiology and medicine and provides the necessary equipment and supplies to permit trainees to return to their countries and establish operating clinics and training centers in the procedures and methods that they have been taught. In addition, it has a follow-up program that sends qualified Americans or third-country nationals to the medical institution of each participant to give further training within the local environment and to assist in developing and maintaining proper standards for the advanced medical procedures that they have learned. Since 1972, 315 physicians from 51 developing countries have received surgical laparoscopy training at one of the PIEGO centers, and 375 AID-purchased laparoscopes are currently distributed in 52 less developed countries among trained gynecological surgeons, many with PIEGO training.

People per physician is a measure that varies greatly in the developing countries. For example, the number per doctor ranges from 530 in Argentina (below the average for the developed countries), to 27,240 in Indonesia, 51,200 in Nepal, and 75,200 in Ethiopia. The problem is intensified in some developing countries by the emigration of physicians seeking to improve their prospects in Northern America, Europe, or other developed areas—an out-movement often referred to as a "brain drain."

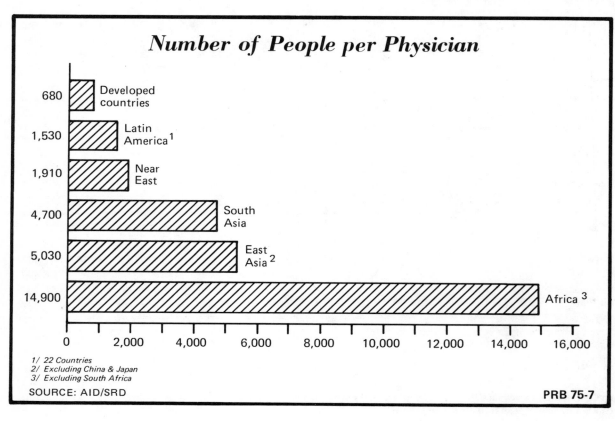

Number of People per Physician

680	Developed countries
1,530	Latin America[1]
1,910	Near East
4,700	South Asia
5,030	East Asia[2]
14,900	Africa[3]

1/ 22 Countries
2/ Excluding China & Japan
3/ Excluding South Africa

SOURCE: AID/SRD

PRB 75-7

Private Organizations

Airlie Foundation

The Airlie Foundation, a private nonprofit institution located near Warrenton, Va., in association with the Department of Medical and Public Affairs of the George Washington University Medical Center, has been actively involved in fostering communication on population subjects.

U.S. Agency for International Development (AID) grants have supported projects along three lines: The operation of an Inter-American Dialogue Center, the support of a Population Information Program, and film productions on population-related subjects.

By the end of fiscal year 1975, the Inter-American Dialogue Center had sponsored 49 meetings both in the United States and Latin America for leaders from government, academia, mass media, military, doctors, bankers, women lawyers, soap opera producers, as well as representatives of the physical and social sciences.

The Population Information Program which publishes population reports aims to make rapid diffusion of population research findings in fields of fertility control technology, family planning programs, and law and public policy. Some 85,000 copies of each of the 40 reports published by the end of 1975 were distributed overseas in four languages—English, French, Spanish and Portuguese. Abstracts and citations are available through a computerized storage and retrieval system.

Nearly 100 16-mm color motion picture films have been produced by Airlie Foundation in the population field under AID sponsorship. Most of them were developed in collaboration with family planning programs of 13 Latin American countries. They are available on free loan for Spanish- and English-speaking audiences in Latin America.

American Home Economics Association

The American Home Economics Association (AHEA), through its International Family Planning Project, has been working since 1971 to help establish population education and family planning as an integral part of home economics programs in developing countries. This project is supported by a grant from the U.S. Agency for International Development.

The first planning conference, held at the University of North Carolina in November 1971, brought 50 participants from 13 developing countries and the United States together to discuss the family planning aspects of home management. Since then, some 3,000 home economists have participated in in-country workshops and institutes including family planning subject matter. These specialists, in turn, have carried family planning information to many thousands of households in their countries.

Country surveys and consultations—the first steps in providing information and stimulating both government officials and home economists to become leaders in family planning/population activities—have been made in 19 countries since January 1972.

Following the surveys, in-country workshops and seminars are conducted by local home economists in consultation with AHEA staff, emphasizing family planning and population education as a component of home economics programs in schools and colleges and in extension and community development programs. In-country funds, personnel, and other resources are used as much as possible.

Thirty-five workshops were held in 30 countries in 1972 through 1974 and are planned for additional countries in 1975-76. These workshops are for the purposes of orientation, curriculum development, and resource development. In Jamaica, for example, most of the 46 workshop participants were teachers. The program included lectures and discussions of the effects of overpopulation and of ways of integrating family planning and home economics education. Three followup workshops were held for 90 teachers in rural schools. As a result of this activity, family planning education became a part of the school curriculum in September 1974 and will reach about 34,000 students each year.

In-depth training on a regional or international basis has been provided. Two month-long workshops were held in Taiwan in 1973 with 10 countries represented. The Philippines Home Economics Association, with AHEA assistance, conducted a 3-week family planning/population education workshop in 1975 for participants from Afghanistan, Nepal, Sri Lanka, Indonesia, Thailand, and the Philippines.

In addition, 6-week summer institutes have been

Family Planning Programs and Fertility Rates

Impacts of vigorous and less-vigorous programs

Countries with vigorous programs in the 1960s

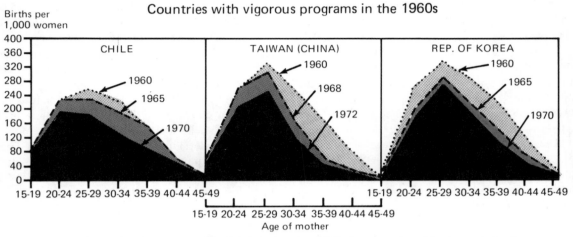

The fertility of women declined during the 1960s in countries with vigorous family planning programs.

Countries not having vigorous programs in the 1960s

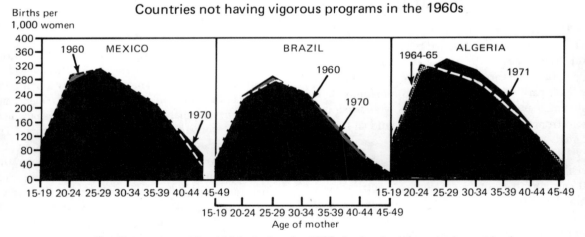

Fertility rates remained high during the 1960s in developing countries not having vigorous family planning programs. Private family planning associations did not exist in most of these countries before the 1960s and government policy often actively discouraged contraceptive availability. However, Mexico in 1973 initiated an official program of family planning and Brazil in 1974 announced a policy embracing recognition of the right of couples to determine the number and spacing of their children and the obligation of the government to make the necessary means available.

SOURCE: AID/PHA/POP

PRB 75-5

held in the United States for home economics students from developing countries—students already in the United States for study purposes. Three institutes in 1972 enrolled 42 students representing 21 countries; in 1973, five institutes enrolled 66 from 26 developing countries. Seventeen countries were represented at one general and two specialized summer institutes in 1974. In 1973 AHEA received a grant from the Asia Foundation to fund Asian graduate students at the summer institutes.

AHEA organized a meeting of an *ad hoc* advisory committee of home economists from developing and developed countries in Helsinki in 1972 and a second meeting in Ankara in 1974. Following recommendations of the second meeting, 35 home economists from 20 countries have been designated as representatives for family planning/population education activities in their own countries, including work with AHEA's international family planning project.

The summer institutes tie in with another function of the project—that of providing educational materials. Two packets of prototype teaching materials have been developed.

Other publications of the project include: *Women's Roles and Education, Resource Papers for Curriculum Development*, and a *Resource Catalog for Family Planning and Population Education in Home Economics.*

AHEA works closely with other organizations. AHEA and IPPF have prepared a 15-minute slide and taped-sound production for home economists and family planning field workers titled *Partners for Change*. An AHEA staff member works regularly with the International Federation of Home Economists (IFHE) at its headquarters in Paris. IFHE, FAO, and AHEA have collaborated in preparing an international plan of action to incorporate population education and family planning in home economics. Liaison is maintained also with UNESCO, WHO, World Education, Asia Foundation, and other organizations concerned with family planning.

A home economist from a developing country attended the World Population Conference in Bucharest under AHEA sponsorship, and an AHEA representative attended the World Conference in Rome. Home economists in developing countries are being encouraged to take part in national and international observances of International Women's Year, and AHEA funded two IFHE representatives to the International Women's Year Conference.

American Public Health Association

The American Public Health Association (APHA), representing some 25,000 members, is broadly concerned with improving public health through community efforts. For over 100 years it has served as a leader in developing technical standards for delivery of public health services, improving the quantity and quality of health manpower, and working with other groups on matters of public policy that affect the public health and welfare. It has made—and is continuing to make—important contributions to population research and family planning in the United States and abroad.

In 1959, APHA adopted a milestone policy statement calling on all health organizations to support population research and encourage development of family planning services for all population groups consistent with their beliefs and desires. Committees were established by the Association to carry out this policy, and numerous related studies and investigations were made of maternal and child health, in epidemiology, in statistics, in public health nursing, and related fields. These early activities led to several national conferences and other meetings at which data were examined, programs reviewed, and plans made for projects relating to population.

The Association followed its 1959 population policy statement by issuing 12 additional statements, resolutions, and program standards between 1964 and 1974. These concerned family planning programs, standards for abortion services, sex education, and related subjects.

APHA has directed and staffed a number of family planning and population projects since 1965. One of the most important was a 5-year project funded by the Ford Foundation in 1966.

One significant result of this 5-year project was the establishment of a process for disseminating information and educational materials on population to public health workers. Another was the publication of several standard-setting documents, including a family planning guide for State and local agencies and a set of standards for abortion services. Between 1966 and 1971, APHA was a major publisher of technical family planning literature.

Other activities stemmed from the project funded by the Ford Foundation. In 1967 the Association assumed responsibility from the Population Council for the continuance of a family planning project with U.S. medical schools. In this project, each of the participating schools developed a plan to better the health of a low-income area through family planning. All plans provided free family planning counseling and services to clients who met established criteria.

In September 1974, under a grant from the Department of Health, Education, and Welfare (HEW), the Association began a detailed study to obtain information on social and psychological factors in adolescent sexual behavior. Health workers have long been concerned about the inadequacy of quantified knowledge on this subject. Working with colleagues, advisors, and teenagers, APHA staff has developed a questionnaire-interview technique to record adolescent attitudes and experiences, personality and cognitive style, life events, motivation, and self-esteem along with social and demographic information. A sample of 2,700 representative 16- and 17-year old males and females is being surveyed in Washington, D.C.; Atlanta, Ga.; and Bellingham, Wash. Adolescents participating in the survey in Washington, D.C., and Bellingham have agreed to a second interview within a year if it is needed. Results and analysis of the study are expected to be available in 1976.

Also in 1974, APHA's continuing interest and leadership in promoting better understanding of the public health implications of population imbalance led to its publication of a comprehensive guide to family planning information sources for health workers.

As part of its educational work in the population field, APHA collaborates with several universities in the United States, including the Universities of California, Washington, and Hawaii and Loma Linda University. It also works with overseas centers to help development and training of manpower. Such examples are the University of West Indies, Mahadol University, and the University of Indonesia. APHA also has assisted schools and colleges in nine developing countries in improving curricula for teaching family planning techniques and population program methodology.

Since 1970, APHA has cooperated with AID in a program to provide professional consultation and technical assistance in population/family planning and health-related fields. Using its own staff and a registry of some 1,000 qualified consultants, the Association has assisted developing countries in planning, implementing, and evaluating programs; in training professional and technical staffs; in preparing and disseminating technical data and educational information; and in integrating family planning into maternal/child health and other services.

Governments of five Latin American countries have asked APHA to study their family planning programs and help establish goals and priorities. The Association also helped plan and conduct four regional seminars on population and family planning

sponsored by the International Alliance of Women.

Advice and consultation have been provided to professional groups throughout the world on the management and utilization of fertility control measures and contraceptive techniques. In the past 5 years, some 200 physicians, nurses, demographers, management specialists, educators, and other professionals have served as short-term consultants in more than 45 developing countries.

One example of this type of assistance is a project initiated in 1971 with the Government of Indonesia. It was designed to increase the number of health education specialists and to involve a major percentage of fertile couples in the national family planning program. A cadre has received in-country training at the undergraduate level, 42 health education specialists have received graduate training in the United States, and a postgraduate program has been established at the University of Indonesia. Health education services have been strengthened at all levels to assure a continuation of support for maternal/child health and family planning programs.

From 1970 through 1974, the Association made a study of the role of voluntary health organizations in developing countries to find ways of increasing citizen and group participation in improving health, family planning, and nutrition services. As a result of demonstration projects in Costa Rica and the Philippines, future plans are directed to expanding and strengthening organized voluntary efforts in support of national health goals.

Since May 1972 the Association has directed a program to assist developing countries plan, establish, and evaluate integrated delivery systems for health, family planning, and nutrition. A procedure has been set up to gather, store, and retrieve information about health delivery systems worldwide; to identify interesting innovations; and to evaluate them and study reasons for their success or failure.

A demonstration project in Thailand—and others currently being planned—will include host-country planning with APHA assistance, involvement of national and community groups, and a focus on integrated services for women 15 to 55 years of age and for children under 5 years. It is anticipated that the demonstrated services can later be carried out and replicated by the host countries without assistance.

APHA collaborates with other organizations—such as the Christian Medical Commission, the Population Council, the Ford Foundation, and The Pathfinder Fund—in international projects. It has worked closely with the World Health Organization and is a sponsor and participant in the National Council on International Health.

American Universities Field Staff

For the past 5 years, 1970-75, the American Universities Field Staff has been engaged jointly with the California Institute of Technology (CIT) in a program studying the consequences of population growth. Launched in 1970, the pilot phase of the program was established to bring together the demographic expertise of selected members of the CIT faculty and area knowledge of the Field Staff Associates. The purpose was to study social and political factors affecting and affected by population problems.

Situated in different parts of the world, Field Staff Associates observe what is happening with respect to population in different developing and developed countries. Pooling their knowledge with that of discipline-oriented scholars of the CIT, they write reports after a process of comment and criticism by all project participants, understandable to the general public. The CIT comments bring into consideration the concern of the economist, demographer, anthropologist, and sociologist.

Field Staff Reports on population have covered many aspects of the problem.

They have included explorations of family planning and the political and religious issues involved, general population reviews discussing population issues in each world area, analyses of the role of multinational political bodies in determining population policy, and studies of the relation of economic development and population pressures.

The result has been over 125 articles and three collections of articles in books: *Population: Perspective, 1971, 1972,* and *1973.*

In addition, annual working conferences have been held. The program's first conference in December 1970 in Pasadena, Calif., dealt generally with the population issue, each field Staff Associate presenting a review of population trends in his area of foreign residence. A second conference in 1971 at the Field Staff's Center for Mediterranean Studies in Rome, Italy, explored relevant problems of migration with special geographical emphasis on sub-Saharan Africa. In January 1973, a third conference dealt with the relations between a society's perception of its population problems and the relevant policies adopted. At the most recent conference, population problems and the food situation in countries around the world were related.

The project has been governed by a steering committee made up of two persons from each of the participating institutions.

Asia Foundation

Following several years of exploratory assistance for population activities, the Asia Foundation in mid-1972 entered into a program of expanded action. (A nonprofit philanthropic institution, the Foundation has been helping Asians and Asian institutions for over 20 years in promoting economic and social progress.) Assistance is mainly for country and institutional improvements in public information, education, and communication on population and family planning matters; but help is also provided in analyses of laws and manpower aspects relating to population policies and programs.

Funding for its activities has been provided by the U.S. Agency for International Development since 1972.

The Foundation encourages and supports programs that fit into national and regional strategies for reaching population/family planning goals. It supports innovative projects and provides resources for exchange and cooperation among Asian population institutions. The Foundation also assists efforts of individual countries in informational education, training in population-related social science research, improving program management, and in spreading public awareness, acceptance, and adoption of fertility-control measures.

The Foundation has resident representatives, or officers-in-charge, in 12 countries.

Those where it now provides direct assistance are Afghanistan, Bangladesh, Hong Kong, Indonesia, Korea, Malaysia, Pakistan, the Republic of the Philippines, the Republic of China (Taiwan), Singapore, and Thailand.

Also, it is exploring ways in which the Japanese population/family planning experience can be helpful to other Asian countries.

Among activities supported by the Foundation are: the Intergovernmental Coordinating Committee in Southeast Asia for Population and Family Planning that assists regional cooperation and exchange, the provision of advisors in population to institutions, and the Asian Broadcasting Training Institute that has workshops for upgrading the planning of radio and television broadcasts.

Association for Voluntary Sterilization

The Association for Voluntary Sterilization (AVS) is a private nonprofit organization in the United States working for voluntary sterilization as a method of family planning and fertility regulation. Its efforts have resulted in substantial gains in the acceptance, availability, and use of voluntary sterilization. In 1974, almost 1½ million Americans elected to be sterilized.

Numerous groups in other countries have turned to AVS for guidance in advancing their voluntary sterilization programs. In response, AVS, with the assistance of AID and funds from private sources, created the International Project (IPAVS) in June 1972 to stimulate and support voluntary sterilization programs around the world. IPAVS provides no direct services; rather, it supports projects through grants to medical and health groups to meet local needs.

Through June 1975, IPAVS had awarded 125 grants totaling $1.9 million to recipients in 24 countries. Its 1972-74 record reflects both increased numbers of grants and an expanding geographic coverage. In 1972, two grants were made; in 1973, 22 grants to 11 countries; and in 1974, 70 grants to 21 countries. Geographic areas receiving assistance have included South America, Central America and the Caribbean, East Asia, and South Asia and the Mideast. Projects have been funded for medical equipment, information and education programs, training paramedical and auxiliary health workers, and medical-scientific conferences. The largest number has been for service and training projects and for medical equipment. Purchase of equipment has amounted to about 40 percent of all funds awarded.

Approximately 22,000 sterilization procedures were performed by IPAVS subgrantees in 1973 and 1974—20,000 female and 2,000 male. About 69 percent of the female acceptors were under 35 years of age compared with 39 percent of male acceptors. During 1974, the largest number of female sterilizations (12,000) was in East Asia and the largest number of vasectomies (1,000) in South America.

A variety of surgical techniques has been used in female sterilizations—laparoscopy, culdoscopy, colpotomy, paparotomy, mini-laparotomy, and postpartum tubal ligation. Laparoscopy accounted for about 40 percent of the female sterilizations.

A significant accomplishment in 1974 was the promotion of mini-laparotomy—a simplified, inexpensive outpatient procedure suitable for programs in both rural and urban settings. The procedure has been widely used in Thailand, where it was perfected, and where rural physicians throughout the country are now being trained for its wider use. In 1974, 578 procedures were performed at an IPAVS-funded program at Ramathibodi Hospital in Bangkok, and hundreds more were performed by Ramathibodi-trained physicians at rural health centers. This procedure is now being used in the Philippines and Colombia and the IPAVS has provided related training to physicians from Bangladesh, Costa Rica, Indonesia, and Korea.

Increased use of this technique in 1975-76 is indicated by the large numbers of requests from governments and physicians throughout the world for training and equipment.

A major IPAVS activity has been physician training. From 1972 through March 1975, 412 physicians were trained in female procedures and 71 in vasectomy. These physicians were from 18 countries, representing all major regions of the developing world except Africa.

Training grants are either major awards to key government or university teaching institutions or small awards for training individual physicans in surgical techniques or in the organizing and planning of voluntary sterilization programs. Since the impact of national training grants is potentially larger, IPAVS has emphasized such projects as a nationwide Philippine program to train 80 physicians. To date, paraprofessional training has been limited to a few programs with Colombia's PROFAMILIA and Guatemala's APROFAM. IPAVS also has provided physicians with orientation trips to other countries to observe various types of service programs.

In 1974, IPAVS funded information and education projects in 14 countries with 62 percent of assistance going to South and East Asia.

The vast majority of these programs, 75 percent, were for patient education and did not extend beyond the confines of a hospital or family planning clinic. Many were coordinated with government family planning and voluntary sterilization services. Others were connected with training and service projects in university, government, or private hospitals. One grant was for a national public education program, and a few were for health personnel education.

Since its Second International Conference in Geneva in 1973, IPAVS has escalated its conference activities. IPAVS sponsored or assisted six conferences in 1974, and directors participated in nine other international meetings. Activity the first half of 1975 included a regional conference in Dacca sponsored by the IPAVS-funded Bangladesh AVS, a regional Asian conference in Taipei, Taiwan, the Korean AVS national conference, and the Egyptian

Fertility Control Society regional conference.

The Second International Conference recommended that IPAVS help groups in various countries develop national voluntary sterilization associations with the ultimate goal of establishing a world federation. To date, IPAVS has funded associations in Bangladesh, Iran, Taiwan, Turkey, Egypt, Indonesia, and Korea. Associations in 15 other countries are in various stages of organization.

The first Developmental Conference on National Associations was held in June 1974. A statement setting forth an Interim Commission was drafted and was signed by health and medical leaders from 16 countries. IPAVS will represent all member associations and affiliates at the international level. It will serve as a forum for the exchange of information, knowledge, and research findings, and it will work toward establishment of nongovernmental organization status with the World Health Organization.

IPAVS is planning a Third International Conference to be held in Tunis in 1976. Emphasis will be on program planning and implementation and management of voluntary sterilization services.

CARE

CARE, Inc. (Cooperative for American Relief Everywhere, Inc.) is well known for its objectives of helping the less fortunate peoples of the world by converting voluntary contributions from Americans and Canadians and the support of host governments into various forms of relief and assistance.

CARE's activities in the family planning field, beginning in 1965, have grown from providing equipment to family planning clinics to carrying out carefully developed multielement projects. The organization does not measure its success in terms of contraceptive delivery or number of acceptors. Its work is through projects that combine education, child nutrition, and family planning.

In Korea, CARE has recently developed and is operating an integrated program combining nutrition supplementation for preschool children with nutrition education and information on family planning for mothers. Up to 15,000 women and 50,000 children will be involved in 1975 and 1976.

In India, CARE's Pre-School Health Services Program in Tamil Nadu began in 1975 and will assist through 1979 in strengthening maternal/child health services of a post partum program. During the first year, 2,500 preschool children and 1,250 mothers were scheduled for special services; by 1979 the number of recipients is expected to triple. Acceptance of family planning is a prerequisite.

CARE has supported population projects in India since 1968 when funds were furnished to print comic books to carry the family planning message. For several years food supplements were provided to patients who underwent sterilization. In 1971 there were more than 63,000 acceptors in a district that had a goal of 20,000.

In 1970, CARE furnished a traveling education unit to the Honduran Family Planning Association. Also, booklets on the use of contraceptives were printed in the Vietnamese language, and other family planning assistance was provided in South Vietnam.

CARE has been involved in family planning programs in Turkey since 1970 and has provided 10 vehicles for mobile teams serving rural and mountain villages. In 1968 family planning demonstration kits were sent to Tunisia, and hospital equipment and instruments were dispatched to a family planning clinic in Hong Kong.

Earlier in the decade CARE provided technical equipment including medical equipment to family planning clinics in Jordan and teaching aids for medical schools in Poland that benefitted 7,000 to 8,000 nurse/midwives and medical students between 1967 and 1970.

CARE's family planning programing in Hong Kong has been in direct support of the Family Planning Association of Hong Kong, a private organization begun in 1936. The Association's main objective is to reduce the high birth rate of Hong Kong through family planning education and by providing services—including the provision of contraceptive devices. It also offers advice to infertile couples and has programs in family life education and related social work. The Family Planning Association operates 54 clinics in Hong Kong, two of which CARE helped to establish. In addition, CARE has provided furnishings, equipment, instruments, and fixtures for a number of other Association clinics.

Church World Service

The planned parenthood program of Church World Service (PPP/CWS) began its work in 1965 with a small staff and limited budget. Since then the program has expanded each year with generous support from church denominations and individual donors.

Within a decade the program has become worldwide in scope and is carried on primarily through church-supported hospitals and organizations. Clinics and doctors receive equipment and supplies. Contacts in additional countries are provided with information and educational materials. In rural areas and remote mountain communities, mobile family planning teams bring medical services and information to otherwise inaccessible people.

In early 1975 the largest country program of CWS was in Indonesia. This family planning project started in 1969 with the cooperation of 50 physicians and included development of educational materials for both the Christians and the Moslems of Indonesia.

Previously, the largest program was in India, where in 1966, the planned parenthood program of CWS began financing a major portion of the family planning project of the Christian Medical Association. Less than a year afterward, more than 100 hospitals had joined the program, and by 1969 over 450 church-related hospitals and clinics were being served. This project is receiving grants from various donors—mainly from abroad. But with 261 member Mission hospitals spread through India, additional funding support became necessary during 1975. Church World Service has moved to meet this need with further assistance so that the India project has once again become the largest country program.

Another major program is in Brazil, where opposition to family planning was once strong. Working with concerned church and medical people, particularly DIACONIA and the Hospital-Escola S. Francisco de Assisi, CWS has helped promote a change in attitude. The Government has now adopted the view that every couple should have the right to receive family planning information and services.

Several pilot programs in leadership training were initiated in the Philippines in 1974 through churches, church-related institutions, and cottage industries. Also, the Coptic Evangelical Organization for Social Services in Egypt has been given a 2-year commitment recently to make family planning a part of its self-help program, and a 3-year leadership training program has been launched in the West Indies.

New programs being developed will emphasize multidisciplinary action—literacy, agriculture, nutrition, maternal/child health, and family planning. The first project now being planned with these elements is a joint one in Venezuela with CWS and Agricultural Missions to support a husband-and-wife team trained in agriculture and public health.

The CWS program has worked in partnership since 1971 with Family Planning International Assistance (FPIA)—the international division of the Planned Parenthood Federation of America. FPIA now handles all shipping of medical and other equipment, contraceptives, and information and educational materials for the overall activity. A fulltime multidisciplinary team of family planning specialists is available to provide on-the-spot expertise.

The number of countries benefitting has increased steadily during the decade. In the first year of the program, approximately 200 church-related doctors in 39 countries in Africa, Asia, Latin America, and the Middle East were furnished information and supplies of intrauterine contraceptives. Ten shipments of contraceptive aerosol foam were made to seven countries that year, and more than 19,000 family planning leaflets were distributed to contacts in 66 countries. One year later, PPP/CWS was supplying information and contraceptives to more than 300 doctors in 46 countries and had contacts in 88 countries. Limited grants were made to clinics in Brazil, Jordan, and Mexico and special assistance went to projects in Haiti, Bolivia, Ghana, Peru, and the Philippines.

By 1968 the value of materials and literature supplied during the year was $1.3 million, and the program had established contact with over 1,000 Christian-supported hospitals in 81 countries. Specific projects had been added in India, Indonesia, Korea, Taiwan, Hong Kong, the Ryukus, and the West Indies.

Along with partnership with FPIA and grant arrangements with the U.S. Agency for International Development, 1971 saw other major developments. An invitation from Chile's Minister of Health to participate in a conference on maternal/child health and family planning was an early step in Chile's becoming the first country in Latin America to establish a national population program. CWS programs also began to be more effective in other countries, such as the Dominican Republic and Costa Rica. By 1972, Colombia had the world's largest vasectomy clinic.

With FPIA assistance, CWS programs were expanded in Peru and Bolivia in 1973. Program activity increased in Africa with assistance going to Ghana, Kenya, Nigeria, Uganda, Zaire, Zambia, Burundi, and Tanzania. FPIA/CWS support also was extended to Thailand, Laos, Malaysia, Singapore, Nepal, Bangladesh, and Israel.

East-West Communication Institute

The Communication Institute of the East-West Center, one of the Center's five problem-oriented institutes, since 1970 has been contributing importantly to improvement of the public information, education, and communication (IEC) elements of population and family planning programs. The East-West Center was established in 1960 by the U.S. Congress to promote better understanding and relations between the United States and nations in Asia and the Pacific through cooperative study, training, and research. The Communication Institute's work in the population field is part of its broad program for improvement in IEC support for development programs in general.

In the population field, the Institute has been developing a comprehensive resource to serve the needs of population programs and their IEC personnel. The Institute draws upon the experience of other types of development communication as well as that for population programs. It provides specialized training in IEC support for family planning programs, conducts collaborative research, maintains a major collection of IEC materials for analysis and inter-country exchange, carries out information-sharing and utilization work, hosts international conferences on population communication and education, and provides support for internships for degree and non-degree study. Its population IEC work has been funded primarily through a grant from the U.S. Agency for International Development (AID). Organizations in addition to AID that have provided financial support for Institute activities include the Ford Foundation, The Pathfinder Fund, the United Nations Educational, Scientific, and Cultural Organization (UNESCO), the Asia Foundation, the United Nations Children's Fund (UNICEF) and the Food and Agriculture Organization (FAO), the Population Council, the United Nations Center for Economic and Social Information, the United Nations Fund for Population Activities, and World Education.

The Institute maintains collaborative relationships with a number of other institutions, including those of developing countries. Close at hand are the East-West Population Institute and the University of Hawaii's School of Public Health.

The Institute also cooperates with the International Planned Parenthood Federation (IPPF), UNESCO, The United Nations Economic and Social Commission, Asia and the Pacific, the Ford Foundation, the Asia Foundation, and the Inter-Government Coordinating Committee in Kaula Lampur.

Although the primary focus of the East-West Center is Asia and the Pacific, the Institute from 1971 through 1975 established regular contacts with IEC personnel in 127 countries. Beginning with a pilot workshop in 1971, 20 different workshops, conferences, and seminars involving a total of 349 people from 42 countries have been held.

The current Modular Professional Development Program is the major training activity conducted by the Institute. The modular program is based on learning materials developed collaboratively by Asian and American IEC experts. The first modular program held in the spring of 1974 consisted of 15 individual modules. Following the third modular program in the fall of 1975, the Institute's work in professional training for family planning communicators entered a new phase. In place of full-length workshops at Honolulu, the program now emphasizes collaboration with Asian, Pacific, and American institutions in country/locality adaptations and use of modular materials.

Each year, in December, the Institute has conducted a 1-week conference on major issues in population IEC for program administrators, practitioners, and scholars from Asia and the United States.

Institute research activities are organized under three subdivisions—International Communication, Developmental Communication, and Popular Culture.

A direct contribution to the research program activity has been a series of case studies of innovative approaches in family and population planning communication problems. Since the initiation of the program in 1971, 11 case studies have been undertaken on topics such as: the use of mothers' clubs to spread family planning information in rural Korea; the use of traditional midwives as communication operatives; strategies for increasing elite support for family planning in Kenya; a comparison of themes, slogans, and nonverbal symbols used for family planning communication; family planning communication in the People's Republic of China; and the uses of commercial resources.

Family Planning International Assistance

Family Planning International Assistance (FPIA) was organized in 1971 as the international division of the Planned Parenthood Federation of America (PPFA). Its purpose is to provide assistance to governmental and nongovernmental agencies and institutions (including church-related ones) in developing countries to enable them to conduct and expand family planning programs. It receives funds from the U.S. Agency for International Development, Church World Service, and other donors as well as from PPFA.

Since its establishment, FPIA has made grants for more than 90 projects in 23 developing countries for a total of $5.3 million. In its first year of operation (1971-72), FPIA funded 27 projects at a cost of $657,000. Obligations in the 1974-75 program year were $2.1 million, 21 percent over the previous year. During the 4 years since 1971, 34 percent of the expenditures have been for projects in Latin America;

30 percent, East Asia; 13 percent, Africa; 5 percent, West Asia; and 18 percent, interregional.

FPIA puts high priority on projects that can lead to the development of other projects in the same country or serve as models for projects elsewhere. For example, an FPIA-funded voluntary sterilization project in the Philippines—the first in that country— encouraged several other agencies to establish similar programs.

Continuing another innovation, FPIA in 1974-75 responded to opportunities to assist agencies of the Catholic Church in responsible parenthood programs. To date, $1.6 million has been obligated for such programs. In Peru, FPIA is working with two Catholic lay groups to operate 48 clinics in urban slum areas and coastal cities. The program is supported by the Church and local priests. Similar projects are planned or underway in other countries including Costa Rica, Colombia, Mauritius, and the Philippines.

Another FPIA objective is developing effective low-cost, high-benefit family planning programs to make contraceptives readily available. With this end in view, FPIA will fund 26 service projects for a total of $1.1 million in the current program year, or more than triple its first year's expenditures. An example of this type of project is the Iglesia Ni Cristo Mobile Family Planning Clinic in the Philippines, which began as a small FPIA-funded demonstration project. It has become a nationwide operation serving more than 100,000 clients. Currently, it is enrolling about one-fourth of all family planning acceptors in the country. Another example is FPIA's support of the Korean National Council of Churches, which is using a cadre of church women to distribute oral contraceptives door to door and is conducting an educational campaign to recruit IUD acceptors.

Besides making direct project grants, FPIA provides contraceptives, medical equipment and supplies, and educational materials. In calendar year 1974, commodities valued at about $800,000 were shipped to more than 23 institutions in 53 countries.

FPIA has identified more than 1,000 church-related hospitals, clinics, dispensaries, and other private groups engaged in family planning services. During its first 3 years, FPIA has become the largest single source of contraceptives and other family planning supplies to this network, which aided an estimated 500,000 users in calendar 1974.

Support for training programs is an integral part of FPIA's activities. An African program, for example, is a collaborative effort with the Family Guidance Association to establish a training program in Ethiopia for nurses and public health officers. This is an important breakthrough in providing family planning services in rural areas. Since 1971, FPIA has provided training for 7,000 family planning personnel.

During its first 4 years, FPIA has funded 41 information, education, and communication projects for a total of $1.9 million. Fifteen projects received a total of $558,000 of support in 1974-75 with the largest share (26 percent) designated for Africa. An example of the work being done in this field is the development of daily radio programs, pamphlets, and a film for use in the Philippines and in East Asia. Also, a series of family planning communications workshops were held in East Asia and Latin America, and another is planned to bring together Christian and Muslim leaders in the Middle East.

Since 1971, FPIA has helped to produce 1.5 million copies of 175 different family planning pamphlets, to broadcast 3,500 family planning radio programs, to provide family planning counseling for more than 400,000 people with another 700,000 attending family planning lectures, and to distribute 291,000 posters and 260,000 books. A quarterly newsletter was started in 1975 to disseminate information about project activities and to encourage replication of successful projects.

Finally, FPIA established regional offices in Africa (Ghana), East Asia (Philippines), and Latin America (Costa Rica) during the 1974-75 year and is planning to open another in West Asia.

Ford Foundation

Since 1952 the Ford Foundation has devoted almost $200 million to work directed to world population problems with the overall purpose of helping to reduce the rapid rate of world population increase. It is convinced that progress in limiting population growth is a necessary condition, especially in developing nations, for attaining economic and social progress and improving the quality of life.

In pursuing this purpose, it takes into account the wide diversity of conditions existing from country to country—needs and requests for assistance, the impact of population growth on national development efforts, the acceptability of population planning, and country capacities for population analysis and action. Thus, it has no blueprint for population work but instead adapts its activities to circumstances in different parts of the world.

Since population change cuts across the knowledge and interest areas of a variety of disciplines and professions, the Foundation is involved in programs of substantive as well as geographic diversity. Its strategy involves pursuing five related objectives:

The Ford Foundation's Total Commitments in Population Activities by Region and Country Through Fiscal Year 1974

Country or region	Commitments in dollars
Asia and the Pacific	
Bangladesh	421,824
Formosa	42,619
Hong Kong	54,450
India	10,583,699
Indonesia	990,260
Japan[1]	14,987
Malaysia	681,000
Pakistan	4,224,373
Philippines	1,064,134
Singapore	191,898
Sri Lanka	153,116
Thailand	129,287
South Central Asia	75,000
Southeast Asia	877,000
Asia	94,000
Total	$19,597,647
Middle East and Africa	
Algeria	347,480
Arab Republic of Egypt	1,363,205
Ghana	210,000
Israel[1]	2,160,000
Kenya	76,000
Morocco	565,625
Nigeria	593,257
Tunisia	727,025
Turkey	915,500
Middle East	428,446
Eastern Africa	241,500
North Africa	202,625
Western Africa	924,000
Africa	188,726
Total	$8,943,389

Country or region	Commitments in dollars
Latin America and the Caribbean	
Argentina	134,800
Barbados	69,000
Bolivia	7,500
Brazil	3,951,805
Chile	572,858
Colombia	1,240,384
Costa Rica	446,000
Ecuador	35,725
Haiti	70,000
Mexico	2,715,677
Peru	505,000
Venezuela	454,700
Central America	236,000
West Indies and Caribbean	69,999
Latin America and Mexico	3,401,983
Total	13,910,432

[1] Considered by the Ford Foundation to be developed.

• increasing awareness of the facts of population growth and their implications for human welfare and expanding and strengthening the commitment to deal with population growth as a major problem.

• expanding, improving, and evaluating the systems through which birth control technology becomes known and used.

• developing more satisfactory birth control methods.

• focusing social science and management competence on problems of lowering fertility.

• encouraging study of the interrelationship between economic and social policy and growth and distribution.

It has been a major force in three general areas of population work:

• assistance to population programs in developing countries.

• research and training in reproductive biology.

• establishment of university population studies centers in the United States.

Most of the Foundation's work in these fields is initiated and carried out by its International Division through the Population Office in New York and 16 field offices in Asia, the Middle East and Africa, and Latin America. The Population Office both supports institutions in the United States and the developed world and—an important activity—provides advisory services to the Foundation's field offices.

Growth of population activities. The Foundation's population commitments have grown to substantial magnitude over the past 10 years, after beginning modestly in 1952 with a $60,000 grant to the Population Reference Bureau, Inc. The program expanded into the international arena in 1959 with a $350,000 grant to the Government of India. Since then, directly or indirectly through the Population Council or other grant recipients, the Foundation has supported family planning activities in more than 30 countries in the developing world.

Its total support for population activities from 1952 through 1963, including $8.3 million in 1963, was $20.8 million. In subsequent years, with the growth of world and country concern for population problems, annual commitments have ranged between $10.7 million and $26.8 million. This funding includes assistance for regional as well as country programs in Asia and the Pacific areas, the Middle East and Africa, and Latin America and the Caribbean areas.

Through 1974, almost $20 million had been committed to population activities in the developing countries of Asia and the Pacific. Half of this total has gone to India. In addition, about $7 million had been channeled to countries in the Middle East and Africa plus $2 million to Israel (which the Foundation considers a developed country). Latin America and the Caribbean received almost $14 million for population activities. For a more detailed breakdown of expenditures see the table, p. 241. In addition to the above, substantial support has been extended to research and training institutions in the United States, Europe, Japan, and Australia whose work is related to the developing regions.

In Asia and Africa the Foundation's work has been directed primarily toward assisting family planning action programs with supplementary assistance to training and research. In Latin America where, until recently, efforts to reduce national birth rates were not a customary part of public policy, the Foundation's emphasis has been on the study of population problems and on reproductive biology.

Since 1959, the Foundation has committed over $90 million—approaching half of its total devoted to the population field—to support fundamental research and training in reproductive biology and to broaden knowledge upon which to build improved contraceptive technology. This work has been carried out principally in university-based laboratories and clinics, mostly in the industrialized world. But increasing emphasis is now being placed on research and training programs in the developing world. In this field, the Foundation has provided assistance to 74 institutions in the United States and Europe, 21 in Asia, 13 in Latin America, and 7 in the Middle East, including Israel.

Grants totaling more than $22 million have gone to some 15 university centers in the United States, each with a different pattern of specialization in the social sciences, demography, and population planning. As a result, more demographers are now involved in the design and evaluation of family planning programs; schools of public health have developed curriculums for training family planning administrators; and behavioral scientists are working to solve problems of education and communications for family planning and in understanding factors in the social and cultural environments that affect fertility. Much of the Foundation's support to U.S. population centers has been directed toward research on the causes and consequences of population growth in the developing world and toward training individuals for responsible positions in national family planning programs.

The next 5 years. Ford Foundation budgets for work in the population field as for other fields are being reduced at present, but population will continue to have a high priority. The Foundation has budgeted $12.7 million for it in 1975 and $11.5 million in 1976. The 1972 total was $14.7 million.

The overriding theme of the World Population Conference at Bucharest was the role of population change as an integral part of development, thus reinforcing the Foundation's decision to give priority attention to matters in this sphere. The Bucharest Conference also indicated the increasing willingness on the part of governments throughout the world to provide family planning information and services, whether as an instrument to improve the health and welfare of the mother and child or as a part of an effort to lower national rates of population growth for the benefit of the country. This concern is reflected in the Foundation's continuing efforts to encourage research aimed at improving contraception as well as making family planning programs more effective through improved management and better information and education programs.

Under current plans, the Foundation's population activities during the next 5 years are expected to take the following shape.

Funding for reproductive science and contraceptive development will be reduced from the $6 to $7 million annually of the past few years to $2 to $3 million per year. Increasing priority will be given to overseas programs, where access to financial support is more limited than in the United States. Effort will be made to stimulate local financing in such countries as Japan and Australia, to emphasize innovative approaches to fundamental research on an interdisciplinary basis, to attract young scientists into the field, and to help provide guidance to the field through activities such as the Review of Reproductive Biology and Contraceptive Development which is being carried out jointly by the Ford Foundation, the Rockefeller Foundation, and the International Development Research Center.

To improve the effectiveness of systems for contraceptive delivery and information and education, the Foundation is particularly interested in the possibility of linkage between indigenous management institutions in family planning programs and the management resources of industralized countries. Management interests also include the planning, administration, and evaluation of information and educational programs and the development of ways to combine maternal and child health services with nutrition and family planning education. Annual budgets for this major area of interest are projected at $1 million.

Social science research is expected to receive increased emphasis, especially with regard to relationships between population change and economic and social variables. This includes prepolicy research as well as analysis of the policy-making process and evaluation of policy implementation. As in the field of reproductive biology, the Foundation expects to place major emphasis on encouraging the development of capacity for research and linkages to policy in the developing world. Three examples of programs currently being supported by the Foundation along these lines are: the Ford Foundation-Rockefeller Foundation program of awards for social science and legal research related to population policy; the regional program of social research on problems relevant to population policy in Latin America (PISPAL); and the southeast Asia population research awards program (SEAPRAP).

Emphasis also will be given to the "population growth-distribution-development nexus" with attention to such problems as marriage age, status and roles of women, infant mortality, incentive schemes, social security schemes, income distribution, family structure, divorce, community structure, education, and literacy.

Finally, the Foundation feels that important opportunities remain for collaborative efforts between it and other agencies, and it will continue to encourage joint funding with other donors for large multicountry activities.

General Service Foundation

The General Service Foundation has provided support since 1965 for selected educational and research activities in the population/family planning field, including public education regarding the social and personal impacts of population growth and change. Through calendar 1974 its grants in this field, for both national and international projects, have totaled over $1.5 million. Included are projects in sex education, leader education, population education, information and education, research, family planning assistance, program training, legal aspects of population matters, and provision of counseling services.

International Confederation of Midwives

The International Confederation of Midwives (ICM) initiated a program in 1972 to encourage and help midwives around the world to supply family planning information and services for their clients and local groups as part of their basic work for maternal and child health. Since then, the ICM has been conducting a series of regional programs for midwifery leaders from nearly all developing countries. Funding is provided through a grant from the U.S. Agency for International Development.

International Planned Parenthood Federation

The International Planned Parenthood Federation (IPPF), with its network of family planning associations in individual countries, has long played a major and uniquely important part in the world spread of family planning and awareness of population problems. In the last decade its role in family planning education and in the provision of technical services and supplies has expanded dramatically— between 1965 and 1975 the number of member associations rose from 40 to 84. Also, groups in 17 additional countries were working toward membership in 1975.

From its inception, IPPF has, in effect, been a women's rights organization staunchly upholding a woman's basic right to determine the number and spacing of her children. It has also campaigned for the right of parents to family planning information and services to be recognized universally as a basic right.

Organization

Much of IPPF's strength comes from the fact that member associations are indigenous national organizations. Each is self-governing, working in its own cultural and political environment to meet the needs of its own people while carrying out basic aims of promoting family planning and disseminating knowledge of the consequences of rapid population growth.

Through the individual country associations, thousands of clinics are being operated and millions of people in all regions of the world are receiving family planning information, services, and supplies. Many hundreds of volunteers and staff workers are going into schools, factories, community centers, and isolated rural areas to reach additional thousands.

In well over 100 countries some form of family

planning program, either government- or non-government-sponsored, has been established or is underway. More than 60 countries have national population commissions, and more than 40 have announced official policies on population growth. In almost all of these countries, the pioneering activities of their own family planning associations, assisted by IPPF, were the forerunners to development of the government programs. Many governments now include family planning or child spacing as part of their public health or maternal/child health programs. Such projects receive strong IPPF support and are particularly important in countries where large families have traditionally been desirable.

Through its central office in London and six regional offices, the IPPF is a supportive and uniting body for all these activities. It helps individuals and groups organize family planning associations and gain public understanding and political support; and it provides them with financial assistance, technical advice, supplies, and education and information services to enable them to become more competent in planning, programming, budgeting, and reporting. As part of its services to member associations, IPPF arranges for field visits, seminars, and workshops and trains more than 25,000 workers a year.

Cooperation With Others

Close cooperation is maintained with other voluntary agencies such as the International Council of Women, Associated Country Women of the World, International YWCA, Girl Guides, World Assembly of Youth, and International Cooperative Alliance as well as with trade unions, professional associations, and many health and welfare groups.

IPPF has given special consideration during the last 3 years to integration of family planning into other efforts to raise living standards and particularly into rural development. This is done primarily by working closely with other groups. In the Philippines, the family planning association cooperates with government departments in an annual educational motivation campaign; more than half a million people attended over 7,000 meetings in Indonesia under a community education project; and the family planning association in Korea serves 400,000 members of 20,000 Mothers Clubs. An IPPF Centre for African Family Studies, based on an international agricultural extension college in Kenya, is launching a program for the training of agricultural extension workers throughout Africa in community development and family planning communication. The Allahabad project in India and the Shadab project in Pakistan are two extensive demonstrations of family planning becoming an integral part of community development in largely rural areas.

IPPF has developed an expanding work relationship with the United Nations and its specialized groups. The Economic and Social Council (ECOSOC) has granted IPPF Category I status, up from the consultative status granted in 1964 and Category II status in 1969. IPPF is on the technical panel of the United Nations Fund for Population Activities (UNFPA), has acted as its agent in handling grants for some countries, and has cooperated with it in raising funds from governments. Consultative status is maintained with the World Health Organization (WHO), the United Nations Children's Fund (UNICEF); the United Nations Education, Scientific, and Cultural Organization (UNESCO); the Food and Agriculture Organization (FAO); and the International Labour Organisation (ILO). Programs are carried on in collaboration with several of these agencies.

The International Audio-Visual Resource Service, funded by the United Nations Fund for Population Activities (UNFPA) and jointly run by UNESCO and IPPF, was set up late in 1974 to help government agencies and organizations and family planning associations to make the best possible use in their programs of the growing wealth of audiovisual materials around the world.

World Population Year

High priority was given by IPPF to cooperation with the United Nations on World Population Year. Member associations sponsored or participated in a great range of special activities with information and support from the central and regional offices. Many volunteers from the member associations were included in the national government delegations to the 1974 World Population Conference in Bucharest, which itself reflected growing international acceptance of IPPF aims and programs and a marked change in attitudes toward family planning in the last decade.

IPPF ran a daily newspaper, *Planet,* throughout the Bucharest meetings. The paper served to point to the issues and clarify the simultaneous debates in the various commissions of the governmental conference and in the sessions of the NGO Tribune.

In its 9-point position paper presented at the Conference, IPPF strongly backed a target date of 1985 to bring family planning education and services to 2.5 billion men and women in their fertile years. While this was not included in the World Plan of Action as a goal for governments, there was no doubt that delegates believed it should remain the objective of the private sector and that each government should be encouraged to fix a target that would be realistic in terms of its own needs and resources.

This is a continuation of the forward movement demonstrated at the United Nations Human Rights Conference in Teheran in 1968 when 84 nations passed, without dissent, a resolution strongly supported by IPPF stating that couples have a basic human right to decide on the number and spacing of their children. And it is a decided change since the 1965 World Population Conference in Belgrade when IPPF was one of two nongovernmental sponsors and considered it a significant accomplishment that family planning was included in the agenda and one session dealt with contraceptive methods.

Contributions

IPPF's eminent position in the family planning field is evidenced also in the sources and amounts of the contributions it receives. For IPPF's first decade, beginning in 1952, funds were woefully short, coming mainly from private donors in the United States and the United Kingdom. In 1965 support was beginning to come in also from governments, and IPPF was able to budget $895,000 (compared with $30,000 in 1961). As interest and support increased, expenditure levels reached $14.3 million in 1970; $33.7 million in 1973; and the estimated cost of programs for 1975 was $46.7 million, with about $30 million of this in grants to the Federation from governments and the remainder being contributions by governments or local authorities to those associations which are also funded by the Federation.

Funds are used to support and maintain existing organizations and services in needy countries, to assist the development of promising new organizations, and to stimulate innovations. The central office engaged in 89 separate projects in 1974, each in response to an identified need. Financial support was provided to 65 member associations and to 20 others in countries without member associations. The central office also distributed $5 million worth of contraceptives through its affiliates.

The number of donor countries, as well as amounts given, has grown steadily. Sweden in 1965 was the first country to make an official grant. It was followed shortly by the United States, Japan, Great Britain, Denmark, and Norway. In 1974, 23 countries made direct financial contributions, including 10 developing nations. IPPF hopes to have 50 contributing countries by 1976, with 20 from the ranks of the developing nations.

U.S. Government grants to IPPF, channeled through the Agency for International Development, began with $121,000 in 1966, increased to $4 million

in 1968, and had reached $12.4 million in 1974.

Assisted countries are making noteworthy contributions of funds, goods, and services. For instance, especially substantial financial support has been provided to their own associations by the Governments of India, Pakistan, Korea, the Philippines, and Ghana. Many provide space and facilities for clinics. The Family Planning Association of Venezuela, for example, which was just getting underway in 1966, was by the end of 1974 operating 136 clinics, 132 of them in Government premises. In Kenya, where a clinical program was started in 1968, IPPF and the Government have a cooperative project which sends seven mobile teams into rural areas and which will be taken over entirely by the Government in 1976.

Substantial support comes from private organizations and foundations. Oxfam was one of the earliest donors (1965), and the Victor Fund gave great impetus to such contributions the same year with a pledge of $3 million to be spread over 3 years. IPPF estimates $2.2 million will be received from such sources in 1975.

Member associations are encouraged to conduct their own fund-raising activities and where possible to contribute to central funds. The Family Planning International Campaign in England was launched in 1963, the forerunner of many successful campaigns in other countries, such as Canada. The 189 affiliates in the United States hoped to raise $120 million in 1975, part of which would support the international movement.

Through the years IPPF has expanded its services to cover far more than assistance to its member associations. It makes grants to universities and individuals for family planning research in the fields of biology and sociology and supports studies in contraceptive methods and problems of fertility. Many training courses to prepare medical and paramedical personnel for family planning activities are conducted or underwritten.

Conferences

International and regional conferences are another important activity. IPPF has sponsored nine international conferences; and numerous regional meetings serve to diffuse knowledge and experience. In 1971, the Middle East and North African regional office brought together 80 Muslim specialists and scholars from 24 countries to consider the religious implications of family planning. Their two-volume study, published in Arabic and English, represents one of the major sociological documents produced in the Islamic world in recent times. The scholars, from countries as far apart as Morocco and Indonesia, concluded that Islamic teaching permits family planning and the use of contraceptives—a major breakthrough toward realizing IPPF's goals in that part of the world.

The International Conference in Brighton, England, in October 1973, commemorated IPPF's 21st anniversary and was called to consider its role in the next decade. As a preliminary to this meeting, IPPF conducted a survey of unmet needs in family planning in 209 countries. Results showed that while 31 percent of couples use some method of contraception, only about a quarter of the world's population has adequate access to family planning information and supplies.

Following the Anniversary Conference, the IPPF Governing Body formulated guidelines and objectives for 1974-76. It will seek to:
• Increase the awareness of peoples and governments about the human rights implications of population growth on family health and welfare and its national and global impact.
• Improve and expand family planning services with emphasis on effective distribution of contraceptives.
• Promote family life and planning courses in schools and for out-of-school youths and adults.
• Undertake or stimulate action-oriented research in biomedical and social sciences.
• Increase systematic evaluation of Federation activities.
• Promote activities to broaden IPPF's membership base, especially among young people.
• Make special efforts to expand rural area programs.
• Upgrade volunteer and staff training and skills.
• Increase efforts to obtain support from all sources.
• Develop information, education, communication, and motivation techniques to achieve these goals.

Rural Areas, Youth

Programs are already underway to implement many of these objectives. IPPF is intensifying its efforts to reach the millions of people in rural areas who have no access to family planning education. In Latin America, 50 to 70 percent of the population is classified as rural; 80 to 90 percent in Africa; and 70 to 80 percent in Asia. India is pioneering a broad education program in rural areas. The Dominican Republic, Sri Lanka, Honduras, Pakistan, and Lesotho are among other countries developing similar programs. In the Dominican Republic and other countries, radio is being successfully used to reach rural communities and to stimulate a demand for provision of government services.

IPPF's newly instituted program of community-based distribution of contraceptives is expected to be especially effective in rural areas. Distribution will be through a variety of commercial and noncommercial channels with shopkeepers, teachers, housewives, and community leaders being recruited to act as suppliers and to supplement the work of auxiliary health personnel. Successful pilot projects in Colombia, Sri Lanka, Thailand, and Brazil are serving as models for a dozen other countries. UNFPA, the Population Council, and several other agencies have joined IPPF in designing and launching this major new effort to make family planning a practical possibility for rural millions.

Associated with this approach had been the recruitment and training of paramedical personnel. Midwives, nurses, health auxiliaries, and traditional birth attendants are being brought into pilot projects.

Associations are being urged to involve more youth in education and motivation activities and in leadership roles. Sex education programs for both in-school and out-of-school youth are being strengthened in an effort to reach young people before their reproductive years. Many associations in Latin America and the Middle East, for instance, are working with their governments to introduce sex education in school curriculums.

A special contingency fund of $100,000 has been approved by IPPF for youth activity expansion in 1975, building on a youth workshop held in Singapore in May 1973 at which nine associations elaborated projects for their countries. A youth leaders' consultation workshop on population education and family planning programs later brought together 56 young leaders from 28 Philippine family planning organizations; and at the end of 1974 another youth workshop was held in Nepal to stimulate activities and involvement in Pakistan, Ceylon, Bangladesh, India, Iran, and Nepal.

Association volunteers and regional and central staff met early in 1975 with outside experts to study a 1973 survey of training needs and activities within IPPF and to map out the first steps towards designing a strategy for a major effort in training generally and in management development in particular. This effort is being allotted top priority for the Federation as a whole. Member associations also regularly turn to IPPF for motivational and educational materials, and these are subject to continuing review, renewal, and addition. A fieldworkers' kit containing slides, film strips, and printed matter was tested in 1974 and was scheduled to be used widely in 1975.

Dissemination of information to bring about an awareness of population problems and create an understanding of the necessity for family planning is a fundmental service of IPPF. The library and information center in London (with 6,000 volumes) is a major world resource on all aspects of family planning and of population education. Audiovisual as well as printed materials are made available to researchers, students, and program planners and managers. A regular flow of technical handbooks and other aids is maintained for workers in specific family planning and population fields.

Publications

Crucial to the success of IPPF member associations in their own countries is the ability of IPPF as a whole to influence opinion leaders and, through them, governments, the United Nations agencies, and other international and national organizations. The central office has always maintained an active publications program and adapted its output to the needs of the time. Rapid success has been achieved by the quarterly magazine *People,* launched for the opening of the World Population Year. The periodical aims to provide decision makers and other persons of influence with a regular flow of lively information on developments and ideas in the family planning and population fields. Like most other IPPF publications, *People* is produced in English, Spanish, and French. Other influential quarterly publications are the *Medical Bulletin* and *Research in Reproduction. IPPF News*, produced in Arabic and Portuguese as well as the three basic languages, provides a monthly news flow for volunteers and staff throughout the Federation and many thousands of other workers in the family planning movement.

Some Background

While this report deals primarily with highlights of the last 10 years, IPPF's work in the field of family planning actually goes back 23 years. Founded in 1952 in Bombay, it was the outgrowth of small, national, planned parenthood groups that had struggled in a hostile climate for many years. By 1922, Mrs. Margaret Sanger—an outspoken champion of women's liberation—was working with a planned parenthood group in the United States and was in close contact with similar groups in other countries. IPPF came into being largely through the efforts of some of these early believers in women's rights.

Today IPPF is the largest voluntary family planning organization in the world. Full membership is limited to one nongovernmental family planning association in each country; associate and affiliate memberships are also accepted. Member associations name representatives to the six regional councils—Africa, Europe, Indian Ocean, Middle East and North Africa, East and South East Asia and Oceania, and Western Hemisphere. These councils choose delegates to sit on IPPF's supreme policy group, the Governing Body. These representatives from different cultures and associations in different stages of development work together to promote IPPF's goal, stated in its constitution, "to advance the education of the countries of the world in family planning and responsible parenthood in the interests of family welfare, community wellbeing and international goodwill."

Western Hemisphere Region. Headquartered in New York City, IPPF's Western Hemisphere Region (IPPF/WHR) has been developing and supporting family planning in Latin America, the Caribbean, and northern America for over 20 years. The past 10 years have seen the movement sweep through the region, bringing affiliated family planning associations to all except two countries—Cuba and Haiti—and attracting nearly 2.9 million acceptors of family planning by the end of 1974. These years also brought immense increase in the region's program resources—from a budget in calendar year 1965 of $196,000 to the 1974 level of $8.59 million in funds and $4.3 million in commodities for distribution.

The country associations in the Western Hemisphere organize their programs around family planning clinics, generally founded and operated in Latin America by doctors and in the Caribbean by volunteers from all walks of life. The number of clinics reached a peak in 1972 of about 750. These serviced 3.5 million visits by clients in that year, of which almost 500,000 were first visits. The number of association clinics has decreased to about 500 in 1975 largely because more governments are now providing family planning services.

In the past 5 years, IPPF's affiliates have begun operations in rural Latin America and in the Caribbean. The first rural effort was by the Colombian association PROFAMILIA; it set a pattern that has come to be known as community-based distribution. In the past 3½ years, PROFAMILIA's program has set up 370 distribution points serving 12,000 acceptors in a low-cost system enjoying exceptionally high continuation rates. This success has led to a transfer of the community-based distribution techniques to urban slums, beginning with Bogotá in 1973. Costa Rica, the Dominican Republic, and Brazil are among the other countries with programs bringing family planning to rural areas via mobile units, radio programs, and special training courses.

This broad trend toward bringing services directly to potential acceptors came to be supplemented by other innovations and new attitudes as the 1970's advanced. These include a much wider use of paramedical personnel, renewed emphasis on postpartum/postabortion programs, and establishment of the first voluntary sterilization program in Latin America.

From the outset, the associations were challenged to find ways of telling the public that family planning services are available and beneficial. And by 1970, information and education units had been established throughout the Western Hemisphere region and all but a very few associations were making use of mass media. In 1975 the Center for the Training of Latin American Communicators in Family Planning had graduated four classes of about 40 students, each from courses lasting 10 weeks.

W. K. Kellogg Foundation

As part of its broader program, the W. K. Kellogg Foundation has provided financial support over the past decade to organizations active in the fields of family planning and population education.

Grants to the Alan Guttmacher Institute, formerly the Center for Family Planning Program Development, totaled $1,850,000 for fiscal years 1968-69 through 1974-75. Funds provided for the first 6 years of this period were to support the Institute's overall activities in the field of family planning/population education. For 1974-75, the grant was for a project to increase the availability of family planning services in rural areas of the United States. An additional $325,000 has been budgeted for this purpose through 1977.

From 1966 through 1975, the Foundation granted $700,000 to the International Planned Parenthood Federation (IPPF) to be used for information and education programs in its Western Hemisphere region. Its funding for 1974 and 1975 enabled support of an education and training project conducted jointly by the Sociedade Civil de Bem-Estar Familiar no Brasil (BEMFAM) and the government of the State of Rio Grande do Norte in the poverty stricken northeastern part of the country. BEMFAM, a nonprofit family welfare society, is the IPPF affiliate in Brazil and operates an extensive family planning program. The educational and motivational program in Rio Grande do Norte includes participation of specially trained teachers and other community leaders.

Assistance also has been provided, beginning in 1971, to the Population Reference Bureau, Inc., for its information/education activities in Latin America. Grants to the Bureau for 1971 through 1974 totaled $325,000.

Two other major Foundation-supported projects

in Latin America with emphases on population planning are the Pan American Health and Education Foundation's Regional Maternal and Child Health Project based in São Paulo, Brazil, and the Javeriana University's model maternal and child health program in Bogotá, Colombia.

Lutheran World Relief

Lutheran World Relief has shipped family planning supplies to missionary hospitals for many years. In 1964, a special family planning project received financial underwriting. At that time Lutheran World Relief began providing funds to Korea for a mobile medical unit, which served as a pilot family planning program in rural areas. This was followed by funds for family planning seminars, with travel costs for leaders. Beginning in 1967, funds were authorized for family planning projects in India. Lutheran World Relief continues to give regular help to the Taiwan Christian Service for its family planning work in low-cost housing developments in Taipei.

Mennonite Central Committee

The Mennonite Central Committee (MCC) has assisted family planning activities in Indonesia, India, South Vietnam, Haiti, and Paraguay in conjunction with broader medical and community development programs. In most of these countries, MCC is associated with the Planned Parenthood Program of Church World Service and with local government programs.

Milbank Memorial Fund

The Milbank Memorial Fund was active in the population-demographic field from 1928 through 1971. It explored the question of differential fertility according to socioeconomic status, investigated contraceptive practices, and studied social and psychological factors affecting fertility. During part of the last decade, the Fund continued to award an annual fellowship to the Office of Population Research at Princeton University. These grants were initiated in 1936 and the last was made in 1972. A series of grants in general support of the Office of Population Research also continued during this period.

Four biennial conferences were held from 1965 through 1972 and the proceedings published in the Milbank Memorial Fund Quarterly. The last conference was "Forty Years of Research on Human

Fertility." Earlier conferences were: "Demographic Aspects of the Black Community" in 1969; "Current Research on Fertility and Family Planning in Latin America" in 1967; and "Components of Population Change in Latin America" in 1965.

The Fund's major program emphasis is now on health services.

National Abortion Rights Action League

The National Abortion Rights Action League (NARAL) was organized in 1969 as the National Association for the Repeal of Abortion Laws. It adopted its present name after the Supreme Court abortion decision in 1973. NARAL's registered lobbyists monitor legislation and provide relevant information to public officials and agencies. By 1975 it represented a coalition of more than 70 State and national groups. Political action networks have been established in every State to inform both the U.S. Congress and the State legislatures of support for the right to choose abortion.

During the earlier period, NARAL concentrated its efforts and resources in States, such as New York, that were considering acceptable bills with a realistic chance of passage. It also promoted and assisted in the organization of State repeal groups and helped initiate challenges to restrictive laws.

Recently, NARAL sent representatives to the U.N. World Population Conference in Bucharest in 1974 and to the U.N. International Women's Year Conference in Mexico City in 1975 to help organize the International Association for the Right to Abortion.

National Right to Life Committee

The National Right to Life Committee is an affiliation of State right-to-life organizations opposed to abortion in the United States. Their objective is to secure the right of "personhood" to every unborn child. While each of the United States is represented, the State organizations and structures differ widely. In California over 100 right-to-life groups are affiliated with a State coalition. Other States may have but one organization; number of members differs considerably from State to State.

The National Committee's stated functions are to:
• Promote respect for the worth and dignity of all human life, including the life of the unborn child from the moment of conception.
• Encourage, promote, and sponsor legislation and other measures for the protection of human life before and after birth—particularly for the defenseless, the incompetent, the impaired, and the incapacitated.
• Engage in activities that will help to accomplish the above purposes.

Objecting to the 1973 decision of the U.S. Supreme Court which liberalized restrictions on abortion, the Committee holds that the abortion question involves a true balancing between two innocent lives. The mother, because she is pregnant, has not forfeited her life. The child conceived has done nothing to indicate that its life should be taken. Both deserve the utmost in competent medical care. No action should be taken, however, to eliminate the life of the child, and every precaution and medical measure must be used to assure that neither life be sacrificed for the sake of the other.

Recognizing the difficulties involved in problem pregnancies, the National Right to Life Committee endorses programs such as Birth Right and Pregnancy Aid.

It favors adoption of a proposed human life amendment designed to afford the protection of the U.S. Constitution to all human beings—including their unborn offspring at every stage of their biological development irrespective of age, health, function, or condition of dependency.

Negative Population Growth

This organization, begun in 1972, has worked to promote drastic reduction in world population during the next 70 to 100 years in order to make possible a world economy it believes would be sustainable indefinitely in a sound and healthy environment. As an initial goal, it seeks to encourage first the United States and then all countries to put into effect national programs of population control in order to reduce the population to not more than half the 1970 levels.

Two grants have been received to be used for a membership campaign and for education-information projects. Four position papers have been issued, and four others are in preparation. Officers have been participating in workshops and conferences sponsored by population and environmental groups. And the organization is now issuing a quarterly newsletter, the first issue distributed in 1975.

Office of Population Research

The Office of Population Research at Princeton University is one of the nation's oldest centers for demographic research and teaching. Since its founding in 1936, the Office has consisted of a professional staff of moderate size and a large number of visitors and students who come for research and training.

Over the years methods have been developed for analyzing fertility, mortality, nuptiality, and migration and their relation to the growth rates and age structures of populations. Several researchers are currently engaged in studies of the classical core of mathematical demography—namely, the theory of stable populations and related concepts. Another continuing concern of the Office is methods for estimating standard measures of fertility and mortality from inaccurate and incomplete data. Progress in this area can be helpful both in analyzing data from developing areas and historical demography.

Various studies, continuing an interest begun decades ago, also are being conducted within the broad heading of population growth in developing countries. For example, a current project examines available evidence on population policy and income distribution.

Two major on-going research projects deal with fertility. An international team of scholars—some working at the Office and some in their native countries—are analyzing demographic trends in each of more than 700 European provinces with relation to declining birth rates. In the United States, the 1975 National Fertility Study is underway. Re-interviews will be scheduled with 3,000 women who participated in a study in 1970, and first interviews will be solicited with 1,000 women who have married since then. Complete pregnancy histories and a record of use of various modes of fertility regulation will be collected from each respondent along with other data.

The Office of Population Research offers instruction to doctoral candidates in such fields as economics, sociology, and statistics; to visiting students enrolled in a special nondegree program; and to post-doctoral research fellows who come for training under grants. In addition to formal courses, the Office regularly schedules seminars on research in progress to acquaint students with new findings and new techniques. In the past 2 years, students from Colombia, England, Egypt, India, Mexico, Morocco,

Nigeria, Scotland, and the United States have received training in demography.

Population Index, published quarterly, provides a special service to the field of demography—the collection of bibliographic information.

The staff, in addition to research, teaching, and publication of the quarterly, engages in extensive public service activities. Members have served as consultants to the United Nations, the U.S. Government, and governments around the world as well as to private foundations and colleges and universities.

Oxfam

Oxfam, a voluntary British-based organization, began supporting family planning activities in 1965 and since then has provided assistance for projects in 34 countries. From 1965 until April 1973 grants totaled slightly less than half a million pounds with approximately £80,000 awarded for projects in Africa, £325,000 in Asia, and £87,000 in Latin America and the Caribbean.

Early assistance was modest, averaging about a dozen grants a year and totaling £30,000 to £40,000. By 1972-73, some 30 projects received £40,000 and in 1973-74 grants of approximately £164,000 were made for projects including family planning. Of this, £39,000 went to Africa, £84,000 to Asia, and £41,000 to Latin America and the Caribbean.

Oxfam seeks out small, needed projects and makes a special effort to encourage the smaller medical institutions to provide family planning. High priority is given to preventive health programs in which family planning is closely associated with maternal and child health services. Training and motivation are emphasized and related to an overall philosophy of integrated family care and welfare.

Family planning programs in India have accounted for a large proportion of Oxfam's grants. For example, continuing support has been given to the Christian Medical Association of India for a nationwide family planning program, and aid has been approved through 1977 for a project in Bombay that incorporates family planning with other health work.

Among its activities in other areas, Oxfam has provided motivational materials and clinic support to the Indonesian Council of Churches since 1971 for its family planning activities and has agreed to support a family planning services and training program in Tanzania until 1976. Other Oxfam-supported projects include an evaluation study of a family planning method being used in El Salvador, support since 1967 of the St. Vincent Planned Parenthood Association, and a family planning program administered by a missionary nurse in Kenya.

In 1969 Oxfam's Council of Management decided to allow funds to be used to support vasectomy and tubectomy programs if local situations make these family planning methods appropriate.

Oxfam—Canada

Oxfam—Canada, sister organization of the British Oxfam, was established in 1963 as an autonomous charitable organization under the patronage of the Governor-General of Canada. It has its own board of directors and its own projects committee. It is one of the largest nongovernmental agencies in Canada that funds indigenous self-help projects and offers emergency relief and assistance in the less-developed countries of the world.

Since 1963, it has provided grants for population/family planning activities in Bolivia, India, Indonesia, Mexico, the Philippines, Trinidad and Tobago, and other countries.

Pathfinder Fund

The Pathfinder Fund was formed in 1957 to continue the life work of the late Clarence Gamble. Beginning in 1929, Dr. Gamble had worked to make family planning services available to those who could not obtain them. During the 1930's and 1940's, he concentrated his work in the United States, where he was responsible for the opening of the first public family planning clinics in 40 cities and 14 States. He made a grant to the Department of Health in North Carolina that made possible the world's first government-operated birth control program. He also gave significant help in the development of a family planning association and a family planning program in Puerto Rico. After World War II, he began offering assistance abroad to initiate or expand family planning in many countries of Europe, Asia, Africa, and Latin America.

At the time of his death in 1966, The Pathfinder Fund was a relatively small organization employing a few field workers who visited cities and countries overseas, stimulated interest in family planning, and helped start national family planning associations through small grants. Some 20 national associations were given such assistance.

Beginning in 1967, grant assistance from the U.S. Agency for International Development and increasing philanthropic interest in family planning have made possible the expansion of Pathfinder programs. Over the 1965-75 decade, the total of Pathfinder grants and the variety of supported activities have grown greatly. In 1965, Pathfinder grants were less than $100,000; in 1975, grants totaled $3.5 million. In 1965, Pathfinder's primary role was to stimulate interest in family planning among the leaders of the countries its field representatives visited. Grants were made to start activities—but necessarily these grants were small. In 1975, not only were the number and size of grants much larger, but the range of activities had multiplied. In 1975 approximately 150 grants were made in more than 40 countries.

Pathfinder continues to make some grants as small as $500 to help countries or cities or organizations start family planning activities. In these cases, a little money made available very quickly can often have substantial impact or even be the key to the starting of a larger project.

As family planning services have become available in more and more cities and countries, it is often no longer a question of whether family planning services would be offered—but of where and how they would be offered. Will they be sufficiently inexpensive—so that a large population may be served? Will they be presented in a manner sufficiently sympathetic so that couples not highly motivated might use them? Additionally, there is an evident need to inform people about family planning services so they know of their availability, know what they are all about, and want to use them. The Pathfinder Fund has responded to these needs in many ways.

Pathfinder, also has sponsored paramedical training programs and encouraged countries' health systems to allow paramedical personnel to deliver family planning services. Where overseas training for health personnel has seemed beneficial, the Pathfinder Fund has funded travel and training.

It also has conducted an extensive research program on intrauterine devices and helped to introduce new contraceptive methods in several countries.

Increasingly, The Pathfinder Fund has provided support to leadership groups, professional groups, and social service and social welfare organizations to enable them to consider the need for family planning in their own countries, to discuss the effects of rapid population growth on economic development and the welfare of their citizens, and to consider possible actions. The Fund's view is that solutions to questions of family size, unwanted pregnancies, and rapid population growth must be determined for each country by the people of the country in terms of their own needs, culture, and resources.

More recently, The Pathfinder Fund—taking a broader look at the social changes that inevitably occur as countries develop—has begun to make grants to individuals and to groups to consider the effects of the changes, how populations respond to those changes, and what the leadership and citizenry might do to improve life and welfare under the new conditions that are evolving. Economic development, improved health, and the increased chances of child survival have wrought substantial changes for a large part of the world's population. Increasing attention in the future may go toward programs that seek to understand, accommodate, or stimulate beneficial change.

Pathfinder's field staff, none of whom are Americans, has been carefully built up over a decade. Five of its members are physicians with public health degrees and experience. In 1964, the field office for Africa and the Middle East was established in Geneva, Switzerland. A national office for the Philippines was opened in Manila the same year. Then a national office was opened in Djakarta, Indonesia; The Pathfinder Fund, India, was organized with offices in New Delhi; and regional offices for Latin America were opened in Santiago, Chile, and Bogotá, Colombia. In 1974 a regional office was opened in Nairobi, Kenya, to cover sub-Saharan Africa and to enable the Geneva office to concentrate on North Africa and the Middle East.

Planned Parenthood Federation of America

The Planned Parenthood Federation of America (PPFA), the pioneer family planning organization of the United States, is the largest national association within the International Planned Parenthood Federation (IPPF)

Beginning with the founding of the Nation's first birth control clinic by Margaret Sanger in Brooklyn, New York, in 1916, the U.S. Planned Parenthood movement spread. By 1974 it was serving 930,000 acceptors. Meantime, there has been a virtual tripling of the service load since 1966, including services in sex education, abortion referrals, vasectomy, and other activities.

PPFA provides the largest private network of reproductive health services for low-income women in the United States. No one is turned away from its clinics because of inability to pay. More than three in four of its acceptors during 1974 were of low or marginal income. Eleven percent were recipients of public assistance.

In addition to contraceptive services, it provided 6 million diagnostic tests and examinations in 1974—pap smears, pelvic and breast examinations, blood pressure measurements, blood tests, and VD tests. It conducted more than 1¼ million individual

counseling sessions on birth control, infertility, problem pregnancy, and other medical needs. And it made roughly 100,000 referrals to other sources of health care—reflecting the organization's concern for all medical conditions uncovered during the client's visit.

PPFA also provides the Nation's largest network of help and advice for those with a problem pregnancy, handling more than 200,000 such cases in 1974. Those who wished to carry a pregnancy to term were recommended to a source of prenatal care and, on request, were referred to adoption services. Those who wished an abortion were guided to a high-quality medical service. During the year, 19 of the 187 affiliates provided abortion service and follow-up contraceptive guidance in their own facilities—eight more than a year earlier.

The organization also serves as a major source of service and referral for persons seeking voluntary sterilization. More than 50 of the affiliate organizations offered vasectomy service in 1974. In all, more than 13,000 women and more than 11,000 men received voluntary sterilization service, counseling, or referral through PPFA clinics in 1974.

The national headquarters of PPFA serves three major roles: as guide to its national network of community services; as major advocate and analyst in the U.S. family planning field; and as a continuing source of family planning assistance to other nations, both through its own programs and through its important financial support to the International Planned Parenthood Federation.

PPFA develops its own international programs through its international division, Family Planning International Assistance (FPIA).

Population Council

The Population Council is a private, nonprofit organization with a twofold role in population activities. It undertakes and supports research, training, and technical assistance in the social, health, and biomedical sciences and also acts as a center for the collection and dissemination of information on significant developments and ideas related to population questions.

Established in late 1952 by John D. Rockefeller 3d, the Population Council is one of the oldest private organizations in its field. Initially confining its activities to small demographic and biomedical research grants, the Council in the early sixties began technical assistance to family planning projects in developing countries. During the past decade, however, its program activities have centered increasingly on research in demography, physiology of reproduction, and public health/family planning and on making population-related training available to institutions in developing countries. Research activities are carried out both in-house and through grants and fellowships. The institution-building activities are carried out through cooperative relationships with private organizations and government agencies in 27 developing countries in Africa, Asia, and Latin America.

In 1975 the Population Council operated with a budget of $13 million and a staff of 125, of whom 28 were stationed in 16 countries. This represented a near tripling of its budget and a doubling of its staff over the past decade. The organization's 1975 budget was drawn from Rockefeller sources, the Ford Foundation, other foundations and individuals, and U.S. AID.

Through its Demographic Division, the Council in 1975 provided major training assistance to universities and university-institutes in 14 countries and minor assistance to other groups in Africa, Asia, and Latin America. In all such efforts, it sought to help recipient organizations in developing institutional capacities for local demographic training and research relevant to national situations. The application of social science, and particularly economic analysis, in the study of population policy was the aim of assistance to development planning bodies and related research institutes in four countries. Support for professional interchange was provided through international professional associations—notably the Population Association of Africa.

Research and publications of the Demographic Division in 1975 involved six major fields, all supported by grants or conducted by the Council's own professional staff. The fields included demographic measurement, detailed assessment of the demographic situation in selected countries, models of fertility determination, models of economic-demographic processes, population projection techniques and results, and migration. Workshops and specialists' meetings in a variety of scientific and policy-related subject areas were also conducted or supported by the Council.

Through its Technical Assistance Division, the Council provides major support to family planning programs in Colombia, the Dominican Republic, and Venezuela in Latin America; Morocco and Tunisia in Africa; Iran in the Near East and South Asia; and Indonesia, Korea, Taiwan, the Philippines, and Thailand in East Asia. As the basic needs of family planning programs have been met by governmental and international agency funding, emphasis has been increasingly turned to experimental, innovative, and evaluative activities. Information and education pilot activities were conducted in Iran and Korea and are serving as the basis for expanded programs in these countries. In Turkey, Indonesia, and the Philippines, work has been completed on the development of family planning delivery assistance through the urban hospital-based international postpartum program. Similar efforts are now being extended in the rural areas through family planning demonstrations coordinated with maternal/child health care.

Postpartum programs previously supported by the Council's technical assistance activities have been transferred to other funding approaches, including those of WHO, UNFPA, and local governments. Research and evaluation continued as a major thrust with significant activities in Colombia, Venezuela, the Dominican Republic, Tunisia, Iran, Thailand, South Korea, and Indonesia. In addition, the International Committee on Applied Research in Population continued to identify and quickly test out promising ideas for improved fertility-reduction measures.

An unchanged primary objective of the Biomedical Division of the Council is the development of improved, new methods of fertility control. Earlier activities toward this end were given new impetus in 1970 when U.S. AID awarded a $3-million, 5-year contract for the development of a once-a-month pill. Under this program, the Division conducted and coordinated efforts to develop agents with useful contragestational activity. Nearly 300 compounds were evaluated for contragestational potential in a variety of animal and biochemical tests. Several compounds identified as having possible utility are undergoing continuing investigations.

The Biomedical Division's contraceptive development efforts scored a success in the early sixties with its work on the plastic intrauterine device (IUD). The Division furnished the lion's share of the research funds, programmatic help, and manufacturing aid that brought the IUD to its present stage as a major contraceptive in national family planning programs. In 1971, the Division's research efforts were enlarged with the founding of the International Committee for Contraceptive Research (ICCR), which was established to carry work on new methods of fertility control through to the final stages of testing and development. The Committee has focused on 12 potential new fertility control methods and has evaluated nearly 100 different dosage regimes and six IUD's in the pursuit of these methods. Approximately 50,000 men and women have participated in these trials. The "Copper T," an IUD, is the first of the ICCR's potential new methods to complete testing and development. It is now being distributed in over 20 countries.

The Biomedical Division has sought to stimulate research and training in reproductive biology and allied fields in both developing and developed countries through its Visiting Scientist, Fellowship Training, and Grant Programs. Small numbers of international scientists and scholars are invited to spend their sabbatical leaves working in the Division's laboratories. The Division's Fellowship Program enables biomedical scientists from both developing and developed countries to carry out advanced training in their specialties at institutions of their choice. In addition, the Division provides post-doctoral training for selected scientists in its own laboratories.

Population Crisis Committee

The Population Crisis Committee (PCC) has played a key role in strengthening programs to curb world population growth during the past decade, especially through its educational work with leaders and policymakers in many parts of the world. Established in 1965 by the late Hugh Moore, Kenneth B. Keating, and William H. Draper, Jr., the PCC seeks to generate knowledge, understanding, and action throughout the world to help bring birth rates into balance with reduced death rates at the earliest possible time.

A nonprofit educational organization, the Committee works with concerned citizens in all walks of life and with leaders in business, the professions, science, religion, and government. Its aim is to reach an ever-widening audience through meetings, discussions, and the publication and distribution of educational and policy statements on population problems.

Over the past decade, General Draper and other PCC members marshalled some $10 million of individual, corporate, and foundation support for the International Planned Parenthood Federation (IPPF). Such contributions from the private sector were made through the Victor Fund and Victor-Bostrom Fund. In 1975, however, a new fund, the Draper World Population Fund, was established by PCC to further expand such support. Named in honor of General Draper, who had served as National Chairman of PCC and who died in late 1974, the fund will give primary support to the IPPF with emphasis on innovative programs that promise maximum impact in reducing excess fertility. Distinguished volunteers, under the direction of Mrs. Angier Biddle Duke, are contributing their time to the work of this fund.

Working with officials of the United States Government, the Population Crisis Committee has encouraged the development of the population assistance program of AID. Committee members have also worked with officials in the Department of Health, Education, and Welfare (HEW) to support programs that will make family planning available to all women in the United States who need but cannot afford such services. To emphasize the continuing value of biomedical research and to develop and perfect better methods of voluntary fertility control, PCC members have worked with the National Institutes of Health in organizing conferences, briefing sessions, and publications on population research issues.

Since the inception of U.S. programs in 1968, Committee members have been increasingly involved in United Nations programs in population. General Draper, as National Chairman of PCC, was a pioneer supporter of the United Nations Fund for Population Activities (UNFPA). As U.S. Representative on the United Nations Population Commission, he and other PCC members were influential in formulating plans for the World Population Conference held in Bucharest, August 1974, and for the World Population Year, 1974. PCC also organized educational tours for German and Japanese parliamentarians in 1972 and 1973, respectively, to see at first hand population problems and programs in a number of developing countries.

During 1974, PCC was accorded consultative status to the United Nations and was active in a number of international conferences. In February, the Women's International Conference on Population and Development, first proposed and then substantially assisted by PCC, was held under U.N. sponsorship and laid the groundwork for new emphasis on improving the status of women as a factor in reducing excess fertility. In March, PCC helped to arrange a conference for Latin-American military leaders and officers on Population and Continental Security. In August, PCC members participated as delegates, advisors, and nongovernmental participants in the World Population Conference and the Population Tribune. PCC coordinated a team of demographers to prepare population projections of 40 countries for the Conference to demonstrate implications of alternative population growth assumptions into the 21st century.

Throughout 1974, PCC worked to publicize and promote action on the world food crisis, emphasizing the close relationship between rapid population growth and food deficiencies in the developing world. A "Declaration on Food and Population," which was drafted in consultation with food experts from all over the world and signed by over 3,000 prominent citizens from more than 100 countries, was presented to the Secretary General of the United Nations in April. Based on this Declaration, a resolution sponsored by 24 developing countries was adopted by the World Food Conference in Rome in November 1974. The resolution urged that birth rates be brought "into reasonable balance with the lowered death rates that have been achieved."

In 1975, PCC worked to maintain the momentum gained during World Population Year (1974). The establishment of a program on Women, Food, and Population enabled PCC members and staff to play a major role in preparations and implementation for the U.N. International Women's Year Conference. An international "Call to Action" has been formulated and widely circulated by PCC.

Throughout the last decade, the PCC has developed a key educational role. The PCC has consistently recruited influential volunteers, prepared pioneering publications and reports on crucial issues in the population field, and helped to develop a broader base of understanding for population issues among policymakers in many parts of the world. In the post-Bucharest era, as an increasing number of governments are moving to implement constructive population policies and to integrate these with overall economic and social development, PCC will continue to encourage wider understanding and support for such programs.

Population Institute

The Population Institute, established in 1969, enlists and assists key leadership groups in bringing population growth into balance with resources as quickly as possible by means consistent with human dignity and freedom. Each of its four divisions contributes to expanding public knowledge of and interest in population problems in the United States and abroad. The Institute's essential role is motivation: identifying for a world public its own responsibility for population issues and providing programs and other resources for action. By reaching out to leadership, it employs the principle of leverage, engaging a vast constituency through the institutions, structures, and media to which millions give attention and allegiance.

The Organization Liaison Division. Beginning in May of 1972, the Liaison Division has given increasing help to U.S. national organizations in informing their members on population-related issues. Through regular communications with more than 500

major organizations—including the Camp Fire Girls, the Boys Clubs of America, the American Association of University Women, the YWCA, and the PTA— millions of individuals are being reached. A bi-monthly publication (first distributed in 1974) and issue-oriented bulletins channel information to these groups; frequent programs of activism or involvement in issues give them a means of contributing directly to the solutions of problems.

The Youth and Student Division. The Institute's first department, started in 1970, is focused on sensitizing America's youth to the problems of population growth. Now the Division's work has grown to international dimensions. At the request of the United Nations, it called together youth leaders from around the world in January 1974 to plan participation in World Population Year (1974); since then it has continued to assist international youth groups. Earlier, in 1973, it had initiated and chaired a coalition of U.S. youth organizations working on population policy matters in preparation for the World Population Conference, and it conducted a group of students to this Conference.

Through these U.S. students, a nationwide campus action network has been established to promote student involvement in population activites. In addition, *The Population Activists' Handbook,* published by Macmillan in November 1974, was prepared by the Division to assist students in becoming involved in population issues. Other activities include a project, initiated in January of 1972, that provides student interns to assist state policy makers in researching and developing population-related programs. And in January 1975 a National Resource Center/Clearing House on Population was organized to provide materials and resources to college and high school students.

The Education Division. Division personnel assists educators, associations, textbook authors, and publishers in carrying population-related issues into classrooms. The Division seeks an interdisciplinary inclusion of population-related themes and information in all curricula. It identifies the need for students to understand the interrelationship of all social issues and the population growth component of each.

The Communication Center. The Center works extensively with radio and television in the United States and abroad to help spread population information. For example, after background briefings by the Institute for 600 TV writers and producers in Los Angeles on November 17, 1971, and 400 in New York on March 15, 1972, major network executives requested briefings for all their producers and story editors. These have led to effective discussions on TV programs. A series of Institute-sponsored annual TV awards first presented in May 1973 helps to motivate producers and writers to include population issues in network entertainment television.

The Center also maintains liaison with radio and TV network news staffs and helps them perceive and report the relationship between rapid population growth and world problems in food, energy, and housing. As a result of efforts of the Communication Center, a worldwide association of religious broadcasters is focusing radio-TV programs on population problems. These broadcasters, convened by the Institute in London in August 1973, operate the two largest networks in the Third World. Using hundreds of transmitters, they provide news and information to a large segment of the population in Asia, Africa, and Latin America.

Other Communication Center activities have included: a national seminar, "The Population Issue and the Role of the Press," for over a hundred newspaper editors in the United States in April 1973; workshops in collaboration with Zero Population Growth and other organizations to help local population activists improve their media coverage; an annual cartoon contest, now in its third year; and cooperation with other groups in promoting International Women's Year, World Population Year, Food Day, and other special events. The Communication Center was a leader in organizing World Population Day in 1974.

Population Reference Bureau

From its beginning in 1929, the Population Reference Bureau (PRB) has been a pioneering force for increasing public knowledge and understanding in the United States and the world regarding population-dynamics-related changes and their present and future effects for individuals, societies, and the environment.

A private nonprofit organization, the Bureau's information-education program is carried out through the issuance of frequent reports and analyses to its broad membership and to public information media. In addition, it offers special services for population education through school systems, sponsorship and/or participation in important seminars and conferences on population problems, and assistance to scholars and private and public agencies in the study and analysis of changing population situations and problems. Further, the Bureau cooperates with other population organizations and institutions in producing or providing information-education publications, visuals, and services needed in their programs.

Under its charter, the PRB is continuously concerned with all aspects of population developments in the United States and abroad, including those in cities, nonmetropolitan areas, States, individual countries, and geographic regions. Its approach is guided by the belief that both individuals and governments are more apt to make sound decisions on future action when they are fully informed about the influence of population dynamics upon individuals and societies.

Population Services International

Population Services International (PSI), established in 1970 as a nonprofit family planning organization, directs its programs primarily to marketing the concept and means of fertility regulation. It stresses methods of contraception that do not require scarce medical services and facilities. Its mode of programming utilizes mass media, consumer goods distribution networks, and local business expertise. Population Services International estimates that its activities in 1974 were responsible for averting more than 22,000 births.

PSI follows a "social marketing" approach—the application of marketing principles to programs designed to enhance human welfare. This approach focuses on the use of commercial facilities and techniques, such as market analysis, sales promotion, and consumer education to bring birth control information and low-priced services to large numbers of people—particularly in areas where family planning clinics are lacking or inadequate. In this work, it cooperates with local researchers, marketers, advertising and consumer products distribution firms, and with community leaders and educators. Its long-range objective is to alleviate problems of population growth, unwanted pregnancies, and substandard health. Its medium-range objective is development of projects that can be adapted for large-scale, demographically significant programs in developing countries and also reduce unwanted pregnancies in developed areas.

Its largest program in 1975 was a nationwide, AID-funded project in Bangladesh. There, PSI is working with local firms to educate consumers about birth control and to distribute 36 million condoms and 7 million monthly cycles of oral contraceptives through thousands of shops over the next 3 years.

Another contraceptive marketing program started in late 1973 in Sri Lanka with a grant from the International Planned Parenthood Federation (IPPF), the support of the Sri Lanka Government, and the aid of a local family planning association. Extensive advertising was used to promote sales through 4,600 local retail outlets and by mail. First-year sales of condoms totaled over 4 million—exceeding the original goal of 2.5 million. As a result, a sister project has been set up to market oral contraceptives.

Other projects are underway or in the planning stages in Latin America, Haiti, India, Nepal, and East and Central Africa.

A grant from the Population Council is enabling PSI to work with private contraceptive manufacturing firms operating in Latin America, Southeast Asia, and Africa to increase the use of their products in developing countries. Working relationships also have been established with advertising firms in Kenya, India, Colombia, Indonesia, the Philippines, Ghana, and Sri Lanka. These have worked with PSI to test and refine advertisements to promote family planning in their own locales. Also, marketers in developing countries receive PSI support for family planning activities.

One of PSI's earliest projects, started in Kenya in 1972, was a campaign using newspapers, radio, direct mail, and cinema advertising to sell contraceptives at a subsidized price. Followup surveys showed that in the project 120,000 condoms were sold to an estimated market of 50,000 people. In addition, 14,000 condoms were sold by mail to purchasers in Uganda and Tanzania. A grant from Oxfam has enabled PSI to purchase a mobile unit and hire a fieldman to continue this project in remote areas.

In addition, some PSI projects relate to medical procedures. For example, widely distributed leaflets have recruited candidates for vasectomies and laparoscopies in the Philippines. Also a Scaife grant is being used for a clinical project in Australia to demonstrate the use of menstrual regulation techniques.

In the United States, PSI gives high priority to programs for teenagers with special emphasis on young men 13 to 20 years old. A 2-year project supported by the Office of Economic Opportunity brought contraceptives and sex information to over 25,000 young men by direct mail and indirectly to over 40,000 more via high school athletic coaches.

Foundations that have contributed to PSI activities, in addition to those donors previously mentioned, include the Hugh Moore Fund, Ford Foundation, Sunnen Foundation, Playboy Foundation, and the Henry B. Plant Memorial Fund, Inc.

Resources for the Future

Demographic work as such became a formal part of the research program at Resources for the Future only in late 1970 though it had been an integral part of nearly every project since the organization's founding in 1952 because one cannot consider environmental quality and natural resources without taking into account the impact of population growth, size, and distribution. It became clear, however, that the population factor should have explicit programmatic recognition, and a major project was developed, at the initiative of the President's Commission on Population Growth and the American Future. The project's goals were to forecast the dimensions and nature of the resources and environmental questions that the Nation is likely to face in the year 2000; to determine the extent to which changes in population, patterns of consumption, and technology contribute to these problems; and to suggest ways of handling such major issues. In addition to in-depth studies of key areas, a comprehensive simulation model was developed, the principal variants of which were population growth and geographic distribution, standard of living, and technological possibilities.

Work continues on long-term perspectives for the United States, with major support coming from the National Institutes of Health. Additional variables being taken into account include size and composition of the labor force, international relations, and institutions and policies.

In the developing countries, studies have been undertaken to explore the long-term consequences of population growth, economic development, and resource consumption. Particular attention is being paid to patterns different from those experienced by the United States and Western Europe so that a better base might be developed for making projections of resource supply and demand for the world. A study in Baroda, India, in cooperation with the Operations Research Group, is nearing completion, one in Indonesia will conclude in mid-1976, and two more are planned—one in Colombia and one in Africa.

Resources for the Future, in work supported by the Rockefeller Foundation, also has been involved in researching the socioeconomic determinants of fertility. Important to the United States, this work gains even greater significance when viewed from the perspectives of the developing countries. In brief, its premise is that demographic variables are affected by such factors as female labor force participation, female educational achievement, degree of urbanization, and the degree of public support for health, family planning, and social security measures. A collection of essays on population policy from this perspective was recently sponsored by Resources for the Future and is nearing publication.

Two features stand out about population studies at Resources for the Future: they have a strong international orientation, and they are much more than demography. Indeed, the emphasis is on resources and the environment—on a view of population as both cause and effect in the total scheme of things.

Rockefeller Foundation

With a four-decade history of support in the population field, the Rockefeller Foundation in 1974 devoted between $6 million and $7 million to help for related programs—approximately the same as in 1973. Grants in 1973 covered programs in 18 countries plus 47 projects in the United States. In 1968, grants were made for 9 projects overseas and 12 in the United States.

Specific goals and interests of the Foundation have changed through the years as needs have changed. In the 1960's, emphasis was on strengthening demographic resource centers, promoting reproductive biology research in developing countries, supporting field programs providing family planning on a research and demonstration basis, and developing information and education programs.

Public and government interest in population programs increased greatly in the 1966-75 decade, as did available funds. By 1973, the Rockefeller Foundation was one of the 10 major sources for the $330 million contributed to population programs. (The $330 million included $125 million from AID and $15 million from other countries' foreign aid programs.) Since these funds were being used largely for family planning projects in developing countries, the Rockefeller Foundation shifted its own priorities. Its main thrust is now research. Particular attention is devoted to the interrelationships between population growth rates and economic and human development and social factors and to a search for better contraceptive methods.

The new orientation includes providing assistance for establishing major centers for research and training in reproductive biology. Grants have been awarded to the Universities of California (San Diego, and the San Francisco Medical Center) and North Carolina, the Salk Institute, Rockefeller University, and Harvard Medical School. Other recipients have been the University of Bristol, England, and the Sloan-Kettering Institute in the United States. The Foundation also awards a limited number of special postdoctoral fellowships—nine in 1974—for advanced laboratory training.

In September 1974 a grant of $1.5 million was approved for the Population Council's international program of laboratory and clinical research to test the effectiveness and safety of new contraceptive methods.

A special program established basic science research positions in medical school departments of obstetrics and gynecology and thus is bringing the approaches and point of view of the laboratory investigator to the more action-oriented clinical departments. Between 1972 and 1975, 10 such grants were approved at an average 3-year cost of $120,000.

Training and educational programs have also been supported. Examples include grants to the University of Texas (San Antonio) for a project involving both social and biological sciences and the clinical aspects of fertility control, to the Planned Parenthood Association of Maryland for developing instructional materials and methods for population education in the Baltimore public schools, and to the Planned Parenthood Federation of America for training nurses as primary providers of family planning services.

Interest in training demographic and other social science personnel in low-income countries led the Foundation to provide a grant to enroll African, Asian, and Latin American students in the demographic training program of the London School of Economics and Political Science. El Colegio de Mexico also received support for research and training graduate students in economics and demography.

In 1970 the Rockefeller and Ford Foundations jointly began supporting a program of competitive research and awards on population policy questions. Since then, support has been provided for more than a hundred projects. In 1974 they included studies on child mortality and compensatory reproductive behavior, policy implications of migration into medium-sized towns in Nigeria, voluntary limitation of family size, and trends in U.S. abortion policy. Awards were made to researchers from the United States, Nigeria, Pakistan, Sierra Leone, Sri Lanka, Hong Kong, Sweden, Israel, Tanzania, Belgium, Colombia, France, and Australia.

The Foundation also funded research on the consequences of population growth with grants to the Instituto di Tella, the Universities of Ghana and Ibadan (Nigeria), Njala University College (Sierra Leone), and the Universidade Federal do Ceara in Brazil. Also, recognizing the importance of training foreign experts to advise their own governments on population issues, the Rockefeller Foundation has encouraged programs at the Universities of Ibadan, Nairobi, and the Philippines; Mahidol University (Bangkok); and Gadjah Mada University (Indonesia).

The Foundation's interest in strengthening regional associations is reflected in its support in 1972 of a social science research program on problems relevant to population policies in Latin America conducted under the supervision of the Commission for Population Development of the Latin American Social Science Council. It includes an emphasis on institution building as well as on population research. Three areas are being given priority: agarian structure and population; urbanization and population; and political systems and population policies. The Foundation also provided support in 1974 for the Council for Asian Manpower Studies, an association of Asian scholars.

The Rockefeller Foundation has consistently tried to concentrate its support in critical areas in the population field not adequately covered by others. It believes that family planning programs can now generally be left to the support of government and international agencies. Thus, it will give its major support to population research and to training in relevant social sciences in low-income countries.

Smithsonian Institution

The Smithsonian Institution, through its Interdisciplinary Communications Program, initiated the International Program for Population Analysis (IPPA) in 1972. IPPA is aimed at generating analysis of population policies and dynamics by scholars and analysts in the developing countries and is supported by the U.S. Agency for International Development. It emphasizes research and interdisciplinary communication among researchers and policymakers to help solve an individual nation's population problems. It seeks especially to attract younger social scientists to population research. This is accomplished through short-term work agreements with individuals to conduct and report on specific research projects and through workshops, conferences, and publications.

With interest and participation expanding steadily, 98 study proposals were received by mid-1975. Of these, 27 were for work in 16 African countries, includng the first request for a project in Niger. Funds for research in 17 Asian countries were sought in 33 proposals, and 35 requests were received for Latin American-Caribbean projects—up 40 percent from the preceding year. From the beginning of IPPA through June 1975, 41 study agreements obligating slightly more than $1 million had been signed. Of these agreements, 8 relate to Africa, 18 to Asia, and 14 to Latin America and the Caribbean.

Over the first 3 years of the international program, the Interdisciplinary Communications Program has been increasingly utilized for technical support, special projects, and staff assistance to various governments and to institutions in the population field. By mid-1975, the program had received 278 support proposals.

Close cooperation is maintained with such groups as the World Bank, the Ford Foundation, the Social Science Research Council, United Nations agencies, and various population organizations. An example of technical support in a cooperative project is the work carried on with the World Bank on the research, design, and administrative arrangements for a demographic and socioeconomic study of the causes and consequences of migration in West Africa. This project, supported by several groups, is administered by the University of Ghana, the Centre Ivoirien de Recherches Sociales of the University of Abidjan, Ivory Coast, and the Centre Voltaique de la Recherche Scientifique, Upper Volta.

In 1974-75, a workshop in Accra, Ghana, on the development and utilization of human resources was sponsored jointly with the University of Ghana. Six African countries were represented. A workshop in Rawalpindi, Pakistan, under joint sponsorship with the Government of Pakistan, explored that country's experiences in the population field. A third overseas workshop was cosponsored with the Government of Turkey and the University of Istanbul and dealt with the impact of planned urbanization on population dynamics in the East Marmara region. In 1973-74, similar workshops were held in Lomé, Togo; Tampaksiring, Bali; and San Salvador, El Salvador. In addition, projects in Pakistan, El Salvador, and African countries have been provided on-site consultations and support by the program's specialists.

Publications are an important part of the program. A trilingual quarterly newsletter is issued as well as semi-annual bibliographies compiled and annotated by the staff of the Interdisciplinary Communications Program. Occasional monographs, proceedings of workshops and conferences, and special reports are published. Also, individuals with work agreements are encouraged to seek publication of their research reports in appropriate professional journals.

In all aspects of the program, technical resources are provided by social science analysts on the staff of the Interdisciplinary Communications Program and by members of an independent panel of more than 45 individuals with special expertise in population-related areas.

Sunnen Foundation

The Sunnen Foundation is a private philanthropic institution founded by Joseph Sunnen in 1945. It is devoted to the support and encouragement of public education regarding the effects of population growth in the developed countries (especially the United States) as well as the developing ones with high rates of population increase.

The Foundation is primarily concerned with the effects of U.S. population growth on the United States and other areas of the world, the effects that population growth in the developing countries have on the United States, and the economic effects on the developed nations of providing massive aid to developing countries with burgeoning populations.

Its activities consist wholly of making grants for educational projects and studies. Major funding goes to specific goal-oriented programs of organizations active in some aspect of the population field. Among its key fields of interest is support for development and adoption of appropriate population education curricula for use by school systems.

Its interests include action-oriented programs in the population field, improvement in the status of women, development of policies tying population growth to demands on world resources, and recognition of effective fertility control as an essential part of national and regional development programs.

Tinker Foundation

Concentrating on programs for better understanding among the peoples of Latin America and the United States, the Tinker Foundation's assistance priorities are demographic education and information, social science research, and postgraduate education programs for Latin Americans. In a 10-year period from 1965 to January 1975, a total of $1,156,479 has been awarded to population projects. The Foundation concentrates on programs that educate or inform national leadership about the serious inplications of rapid population increase for social and economic development. The Foundation plans to continue to assist similar programs in the future, giving primarily to activities which are initiated from within the Latin American region or which complement such initiatives. The Foundation has not given support to medical research, training, or clinical programs. Examples of its recent grants are listed below.

In 1974 a grant of $16,250 was made to Planned Parenthood of New York City to assist the Margaret Sanger Center launch a population education program for foreign students studying in the metropolitan area. The objective of this program is to help familiarize the students with the broad concepts of demography, population dynamics, and public health problems.

A grant to the American Universities Field Staff was renewed in 1973 for a second 3-year period and increased from $75,000 to $90,000. This supports a series of reports analyzing the population issue in Latin America. The project is part of a worldwide study being conducted in collaboration with the California Institute of Technology.

Several 2- and 3-year grants were made in 1971. The Foundation awarded a 2-year grant of $43,000 to Duke University to send an economic demographer to Brazil to work with the Sociedade Civil de Bem-Estar Familiar no Brasil (BEMFAM), the Getulio Vargas Foundation, and the Pontificia Universidad Catolica on population projections for the 1970's and analyzing the impact of population growth on the social and economic structure of the nation.

The same year the Foundation initiated a 3-year grant of $75,000 to the Center for Studies in Education Development at Harvard University to develop a program in population education to meet the needs of Latin American countries. Foundation support was used for fellowships, to enlarge the Center's library, and for an additional faculty member.

A 3-year grant (1971-73) was awarded to the North American Educational Foundation to permit the Instituto Tecnologico y de Estudios Superiores de Monterey to add a course in demography to its curriculum. The course has now been absorbed into the Instituto's own budget.

In 1971 the Foundation began a $150,000 3-year grant to the University of Florida to develop an intensive training and research program on Latin American demography and population studies. Programs for Masters and Doctors degrees in Latin American demography were improved, and the capacities of the data bank and cartographic laboratory were increased.

The Foundation's initial grant in the field of population was a $500 award in 1965 to the publications program of the Latin American department of the Population Reference Bureau. This support continued from 1968 through 1973 and totaled $343,125. In 1969 the Foundation began supporting an annual series of population dialogues in Latin America organized by the Bureau. It awarded a total of $323,104 for these conferences through 1973.

Unitarian Universalist Service Committee

The Unitarian Universalist Service Committee uses a multidisciplinary, multidimensional approach in its international program in the population field. This activity is a major component of maternal and child health care services.

The Committee is a private, nonprofit, nonsectarian organization.

Family planning activities have been included in its program in Nigeria, Haiti, and other countries. The work in Haiti began in March 1966 and was reorganized in January 1969 into a family planning field laboratory in urban and rural settings. In cooperation with the Pan American Health Organization, the Haitian Government has now absorbed the urban component as a first step toward building a national program.

World Assembly of Youth

The year 1974 marked the 25th anniversary for the World Assembly of Youth (WAY) and its widespread economic, cultural, and social programs which were designed to help increase the involvement of youth in meeting the major challenges of our time.

In 1948 a number of youth leaders in Europe and North America, sensing the need for an international youth organization dedicated to human rights, invited the youth councils of all member countries of the United Nations to be represented at a conference held in London. The following year, 29 national youth councils ratified a charter and WAY began its work.

Today, WAY serves as a coordinating body for some 67 national youth councils and cooperates with youth organizations in 40 additional countries. It has gained international recognition and support, and its programs and services have expanded rapidly.

During the last decade—and particularly since 1969—WAY has placed increasing emphasis on information and education programs related to family planning and responsible parenthood. WAY believes young people constitute a dynamic resource in worldwide efforts to eliminate poverty, sickness, ignorance, and social injustice and to build a productive and peaceful life for all people. If these goals are to be reached, young people must be made aware of the damaging effects of rapid population growth on family life, community development, and national progress.

WAY has been carrying on its population work primarily through conferences, seminars, and workshops.

In 1973, a 3-week seminar was held in Brussels, Belgium, for youth leaders from developing countries. Other international conferences have been sponsored in Vienna, Austria, and in Washington, D.C., in the United States. The International Youth Seminar in Vienna was attended by 42 participants from 23 countries.

Regional and national conferences have been sponsored in Africa, Asia, and Latin America. Participants at these conferences have, in turn, spearheaded thousands of local workshops throughout the world. Well over 250,000 young people have attended these sessions.

National and regional conferences are planned in cooperation with area youth councils and with the support of government officials and national leaders. Officials of family planning associations often are featured speakers. The conferences point out the relationship between family planning and economic and social progress and, conversely, between rapid population expansion and economic and environmental problems. Young people are encouraged to discuss these matters further in student and youth meetings and in their homes. Debates, contests, and discussion groups often are arranged to precede or follow a conference.

Programs developed by national youth councils are coordinated by the international secretariat based in Brussels. Regional offices for Africa are located in Accra, Ghana, and Nairobi, Kenya; for Asia, they are in Djakarta, Indonesia; and for Latin America, in Managua, Nicaragua.

As part of its population information/education program, WAY provides handbooks, special publications, slides, charts, posters, and graphs for use in seminars and by local groups. A monthly population bulletin also is issued.

The international secretariat places importance on the principle of channeling support from youth organizations of developed countries to youth activities in developing areas. Many programs are carried out with the collaboration and support—both in facilities and funds—of the United Nations and its specialized agencies such as the Educational, Scientific, and Cultural Organization (UNESCO), the Food and Agriculture Organization (FAO), the Children's Fund (UNICEF), the International Labor Organization (ILO), and the World Health Organization (WHO).

The U.S. Agency for International Development (AID) provided support from 1969 to 1974.

World Education

World Education works in partnership with about 45 organizations in developing countries and in collaboration with a number of international agencies to provide innovative educational approaches, financial assistance, and skilled consultants to 30 literacy projects in 17 countries. It develops integrated functional literacy programs for adults that include education on population matters, family planning, nutrition, and food production. Its long-term program of functional literacy training has been assisted since 1969 by grants from the U.S. Agency for International Development.

World Education's program includes: identification of learner needs through individual and group interviews and baseline surveys; design of training programs and curriculums; development of learner-oriented methods and materials focusing on problems of everyday concern to the learners; training of staff and teachers; and development of evaluation strategies and techniques for assessment of program activities and learner gains.

Its communication program disseminates information and results of project activities through publications and audiovisual media.

World Neighbors

World Neighbors has been active since 1952 in self-help programs of community betterment in the villages of many developing nations. Program emphasis has been on food production, literacy, public health, village industries, and leadership training. Although family planning has always been a part of the program, since 1964 it has become second only to food production in emphasis and expenditures. World Neighbors has self-help programs in numerous countries.

A Production Center for rural development training materials, established at the World Neighbors headquarters, produces materials designed for village-level use by workers and volunteers. Filmstrips and manuals include material on family planning, public health, and food production. In addition, staff members have conducted communications training sessions in selected countries.

World Neighbors' project directors are usually nationals of the countries where its projects are located. Overall direction is given by World Neighbors' director of the overseas program and five resident representatives. Work is done principally through local personnel indigenous to project areas.

World Population Society

The World Population Society is an international, nonprofit professional society that promotes a multidisciplinary approach to questions of population dynamics and their interaction with other variables such as food, economics, natural resources, and development. The Society provides channels of communication between laymen and professionals through the publication of a newsletter, a student newspaper, conference proceedings, and through sponsorship of meetings, symposia, conferences, and workshops. An International Population Conference—which brought together international experts in population, food, law, economic development, and social justice—was held in Washington, D.C., November 19 through 22, 1975.

Worldwatch Institute

Worldwatch Institute is an independent, nonprofit research organization funded by a group of private foundations, the U.S. Government, and agencies of the United Nations which share an interest and concern for problems of the future. As an "early warning system," Worldwatch identifies trends relating to population growth, food, and the environment that could develop into crises during the final quarter of this century. Worldwatch focuses global attention on these problems and presents decision makers with a range of public policy alternatives. The approach to problem solving is international and interdisciplinary and reflects the Worldwatch view that the complexity of tomorrow's important problems requires solutions not to be found within the narrow confines of national frontiers and traditional academic perspectives.

Current Worldwatch projects focus on: redefining national security in a time of increasing global interdependence; ecological undermining of food production systems as a result of deterioration and losses of agricultural land; economic, demographic, and political problems facing the world in the last quarter of this century; global energy resources, needs, conservation, and distribution alternatives; the changing role of women; and environmental and social threats to human health.

Worldwatch research results are communicated through Worldwatch Papers, articles in popular and scholarly international periodicals, in books written for both opinion leaders and the general public, and seminars. Worldwatch publications are aimed at a worldwide audience of persons whose thoughts and actions involve them in mankind's future problems.

Zero Population Growth

Since its establishment in 1968, Zero Population Growth, Inc. (ZPG) has conducted and supported programs of education and information "stressing the need for achieving zero population growth in the United States and elsewhere as soon as possible." By mid-1975, ZPG had a nationwide membership of about 10,000 and a network of 100 chapters. It is the only registered national population lobby.

In the spring of 1975, the organization reaffirmed its long-standing interests in promoting small families, improving birth control options, preserving the right to select abortion, and reducing immigration to the United States. At the same time, it has stepped up attention to population distribution and per capita consumption of natural resources. ZPG is currently giving detailed consideration to the possible components of a comprehensive U.S. policy on population size and distribution.

Combining these new initiatives with traditional concerns, ZPG is presently working to foster public attitudes supportive of small families, child-free couples, fertility control, population stabilization, provision of fertility control services to all persons, reduction in levels of teen-age pregnancy, U.S. assistance for fertility-control programs in other nations and for stabilization of the world population. ZPG is also working to lower levels of per capita resource consumption in the United States and to stimulate stewardship of U.S. land resources and desired policies in growth-determinant fields such as transportation and other public facilities.

ZPG assigns top priority to educational work with public officials and to broad public education on population matters through news media, its newsletter, special studies and reports, and work with a special correspondence group.

Its school-oriented role is one of encouraging school systems at regional and State levels to apply modern population education concepts. Heavily involved in past years with the development of population education materials and curricula for use on the Nation's schools, ZPG has recently decided that it should now concentrate on the implementation of such materials and curricula.

Note: *It is recognized that, in addition to the organizations discussed above, scores of other institutions and organizations in the United States and elsewhere throughout the world also have given attention to population matters during the 1965-75 decade. The above descriptions cover the most significant of such activities for which information has been available to the Population Reference Bureau. Of special note have been the activities of many U.S. universities and colleges in the area of population studies and technical assistance. A number of foreign organizations and foundations, including the Colombo Plan, also have rendered valuable assistance to population programs during the decade.*

Estimating Population of World and Individual Countries for Mid-1975

For almost all countries, the midyear 1975 estimates presented here were derived from the midyear 1974 Government or United Nations' estimate for that country. That estimate was projected to midyear 1975 by applying what was considered to be an appropriate growth rate for the 1-year period. In most instances the growth rate used was that experienced by the country in the 1973-74 or the 1972-74 periods or that is implied for the 1970-75 period by the United Nations' population projections as assessed in 1973 (medium variant).

Other methods used to derive midyear 1975 population estimates would usually result in different figures. One generally accepted method is to project the separate components of population change; that is, to apply fertility, mortality, and international migration assumptions to the latest age-sex distribution—usually data derived from the latest census. Such longer range projections may vary from the 1-year projections presented here because of two principal factors: (1) whether or not the 1974 Govern-

ment or United Nations population estimates are accepted as valid; and (2) whether or not the 1974 estimates or the base data for the projections take underenumeration into account; i.e., the population totals are increased on the basis of knowledge regarding the degree to which the latest census underenumerated the population. Also, differences in timing and other factors may result in estimates which differ from those officially accepted by the various countries.

It is not known whether the estimates presented here are closer to the actual populations in the various countries than those which would result from the longer range component projections or from other projection techniques, particularly those based on adjusted totals and age-sex distributions. It would be fortuitous if any estimate now were to prove identical with the final official figure when the latter is known, but it is believed that the estimates given here by the Population Reference Bureau are technically sound, although differing in some cases with estimates from other sources.

World Population Data—1965 and 1975 Compared

Region	Estimated population, July 1		Births per 1,000 population		Deaths per 1,000 population		Rate of natural increase		Time to double population[1]		GNP per capita[3]	
	1965	1975	1965	1974[2]	1965	1974[2]	1965	1974[2]	1965	1974[2]	1965	1973
	Thousands	*Thousands*	*Number*	*Number*	*Number*	*Number*	*Percent*	*Percent*	*Years*	*Years*	*Dollars*	*Dollars*
World	3,289,308	3,947,039	34	30	15	12	1.9	1.8	36	38	920	1,250
Northern America . . .	214,073	236,552	20	15	9	9	[4]1.0	0.6	69	116	4,950	6,130
Latin America	241,078	317,083	39	37	11	9	2.8	2.8	25	25	590	770
Mainland	218,998	290,271	39	38	11	9	2.8	2.9	25	24	590	770
Caribbean Islands . . .	22,080	26,812	36	31	10	9	2.6	2.2	27	32	560	780
Europe[5]	666,604	718,682	18	16	9	10	0.9	0.6	77	116	1,900	3,010
Africa[6]	278,176	365,003	48	47	23	21	2.5	2.6	28	27	250	310
Near East[7]	126,270	163,536	42	41	16	14	2.6	[4]2.6	27	27	470	710
South Asia	635,210	799,886	44	38	20	16	2.4	2.2	29	32	110	120
South East Asia	247,911	319,281	44	38	18	15	2.6	[4]2.4	27	29	140	180
East Asia	862,433	1,005,787	33	26	15	9	1.8	1.7	38	41	350	680
Oceania	17,553	21,229	24	22	10	10	1.4	1.2	50	58	2,660	3,300

[1]Based on the rate of natural increase shown and assuming no change in the rate.

[2]Data refer to 1973, 1974, or to the 1970-75 period.

[3]For the Communist countries and for nearly all countries with populations of less than 1 million, the estimates were derived by applying the annual growth rate for the 1965-72 period to the 1972 estimate. The figures were published in the 1974 edition of the *World Bank Atlas: Population, Per Capita Product and Growth Rates*. The 1972 estimates are in market prices and are based on a multiyear period (1965-71) to convert domestic currencies to dollars. For the remaining countries, the figures are in 1973 constant dollar equivalents.

[4]Difference due to rounding of birth and death rates.

[5]Excludes Greece, shown in Near East section of World Population Data, page 269, and includes over 60 million in Asiatic U.S.S.R. See text.

[6]Excludes population of Egypt, shown in Near East section of *World Population Data*, page 269. See text.

[7]Excluding Greece as European, 1975 total for Near East as 117.3 million.

Note: For general sources and methods, see the notes of the table **World Population Data.** The estimates given above are the weighted averages for the countries within each region for which data are available or estimates were derived.

WORLD POPULATION DATA[1]

Region and country	Estimated population, July 1, 1975	Births per 1,000 population[2]	Deaths per 1,000 population[2]	Rate of natural increase	Time to double population[3]	Population under age 15	Life expectancy at birth	Urban population	GNP per capita[4]
	Thousands	Number	Number	Percent	Years	Percent	Years	Percent	Dollars
World	3,947,039	30	12	1.8	38	36	59	38	1,250
Northern America	236,552	15	9	0.6	116	27	71	74	6,130
Bermuda	55	19	7	1.2	58	30	69	100	4,710
Canada	22,811	15	7	0.8	87	29	73	76	5,370
Greenland	50	20	6	1.4	50	43	61	67	2,780
St. Pierre and Miquelon ..	5	30	13	1.7	41	32	NA	NA	NA
United States (the 50 States and the District of Columbia) ..	213,631	15	9	0.6	116	27	71	74	6,210
Latin America (Mainland)	290,271	38	9	2.9	24	42	62	60	770
Argentina	25,376	22	9	1.3	53	29	68	81	1,250
Belize	139	39	5	3.4	20	49	NA	54	700
Bolivia	5,612	44	18	2.6	27	43	47	35	200
Brazil	107,162	37	9	2.8	25	42	61	58	750
Chile	10,585	28	8	[5]1.9	36	39	63	76	780
Colombia	22,273	41	9	3.2	22	46	61	64	410
Costa Rica	1,967	28	5	2.3	30	42	69	41	780
Ecuador	6,716	42	10	3.2	22	47	60	39	370
El Salvador	4,099	40	8	3.2	22	46	58	39	340
Falkland Islands	2	20	6	1.4	50	27	NA	55	NA
French Guiana	55	37	9	2.8	25	38	NA	66	1,000
Guatemala	5,509	43	15	2.8	25	44	53	34	450
Guyana	786	36	6	3.0	23	44	68	40	380
Honduras	2,747	49	14	3.5	20	47	54	28	290
Mexico	60,152	46	8	[10]3.8	18	46	63	61	870
Nicaragua	2,153	48	14	3.4	20	48	53	49	500
Panama	1,668	31	5	2.6	27	43	66	49	900
Panama Canal Zone	40	14	2	[5]1.1	63	32	NA	6	2,910
Paraguay	2,547	40	9	3.1	22	45	62	38	400
Peru	15,510	41	12	2.9	24	44	56	60	620
Surinam	416	41	7	3.4	20	50	66	49	880
Uruguay	2,764	21	10	1.1	63	28	70	80	860
Venezuela	11,993	36	7	2.9	24	44	65	75	1,360
Caribbean Islands	26,812	31	9	2.2	32	41	64	43	780
Antigua	73	18	7	1.1	63	43	62	40	480
Bahama Islands	205	22	6	[5]1.7	41	44	66	58	2,320
Barbados	239	21	9	1.2	58	34	69	4	950
British Virgin Islands ...	11	25	6	1.9	36	39	52	12	NA
Cayman Islands	12	32	8	2.4	29	39	NA	39	NA
Cuba	9,252	25	6	[5]2.0	35	37	70	60	540
Dominica	75	36	10	2.6	27	49	58	17	360
Dominican Republic ...	4,694	46	11	3.5	20	48	58	40	510
Grenada	96	26	8	[5]1.9	36	47	63	8	460
Guadeloupe	352	28	7	2.1	33	40	69	9	1,050
Haiti	4,574	36	16	2.0	35	41	50	20	130
Jamaica	2,052	31	7	2.4	29	46	68	37	870
Martinique	347	22	7	[5]1.6	43	41	69	33	1,330
Montserrat	11	25	9	1.6	43	40	52	11	NA
Netherlands Antilles	233	25	7	1.8	38	38	73	32	1,650
Puerto Rico	3,128	23	6	1.7	41	37	72	58	2,270

See footnotes at end of table.

266

WORLD POPULATION DATA[1]

Region and country	Estimated population, July 1, 1975	Births per 1,000 population[2]	Deaths per 1,000 population[2]	Rate of natural increase	Time to double population[3]	Population under age 15	Life expectancy at birth	Urban population	GNP per capita[4]
	Thousands	Number	Number	Percent	Years	Percent	Years	Percent	Dollars
Caribbean Islands (Continued)									
St. Kitts, Nevis, and									
Anguilla	68	26	11	1.5	46	46	60	28	450
St. Lucia	107	41	9	3.2	22	50	57	5	480
St. Vincent	94	34	10	2.4	29	51	59	5	300
Trinidad and Tobago . . .	1,088	26	7	[5]2.0	35	40	66	12	1,200
Turks and Caicos Islands .	6	32	10	2.2	32	47	NA	41	NA
U.S. Virgin Islands	95	40	8	3.2	22	36	NA	24	5,910
Europe	718,682	16	10	0.6	116	26	71	63	3,010
Albania	2,411	30	8	2.2	32	40	71	34	460
Andorra	23	18	6	1.2	58	29	NA	NA	NA
Austria	7,540	13	12	0.1	693	24	71	52	3,710
Belgium	9,803	13	12	0.1	693	23	71	87	4,690
Bulgaria	8,741	17	10	0.7	99	22	72	59	1,590
Channel Islands	123	12	13	-0.1	—	22	NA	80	2,400
Czechoslovakia	14,804	20	12	0.8	87	23	70	56	2,870
Denmark	5,065	14	10	0.4	173	23	73	80	5,340
Faeroe Islands	40	20	7	1.3	53	32	NA	85	3,840
Finland	4,706	13	10	[5]0.4	173	24	69	58	3,660
France	52,694	15	10	0.5	139	24	73	70	4,850
Germany, Democratic Rep.	16,885	11	14	-0.3	—	23	71	75	3,000
Germany, Federal									
Republic	61,947	10	12	-0.2	—	23	71	88	5,620
Gibraltar	30	18	6	1.2	58	26	NA	100	1,580
Hungary	10,546	18	12	0.6	116	20	70	49	1,850
Iceland	220	20	7	1.3	53	32	74	86	4,840
Ireland	3,109	22	11	1.1	63	31	72	52	2,160
Isle of Man	56	13	19	-0.6	—	20	NA	56	1,690
Italy	55,805	16	10	0.6	116	24	72	53	2,520
Liechtenstein	24	17	8	0.9	77	28	NA	28	NA
Luxembourg	358	11	12	-0.1	—	21	71	68	5,230
Malta	325	18	9	0.9	77	26	70	94	1,100
Monaco	24	11	11	0.0	—	13	NA	100	NA
Netherlands	13,654	14	8	0.6	116	27	74	77	4,440
Norway	4,010	15	10	0.4	173	24	74	45	4,740
Poland	34,022	18	8	1.0	69	25	70	55	2,090
Portugal	8,499	19	11	0.8	87	28	68	26	1,310
Romania	21,245	20	9	1.1	63	25	69	42	NA
San Marino	19	17	8	0.9	77	26	NA	92	NA
Spain	35,596	19	8	1.1	63	28	72	61	1,730
Sweden	8,195	13	11	0.2	347	21	75	81	6,160
Switzerland	6,489	13	9	0.4	173	24	73	55	6,350
U.S.S.R.	[11]254,300	18	9	0.9	77	28	70	60	2,300
United Kingdom	56,024	13	12	0.1	693	24	72	76	3,120
Yugoslavia	21,350	18	8	[5]0.9	77	27	68	39	1,100
Africa	[12]365,003	47	21	2.6	27	44	45	21	310
Algeria	16,792	49	15	3.4	20	48	53	50	500
Angola	6,262	47	24	2.3	30	42	38	15	490
Botswana	677	46	23	2.3	30	46	44	13	280
Burundi	3,770	48	25	2.3	30	45	39	3	70
Cameroon	6,398	40	22	1.8	38	40	41	20	230

See footnotes at end of table.

WORLD POPULATION DATA[1]

Region and country	Estimated population, July 1, 1975	Births per 1,000 population[2]	Deaths per 1,000 population[2]	Rate of natural increase	Time to double population[3]	Population under age 15	Life expectancy at birth	Urban population	GNP per capita[4]
	Thousands	Number	Number	Percent	Years	Percent	Years	Percent	Dollars
Africa (Continued)									
Cape Verde Islands	298	33	10	2.3	30	44	50	6	340
Central African Republic .	1,790	43	22	2.1	33	42	41	27	180
Chad	4,028	44	24	2.0	35	41	38	12	90
Comoros	298	44	20	2.4	29	43	42	5	170
Congo	1,350	45	21	2.4	29	42	44	37	420
Dahomey (now Benin) . . .	3,111	50	23	2.7	26	45	41	13	120
Equatorial Guinea	320	37	20	1.7	41	37	44	9	290
Ethiopia	27,920	49	26	2.3	30	44	38	11	80
French Territory of Afars and Issas	106	42	21	2.1	33	NA	NA	NA	1,580
Gabon	528	32	22	1.0	69	32	41	17	1,250
The Gambia	516	43	24	1.9	36	41	40	14	160
Ghana	9,867	49	22	2.7	26	47	44	29	290
Guinea	4,416	47	23	2.4	29	43	41	16	140
Guinea-Bissau	522	40	25	1.5	46	37	38	20	280
Ivory Coast	6,673	46	21	2.5	28	43	44	28	510
Kenya	13,351	49	16	3.3	21	46	50	10	170
Lesotho	1,038	39	20	1.9	36	38	46	5	100
Liberia	1,567	50	21	2.9	24	42	45	28	250
Libya	2,437	45	15	3.0	23	44	53	29	2,980
Madagascar (Malagasy Republic) . . .	7,518	50	21	2.9	24	45	44	14	170
Malawi	5,012	48	24	2.4	29	45	41	4	110
Mali	5,629	50	26	2.4	29	44	38	12	400
Mauritania	1,316	39	25	1.4	50	42	38	10	200
Mauritius	885	28	7	2.1	33	38	66	44	400
Morocco	17,370	46	16	3.0	23	44	53	37	290
Mozambique	9,120	43	20	2.3	30	43	44	10	330
Niger	4,596	52	25	2.7	26	46	38	8	120
Nigeria	63,022	49	23	[5]2.7	26	45	41	16	250
Reunion	493	28	7	2.1	33	43	63	43	1,210
Rwanda	4,241	50	24	2.6	27	44	41	3	70
St. Helena	6	23	11	1.2	58	39	NA	32	NA
Sao Tome e Principe . . .	79	45	11	3.4	20	33	NA	23	470
Senegal	4,383	48	24	2.4	29	43	40	30	250
Seychelles	'60	30	9	2.1	33	43	65	26	370
Sierra Leone	3,042	45	21	2.4	29	43	44	13	160
Somalia	3,156	47	22	2.5	28	45	41	26	80
South Africa	24,964	43	16	2.7	26	41	52	48	1,080
Namibia (South-West Africa)	852	46	23	[5]2.2	32	41	41	23	[6]
Southern Rhodesia	6,308	48	14	3.4	20	46	52	19	410
Spanish Sahara	122	45	26	1.9	36	41	NA	41	NA
Sudan	17,757	48	18	3.0	23	45	49	13	140
Swaziland	493	49	22	2.7	26	46	44	8	310
Tanzania	15,162	50	22	2.8	25	47	44	7	130
Togo	2,230	51	23	[5]2.7	26	46	41	15	180
Tunisia	5,776	38	13	2.5	28	44	54	40	460
Uganda	11,546	45	16	2.9	24	44	50	8	160
Upper Volta	6,032	49	26	2.3	30	43	38	7	80
Zaire	24,900	45	20	2.5	28	44	44	25	150
Zambia	4,898	51	20	3.1	22	46	44	34	500

See footnotes at end of table.

WORLD POPULATION DATA[1]

Region and country	Estimated population, July 1, 1975	Births per 1,000 population[2]	Deaths per 1,000 population[2]	Rate of natural increase	Time to double population[3]	Population under age 15	Life expectancy at birth	Urban population	GNP per capita[4]
	Thousands	Number	Number	Percent	Years	Percent	Years	Percent	Dollars
Near East[13]	163,536	41	14	[5]2.6	27	43	54	42	710
Bahrain	240	44	15	2.9	24	44	61	78	940
Cyprus	646	18	10	0.8	87	32	71	43	1,460
Egypt, Arab Republic of . .	37,218	38	15	2.3	30	41	52	43	260
Greece	9,005	16	8	0.8	87	25	72	53	1,780
Iran	33,103	45	16	[5]3.0	23	47	51	43	760
Iraq	11,018	48	15	3.3	21	48	53	61	640
Israel	3,377	28	7	2.1	33	33	71	86	2,730
Gaza Strip	387	50	16	3.4	20	49	52	79	NA
Jordan	2,706	48	15	3.3	21	48	53	43	290
Kuwait	1,007	45	8	3.7	19	43	69	22	7,050
Lebanon	2,656	40	10	3.0	23	43	63	61	870
Oman	766	50	19	3.1	22	NA	NA	NA	490
Qatar	92	50	19	3.1	22	NA	NA	NA	5,940
Saudi Arabia	6,231	49	20	2.9	24	45	45	18	1,300
Syria	7,355	45	15	3.0	23	49	54	44	340
Turkey	39,180	39	12	2.7	26	42	57	39	580
United Arab Emirates . . .	224	50	19	3.1	22	34	NA	65	6,740
Yemen (Aden)	1,657	50	21	2.9	24	45	45	26	110
Yemen (San'a)	6,668	50	21	2.9	24	45	45	7	80
South Asia	799,886	37	16	2.1	33	40	49	19	120
Afghanistan	19,108	43	21	2.2	32	44	40	15	80
Bangladesh	74,000	47	20	2.7	26	46	43	9	100
Bhutan	1,176	44	21	2.3	30	42	44	3	60
India	608,540	35	15	2.0	35	40	50	20	120
Maldive Islands	136	50	23	2.7	26	44	NA	11	90
Nepal	12,591	43	20	2.3	30	40	44	4	90
Pakistan	70,329	44	15	2.9	24	46	50	26	130
Sikkim	222	NA	NA	2.0	35	40	NA	5	90
Sri Lanka (Ceylon)	13,784	28	8	2.0	35	39	68	22	200
South East Asia	319,281	38	15	[5]2.4	29	43	51	20	180
Brunei	153	33	4	2.9	24	43	NA	64	1,640
Burma	30,470	40	16	2.4	29	41	50	19	80
Indonesia[7]	131,920	38	17	2.1	33	44	48	18	120
Khmer Republic (Cambodia)	8,110	47	19	2.8	25	45	45	19	80
Laos	3,303	45	23	2.2	32	42	40	15	100
Malaysia (including West Malaysia, Sabah, and Sarawak)	12,039	39	10	2.9	24	44	59	27	550
Philippines	42,761	41	11	[9]3.0	23	43	58	32	250
Portugese Timor	670	44	23	2.1	33	42	40	10	130
Singapore	2,250	20	5	1.5	46	39	67	100	1,930
Thailand	42,277	36	11	2.5	28	45	58	13	230
Vietnam, North	24,323	32	14	1.8	38	41	48	12	110
Vietnam, South	21,005	42	16	2.6	27	41	40	19	160
East Asia	1,005,787	26	9	1.7	41	32	63	30	680
China, People's Republic of	822,763	[8]27	10	1.7	41	33	62	23	270

See footnotes at end of table.

WORLD POPULATION DATA[1]

Region and country	Estimated population, July 1, 1975	Births per 1,000 population[2]	Deaths per 1,000 population[2]	Rate of natural increase	Time to double population[3]	Population under age 15	Life expectancy at birth	Urban population	GNP per capita[4]
	Thousands	Number	Number	Percent	Years	Percent	Years	Percent	Dollars
East Asia (Continued)									
China (Taiwan)	16,040	23	5	[5]1.9	36	43	69	63	660
Hong Kong	4,339	19	5	1.4	50	36	71	90	1,440
Japan	110,944	19	6	[5]1.2	58	24	73	72	3,810
Korea, North	15,852	36	9	2.7	26	42	61	38	340
Korea, South	34,128	29	9	2.0	35	40	61	41	380
Macao	277	25	7	1.8	38	38	NA	97	270
Mongolia	1,444	40	10	3.0	23	44	61	46	550
Oceania	21,229	22	10	1.2	58	33	68	71	3,330
American Samoa	29	37	5	3.2	22	47	67	0	1,020
Australia	13,623	18	9	[5]1.0	69	29	72	86	4,000
British Solomon Islands . .	191	36	11	2.5	28	44	NA	9	280
Cook Islands	23	33	6	2.7	26	52	NA	NA	NA
Fiji	570	28	5	2.3	30	41	70	33	640
French Polynesia	128	34	7	2.7	26	44	58	38	2,680
Gilbert and Ellice Islands. .	63	35	8	2.7	26	45	58	24	360
Guam	111	35	5	3.0	23	40	NA	25	4,130
New Caledonia	134	36	10	2.6	27	39	NA	44	5,010
Papua New Guinea	2,762	41	17	2.4	29	45	48	11	360
New Hebrides	94	45	20	2.5	28	46	NA	19	480
New Zealand	3,129	19	8	1.1	63	32	72	81	3,930
Pacific Islands	116	35	5	3.0	23	46	NA	32	450
Tonga	97	35	10	2.5	28	46	NA	20	210
Western Samoa	159	37	7	3.0	23	50	63	20	250

NA = Not available.

[1]Aside from GNP per capita, the sources for which are given in footnote 4, most of the data in this table were reported in various United Nations' publications or were estimated by the Population Division of the United Nations or by the International Statistical Programs Center of the U.S. Bureau of the Census. Estimates for the world regions and the world total are weighted averages for countries for which data are available.

[2]For the more developed countries, with complete or nearly complete registration of births and deaths, nearly all the rates shown pertain to 1973 or 1974. For nearly all the developing countries, with incomplete registration, the rates shown refer to the 1970-75 period and are taken from the United Nations' medium variant estimates as assessed in 1973 (United Nations, *Selected World Demographic Indicators by Countries, 1950-2000*, ESA/P/WP.55, May 28, 1975). These figures should be considered as rough approximations only; for many countries they probably differ significantly from the actual rates.

[3]Based on the rate of natural increase shown and assuming no change in the rate.

[4]Data refer to 1973. For the Communist countries and for nearly all of the countries with populations of less than 1 million, the figures shown were released by the World Bank on December 21, 1975. They are to be published in the tenth edition of *World Bank Atlas: Population, Per Capita Product and Growth Rates.* For the remaining 136 countries, the figures shown were published by AID in *Gross National Product, Estimates for Non-Communist Countries for 1973*, RC-W-137, July 1975. However, the figures for French Guinea, Grenada, Kuwait, Mali, Netherlands Antilles, the United States, and Yugoslavia are later estimates to be published soon by U.S. AID in an updated report on GNP.

[5]Difference due to rounding of birth and death rates.

[6]Included with South Africa.

[7]Includes West Irian.

[8]Since about one-fifth of the world's population lives in the People's Republic of China, its birth rate is especially significant to the birth rate for the world as a whole. A change of five per 1,000 in China's rate changes the rate for the world by one per 1,000. In the absence of official information on the birth rate in the People's Republic, the United Nations' medium variant estimate was used in this table. Some observers, however, consider the rate of 27 per 1,000 population too high at the present time because of China's vigorous family planning program in the recent past.

[9]Preliminary data from the 1975 census indicate a 2.7 percent rate of natural increase in 1974.

[10]Based on United Nations data for 1973 published October 1975.

[11]Includes over 60 million in Asiatic U.S.S.R.

[12]Including Egypt's population, 1975 total for Africa is 402.2 million. See text.

[13]Excluding Greece and Egypt, 1975 population total for Near East is 117.3 million. See text.

Glossary

Acceptor: One who adopts a given method of regulating births and/or receives advice through a family planning program.

Antinatalist: Policy of government, society, social group, or religion aimed at slowing population growth.

Birth control: Measures of individuals, countries, or societies aimed at influencing—decreasing or increasing—numbers of births. The expression is often used synonymously with family planning, fertility control, and responsible parenthood.

Birth order: Rank of each live child a woman has borne.

Birth rate: A measure of the frequency of live births in the whole population, generally expressed as the number of births during the year per 1,000 population at midyear.

Commodities: Contraceptive materials, such as pills, IUDs, condoms, used in a family planning program. Broadly the term also includes medical equipment needed to perform examinations and sterilizations, office supplies, or even field equipment, such as jeeps.

Death rate: A measure of the frequency of deaths in the whole population, generally expressed as the number of deaths during the year per 1,000 population at midyear.

Demography: The empirical, statistical, and mathematical study of human populations.

Family planning: The conscious effort of couples to regulate the number and timing of their children's births. Although family planning usually involves reducing the number of births, it also includes efforts of childless couples to induce pregnancy.

Fertility control: A deliberate effort on the part of individuals, societies, or social groups to regulate the number of offspring.

Fertility rate: A measure of the number of births during a given year per 1,000 women of childbearing age, usually defined as ages 15 to 44 or 15 to 49.

Net reproduction rate: A measure of the number of live daughters that would be born to a group of newborn girls if up to the end of their reproductive age span they were exposed to the same mortality rates by age and bore daughters at the same rate by age as all women in a given year. An NRR of 1.0 means that if current mortality and fertility rates were to continue, the group would produce on average one daughter per woman, with the *eventual* result that population growth would cease.

Nurse-midwife: A fully accredited nurse trained to handle uncomplicated delivery of babies and to examine women and prescribe birth control methods.

Oral cycle: A 1-month supply of oral contraceptive pills designed to prevent pregnancy within a woman's menstrual cycle.

Parity: The number of live children a woman has borne.

Pronatalist: Policy of a government, society, social group, or religion aimed at increasing population growth.

Rate of natural increase (percent): A measure of annual population growth based on the difference between the birth rate and the death rate per 1,000 population.

Specific fertility rate: A measure of live births in a specific group. Often refers to births to women in specified age groups, in which case it is called an age-specific fertility rate.

World Population Year: The year 1974 was proclaimed "World Population Year" by the United Nations to focus world attention on population problems and specifically on the UN's World Population Conference, which was held in Bucharest in August 1974.

271